HENRY II
THE VANQUISHED KING

HENRY II

THE VANQUISHED KING

BY

JOHN T. APPLEBY

THE MACMILLAN COMPANY
NEW YORK
1962

First Published in
the United States of America
by the Macmillan Company, 1962

Printed in Great Britain by
ROBERT CUNNINGHAM & SONS LTD, ALVA

FOR MY MOTHER
GERTRUDE BAYLOR APPLEBY

FOREWORD

IN July 1189 the greatest king of the Europe of his time and one of the greatest kings that England has ever had lay dying at Chinon, in the Loire Valley. Henry II had started his life as the eldest son of the Count of Anjou and Maine and of the daughter of King Henry I of England. Through his birth, through his father's bravery and his mother's persistence, through his marriage with Eleanor of Aquitaine, and through his own skill and cunning, he had become Duke of Normandy, Count of Anjou and Maine, Duke of Aquitaine, King of England, and Lord of Ireland, with the King of Scots and the Duke of Brittany as his vassals. His empire stretched from Scotland to the Pyrenees. No King of England before or after him wielded such power over so vast a territory as did Henry II.

And yet, for all his great power and vast territories, Henry met death almost alone, in the most abject misery. His Queen was in prison, kept there by her husband for some sixteen years. His best friend had been savagely hacked to death at Henry's instigation because he placed his God before his King. Of his four sons who reached maturity, two had died while they were in rebellion against their father, one had joined the King of France to vanquish Henry and force him to the most humiliating submission, and the youngest, whom he loved the best, had betrayed him at the end and joined his enemies. His barons deserted him, and as Henry lay in his last agony, crying hoarsely, 'Shame, shame on a vanquished King!' his servants stripped him even of his clothes and left him lying naked on the ground.

How did such a man come to such an end?

In an effort to answer that question, I have tried to assemble a life of Henry II from the accounts of men who lived during his time or shortly thereafter. My aim is modest: to tell the story of Henry's life as accurately as I can. I have invented no conversations: such talk as is here written was reported by Henry's contemporaries. Nor have I ventured to 'interpret' Henry, after the modern fashion. From the facts of Henry's life the reader can draw his own conclusions without needing any help from me.

vii

The story of Henry's life is a fascinating one, and no one needs an excuse for trying to tell a good story. Apart from the drama of his life, however, Henry has a special claim to our interest, for he was in the truest sense the father of English law. Before his time, the law was little more than a set of tribal customs. Henry introduced such profound and far-reaching reforms and innovations that one cannot attempt to write of his life without devoting a great deal of attention to his legal measures. Since a biography of Henry is hardly the place for the detailed examination of his great enactments that those measures deserve, the reader is referred to Pollock and Maitland's *History of English Law* for a comprehensive analysis of them.

I am grateful to the staff of the Library of Congress for having made their facilities available to me and particularly to the Messrs Stewart Dickson, L. H. Thacker, and Raphael Brown, who not only helped me in every possible way but also took a warm and friendly interest in my work.

My gratitude is due also to my brother-in-law, John A. Fogleman, Esq., for his generous assistance, and to J. M. Lalley, Esq., for his helpful suggestions.

Finally, I should be little better than a churl if I were not to express my thanks to my dog Fritz, who patiently stayed at home alone day after day while I was consorting with strange dogs at the Library of Congress.

JOHN T. APPLEBY

Washington, D.C.
1962

CONTENTS

TABLES

MAPS

PART I

THE KING AND THE ARCHBISHOP

I

HENRY, SON OF THE EMPRESS
1133 - 1148

W HEN old King Henry died, on December 1, 1135, of a fever brought on by gorging himself on lampreys after a hard day's hunting, the England over which he had ruled with ferocious severity for thirty-five years was a rich and prosperous country, with a population of around two million.[1] One should not think, however, that where there are some thirty Englishmen at the present day, there was only one in the twelfth century. The distribution of population was radically different. London scarcely filled the square mile within the city walls; such great centres of population as Liverpool, Birmingham, and Manchester, which grew out of the Industrial Revolution, either did not exist at all or were mere villages; and vast areas in the North were still deserted after the harrying inflicted by William the Conqueror. The favourable climate, the fertile soil, and the peace that King Henry had sternly enforced had contributed to produce a state of plenty unknown in the strife-torn lands across the Channel. The country was almost wholly agricultural, and wool was already the chief article of export and the main source of England's wealth.

The country was still covered by vast forests. The people lived for the most part in small villages, clustered about the church and the hall of the lord of the manor and surrounded by the fields, which they worked in common, and the meadows on which they pastured their scrawny livestock. The great majority of the people were, of course, English, thoroughly cowed and subdued by their Norman masters. Their language, the most beautiful and highly developed vernacular in Western Europe, had almost disappeared as a literary vehicle, written by only a few monks at Peterborough, one of the last strongholds of the Old English culture. The Normans, who occupied every position of importance

[1] A. L. Poole: *From Domesday Book to Magna Carta* (Oxford, 1951), p. 36.

3

in Church and State although they formed only a minute proportion of the population, spoke their own variety of French.
The clergy used a debased Latin as a written language, adequate,
no doubt, for the conveying of information, but lacking the flexi-
bility, colour, and poetic beauty of the English it had displaced.

Society was rigidly stratified. At the top were the king, a
few earls, less than two hundred great barons, and the dignitaries
of the Church. These men formed the Great Council, which
met with the king to consult with him and advise him as to the
state of the realm.

The great barons were in most cases the descendants of the men
who had come over with the Conqueror or joined him later to
share in the great land-grab that followed the dispossession of the
English. When William the Conqueror divided up the land of
England, no Englishman who had borne arms against him was
allowed to retain his holding; all the English landowners of any
importance were dispossessed and their lands taken over by the
King. William so divided the land that roughly two-sevenths
in value was reserved for himself and his household, two-sevenths
was given to the Church, and the remainder was divided among
his followers.[1]

These men, who held their land directly of the king, were
known as barons. The lands they received were intended to
provide for the needs of the barons and their following. In
return for the land, the barons were expected to serve in the king's
army when they were needed, bringing their knights with them;
to help, either in person or by sending a quota of knights, to
guard the king's castles, which William built over the land; and
to appear at the king's court when they were summoned.

In the first unsettled years after the Conquest, when the Norman invaders were aliens living amidst a defeated and hostile
people, the barons kept their knights as personal retainers in their
households. As the years passed and the occupation became
secure, some of the barons gave portions of their lands to their
knights, upon which the knights could live apart from their lords.
The knights in turn held their lands of their lords in exchange for
their military services.

[1] W. J. Corbett: 'The Development of the Duchy of Normandy and the
Norman Conquest of England', in *Cambridge Medieval History* (Cambridge, 1929),
Vol. V, p. 508.

The whole scheme of land tenure and the rank arising from it was purely military. Barons were military leaders who could bring their contingents of knights to the king's army and fight beside him. Knights were skilled fighters, trained to arms from their boyhood, expert horsemen, able to handle their ponderous shield and sword with an ease born of long familiarity, weighted down though they were with a coat of chain mail that reached from neck to knee. Military values were supreme. A baron was judged by how many men he led in battle and how well he led them; a knight was judged by how well he acquitted himself in battle. There was no room in this society for a man who was not a fighter. If a young man of good family felt no attraction to this rough life, the cloister was the only place for him, and the sooner he took himself off to a monastery the better it was for him.

Trained to war, living for the joy of battle, most of these men were at a loss in times of peace. Some of them turned their formidable energies to the task of administering their estates. Some put their abilities at the king's disposal and served either in his household or as sheriffs or judges. For most of them, however, when there was no enemy in sight, their natural inclinations led them to pick a fight with their nearest neighbour on any pretext that offered. That is how the fighting man spent his time in their native Normandy, and that is how the Norman barons, transplanted to England, would have spent their time if the king had not ruthlessly suppressed private wars in England. His barons had rebelled against him more than once, and the fear that they might unite against him again led him to suppress with ferocity any private wars, which always carried the threat of turning into a war against the king.

Left to their own devices, apart from occasional military service in the king's Duchy of Normandy, the earls and barons and knights of England turned to the usual distractions of fighting men when there is no fighting to be done. They feasted and gambled and drank in their draughty halls, in castles built of wood, perched on a mound and surrounded by a palisade of stakes and a moat. Clad in their bright cloaks of scarlet or green or russet brown, sounding their horns in merry flourishes, surrounded by swarms of huntsmen and packs of baying hounds, they hunted from morning till night. The forests of England were full of deer and wild boar, protected by forest laws that punished the unlawful killing of a deer with swift and dreadful mutilation for the lower classes and with crushing fines for the upper. Each baron had his own forests, protected by his own wardens, and in them he and his knights hunted at every opportunity.

In addition to being fighting men, the barons exercised an almost complete jurisdiction over their lands and tenants, not merely as owners of the land but also as feudal lords, with power to settle disputes, punish crimes, and administer what passed for justice. The king claimed jurisdiction over certain offences and strove to maintain the peace, but the barons stoutly resisted every encroachment of the royal justice into their domains. The constant tension between the king and his barons, ready to burst into open rebellion if the king relaxed his stern hold over them, arose primarily from the desire of the barons to be almost complete sovereigns within their individual domains and the corresponding determination on the king's part to make his power and authority felt throughout his realm.

On the knights' shoulders fell the greater part of the administrative work in the counties, in addition to their military duties. In this work were included the obligations of attending the shire and hundred courts, giving evidence, investigating crimes and accusations of crime, assessing land values, and, most important of all, serving as trustworthy remembrancers of how things had been in the past, of who held what land of whom and under what conditions.

Assisting the knights in this onerous and unpaid work, on which the structure of English local government rested, were the 'free and law-worthy men' of the writs of the time. They were small landholders, holding their lands on a great variety of tenures and sometimes supplementing their incomes by working for wages. A special class of free men were the burgesses of the towns, who were growing in numbers and in wealth but who took little part in the governmental machinery, based as it was on a rural concept of the hundred and the county as administrative units.

The manor was the smallest unit in the system of land-holding, apart from the occasional freeholding. It usually embraced a village and its surrounding fields, although as the system grew more complex a village might be divided between two or more manors. The lord of the manor might hold his land as the last member of a chain reaching through king, earl, baron, and an indefinite number of knights, or he might hold it directly of the king. If he had only the one manor, he usually lived on it and took an active part in its affairs; if he owned more than one, he would appoint a bailiff for each manor and move from one to the other in order to consume its produce on the spot.

The open-field or strip system was the most common method of farming. The land of the manor was usually divided into three great fields, two of which were cultivated and the third, in rotation, lay fallow. Each tenant or villein and the lord himself had a certain number of strips, each of which was roughly equal to a day's ploughing, all mingled together. The major portion of the income of the lord of the manor came from the produce of his land, his 'demesne', which was cultivated for him by the villeins.

The face of England was radically different then from what it is now. In place of the comparatively small fields divided by hedgerows, the most characteristic and beautiful feature of the English landscape of today, one must picture the manor with its great open fields set amidst the forest on which it steadily encroached.

At the bottom of the scale were the villeins, who made up more than half the population. They held their land of the lord of the manor in return for working a specified number of days on his land and for a number of other services that varied from manor to manor. They were bound to the land in the sense that they could not leave it without their lord's permission. They were not slaves, but they were subject to such humiliating exactions as the forfeiture of their best beast upon the death of the head of the household and the necessity for securing their lord's permission if they wanted to marry someone from a different manor.

Their lives were hard, rarely rising above the level of mere subsistence. Their food was whatever they could grow on their strips of land, all mingled together with the lord's and their fellow-villagers' in a patchwork quilt of scattered holdings. They grew wheat, oats, barley, rye, peas, and beans. In addition to their plough animals they kept, when they could afford them, cows, pigs, sheep, and poultry. Meat they ate but rarely; bread and cheese, porridge, eggs, and, for those living near a river or the sea, fish were the main articles of their diet. Though the forests were full of game, it was not for the likes of them. They dressed in such clothes as they could make for themselves of rough homespun from the wool of their own sheep, fashioned into a smock-like tunic and leggings. Their lives were circumscribed by the narrow limits of their village and its surrounding fields and pastures. Their sports, when they had time for them, were the simple ones of wrestling, playing ball, and, on the greatest days of the year, drinking all the beer they could hold. Englishmen were noted for their heavy drinking, an evil habit introduced by the Danes.[1]

In addition to these lay people of every degree were the clergy. They ranged from the humble parish priest, often little better than a villein himself, to the highest dignitaries of the Church, who gave counsel to the king and often served as his ministers of state. They were the only educated class and therefore filled many important posts in the government. Monasteries and cathedral schools were the only centres of learning, and all their scholars were clerics.

The clergy were a variegated group. Apart from the parish priests, who could not hope to rise above their station and were content if they could pass their churches on to their sons, the influential members of the clergy came from the same Norman families that produced the barons and knights. Some of them were little better than barons in holy orders, building and fortifying castles, amassing such wealth as they could lay their hands on, and openly violating the precept of celibacy that the Church was trying to impose on her clergy. Others were saints of great holiness and learning. Still others were highly gifted administrators and turned their exceptional talents to the service of their diocese, their monastery, or their king.

All these men, earls, barons, and knights; townsmen, free men, and villeins; bishops, priests, and monks: all were bound together, despite their differences of speech and way of life, in one visible Church and in allegiance to one king, who held the realm of England as his personal property.

No matter who held the land or under what conditions, in the last resort all the land belonged to the king, by virtue of William's

---

[1] *Annales de Wintonia*, in *Annales Monastici*, ed. H. R. Luard (Rolls Series, 5 vols., 1864-9), Vol. II, p. 13.

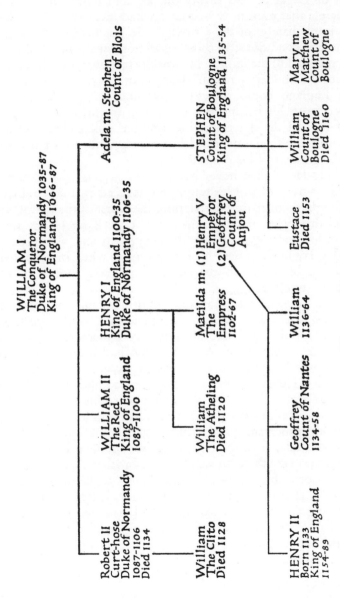

WILLIAM I
The Conqueror
Duke of Normandy 1035-87
King of England 1066-87

Robert II
Curt-hose
Duke of Normandy
1087-1106
Died 1134

WILLIAM II
The Red
King of England
1087-1100

HENRY I
King of England 1100-35
Duke of Normandy 1106-35

Adela m. Stephen
Count of Blois

William
The Clito
Died 1128

William
The Atheling
Died 1120

Matilda m. (1) Henry V
The   Emperor
Empress   (2) Geoffrey
1102-67   Count of
                    Anjou

STEPHEN
Count of Boulogne
King of England 1135-54

HENRY II
Born 1133
King of England
1154-89

Geoffrey
Count of Nantes
1134-58

William
1136-64

Eustace
Died 1153

William
Count of
Boulogne
Died 1160

Mary m.
Matthew
Count of
Boulogne

I Kings of England
1066-1189

9

conquest of England. So firmly did all land tenure rest upon
this principle that even now 'All land whatsoever is held, mediately or immediately, of the Crown'.[1] It was held of the king
under certain conditions; if those conditions were not fulfilled
the land reverted to the king. He was the real owner of the land;
his barons were merely tenants. In this lay his strength, and the
king of England could thereby command a high degree of
obedience from his barons and exert a powerful control over
them, if he had the determination and the will to exercise it.
He was no mere feudal overlord but a king with power to dispossess the greatest of his subjects.

Old King Henry had never hesitated to exercise that power.
In the thirty-five years of his reign he was faced by many rebels,
and he fought them all down, stripping the worst of them of their
lands and driving them into exile. But now King Henry was
dead, and his body, gutted and filled with salt and wrapped in
stout hides, lay in Caen near his father's tomb while men waited
for a favourable wind so that they could take him back to
England and bury him.

Although he had fathered at least twenty bastards, he had had
only one legitimate son, William, who had died in the wreck of
the White Ship in 1120. All his hopes were then centred in his
only other legitimate child, Matilda, who had been married in
1114 to Henry V, Emperor of Germany. When the Emperor
died, in 1125, Henry summoned his widowed and still childless
daughter to him. He had all the members of his council, both
bishops and barons, to swear 'that if he died without a male heir,
they would immediately and without any hesitation accept his
daughter Matilda, formerly the Empress, as their lady'. The
first layman to take the oath was Henry's brother-in-law, David,
King of Scots; the second, his nephew Stephen, Count of
Boulogne.[2] He then impressed upon his daughter the obligation
of producing an heir to his kingdom and arranged with Count
Fulk V of Anjou for her marriage to his son Geoffrey.

Matilda had no more voice in the arrangements than did
Geoffrey. She was ten years older than her husband. She had

---

[1] A. W. B. Simpson: *An Introduction to the History of the Land Law* (Oxford,
1961), p. 1.
[2] William of Malmesbury: *Historia Novella*, ed. K. R. Potter (Nelson's
Medieval Texts, 1955), pp. 3-4.

lived in Germany since she was eight years old; she had been Empress of Germany since she was twelve; she had learned the German language and acquired German ways, and she had developed an arrogance that had endeared her to her German subjects but that made her detested by everyone else. It was a great humiliation for her to accept as her second husband a mere stripling of fifteen, a petty count as the consort of an empress, for so she continued to style herself until her death.

The ill-matched couple were married at Le Mans in 1128. Shortly thereafter, having done all that a father could do for his son, Count Fulk, a carefree widower, turned his counties of Anjou and Maine over to Geoffrey and left him to shift for himself, while he set out for the Holy Land, married the daughter of the King of Jerusalem, and became King himself when King Baldwin died.

Boy though he might be in his wife's eyes, Geoffrey was nevertheless Count of Anjou and Maine in his own right. After a year of his wife's intolerable pride, he drove her out of Anjou. She could go back to England if she liked. Better still, since she was always boasting that the Germans had begged her to stay and rule over them after the Emperor had died, she could go back to Germany. In any case, he refused to live with her or to tolerate her presence in his lands.

Matilda found refuge in Rouen, the chief city of her father's Duchy of Normandy. Henry took her back to England with him in the summer of 1131, with the problem of the succession to the throne unsolved. Geoffrey himself solved the problem by announcing that he would now take back his wife; perhaps he thought that the two years of separation might have taught her a lesson.

Before returning her to her husband, King Henry had his bishops and barons swear fealty to Matilda as his successor, on September 8, 1131. This oath was a repetition of the one they had taken earlier. The bishops and barons took it with many misgivings. England had never been ruled by a woman, and the prospect of such a novelty filled everyone with dismay. Even more dismaying was the prospect of being ruled by such a woman as Matilda. She had the beauty of a woman, the courage of a man, and the insolent arrogance of Lucifer himself. Whether they liked it or not, Henry forced them to swear to the oath.

'After this, the King's daughter was sent back to her husband and was received with a haughty pride worthy of such a virago.'[1]

Matilda had not changed in the least, but Geoffrey resolved to make the best of a bad bargain. After all, a young man so handsome that everyone called him Geoffrey the Fair need not consider himself tied down to a shrew of a wife. Matilda could be kept busy bearing children while he amused himself elsewhere. Their first son, Henry, named after his grandfather the King, was born on March 5, 1133, at Le Mans. On June 1, 1134, Matilda bore their second son, Geoffrey. This was such a difficult confinement that the Empress almost died. It was not until August 1136 that she had her third son, William.

King Henry, meanwhile, had died on December 1, 1135. 'A good man he was, and much awe there was of him: durst no man wrong another in his time,' says the English chronicler of him. 'Peace he made for man and deer.'[2]

At the crucial moment, when the news of the King's death was spreading over Normandy and then to England, a man whom no one had ever considered as a successor to the throne quickly took ship from his port of Wissant, landed in England amidst 'a terrible sound of thunder, with dreadful lightning, so that it was almost thought that the world was breaking up',[3] and laid claim to the crown. Stephen, Count of Boulogne, was the third son of Adela, a daughter of King William the Conqueror, and Stephen, Count of Blois. To be sure, he was the favourite nephew of King Henry, who had brought him up at his court, had him educated with his ill-fated son, William, and knighted him with his own hand. Henry had given him ample lands in both England and Normandy and had arranged a handsome marriage for him with Matilda, the only daughter and heir of Count Eustace of Boulogne, to whose title and estates he had succeeded in due course.

None of this, however, indicated that Henry considered him as a possible heir; indeed, the King's insistence upon the oaths of fealty to his daughter showed quite the contrary. Stephen's long residence in England, his affable, friendly, easy-going ways, and

[1] Henry of Huntingdon: *Historia Anglorum*, ed. Thomas Arnold (Rolls Series, 1879), p. 252.
[2] *The Peterborough Chronicle*, ed. Cecily Clark, Oxford English Monographs (Oxford 1958), p. 54.
[3] William of Malmesbury, p. 15.

his courtesy and consideration for rich and poor alike had won him many friends. When he reached London the citizens elected him King by popular acclaim, for 'he appeared to all as worthy of this, both because of his noble birth and because of his uprightness of character'.[1]

Stephen was crowned King of England by the Archbishop of Canterbury, in the presence of two bishops and only a few nobles, on December 22, 1135. One of the bishops, however, was his brother Henry, Bishop of Winchester, one of the richest and most influential men in England, and the other, Roger of Salisbury, had been King Henry's most trusted minister and had ruled the country during the King's absences in Normandy.[2] When he had gained possession of the royal treasury, containing over a hundred thousand pounds, as well as a vast quantity of gold and silver plate, and when Pope Innocent II had confirmed his title, Stephen could proudly issue the customary charter of liberties at Oxford shortly after Easter 1136 with the resounding opening:

> I, Stephen, by the grace of God, with the consent of the clergy and people, elected King of England, and consecrated by the Lord William, Archbishop of Canterbury and Legate of the Holy Roman Church, and afterwards confirmed by Innocent, the Pontiff of the Holy Roman See . . .[3]

Stephen, however, was too easy-going, affable, and trusting to be able to govern his realm effectively. Haunted by a feeling of insecurity, conscious of his broken oath to recognise Matilda as Henry's successor, and ever aware of that same Empress across the Channel, waiting for the first opportunity to assert her son's right to the throne, he tried to win the loyalty of his greater subjects by lavish gifts of land and, while King Henry's treasure lasted, of money as well. When the barons realised how soft their new King was, they broke out into numberless private quarrels, settling old grudges by waging war on a limited scale against their enemies. A rash of castles sprang up over the land, from which lawless men spread out to burn, steal, and kill.

As strife and dissension spread through England and the King's authority came to mean less and less, Matilda decided that the time was ripe for her to assert the right of her son Henry to be his grandfather's lawful heir. Her bastard half-brother, Earl

---

[1] *Gesta Stephani*, ed. K. R. Potter (Nelson's Medieval Texts, 1955), pp. 2-4.
[2] William of Malmesbury, pp. 15-16.   [3] Ibid., p. 18.

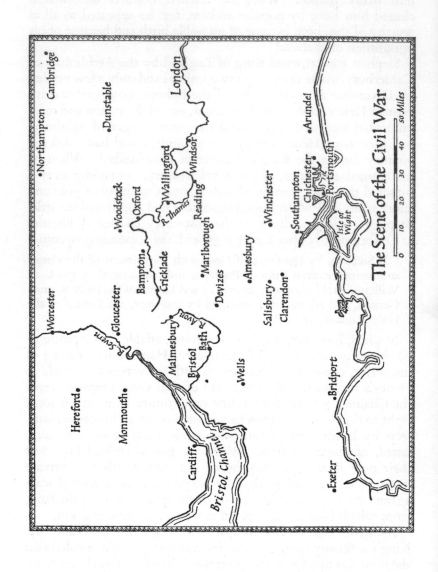

The Scene of the Civil War

Robert of Gloucester, had joined her and offered to help her. Robert had been his father's favourite son, and Henry had given him an earldom and the hand of 'Mabel, a beautiful and excellent woman, a lady both obedient to her husband and blessed with numerous and beautiful children'.[1] A number of barons had advised Robert upon his father's death to claim the throne, but he had refused out of deference to his sister.[2] He would have made a far better king than Stephen, for he was an experienced military leader, highly respected by all the barons and particularly by those of the West Country, and a gifted statesman. He was, in addition, an outstanding patron of letters, to whom both William of Malmesbury and Geoffrey of Monmouth, the two greatest writers of the age, dedicated their works.

Matilda, with Robert's help, set out to conquer her son's inheritance for him. It is not recorded whether or not she invited her husband to join her in this enterprise; at any rate, Geoffrey stayed in Anjou while she and Robert set sail for England. They landed on September 30, 1139, and soon they had control of the West, where Robert's estates lay, with Bristol and Gloucester as his chief strongholds. With the help of their uncle, David, King of Scots, and the leading men of the West, by February 1141 they had captured King Stephen in a battle at Lincoln and held him in prison, in chains, at Bristol. In the following April Matilda was formally recognised by a council of bishops and barons as Lady of England.

Now that her great object had been accomplished, she gave full rein to her arrogance. She failed to realise that her supporters were drawn to her, not by loyalty to her or to her cause, but simply by self-interest. With the King in prison and at her mercy, the barons transferred their allegiance to her because they thought they had more to gain from her than from the fallen Stephen.

She went to London in the summer, and there she completed the work she had begun at Winchester. She began to call herself Queen of the English, although she had not been anointed and crowned. She received the barons with extreme haughtiness and would not rise to greet even the venerable Bishop of Winchester, the King's brother, when he knelt before her. She attempted to cancel Stephen's charters, to take away the lands he

[1] William of Malmesbury, p. 4.   [2] Gesta Stephani, p. 8.

had granted, and to award them to those whom she favoured. She showed the most disagreeable side of her nature to the Londoners and demanded an enormous sum of money from them.

Stephen's Queen meanwhile was collecting an army in Kent, and its ranks were steadily increased by the arrival of many men who could no longer stomach the Empress. She sent a delegation to plead in behalf of her imprisoned husband; the Empress sent them away with insults. The Queen then marched her army close to London. The citizens, cheered by the sight of this body of soldiers and intolerably irked by the excessive demands of the Empress, rose up and drove her and all her supporters pell-mell out of the city, just as they were sitting down to a noble feast. She took refuge in Oxford, and the Londoners welcomed their Queen.[1]

In September 1141 the Empress, at her stronghold in Oxford, heard that Bishop Henry of Winchester was working for his brother's restoration. She and Earl Robert went to Winchester and besieged the Bishop in his castle. No sooner had they invested the castle and settled down for the siege than Stephen's Queen, leading an army that included a thousand Londoners, arrived and encircled the besiegers.

The Bishop's men set fire to part of the city, and the Queen's army on the outer ring soon brought the besiegers to the verge of starvation. At last they decided to make a desperate dash for freedom. In the utter route of the Empress's forces, Earl Robert was captured, the army was hacked to pieces, and the Empress, with only one follower, reached Gloucester more dead than alive.

Stephen's Queen now had a prisoner almost as valuable as her husband, for even the Empress knew that her brother Robert, with his courage, his military skill, his unswerving fidelity, and his friendly relations with the leading men of the West, was indispensable. Negotiations were drawn out for over a month; in the end King Stephen and Earl Robert were exchanged on equal terms.[2]

In order to break the deadlock that now ensued, Matilda sent a delegation of noblemen to her husband in the spring of 1142, bidding him come 'to defend the lawful inheritance of his wife and his sons in England'. The haughty terms in which the message was couched were hardly likely to induce Geoffrey to

[1] *Gesta Stephani*, pp. 79-83.   [2] Ibid., pp. 83-91.

make any effort to help the woman he heartily detested and whose absence in England was greatly to his liking. He accordingly sent a message that was delivered to the Empress and her council at Devizes in June 1142:

> The Count of Anjou is not in the least favourably inclined towards the mission of the noblemen. Furthermore, he recognises amongst all of them only the Earl of Gloucester, whose prudence and good faith, whose magnanimity and industry he knows to be proven from of old. If the Earl crosses the sea and comes to him, the Count will not be wanting in favour to him, as far as he is able; any others will waste their time in coming and going.[1]

Earl Robert accordingly crossed over to see his brother-in-law. He found Geoffrey engaged in conquering the whole of Normandy for his son while his wife was making a fool of herself in England. Geoffrey welcomed the arrival of so skilled a fighter as Earl Robert and enlisted his help in taking a castle he was then besieging. That done, Geoffrey wanted to move on to the next castle. When Robert attempted to tell him of his wife's plight in England, Geoffrey could scarcely conceal his satisfaction and proposed that they try to capture another castle. Thus the summer and early autumn passed, and with Earl Robert's help the Count of Anjou succeeded in taking ten Norman castles.

Late in the autumn came the news that Stephen was closely besieging the Empress at Oxford and that her situation was desperate. Geoffrey refused to accompany Robert to England, since there were still a number of castles to be taken in Normandy and he had no desire to join his wife, but he sent in his place his son Henry, then nine years old. Earl Robert sailed with his nephew and a force of three or four hundred Norman soldiers.[2] He went at once to Oxford, but there he found that his army was too small to offer any threat to Stephen. He turned to Wallingford, hoping that by laying siege to that castle he could force Stephen to divert part of his army there. The King refused to rise to the bait, and Robert took the castle.

Shortly before Christmas, when provisions in the castle at Oxford were running dangerously low and when the river was frozen hard and the ground covered with snow, the intrepid Empress, with three of her knights, had herself lowered by ropes

[1] William of Malmesbury, p. 71. [2] Ibid., pp. 72–74.

from one of the towers and crossed the frozen river at its feet.
Clad all in white cloaks and thus made invisible against the snow,
they passed through the besieging army. They made for
Wallingford, where the Empress met her brother and her eldest
son, and the party then succeeded in reaching Bristol, Earl
Robert's stronghold.[1]

The Empress remained at Bristol and at Gloucester for the next
five years, clinging stubbornly to the hope that she could again
snatch Stephen's crown from his head. There were desultory
engagements between the two forces, with first one side and then
the other scoring a small advantage. Thanks largely to the skill
and wisdom of Earl Robert, the West remained faithful to his
sister. Stephen nominally ruled the rest of England, but his
authority was continually being challenged by his barons, acting,
not as partisans of the Empress, but as rebellious vassals intent on
defying the King and shaking off his rule, weak though it was.

During this stalemate Henry went back to Normandy to join
Count Geoffrey. Earl Robert had seen to it that Henry and his
own son, Roger, who were of about the same age, had had their
first lessons in 'manners and letters' together.[2] Henry's education
was now continued under his father's guidance. In addition to
receiving the usual training in arms and horsemanship and
courtesy that was proper for lads of gentle birth, he was well
educated in such branches of learning as were considered appropriate to a person of his position. He learned to speak Latin, as
well as his native French. English was still the language of a
conquered race, beneath the notice of its rulers, and there is no
indication that Henry ever made any effort to learn it. He may
have learned to write, although he would have had little use for
such a skill, since writing was the business of clerks; at any rate,
he learned to read, which was quite an accomplishment for a
layman.

In addition to his formal education, he heard over and over
again the history of his ancestors, the Counts of Anjou. The
story that most stirred his youthful imagination would without
doubt be the one about the heroic exploits of his great-great-

---

[1] *Gesta Stephani*, pp. 94-95.
[2] William Fitz Stephen, in *Materials for the History of Thomas Becket* (hereafter referred to as *Materials*), ed. J. C. Robertson (I-VI) and J. B. Shappard
(VII), (Rolls Series, 7 vols., 1875-85), Vol. III, p. 104.

great-grandfather, the almost legendary Count Fulk the Black. Before he was fourteen, Count Fulk had defeated a great army of Bretons, captured their leader, Count Conan, cut off his right hand, and seized the city of Nantes.[1] Henry was fired by a passion to emulate these deeds, and his father had the sound idea of letting the lad learn by trying, for the Counts of Anjou were accustomed to assuming their responsibilities at an early age.

Henry, therefore, in 1147, when he too was only fourteen, on his own initiative and without any serious preparation or any thought as to what his expedition involved, collected a small company of high-spirited knights and sailed to England to try conclusions with King Stephen himself, just as Fulk the Black had with Count Conan. He landed at Bristol and marched his little party to Cricklade, half-way to Oxford. Stephen was no great military leader, but he had little difficulty to putting his presumptuous young rival to flight in their first engagement.

None of the English barons had joined Henry, although the lad seems to have expected a great rising in his favour when word of his coming got round. Furthermore, like his great-grandfather William the Conqueror before him, he had not hired his knights with ready cash but with promises of rich pay when he should have succeeded in defeating the King of the English. When Stephen dispersed this venturesome crew, Henry's position was difficult indeed. He had no money either to pay his companions or to transport them back to Normandy. He appealed to his mother, but the Empress was herself sorely in need of money and could not help him. Next he turned to his uncle Robert, but the Earl of Gloucester, 'lying on his money-bags like a miser', had other uses for his wealth.

At last, in despair, he sent messengers to King Stephen to beg him as his kinsman to help him. It was characteristic of Stephen that when he received this appeal he immediately sent the boy, who had just tried to usurp his crown, all the money he needed, and Henry and his crestfallen company of knights were able to return to Normandy.[2]

Earl Robert died on October 31, 1147, and with him died the Empress's hope of winning England. He was succeeded by his son William, 'an effeminate man, more interested in affairs of the

---

[1] Rodolfus Glaber: *Historia*, in *Rerum Gallicarum Scriptores*, Vol. X (Paris, 1760), p. 15.   [2] *Gesta Stephani*, pp. 135-7.

bedchamber than in matters of war'.[1]   The Empress could look
for little help from him.   Early in 1148 she abandoned all her
rosy dreams and went back to join her husband.   The nine years
of civil war were over; Stephen was still King of England; and
he had just knighted, in a magnificent ceremony, his son Eustace,
a most promising young man, who was already married to
Constance, the sister of the King of France.

[1] *Gesta Stephani*, pp. 139-40.

II

HENRY, DUKE OF NORMANDY
1148 - 1154

WHILE his wife and his eldest son had been going from one miserable failure to another in England, Count Geoffrey had conquered the whole of Normandy and was now ruling it in his son's name. He made no attempt to claim the Duchy for himself by right of conquest, although he might well have done so, and after his son returned from England in 1147 he was careful to associate Henry with him in the administration of Normandy. Thus Henry received his education in the art of governing his turbulent Duchy under a capable teacher. Although few records survive of Henry's rule in Normandy at this time, it is evident that the experience was immensely valuable to him during these formative years. By the time he was twenty-one he was already an accomplished administrator who knew what he wanted, what his country needed, and how best to secure it. Matilda, for her part, never let her son lose sight of the fact that he was the rightful heir, not only to Normandy, which his father's bravery had recovered for him, but to England as well.

In spite of his mother's ignominious retreat from England, Henry and his cause still had many friends there. Some of them sent him word, early in 1149, that he should be knighted, so that he might lead an army with propriety, and then 'with renewed strength rise up against the King and with vigour and spirit conquer what was lawfully his'.[1]

This turned out to be poor advice. When Henry, acting on it, landed at Bristol, the only person of any importance who joined him was Earl Roger of Hereford, whose father, Miles of Gloucester, had been a stout supporter of the Empress and had been made an earl by her. Many of the other noblemen who had supported the Empress sent their young sons to join Henry, but they did not give him any more effective help. The lad was still only sixteen,

[1] *Gesta Stephani*, p. 142.

21

and the noblemen on whom he had counted took the view that he could scarcely hope to accomplish, at his tender age, what his uncle Robert had not been able to do.

If there was no popular rising of the West in his favour, Henry at least could count on the support of his great-uncle, David, King of Scots, who had never ceased to consider himself bound by his oath to recognise Matilda as King Henry's heir. Henry and his young companions accordingly went to Carlisle to meet King David. He gave them an enthusiastic reception and knighted Henry and his friends on Whitsunday, May 22, 1149.[1] No chronicler wrote a description of the ceremony on that particular occasion, but one may assume that it did not differ materially from the one in which Henry's grandfather, King Henry, had knighted Geoffrey of Anjou.

At dawn, having taken a bath, as custom demands of the candidate, he was ready. After the washing of his body, Geoffrey put on a fine linen shirt next his flesh. He was vested with a robe woven of gold, he was clothed with a cloak dyed purple, he was shod with silken slippers, and his feet were fitted with shoes that had small golden lions on their tops. He was given a Spanish horse of great beauty and an incomparable coat of mail, double-meshed, so that it could not be pierced by blows from any lance or javelin. His feet were bound with golden spurs; a shield with fanciful golden lions was hung about his shoulders; a helmet, shining with many precious stones, was put on his head; a lance of ashwood was brought to him. And lastly a sword was brought to him from the King's treasury. Thus armed, our new knight, with wondrous agility, leaped on his horse without touching the stirrups.[2]

Earl Rannulf of Chester, the son-in-law of Earl Robert of Gloucester and the most notorious turncoat of his time, joined the party. Rannulf was virtually an independent sovereign, ruling over a territory that stretched from Chester almost to Lincoln, and he had shown great cleverness in playing the rival parties against each other, always to his advantage.

King David, the two Earls, and the young Henry concocted a

---

[1] Gervase of Canterbury: *Chronicle*, ed. William Stubbs (Rolls Series, 2 vols., 1878-80), Vol. I, p. 141.

[2] Condensed from *Historia Gaufridi Ducis Normannorum et Comitis Andegavorum*, ed. Louis Halphen and René Poupardin, in Collection des textes pour l'étude de l'histoire, Vol. XLVIII (Paris, 1913), pp. 179-80.

plan to storm the city of York, Stephen's chief stronghold in the North. David raised a great army of Scots, and with this army they marched on York. When they approached the city, however, they found that Stephen had been warned and was waiting for them with a well-equipped body of knights. David had hurled his half-naked Scots against the English at the Battle of the Standard eleven years before this, and 'all their might was destroyed like a cobweb'. Eleven thousand Scots were killed in that engagement, and of the two hundred knights who accompanied King David into battle only nineteen carried their coats of mail back home with them.[1]

David had no desire to repeat that disastrous experience. Observing that Stephen's army was larger than theirs and growing all the time, the allies prudently gave up the idea of a battle and dismissed their army. The newly-knighted Henry and his English companions fled down twisting lanes and little-used byways to escape pursuit and at last reached Roger's city of Hereford, 'worn out with fear and labour'.

Stephen had warned his son Eustace, who was then in London, that Henry would probably make for the West. Eustace set out to catch him. He laid an ambush for Henry near Bristol, but the young pretender escaped in the middle of the night and took refuge at Devizes.

Henry next led an expedition into the Southwest. His cousin, Earl William of Gloucester, and the Earl of Hereford accompanied him. They captured the town of Bridport by storm and inflicted great damage on the estates of Stephen's adherents in that area. While they were pleasantly engaged in pillaging everything along their way and setting fire to houses and churches, they heard that Eustace was attacking Devizes in their absence. They hurried to the relief of the garrison and arrived just as Eustace and his army had captured the outworks of the castle and were setting fire to the houses around it. The defenders, who had been putting up a poor fight, took heart when they saw Henry's party arrive. Both groups fell with fury upon the attackers and utterly routed them.

Henry was gaining experience in warfare from all this, but at

[1] Henry of Huntingdon, p. 264; John of Worcester: *Chronicle*, ed. J. R. H. Weaver, Anecdota Oxoniensia, Medieval and Modern Series, Part 13 (Oxford, 1908), p. 52.

c

the same time it was obvious that with the forces then at his command he had little chance of accomplishing anything of importance in England. It had been a mistake for him to have come to England without an army large enough to challenge King Stephen successfully, for both this expedition and his similar experience in 1147 had demonstrated that the English barons would do nothing to help him unless he had a good chance of winning. Stephen was a king after the barons' own hearts, for he allowed them to do pretty much as they pleased, and they would make no effort to depose him. Henry's friends therefore advised him to return to Normandy, establish his position there, and then come back to England when he could bring effective help with him. Henry took their advice.[1]

Geoffrey at once relinquished Normandy to him as his rightful inheritance through his mother. It must have given Geoffrey satisfaction to think that it was he who by force of arms had won the Duchy for his son, while the Empress, for all her pride, had met with miserable failure in her efforts to do the same thing in England.

Meanwhile Louis VII, who as King of France was the overlord of Geoffrey, Count of Anjou and Maine, and of Henry, who was in effect Duke of Normandy although Louis had never recognised him as such, had returned from his abortive expedition to the Holy Land in the ill-fated Second Crusade. Louis had been destined for the priesthood, but when his elder brother Philip was killed by a fall from his horse Louis had been taken from the cloister and anointed by Pope Innocent II, in 1131, as the future King of France.[2] His education had been continued under the direction of Suger, Abbot of St. Denis, to such good effect that he always felt most at home in the company of priests and monks.

To console himself for the sorry figure he had cut on the Crusade and perhaps to take his mind off his troubles with his wife, who was clamouring for a divorce, Louis embarked on a series of petty quarrels with Geoffrey and Henry over some castles that Geoffrey had captured in his enthusiasm, although his title to them was by no means clear. Eustace came over from

[1] *Gesta Stephani*, pp. 142-8.

[2] Robert of Torigni: *Chronicle*, in *Chronicles of the Reigns of Stephen, Henry II, and Richard I*, ed. Richard Howlett (Rolls Series, 4 vols., 1884-9), Vol. IV, p. 120.

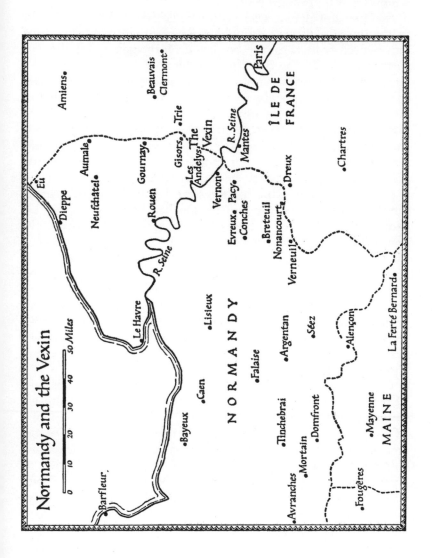

Normandy and the Vexin

Barfleur.

Avranches
•Mortain
•Domfront
•Tinchebrai
Bayeux
•Caen
•Falaise
•Argentan
•Séez
•Alençon
•Lisieux
•Mayenne
La Ferté Bernard•
•Fougères

MAINE

NORMANDY

Le Havre
R. Seine
Rouen
Gournay•
•Verneuil
Nonancourt•
•Breteuil
•Conches
Evreux• Pacy•
Vernon•
Les Andelys• The
Gisors• Vexin
•Trie
•Dreux
•Chartres

R. Seine
Mantes•
•Beauvais
Clermont•

ÎLE DE
FRANCE

Paris

Amiens•

Eu
•Dieppe
Neufchâtel•
Aumale•

0   10   20   30   40   50 Miles

England to help his brother-in-law, and Louis used him to make a number of forays into Normandy.[1]

Geoffrey and Henry, after several indecisive clashes with Louis, in the summer of 1151 assembled a large and capable army of experienced fighters on the border of Normandy to repulse any further attacks by the French. On his part, Louis gathered the largest army he could command. A real war, rather than a game of attacking and defending scattered castles, seemed imminent. At this crucial moment Louis was stricken with fever. 'Wise and religious men' seized the opportunity to point out to him the wickedness of shedding so much Christian blood, especially by one who had worn the Crusader's Cross. He therefore proclaimed a truce to last until he had recovered his health.

Louis had time to think matters over during his convalescence. He decided that Geoffrey and his son had too firm a grasp on Normandy for him to be able to drive them out. He accordingly confirmed Henry in his possession of the territory by accepting his homage for it. This act of homage did not imply that Louis had or claimed any real authority over Normandy. It was the formal recognition of a feudal fiction, but it was necessary in order for Henry to be legitimately established as Duke of Normandy. As the price of this recognition Henry had to surrender to Louis the Vexin, the much-fought-over territory that lay between Normandy and the Ile de France, between the rivers Epte and Andelle on the right bank of the Seine.[2]

Geoffrey and Henry went to Paris together for the ceremony of rendering homage to their overlord. While they were there, Louis's wife, Queen Eleanor, cast an appraising eye on the Duke of Normandy, a young man of eighteen, eleven years her junior, fresh-faced and ruddy, and she liked what she saw. None of this was lost on Geoffrey. He warned his son several times to have nothing to do with Eleanor, both because she was the wife of his lord, the King of France, and because Geoffrey himself had committed adultery with her, which would make any relationship between Henry and Eleanor incestuous.[3] Eleanor, however, was so taken by the young Duke's appearance and manners that

---

[1] Henry of Huntingdon, p. 283.

[2] Robert of Torigni, p. 162.

[3] Gerald of Wales: *De Principis Instructione*, ed. G. F. Warner. Vol. VIII of *Opera* (Rolls Series, 8 vols., 1861-91), p. 300.

she at once set to work to obtain a divorce in order to marry him.[1]

Henry was never considered a handsome man like his father, but his youthful freshness captured Eleanor's fancy. He was a little above the average in height, stocky, square-shouldered, and immensely strong. He had a ruddy, freckled, square face, with clear grey eyes, and tawny hair cropped close to his head. His hands were rough and chapped from exposure. Although his clothes were rich, as befitted his station in life, he wore them carelessly. Instead of the usual long robe and flowing cloak, Henry ordinarily wore a knee-length tunic and a short mantle for ease in riding, which gained him the appelation of 'Curt-mantle' among the English. His legs were covered by woollen hose rather like the long woollen underwear of today, except that the hose were woven, not knit, and cross-wrapped from the ankle to the knee with leather thongs to make them fit better. Henry was a rough man of action, hardened to war, tireless in the saddle, and so full of energy that he could not bear to be still for a moment.

Geoffrey and his son left Paris rejoicing at their success in having had their conquest of Normandy confirmed by their overlord. On their way they discussed Henry's latest plans for the invasion of England. Now that he was recognised as Duke of Normandy and in full control of the Duchy, he was in a position where he could raise the money to pay an effective army to further his ambitions. He had summoned a council of his Norman barons to meet him on September 14, 1151, and consider his return to England.

As they rode along, Geoffrey complained of not feeling well. They stopped at Château-du-Loir, twenty-five miles south and a little east of Le Mans. The Count developed a high fever and made his preparations for death. He designated Henry as his heir to Anjou and Maine, and to his second son, Geoffrey, he gave three castles in Anjou. When Henry gained England, his father specified, he was to turn Anjou and Maine over to his brother. The valiant Count Geoffrey the Fair died on September 7, 1151, and was buried in the Church of St. Julian at Le Mans.[2]

After his father's funeral, Henry received the homage of the

---

[1] William of Newburgh: *Historia Rerum Anglicarum*, ed. Richard Howlett. Vol. I of *Chronicles of the Reigns of Stephen, Henry II and Richard I*, p. 93.

[2] Robert of Torigni, pp. 162-3.

nobles of Anjou and Maine. He assured himself of the loyalty and safety of his domains, and then his thoughts turned once more to England. During the following Lent his uncle Reginald, another bastard son of King Henry, whom the Empress had made Earl of Cornwall during her stay in England, arrived in Normandy to urge him once more to return. He summoned a council to meet at Lisieux shortly after Easter 1152, but again his plans had to be postponed.

The Queen of France secured a divorce from her husband on March 21. She at once offered herself and her great Duchy of Aquitaine, which embraced all of southwestern France, to the young Duke Henry. He accepted with alacrity, for she was the richest prize in Europe.[1] Her reputation might be badly tarnished, but her Duchy made up half the kingdom of France. Count Geoffrey had in the end subdued a wife older than himself and of greater importance, and his son was certain that for the sake of Eleanor's lands he could do the same.

Eleanor, the elder of the two daughters who were the only surviving children of William X, Duke of Aquitaine and Count of Poitou, was born about 1122. When her father died in 1137 he willed the hand of his elder daughter to Louis, the son of his overlord, King Louis VI. Louis at once claimed his bride and her inheritance. He married Eleanor at Bordeaux in June 1137, and on August 1 he succeeded his father as King of France.

Under the influence of the preaching of Bernard of Clairvaux, Louis and Eleanor took the Cross at Vézelay at Easter 1146 and left for the Holy Land in the following year. Louis's motive in setting out on the Crusade was no doubt purely religious, but his wife had no such feelings. Eleanor was gay, impetuous, and pleasure-loving. Her life with the staid and proper Louis was intolerably boring to her. She wanted gaiety, movement, and adventure, and these she found in plenty in the stir and excitement of the crusading army.

When they arrived in Asia Minor, Louis lost almost the whole of his army in various ambushes between Byzantium and Antioch. They were welcomed to Antioch by its Prince, Raymond, who was Eleanor's uncle and only a few years older than she. Eleanor and Raymond fell at once into an intimacy that was a source of great offence to Louis and of much comment among the Crusa-

[1] Robert of Torigni, pp. 164-5.

ders. Antioch was a highly civilised city, and Prince Raymond, a man of the same temperament as his niece, dazzled Eleanor with its refinements. The gossip of the time accused Raymond and Eleanor of incest; even the learned and cautious John of Salisbury, an English cleric who was a member of the papal court at the time, hints that their relations were not above reproach.

In the year of grace 1149 the most Christian King of the French, after his forces had been crushed in the East, came to Antioch, where he was honourably received by Prince Raymond, the brother of William, Count of Poitou, of happy memory. Thus he was the Queen's uncle, and he owed loyalty, love, and respect to the King for many reasons. But while they remained there in order to console, encourage, and put new life into the survivors of the ruined army, the Prince's familiarity with the Queen and their assiduous and almost ceaseless conversation made the King suspicious. His suspicions were greatly increased when the Queen wanted to remain there, although the King was preparing to leave, and the Prince tried his best to keep her, if it could be done with the King's permission.

When the King hastened to tear her away by force, she made mention of their kinship and said that it was unlawful for them to remain together, because there was kinship between them in the fourth and fifth degree. . . .

She was taken away and forced to set out for Jerusalem with the King, and the hearts of both of them burned ever hotter, and, although they hid it as best they could, the injury remained.[1]

They went on to Jerusalem and then to the siege of Damascus, which ended in a fiasco that became the scandal of Christendom. Having accomplished less than nothing, such of the Crusaders as were still alive set out for home. On the way, Louis and his unhappy Queen stopped to visit the Pope, Eugene III.

The Cardinals and officials of the Church went to meet the King, and, having provided everything at his pleasure, they brought him to Tusculum to the Lord Pope, by whom he was received with such kindness and devotion that one would have said the Pope was receiving not a mere mortal man but an angel of the Lord. After hearing the complaints of each one separately, he entirely settled the falling out between the King and the Queen, which had begun at Antioch, and forbade under threat of excommunication that any-

[1] John of Salisbury: *Historia Pontificalis*, ed. Marjorie Chibnall (Nelson's Medieval Texts, 1956), pp. 52-53.

one should dare to speak against the marriage or that it should be dissolved for any reason whatever. This order evidently pleased the King greatly, for he loved the Queen vehemently and in an almost childish fashion.[1]

After they returned to France, Eleanor bore her second child, also a daughter. Her failure to provide an heir to the throne in fifteen years of marriage was probably a more potent reason for

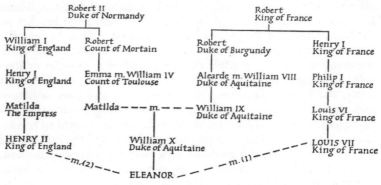

II ELEANOR AND HER HUSBANDS

Degrees of consanguinity are computed by the number of generations back to the common ancestor. Thus Henry II was four degrees removed from Robert II, and Eleanor five degrees.

Louis's agreeing at last to her continued pleadings for a release than was the excuse of consanguinity. Louis and Eleanor were related in the fourth and fifth degrees, having a common ancestor in Robert, King of France. The Church at this time forbade marriages within the seventh degree of kinship. The rule was commonly disregarded, but it made a convenient pretext for dissolving an unhappy marriage.

The Archbishop of Rheims held a council to consider the validity of Louis's marriage to Eleanor. On March 21, 1152, the prelates decided that the couple were indeed related within the forbidden degree and that the marriage was therefore null and void. Apparently no-one mentioned the Pope's validation of the marriage. Since they were presumed to have married in good faith, however, their two daughters, Marie and Alice, were

[1] John of Salisbury: *Historia Pontificalis*, ed. Marjorie Chibnall (Nelson's Medieval Texts, 1956), p. 61.

pronounced legitimate, and they remained in their father's care. Eleanor was at last free of the husband she described as a monk, not a man.[1] Louis, however, was enough of a man deeply to resent Eleanor's contemptuous treatment of him.

Eleanor was not only free; she was also Duchess of Aquitaine in her own right and one of the richest women in Europe. She went at once to Poitiers and sent messengers to Henry to offer herself and her lands to him. Henry set out immediately with only a few companions. He and Eleanor were quietly married at Poitiers without any pomp and almost surreptitiously, for fear that some troublesome canonist might raise the question of kinship at this awkward moment. Eleanor was as closely related to Henry as she was to Louis, their common ancestor being Robert II, Duke of Normandy.

Louis had little enough reason to think well of his presumptuous young vassal. When his wife spurned him and hastened to throw herself into Henry's arms, the French King was filled with jealousy and resentment. Louis's mind worked slowly, but he was a stubborn and tenacious man. He dedicated himself from this time forward to revenging himself on Henry.

An opportunity soon offered itself. Eustace, King Stephen's son, gravely concerned at Henry's great increase in power and prestige and the consequent threat it offered to his prospects of inheriting his father's crown, went to France and urged his brother-in-law, King Louis, to take steps to curb his vassal. Henry had not only taken Louis's wife; her Duchy of Aquitaine, which had once belonged to Louis by virtue of his marriage, was now added to Henry's lands. As Duke of Normandy and of Aquitaine and Count of Anjou and Maine, he controlled the whole western half of France excepting Brittany, an area larger by far than that over which Louis held sway. The kings of France, for all their fine title, had effective control only over the Ile de France.

Louis formed a coalition, sometime after midsummer 1152, that included Eustace and Geoffrey, the brother of Henry, son of the Empress. Geoffrey was not content with the three castles that formed his inheritance and hoped by defeating his brother to force him to share some of his lands with him. The avowed object of this alliance was to wrest Normandy, Anjou, and

[1] William of Newburgh, p. 93.

Maine from him.   The young Duke was at Barfleur, preparing
to cross to England, when the attacks were launched.

Henry was forced to spend the rest of the year in meeting these
threats.   By the end of 1152 he had soundly defeated his brother
Geoffrey and had so capably defended Normandy against Louis
that the allies were glad to agree to a truce with him.[1]   By this
time Henry had organised his defences so skilfully that he felt he
could safely leave his territories in the hands of his mother, his
Duchess, and his captains, while he made another attempt to gain
the crown of England, this time with an army large enough to
ensure his success.   To finance this expedition he borrowed at
least £7,000 from two money-lenders, William Cade of St.
Omer and William Trentegeruns, Viscount of Rouen.[2]

It is impossible to translate medieval sums of money into
modern equivalents.   The economy then was not primarily
based on money, and the major portion of a man's income consisted of goods and services received.   Roughly speaking,
£7,000 was equal to about half the total income of the Crown
as accounted for at the Exchequer during an average year in the
early part of Henry's reign.   One may form some idea of the
value of money from the fact that the ordinary foot-soldier was
paid a penny a day at this time and the knight eightpence.

Henry collected a fleet of 36 ships, and with 140 knights and
3,000 men-at-arms[3] he landed at Bristol on January 6, 1153.   His
cousin, Earl William of Gloucester, and his uncle, Earl Reginald
of Cornwall, met him there.   Soon many of the leading men of
the West, faithful as ever to the Angevin cause and impressed by
the strength of his forces, joined him with their followers.

From Bristol, as the first step in their campaign, Henry and his
army went to lay siege to Malmesbury.   King Stephen and
Eustace, who had returned to England after Louis had made the
truce with Henry, hastened to meet them.   The rival armies in
battle array faced each other across the River Avon.   A violent
winter storm came up from the west, and the wind and the cold
rain beat in the faces of Stephen's men with such fury that they
were forced to withdraw.   Henry, with the storm at his back,

---

[1] Robert of Torigni, pp. 165-6, 169-71.

[2] Sir Hilary Jenkinson: 'William Cade, a Financier of the Twelfth Century',
English Historical Review, Vol. XXVIII (April 1913), pp. 209-20; H. G. Richard-
son: 'The Chamber under Henry II', *EHR*, Vol. LXIX (Oct. 1954), pp. 596-611.

[3] William of Newburgh, p. 88.

was left in undisputed possession of the field. The garrison of Malmesbury surrendered to him, and Stephen and Eustace retreated to London.[1]

This bloodless victory was a great help to Henry's cause. The Earl of Leicester, one of the richest and most powerful men in England, now came out openly on his side, supplied him with everything he needed, and turned some thirty castles over to him. Robert of Beaumont, Earl of Leicester, belonged to one of the greatest of the Anglo-Norman families. His father had fought with William the Conqueror at Hastings and was the first man to breach the English shield-wall. He had lived well into the reign of Henry I and had accumulated vast estates. His son Robert had been brought up in the King's court, and Henry had given him a rich heiress, the daughter of the Earl of Norfolk, as his wife. Although Earl Robert had been faithful to Stephen, he had taken little part in the civil wars and was careful to keep on friendly terms with the Angevin party. He had spent the crucial years of the war in supervising the construction of the great Augustinian abbey of St. Mary de Pré at Leicester, which he built and richly endowed.

The adhesion of so great a man as the Earl of Leicester marked one of the turning points in Henry's efforts to secure the crown. Up till this time, Henry had drawn his active support largely from the adventurous younger men of the West, who had little influence outside their own neighbourhood. That the Earl of Leicester should now lend his backing to Henry turned the scales in his favour. He was no longer a brash young adventurer. For the first time, he had the men, the money, and the support necessary to gain his ends.

The Duke cautiously devoted the spring to consolidating his position in the West. In the summer he felt sufficiently secure to go to the relief of Wallingford, which Stephen had been besieging for more than a year. He laid siege to Crowmarsh, on the other side of the Thames, to relieve the pressure on Wallingford. Stephen came up with his army, and again the two forces prepared for battle.

As the King was riding about and directing the disposition of his forces, his horse reared and threw him to the ground. When this happened three times in succession, it was considered such a

[1] Henry of Huntingdon, pp. 286-7.

bad omen that his advisers seized the opportunity to point out
to him the dreadful results that the impending battle, in which
brothers would be arrayed against brothers and fathers against
sons, would have, no matter which side won.   They prevailed
on him to let them seek a parley with Henry.

When they approached the young Duke, however, his friends
had great difficulty in persuading him even to postpone the
attack, for he saw victory and the crown of England within his
grasp, and he wanted to fight through to a conclusion.   At last
he agreed to meet the King.   He and Stephen, standing on
opposite banks of the Thames at a narrow place in the river, held
a conversation out of earshot of their followers.   At the conclusion of the conference each withdrew to his army and in-
structed his men to lay down their arms.   The battle was called
off; no one save Henry and Stephen knew on what terms.

Eustace was so disgusted by his father's spiritless conduct that
he went into Suffolk burning with rage.

> When he came to the convent of the blessed Edmund [at Bury
> St. Edmunds] he was honourably received there and given a splen-
> did meal, but when he was refused the money he demanded in order
> to pay his followers he went away raging.   On the octave day of
> St. Lawrence he ordered all the country round about, and especially
> St. Edmund's harvests, to be plundered and all the loot to be brought
> to a castle of his that was nearby.   But when he sat down at table
> to eat, as we read in writings, at the first taste of food he fell into a
> miserable madness, and because of the arrogance he had shown to the
> Martyrs he underwent the dire pains of death.[1]

People rarely enjoyed long illnesses in the twelfth century.
Hale and hearty on one day, they would fall into a fever on the
next, make their preparations for death, and die almost immediately.   The wretched state of sanitation, the primitive medicine
of the time, which had hardly advanced a step in the last thousand
years, and the fact that much of the meat they ate was tainted, to
say the least, were more than sufficient reasons for these sudden
and fatal fevers.   For the monastic writers of the time, however,
the sudden illness and death of wicked men like Eustace were
direct punishments from the hand of Almighty God, whereas the
passing of a good man was hailed as a holy and happy summons
to a better life.

[1] Gervase of Canterbury, Vol. I, pp. 153-5.

On the same day that Eustace died, August 17, 1153, Eleanor of Aquitaine gave birth to her first son, who was given the name of William, the traditional name of the Dukes of Aquitaine. It was probably later in this year that Henry's first bastard son was born, of a common English whore named Ykenai or Hikenai, 'who scorned no filthiness'. The child was named Geoffrey, after his grandfather, and Henry later had him brought up with his family.[1]

Towards the end of August, seeking always to bring matters to a conclusion, Henry laid siege to Stamford. With the resumption of open warfare the country returned to the state of confusion from which the truce at Wallingford had briefly rescued it. The bishops, particularly Archbishop Theobald of Canterbury and Bishop Henry of Winchester, and the more responsible barons were appalled at the prospect of renewed and apparently endless civil war. Bishop Henry constituted himself a mediator between his brother and the Duke, urging them to a peaceful settlement, and Archbishop Theobald added his powerful influence to the negotiations. Stephen's wife had died during the previous year, and Eustace's death, coming so soon afterwards, had greatly saddened the gentle King, broken his spirit, and made him even more anxious to avoid further conflict. William, his only surviving son, was well provided for. He had married the daughter of the Earl Warenne and had been given both his title and his estates. Furthermore, William himself showed no desire to succeed his father in the thankless task of ruling England and fighting Henry.

At last, on November 6, 1153, King Stephen and Duke Henry met at Winchester and agreed on the terms of peace. They then went to London together, and in the presence of many of the leading men of the kingdom the treaty was drawn up and ratified.

> Stephen, King of England, to the archbishops, bishops, abbots, earls, justiciars, sheriffs, barons, and all his faithful men of England: greetings.
> Be it known to you that I, the King of England, Stephen, have made Henry, Duke of Normandy, the successor to the kingdom of England after me, and my heir by hereditary right, and thus I have

[1] Walter Map: *De Nugis Curialium*, ed. M. R. James (Oxford, 1914), pp. 238, 246.

given and confirmed to him and his heirs the kingdom of England.

The Duke, therefore, because of this honour and the grant and confirmation made to him by me, has done homage to me and given security by oath that he will be faithful to me and that he will guard my life and honour to the best of his ability, through the provisions discussed between us beforehand, which are contained in this charter.

I also have given security by oath to the Duke that I will guard his life and honour to the best of my ability, and I will uphold him as my son and heir in everything I can, and I will guard him against all men as far as I am able.

My son William has made liege homage and security to the Duke of Normandy, and the Duke has granted to him to hold from him all the lands that I held before I obtained the Kingdom of England, whether in England, whether in Normandy, whether in other places; and whatever he received with the daughter of the Earl Warenne.

The Duke's mother, and wife, and the brothers of this same Duke, and all to whom this treaty might apply are hereby given assurance of security. In the affairs of the kingdom I will act with the advice of the Duke. I, however, in the whole realm of England, both in the Duke's part and in mine, will exercise royal justice.[1]

All the nobles of England were summoned to meet at Oxford on January 13, 1154. There they swore fealty to Henry, saving the honour due the King while he lived.[2]

The Duke was nevertheless in a difficult position in England, where he had no real authority. He had gained his great objective, for he was the acknowledged heir to the throne, with no rival in sight, but he could accomplish little more in England while Stephen still lived. Furthermore, he was receiving disquieting reports about the rebellious attitude of some of his newly-acquired vassals in Aquitaine. He returned to Normandy around Easter, April 4, 1154, made a quick expedition into Aquitaine, and suppressed the disorders there.

These affairs seemed petty indeed when he received the news that King Stephen had died on October 25, 1154. Stephen, of whom the English said that 'he was a mild man and soft and good and did no justice',[3] had fallen sick of 'a chronic flux of hæmorrhoids'[4] at Dover and died after a few days. He was buried beside

---

[1] L. V. Delisle and Elie Berger: *Recueil des actes de Henri II* (2 vols., Paris, 1916), Vol. I, p. 61.   [2] Gervase of Canterbury, Vol. I, p. 157.

[3] *The Peterborough Chronicle*, p. 55.

[4] Gervase of Canterbury, Vol. I, p. 159.

his wife and his son in Feversham Abbey, which he and his Queen had founded.

Archbishop Theobald of Canterbury despatched swift messengers to carry the news to Henry and to urge him to come at once and claim the crown of England.

III

HENRY, KING OF THE ENGLISH
1154 - 1157

AFTER taking counsel with his mother, Henry summoned his brothers, Geoffrey and William, and his leading Norman barons to meet him at Barfleur to take ship to England. When they assembled, however, such violent storms disturbed the Channel that they could not sail. Henry, who could not bear any form of inactivity, was forced to wait for a favourable wind day after day, till a month had passed. At last, he could endure the delay no longer. When the wind slackened only slightly, he and Eleanor and their attendants sailed on December 7. A number of the English barons met him at Winchester and did homage to him. The party then proceeded to London, where the people gave Henry an enthusiastic welcome.

'Among the noble cities of the world, celebrated by fame,' writes William Fitz Stephen, himself a Londoner, 'the city of London, the seat of the realm of the English, is the one whose fame is most widely spread, whose works and wares are carried the farthest, whose head is lifted the highest.' London had at that time, he boasts, thirteen great conventual churches and 126 smaller parish churches. The Tower of London guarded it on the east and Barnard's Castle on the west. It was surrounded on three sides by the city walls, with seven gates, and on the south by the Thames. Two miles up the river was Westminster, with its abbey and royal palace.

Outside the city walls were pleasant gardens, planted with trees. To the north were 'fields, meadows, and pleasant stretches of level ground, with streams where the mill-wheels turn with a merry murmur. Nearby stretches a vast forest and thick woods, the haunt of stags, fallow-deer, wild boars, and forest bulls.' William tells of the disputations of the scholars in the principal schools and of the horse-fairs and races at Smithfield every Friday, attended by many of the earls, barons, knights, and citizens.

He writes sympathetically, 'for we were all children once', of how the schoolboys on Shrove Tuesday bring their fighting cocks to school and spend the morning at cock-fights and the afternoon at playing ball in a field in the suburbs, cheered on by an enthusiastic crowd of parents and city men who have ridden out to watch the sport. He tells of the miracle plays, of the tilting during the Sundays of Lent, and of the sham naval battles on the Thames at Eastertide. During the summer the young men exercise at archery, run, jump, wrestle, throw stones, and stage mock wars, armed with slingshots and shields, while 'Cytherea leads the chorus of girls till moonrise, and the earth is shaken by joyous feet'. In the winter they skate on the Thames, with the shin-bones of animals tied under their boots, while others make sledges of blocks of ice and are pulled by their companions.

Most wonderful of all, according to William, 'there is in London, on the river-bank, a public cookshop. Every day one may find there dishes of various kinds, roasted, baked, fried, boiled: big fish, little fish, coarse meat for the poor, dainty meat for the rich, meat of game, of birds, and of sparrows.' Summing it all up, 'I do not think that there is a city in which there are more praiseworthy customs, in visiting churches, in honouring God's priests, in observing the feasts, in giving alms, in entertaining guests, in plighting betrothals, in contracting marriages, in celebrating weddings, in gracing banquets, in amusing one's fellow-guests, and also in attending funerals and burying the dead. The only bane of London is the immoderate drinking of fools and the frequent fires.'[1]

Henry and Eleanor were crowned King and Queen of the English by Archbishop Theobald of Canterbury in Westminster Abbey on Sunday, December 19, 1154. The Archbishops of York and Rouen, fourteen bishops, and many earls and barons both Norman and English attended the ceremony and the great feast that followed it.[2]

The right to crown the king and queen belonged to the Archbishop of Canterbury alone. The ceremony set, in the most solemn way possible, the Church's seal of approval on the king and raised him above ordinary men. The rite itself was modelled

---

[1] William Fitz Stephen, in *Materials*, Vol. III, pp. 2-8.
[2] Gervase of Canterbury, Vol. I, pp. 159-60.

after that used for the consecration of a bishop and partook of a
sacramental nature. In the solemn procession into the Abbey
walked a host of pages, of knights, barons, and earls in due order
of precedence, of the monks of Westminster Abbey, of the clergy,
priests, abbots, and bishops, their vestments worked with gold
and precious stones gleaming in the light of countless candles, and
lastly the King, the Queen, and the Archbishop, while the great
organ poured forth its peals of joy, the choir of monks sang with
all their might, and the great bells crashed in brazen thunder to
tell all England that the King was being crowned. The Archbishop anointed the King and Queen with the holy oils during the
course of the Mass and placed their crowns on their heads. Henry,
son of the Empress, was now King of the English.

Immediately after his crowning, Henry issued the customary
charter of liberties, in which he harked back to the government
of Henry I as the ideal he proposed to follow:

> Henry, King of the English, Duke of the Normans and Aquita-
> nians, and Count of the Angevins, to all his faithful men, French
> and English: greetings.
>
> Be it known to you that to the honour of God and Holy Church
> and for the common improvement of my whole realm I have con-
> ceded and given and by this my present charter confirmed to God
> and Holy Church and to all my earls and barons and all my men, all
> the concessions and gifts and liberties and free customs that King
> Henry my grandfather gave and conceded to them.
>
> Likewise, all evil customs that he wiped out and remitted I remit
> and concede that they be wiped out by me and my heirs.
>
> Wherefore I will and firmly order that Holy Church and all earls
> and barons and all my men have and hold all those concessions and
> gifts and liberties and free customs freely and quietly, well and in
> peace and wholly, of me and my heirs, for themselves and their heirs,
> as freely and quietly and fully in all things as King Henry my grand-
> father gave and conceded to them and confirmed by his charter.[1]

The new King of England, although he was only twenty-one
years old, was no raw, inexperienced youth. As Duke of Normandy he had learned to hold his own against stubborn barons
who resisted his rule. He had acquired, in his dealings with King
Louis, confidence in his ability both to meet his overlord on the
field of battle and to negotiate with him for the truces that

[1] *Select Charters*, ed. William Stubbs (Oxford, 1913), p. 158.

occasionally interrupted the almost continual skirmishes along
the French border.   During the course of his various attempts to
win the crown of England he had learned to know most of the
leading men of the country.   He came to the throne with a good
knowledge of the land over which he was to rule.

Henry was shrewd.   In observing both his mother, the
Empress, and his cousin, King Stephen, he had realised their outstanding weaknesses and had determined to avoid them in his
own conduct.   His mother had alienated her supporters and lost
her following because of her haughty conduct.   Henry's conduct
was quite the opposite.   He had manners of an easy familiarity,
and he made himself accessible to any of his subjects who wanted
to see him.   King Stephen, on the other hand, had been too soft
in his dealing with his barons to be able to command their obedience.   There was nothing soft about Henry, as he proceeded to
show his barons as soon as the formalities of his coronation were
out of the way.

The King held his Christmas court at Bermondsey, and all those
who had attended his crowning were no doubt present.   He discussed with them 'the state of the realm and the restoration of
peace'.[1]   It was probably at this time that he selected the ministers
who were to help him in his great task.   The most important
post by far was that of the Chief Justiciar, who was in charge of
the judicial system, who sat at the meetings of the Barons of the
Exchequer when the sheriffs rendered their twice-yearly accounts,
who heard the most important cases in the King's court, who
supervised the routine course of the government, and who acted
in the King's stead when he was out of the country.

Henry divided this responsibility between Richard of Luci, who
had served King Stephen faithfully and well and who knew all
the workings of the governmental machinery, and the Earl of
Leicester, to whose support, more than that of any other one man,
Henry owed his crown.   The appointment of these two men
showed the country that the new King harboured no resentment
against those who had served his predecessor loyally and also
that he intended to help, as far as he justly could, those who had
helped him in the past.   Henry, for all his impatience and restless
temper, was an excellent judge of men, and in no way did he
show this quality better than in his choice of these two men to be

[1] Gervase of Canterbury, Vol. I, p. 160.

his chief ministers, for both of them served him with perfect fidelity and great ability for the rest of their lives.

Henry's first object was to secure the demolition of the un-licensed castles that Stephen had weakly tolerated and the expulsion of the hated Flemish mercenaries he had used to prop up his position. Henry sent the Flemings out of the country, to the great relief of the English, and he had most of the unlicensed castles torn down. A few rebellious barons held out and were dealt with in the course of the following year. Henry was determined at the very outset of his reign to make the royal power once more supreme in England.

With characteristic energy the King began in January to bring some of the worst offenders to account. Thus he started on the ceaseless peregrinations over his realms, usually at breakneck speed, that were to be the despair of his court. When the King travelled, as Henry did constantly, all his household and the officers of the government travelled with him. The King and his entourage rode on horseback; his clothes, his bedding, the fittings of his chapel and the relics of the Saints, his money, his silver plate, and the pots and pans of the kitchen were carried in chests and bags slung in pairs over the backs of pack horses or hauled in carts.

In the procession went the clerks of the chancery, who turned out an unending stream of charters and writs under the supervision of the chancellor; the steward and the butler, with their retinue of napiers, cooks and bakers, slaughter-men, cup-bearers, and scullions; and the chamberlain, whose staff included the bearer of the king's bed, the servants of the bedchamber, who had charge of the king's clothes, the tailor, the ewer, who dried the king's clothes and prepared his bath, and the laundress.

The finest show was made by the outdoor departments, under the constable and the marshal, who in time of war were the leaders of the army. They were responsible for the king's horses, for the ushers and sergeants who kept order in the vast establishment, for the watchmen and the stoker, who kept fires burning from Michaelmas till Easter wherever the king stayed, for the king's tent-keeper, in case he should decide, as he often did, to spend the night wherever he happened to be and thus throw all the planning of his household into confusion; and for the hunting staff. This was a small army in itself, for Henry preferred hunting above all other diversions. The cavalcade was enlivened by the horn-blowers; the fewterers, leading the greyhounds and the lime-hounds and the braches; the berners, who fed the hounds; the wolf-hunters, with their twenty-four running hounds and eight greyhounds; the archers; the chief huntsman and his knights and the twenty sergeants of the hunt, and a host of underlings.[1]

Thus the great procession wove its way, usually over the old Roman roads that still formed the arteries of communication, with the King resplendent in the 'ruby scarlet' and Lincoln green that were his favourite wear, with jewelled brooches at his throat and shoulder to serve as clasps for his tunic and cloak and with a richly ornamented buckle on his belt.

For all the richness of his attire and the splendour of his household, Henry led a busy, rather drab and workaday life, hearing the constant suits that arose from the confusion of the civil war, settling disputes among his tenants, and ceaselessly investigating and prying into every aspect of the administration of his new realm. He was a severely practical man of business, and his major concerns were to establish peace and order, to curb the powers of such of his barons as had set themselves up as independent lords, and to increase the revenues of the Crown, which had suffered severely from the lavishness with which both King Stephen and the Empress had given away the lands and manors that were the king's main source of income.

In the course of his progress to the north, Henry received the submission of one of the most turbulent and treacherous men of his time. Hugh Bigod had vast estates centred about Framlingham, in Suffolk. Although Stephen had made him Earl of Norfolk to purchase his support, Hugh had joined whichever side that seemed to him at the moment to have the upper hand. In return for his formal submission, Henry gave him a charter making him Earl of Norfolk, as though Stephen's creation had meant nothing, and thus made sure of Hugh's castle of Framlingham. Earl Hugh was so impressed by Henry's strength and determination that he returned to his estates in East Anglia and kept the peace for almost twenty years. Henry went on to York, where he forced William of Aumale, Stephen's chief supporter in Yorkshire, to do homage to him and to surrender Scarborough

---

[1] *Consitutio Domus Regis*, included in *Dialogue de Scaccario*, ed. Charles Johnson (Nelson's Medieval Texts, 1950), pp. 129-35.

Castle.   Having thus dealt effectively with these trouble-makers, potential or actual, the King returned to London.

Shortly after his return Henry summoned his council to meet him in London, and again they discussed the subject of the un-licensed castles.   Henry had made his intentions clear by his actions in the North.   He now made them even clearer by de-manding an accounting from those barons who continued to keep their castles, contrary to his order.   A castle at this time was not the stately pile of stone of later ages; it was simply any fortified place.   The author of the *Gesta Stephani* tells of a castle built 'on the tower of the church' at Bampton.[1]   Although some of the royal castles were of stone, most of them were wooden towers on the top of a mound, surrounded by a palisade and a ditch filled with water.

The first man to rebel against the new order of things was the one who had supported Henry most faithfully in his struggle for the crown.   Earl Roger of Hereford, 'seduced by the counsel of wicked men, slipped away from the council and fled quickly to Gloucester, for he had decided within himself to undergo all the perils and inconveniences of the earlier rebellion rather than to submit the mastery of the tower of Gloucester and the castle of Hereford to the King's judgment'.[2]   He stocked those strong-holds with arms and food and troops of Welshmen.   The Bishop of Hereford, the most learned and eloquent bishop in England, was related to Earl Roger.   He went to his kinsman, expostulated with him on the folly and wickedness of his brash course of action, and at last induced him to submit to the King.

One more rebel, Hugh Mortimer, attempted to defy the new King, but Henry promptly laid siege to his castles and forced him to submit.   The King treated him with surprising mildness.   At a meeting of the Great Council to determine the articles of peace, Hugh was allowed to keep all his lands.   He seems to have been touched by the King's mercy, for he henceforth devoted himself to building Wigmore Priory and lived in peace.

Henry acted with such energy and despatch in subduing these rebels and securing their castles that all the other barons came to the realisation that the days of anarchy were at an end and that they had a king who intended to rule England with the same firmness that his grandfather had shown.   In little more than six

[1] *Gesta Stephani*, p. 92.   [2] Gervase of Canterbury, Vol. I, p. 161.

months Henry established his rule so securely that his authority
was not challenged in England for almost twenty years.   In part
this was due to the fact that between 1153 and 1155 six earls,
and those six among the most rebellious and troublesome of the
twenty-two earls, had died,[1] leaving few effective leaders for a
possible rebellion.   Partly it was due to the fact that the country
was sick of disorder and civil war and longed for peace.   It was
due most of all to Henry's firmness, strength, and determination
of character.   In no case did he punish the rebels harshly or unjustly; once they had submitted, Henry readily forgave them.

Bishop Henry of Winchester, who had built many castles in
his part of the country, knew that he would soon be called to
account for them.   As a brother of the late King and the richest
bishop in England, Henry did not relish the thought of humbling
himself before the new ruler, but he was too wise to attempt to
rebel against him.   He sent all his treasure ahead of him by Peter
the Venerable, Abbot of Cluny, and secretly left the country
without the King's permission.

He took refuge at Cluny, where he had made his monastic profession and where he was now a most welcome guest, for with his
great wealth he paid off the debt that was sorely troubling the
abbey and supported the community of 460 monks for a year.[2]
They no doubt found him good company, for although he made
no pretence of being a scholar he was a gentleman of cultivated
tastes.   John of Salisbury tells of the impression the Bishop made
when he went to Rome in 1148 or 1149.   He was conspicuous
for his full beard and his grave and stately bearing, and he
attracted much attention by buying old statues ('idols', John calls
them) and shipping them to Winchester.[3]   While the Bishop
was at Cluny, the King had his castles destroyed.

Henry held a council at Winchester at Michaelmas, September
29, 1155, and broached a plan for conquering Ireland and giving
it to his brother William, for whom no provision had yet been
made.   Henry's insatiable appetite for land and yet more land
was probably the chief reason for this plan.   Furthermore,
Geoffrey, who by his father's will should have received Anjou

[1] F. M. Stenton: *The First Century of English Feudalism, 1066-1166* (Oxford, 1950), p. 256n.

[2] Peter the Venerable: *Epistolae*, in *Patrologiae Series Latina*, ed. J.-P. Migne, Vol. CLXXXIX, col, 243.

[3] John of Salisbury: *Historia Pontificalis*, p. 79.

and Maine, had returned to Anjou and was stirring up trouble there. No doubt Henry hoped by promising Ireland to William to gain his support against Geoffrey.

The Empress had come over to England for the only visit she ever paid that country after her son became King. She was present at the council and opposed the Irish scheme because Ireland was such a poor country that it would not be worth conquering in the first place, and because Geoffrey was making so much trouble in Anjou and Touraine that she thought Henry would be better occupied in bringing him to submission.

Because of her long residence in Germany Henry valued his mother's advice on foreign affairs. He therefore abandoned the plan for the time being. However, he commissioned John of Salisbury, who was now a member of Archbishop Theobald's household, to explain the project to Adrian IV, the only Englishman ever to be Pope, and to secure his approval. Adrian readily authorised Henry to conquer Ireland and bring it into submission to the English crown and the Roman See. He issued the bull *Laudabiliter* in formal approval of the undertaking, and Henry kept it for future use.[1]

Henry meanwhile was receiving such alarming reports of Geoffrey's activities that he determined to cross over and deal with him before he succeeded in taking Anjou away from Henry. Geoffrey had stocked his castles of Chinon, Loudun, and Mirebeau in preparation for war and was apparently entertaining ideas of wresting his lawful inheritance away from his brother. Leaving the Earl of Leicester and Richard of Luci to govern the kingdom in his absence, Henry crossed to Normandy in January 1156.

He went first to meet his overlord, King Louis, and did homage to him for all his lands in France, in order to have a perfectly clear title to Anjou. He repeated his homage for Normandy, which he had already made in 1151, and he did homage for Anjou and Maine, to which he had succeeded at his father's death, and for Poitou and Aquitaine, which he had acquired when he married Eleanor. This last act of homage must have been a particularly galling one for Louis to receive.

Geoffrey then came to Rouen to see his brother, and their interview concerning his inheritance was a stormy one. Geoffrey's

---

[1] Gerald of Wales: *Expugnatio Hibernica*, ed. J. F. Dimock, in Vol. V of *Opera*, p. 315.

claim to Anjou and Maine was quite clear, through the terms of his father's will. Henry never gave up any land he had once acquired, as he proved over and over again in his later life, and he certainly had no intention of relinquishing Anjou and Maine, which lay between Normandy and Aquitaine, and thus leaving his two duchies cut off from each other.

Geoffrey went back to Anjou and prepared for war. Henry collected an army in Normandy, set out after his brother; and laid siege to his castles. Geoffrey gave up the struggle and surrendered to his brother in July. By the terms of the peace arranged between them, Henry agreed to pay him a thousand pounds in English money and two thousand pounds Angevin (worth a fourth as much as English money) every year. Just how much these promises of vast sums, for a thousand pounds was a vast sum in those days, and how much Henry's promises in general were worth is shown by the fact that the Pipe Roll for 1157 records that Geoffrey was paid only £40 10s. 10d., and he received the same sum in the next year.[1]

Shortly after this treaty was arranged, Geoffrey had a piece of good luck that no doubt saved him from the temptation to further warfare against his brother. Brittany, after the death of Duke Conan III in 1148, was in its usual state of anarchy, with two rival claimants to the Duchy. The citizens of Nantes, at the southeastern corner of Brittany at the mouth of the Loire, were driven to revolt by this lawlessness. They ejected their Count and offered themselves to Geoffrey. He was of course delighted to accept an offer that freed him from his dependence on his brother and gave him some standing in the world.[2]

Queen Eleanor, meanwhile, was taking an active part in the government of England during her husband's absence. She travelled about the country extensively, living on a lavish scale, with expenditures of over £350 in a little more than six months. Some of the writs authorising the payments were issued by the Queen herself, which indicated that Henry either placed a great deal of confidence in her or was overawed by his wife, so much older and more experienced than he. Normally only the King, or his Chief Justiciars in the King's absence, had authority to order payments to be made from the Exchequer.

[1] Pipe Roll 3 & 4 Henry II, pp. 72, 132.
[2] William of Newburgh, p. 114.

Eleanor's second son was born in London on February 28, 1155, and was baptised by Archibishop Theobald. He was given his father's name. Her first son, William, died in 1156 and was buried at the feet of King Henry I in Reading Abbey. In June 1156 Eleanor gave birth to a daughter, who was named Matilda, after her grandmother the Empress.

The Queen and her surviving children, Henry and Matilda, crossed over to Normandy and joined the King in July 1156. Both in order to please his wife, who loved her Aquitaine more than any other place in the world, and in order to show himself as their Duke to the noblemen of the South, who did not gladly acknowledge anyone's authority over them, Henry took his wife and children to Aquitaine and held his Christmas court at Bordeaux. Eleanor returned to England with her children in February, and Henry followed them shortly after Easter, April 7, 1157, with all his continental possessions at peace and firmly under his control.

IV

THE KING AND THE CHANCELLOR
1157 - 1162

WHEN Henry returned to England in April 1157 he began laying plans for an expedition into North Wales to meet the threat posed by Owain Gwynedd, Prince of North Wales, who had taken advantage of the disorders of Stephen's reign to extend his sphere of influence steadily eastward. By the time Henry succeeded to the throne Owain was threatening the city of Chester. The King had heretofore been too busy establishing his authority in England and reducing Geoffrey to order in Anjou to deal with Owain. Now that both England and his domains on the Continent were at peace and firmly under his control, he turned his attention to the Welsh.

On June 24 he issued the summons for his army to assemble. Instead of calling out the whole feudal host for the customary forty days, he ordered that only one knight in three was to serve, while the remaining two paid his expenses.[1] He recruited a body of archers from Shropshire and ordered supplies of salt pork, grain, and cheese, as well as sixty casks of the wine of Poitou.[2] At a meeting of the Great Council at Northampton on July 17 he laid his final plans for the expedition.

A sizable army assembled at Chester. The summons to a third of the knight-service of England would produce around two thousand knights,[3] and they were supplemented by the archers from Shropshire. A fleet had been gathered and was to meet the army at Rhuddlan. For all his experience in Normandy and England, however, Henry was not prepared for the type of war upon which he was now embarking. With the Welsh warfare was not a form of tournament, as it was with the Normans; they fought through grim necessity, and they paid no attention to the elaborate code of chivalry that regulated the French and Norman procedure.

[1] Robert of Torigni, p. 193.   [2] Pipe Roll 3 Henry II, pp. 89, 105.
[3] A. L. Poole, op. cit., p. 15.

The Normans seek the level ground, the Welsh the mountains: the Normans the fields, the Welsh the forests. To the Normans arms and armour are an honour: to the Welsh a burden. The Normans win by their steadfastness; the Welsh by their fleet-footedness. The Normans capture knights; the Welsh cut their heads off. Amongst the Normans they are ransomed; amongst the Welsh they are killed.[1]

As Henry and his army started out from Chester along the narrow strip of land between the estuary of the River Dee on

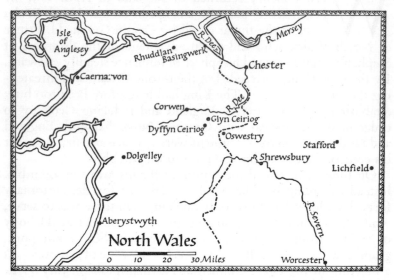

their right and the wooded mountains on their left, Owain Gwynedd held the stronghold of Basingwerk, which blocked their way to Rhuddlan. His sons, David and Cynan, dispersed their fleet-footed men through the forest and up the side of the mountain to prevent Henry from turning their flank and seizing Rhuddlan at their rear. It was the most elementary sort of a trap, but Henry fell directly into it.

He sent the main body of his army, the mounted knights in their cumbersome armour, along the coast, while he took the lightly-armed troops blindly into the forest. The Welsh set upon them with wild fury and killed many of them. Henry

[1] Gerald of Wales: *Descriptio Kambriae*, ed. J. F Dimock, Vol. VI of *Opera* p. 220.

himself was sorely beset. His Constable, Henry of Essex, in the panic cried out that the King was dead. The Constable, it was later alleged, let fall the royal standard and fled. Earl Roger of Clare picked up the standard, rallied the English, and thus saved the King's life.[1]

Henry and his men fought their way down to the coast and rejoined the main army. This was a frightening experience for the young King, who had narrowly escaped with his life, and for the first time it occurred to Henry that he might be killed in battle. Losses were heavy on both sides, in proportion to the small number of men involved. That was not the way they played the game in Normandy.

'In that same wood of Coleshill,' Gerald of Wales relates, 'a young Welshman was killed by the King's army. A week later his greyhound was found standing over his master's body, without food or water, faithfully and admirably guarding it unharmed from the dogs, wolves, and birds with brute affection.'[2]

Owain slowly withdrew before the King's army, and Henry at last reached Rhuddlan, where his fleet was to join him. They came bearing bad news. On the way they had stopped to plunder the Isle of Anglesey. The natives had then assembled and defeated them in battle. They had killed Henry, a bastard son of King Henry I by the notorious Welsh princess Nesta, and seriously wounded his half-brother. The raiders had with difficulty escaped to their ships.[3]

Henry decided that having regained Rhuddlan, the limit of the English penetration into North Wales, he had had enough of the Welsh and their rough ways. Owain, too, was willing to agree to a truce, for he knew that the best he could hope for if he continued fighting would be to hold his own against the English. They therefore agreed to a peace, and Owain gave hostages as a guaranty of his good intentions. Henry fortified the castle of Rhuddlan and built one at Basingwerk. He had by no means subdued North Wales, but he had at any rate pushed Owain Gwynedd back beyond Rhuddlan, and he had established two strongholds to check further forays.[4]

[1] William of Newburgh, pp. 107-8.
[2] Gerald of Wales, op. cit., p. 138. (This anecdote is inserted at the request of my dog Fritz.)
[3] Gerald of Wales, op. cit., pp. 130-1.
[4] William of Newburgh, pp. 108-9.

During the spring of 1158 Henry sent his Chancellor to France on a mission of the utmost delicacy: to propose to King Louis a marriage between the young Henry and Louis's daughter Margaret. Shortly after his divorce from Eleanor Louis had married Constance, the daughter of King Alfonso VII of Castile, and by her he had had yet another daughter. Henry now proposed a marriage between this child and his own eldest son.

The King, shortly after his crowning, had asked the Archbishop of Canterbury for advice about whom he should appoint as his Chancellor. Theobald had recommended Thomas, a cleric of his household, for that important post. Thomas was born in London on December 21, the feast of St. Thomas the Apostle, probably in 1118, of a respectable middle-class family. His father, Gilbert, had been a merchant in Rouen and then had come to London, where he was so well thought of by his fellows that he was elected sheriff. Thomas was educated in London, at the school of the Austin Canons at Merton Priory in Surrey, and, during his father's period of afluence, in Paris.[1]

The most important influence in Thomas's youth was that of his mother, Matilda, who inspired him with her devotion to the Blessed Virgin. She would frequently weigh her child and give his weight in food, clothing, and money to the poor. The second most important influence would seem to have been that of a Norman knight, Richer of l'Aigle, who was a frequent guest in Gilbert's house and whom the lad Thomas regarded with something approaching hero-worship. Thomas's companions at home and at school were respectable but dull; Richer, a dazzling young knight, was passionately addicted to hawks and hounds and all the pleasures of the hunt. Thomas, for some reason not stated, stayed at home from school for half a year and spent much of that time in the company of his dashing hero. Richer opened the lad's eyes to a new world, and under his tutelage Thomas learned to ride and to hunt. The tastes he acquired from Richer he never lost.

When Thomas reached young manhood his life became even duller than it had been before Richer gave him a taste of joys and excitements and sports that now seemed beyond his reach forever. His mother died when he was twenty-one, and his father suffered financial reverses. Gilbert's widowed house was

---

[1] William Fitz Stephen, in *Materials*, Vol. III, p. 14.

'empty and desolate'. The young man who had shown such promise at his studies had to go to work as a clerk to his kinsman, Osbern 'Eight-pence'.[1] For three years Thomas served at the dullest of occupations, sunk in a bourgeois life from which there seemed no escape. Richer of l'Aigle and his dazzling life seemed far away indeed to the young man in the musty countinghouse. Respected though his father and his kinsman might be among their fellow citizens of London, there was a vast gulf between them and the world that Richer represented. The Anglo-Normans were ferociously snobbish. 'If a knight or other free man should perchance sink from the dignity of his state in life by multiplying pennies in public trade (which God forbid!) ...' writes Richard the Treasurer[2] in a burst of snobbishness that hardly sits well on one who was born a bastard.

Thomas was saved from a life of drudgery and obscurity by Theobald, Archbishop of Canterbury. Gilbert and Theobald seem to have come from the same part of Normandy. Someone who knew them both called the Archbishop's attention to the brilliant young man buried in his accounts. Theobald took Thomas into his household, among a group of the most promising scholars in England. The Archbishop had introduced the study of the Roman civil law into England, and his household was a university in miniature, where Thomas could take up this new study under the best of teachers. His quick, alert intellect and his spontaneous charm soon made him stand out even in that brilliant company.

Thomas underwent a great deal of persecution at the hands of Roger of Pont l'Évêque, an ambitious and jealous cleric of a knightly Norman family. Roger was a singularly unsavoury character, if a letter attributed to John of Salisbury is to be believed. Writing to Archbishop William of Sens in 1171, the author reminds the Archbishop in circumstantial detail of an occurrence that had taken place while William was in England visiting his uncle, Bishop Henry of Winchester. John, who was no purveyor of mere idle gossip, wrote as though William were familiar with the whole story of how Roger had seduced a handsome lad named Walter and then, when Walter had denounced him, of how Roger had corrupted the judges and had had Walter blinded

[1] Anonymous I, *Materials*, Vol. IV, pp. 6-8.
[2] *Dialogus de Scaccario*, p. 109.

and strangled on a gibbet. 'We are not inventing this,' John writes; 'we are recalling it to your memory. . . . Even to the present day this sad story is told to the great disgrace and contempt of the Church.'[1]

Roger mocked Thomas for his lowly origin and bourgeois habits. Twice Roger succeeded in having him dismissed from the Archbishop's service. Although Thomas's biographers attribute these dismissals solely to Roger's spiteful jealousy, Theobald was too wise and experienced a man to be wholly under the thumb of one of his clerks. It is possible that Theobald felt that Thomas, for all his brilliance and charm, was not wholly suited, by temperament and character, for the ecclesiastical life. Each time he was dismissed Thomas took refuge with Theobald's brother, Walter, Archdeacon of Canterbury, and each time Walter persuaded his brother to restore Thomas to his favour. When Walter was elected Bishop of Rochester in 1148, Roger of Pont l'Évêque succeeded him as Archdeacon.

Roger, in turn, was consecrated Archbishop of York on October 10, 1154, and Theobald promoted Thomas to the archdeaconry thus made vacant and ordained him deacon. As Archdeacon of Canterbury Thomas had charge of the legal affairs of the archdiocese, a position for which his studies had particularly fitted him.[2] From this post the King raised him to be his Chancellor.

Henry and Thomas quickly became the most intimate friends. The King found in Thomas the perfect servant and a most charming and agreeable companion. Thomas had a quick intellect, a ready charm, and a natural gaiety of temperament that would make him good company at all times. He understood the great problems that faced the new King in his effort to restore order to England, to reduce the barons to submission, and to renovate the whole machinery of government, which had sadly run down under Stephen's carelessness. Thomas's training in the law made him particularly valuable to the young King, for Thomas could grasp the legal aspects of a problem and quickly find the best and surest way of solving it.

---

[1] *Materials*, Vol. VII, p. 528. R. L. Poole contends that this letter is incorrectly attributed to John of Salisbury and that the passage relating to Roger is an interpolation. See R. L. Poole: 'Two Documents Concerning Archbishop Roger of York', *Speculum*, Vol. III (Jan. 1928), pp. 81-84. See also David Knowles: *The Episcopal Colleagues of Archbishop Thomas Becket* (Cambridge, 1951), pp. 13-14.

[2] William Fitz Stephen, *Materials*, Vol. III, pp. 14-17.

The post of Chancellor was a responsible one, carrying with it the custody of the Great Seal and the supervision of the clerks who prepared all the official documents and drew up all the correspondence by which Henry governed his far-flung domains. In itself, however, the office was not comparable in responsibility and power to that of the Chief Justiciar. Thomas proved himself such a capable and adaptable servant, however, that Henry relied more and more on his Chancellor. The routine business of the government was left in the hands of the two Chief Justiciars, while Henry and Thomas devised the plans and directed the operations that aimed always at increasing Henry's power and strength. 'Not only was he the King's friend and second in the realm; he was also the King's guide and, as it were, his master.'[1]

Above and beyond the reasons for Henry's valuing Thomas's services and relying upon his advice, however, the relationship between the two came increasingly to rest upon a vehement affection that the headstrong, burly King felt for this learned and elegant clerk who seemed the gayest of all Henry's knights. Henry felt more than friendship for this charming and versatile companion; more than admiration for his legal skill; more than respect for the soundness of his judgment and the ingenuity of his advice. Henry loved Thomas with all the strength of his rude heart.

Perhaps, on Thomas's side, it was the life he loved, rather than the King, that life of which Richer of l'Aigle had given him a brief glimpse and which then seemed closed to him forever. Thomas loved elegance and magnificence and colour and gaiety; he loved hawking and hunting with as passionate a fervour as had Richer of l'Aigle and as did Henry himself, who would neglect the most pressing and important business to spend the whole day in the forests with his hawks or his hounds. After his drab boyhood and his even drabber and poverty-stricken young manhood, spent among the dull merchants whom he probably scorned in his heart, Thomas found himself, at the age of thirty-seven or so, plunged into the midst of the most turbulent and exciting and colourful life that anyone could imagine.

Henry's household and court were disorganised and often almost chaotic; his domestic arrangements were so slapdash that the bread on his table was half-baked, the meat either half-raw

---

[1] Gervase of Canterbury, Vol. I, pp. 169.

or scorched to cinders, and the fish stinking to high heaven; his movements were so erratic that no one knew from one hour to another where the vast establishment would be next.[1]   Along with all this, there was a stir and bustle, a frenzied coming and going of messengers from every part of Henry's far-flung lands, a constant procession of bishops and abbots and earls and barons, and a restless progress all over England and Normandy and Anjou and Maine and Aquitaine that delighted the heart and satisfied the longings of Thomas, once clerk to Osbern Eight-pence and lately a member of the staid and studious household of the Archbishop of Canterbury.

The contrast in the appearance of the two friends was striking. Henry was only of medium height, square-shouldered and stocky, with a tendency to corpulence even in his twenties; Thomas was tall and gracefully thin.   Henry had a ruddy complexion, and his face was square and freckled; Thomas's face was long and handsome and oval, with a high forehead.   Henry's hands were rough and reddened and chapped by exposure; Thomas's hands were long and white and singularly graceful.   Henry was careless in his dress, looking only for comfort and convenience; Thomas was elegantly and richly dressed in the finest clothes.   To see them thus, one would say that Thomas was the king and Henry his chief huntsman.

Although the Chancellor was some fifteen years older than his master,

> when they had finished with serious matters, the King and he played together like little boys of the same age, at the court, in church, in assemblies, in riding.
>
> One day they were riding together in a street in London.   Harsh winter howled.   The King saw coming from a distance a poor old man, his cloak tattered and thin.   He said to the Chancellor; 'Do you see that fellow?'
>
> The Chancellor replied; 'I do.'
>
> 'How poor, how feeble, how bare he is!' the King exclaimed. 'Wouldn't it be an act of great charity to give him a warm, heavy cloak?'
>
> 'It would indeed,' the Chancellor replied, 'and you, King, should have a mind and an eye for that sort of a thing.'
>
> Meanwhile the poor man was before them.   The King dismounted, and the Chancellor with him.   The King spoke gently to

[1] Peter of Blois: *Epistolae*, Migne, Vol. CCVII, cols. 47-48.

the poor man and asked if he would like to have a good cloak.   The poor man, not knowing who they were, thought that it was a joke and that they were not serious.

The King said to the Chancellor: 'Truly, you shall perform this great act of charity.'   Laying his hands on the hood, the King tried to take away and the Chancellor tried to hold on to the cloak, a new one of the best quality, of scarlet cloth and grey fur, that the Chancellor was wearing.   Then there was a great stir and tumult there. The knights who were following them hastened up in amazement to find out what was the cause for such a sudden struggle between them, but there was no one to tell them.   Each one was intent on his hands, so that it looked as though they were going to fall.   After a while the reluctant Chancellor allowed the King to overcome him, pull off his cloak as he bent over, and give it to the poor man.

Thomas went hawking and hunting with the King and shared in all his sports.   He maintained a magnificent household:

He ordered that every day fresh straw or hay in the winter and fresh rushes or green boughs in the summer be strewn in his hall, so that the crowd of knights who could not find a seat might have a clean and agreeable place on the floor, lest their rich garments and beautiful linen shirts be soiled by a dirty floor. . . .

Often the King ate at the Chancellor's table, sometimes for entertainment and sometimes to see for himself the things that were told about his house and table.   Sometimes the King dismounted and came into the Chancellor's hall while he was sitting at table: sometimes he had his bow in his hand, returning from the chase or going to the forest.   Sometimes he drank and then, having seen the Chancellor, left; at other times he would leap across the table, sit down, and eat.

Never have there been two men who were such friends and of such a single mind in Christian times.[1]

When Thomas set out on his embassy to King Louis, he provided the French with a splendid show.

He had around two hundred mounted men from his household with him, knights, clerks, stewards, sergeants, armour-bearers, and the sons of nobles being brought up to arms by him, all fittingly provided.   All these men and all their followers shone in new holiday attire, each according to his station. . . .

He had with him dogs and birds of every sort that kings and rich men use.   In his train he had eight carts; five horses, matched in body and strength, drew each cart; each horse had assigned to it a

[1] William Fitz Stephen, *Materials*, Vol. III, pp. 20-21, 24-25.

stout lad dressed in a new tunic to go with the cart; each cart had its outrider and guard. Two carts were laden only with beer, made from a decoction of grain in water, in iron-bound kegs, to give to the French, who marvelled at that kind of a liquid, a healthful drink indeed, clear, of the colour of wine, and more pleasant to the taste. . .

When they entered a French village or town, first came some lads on foot, about two hundred and fifty of them, going in groups of six or ten or more together, singing in their native tongue after the manner of their country. After a short interval followed the dogs and greyhounds tied together, in their leashes and muzzles, with their keepers and attendants. Next came the carts, with their iron tyres rattling on the stones of the streets, covered with great hides sewn together. At a short distance followed the pack horses, with their grooms kneeling on the horses' haunches.

Some of the French, coming out of their houses when they heard so much noise, asked who was coming and whose household this was.

They told them that the Chancellor of the King of the English was coming, who had been sent to the Lord King of France.

'Wonderful indeed is this King of the English,' said the French, 'whose Chancellor comes in such great fashion.'

The French King and his nobles entertained the Chancellor and his party at a magnificent feast, and Thomas in turn entertained them even more splendidly. For a long time afterwards the French told how he had paid 100s. for a single dish of eels. Then Thomas, who had once studied in Paris, feasted the students and their teachers and sought out the creditors of the English students. The mission was a success; Thomas easily secured Louis's consent to the match.[1]

Henry and Eleanor held their Easter court at Worcester on April 29, 1158, and wore their crowns in state. At the offertory of the Easter Mass the King and Queen took off their crowns and laid them on the altar, vowing never to wear them again. The King, at any rate, was glad under the guise of an act of piety to give up a practice distasteful to him. The elaborate pageant of the crown-wearing on the great festivals of Christmas, Easter, and Whitsunday, with the solemn placing of the crown on the king's head by the Archbishop of Canterbury, the formal procession into the church, and the ceremonies surrounding the king's offering and communion, was repugnant to a man of Henry's

[1] William Fitz Stephen, *Materials*, Vol. III, pp. 29-33.

impatient and informal temperament. Henry, unlike his grandfather, placed no value upon the trappings of royalty and avoided
showing himself in kingly state to his subjects.

Henry's brother Geoffrey died on July 26. In August the
King crossed over to Normandy, both to conclude the treaty his
Chancellor had arranged with Louis and to make sure of Geoffrey's
city of Nantes. Leaving the Queen in England with their infant
son Richard, who was born on September 8, 1157, Henry went
first to Rouen, probably to visit his mother, and then met Louis
near Gisors. They agreed on the terms of the marriage between
Henry, then three years old, and Margaret, not yet a year old.
Louis promised to give his daughter as her dowry the whole of
the Vexin with all its castles.[1]   There was no region in the world
that Henry coveted so much as the Vexin, to provide a buffer
between his Duchy of Normandy and the Ile de France, and he
had never ceased regretting having had to surrender it to Louis
as the price of his recognition as Duke of Normandy.

In this friendly atmosphere Henry brought up the subject of
Brittany. Conan, the grandson of the late Conan III, seemed to
be the most successful contender for the title of Duke of Brittany,
and Henry wanted to make sure that Nantes did not fall into his
hands. Louis agreed to recognise Henry as overlord of Brittany,
a position for which the Dukes of Normandy had long struggled
but had never attained. Henry now had the right to receive the
homage of the Duke of Brittany on his own terms, Louis conceded.

Henry hastened to Avranches, near the northeastern border of
Brittany. There he learned that Conan had indeed invaded the
County of Nantes and was threatening to take the city. On
September 8 the King summoned his Norman barons to gather
at Avranches at Michaelmas to march against the presumptuous
Conan.

While his army was assembling, Henry went to Paris to visit
Louis. His entrance into the city was in marked contrast to that
of his Chancellor, for Henry, with characteristic informality,
took only a few followers with him. There was a touch of
shrewdness in this studied informality. Henry was anxious to
gain Louis's support in his designs upon Brittany. He was
already king over a much greater area than Louis was, and his

---

[1] *Continuatio Beccensis*, ed. Richard Howlett, in Vol. IV of *Chronicles of the
Reigns of Stephen, Henry II, and Richard I*, p. 318.

income from these lands was far larger than was that of Louis. For Henry to make a display of his power at this moment would hardly be likely to put Louis in a state of mind receptive to Henry's proposals. Henry therefore assumed the part of a vassal coming to pay his respects to his liege lord.

Louis and Constance received him with every honour they could shower upon him. Henry received all these attentions with great modesty. Louis, still the monk at heart, thought that the best way of entertaining his visitor and doing him honour would be to take him on a tour of the principal churches of Paris and the neighbourhood, so that Henry could be welcomed at each church by a solemn procession of the clergy. With great humility and a due sense of the honour intended to him, Henry steadfastly declined. He more than made up for his refusal, however, by distributing large sums of money amongst the churches and the poor.

The people, too, gave him an enthusiastic welcome, for they saw in this new friendship an end to the warfare along the Norman border. When Henry left Paris he took with him the infant Margaret, to be brought up, as was the custom of the time, with his family till she and his son were old enough to be married.[1]

While her husband was thus arranging for the marriage of their eldest son, Queen Eleanor gave birth to her fourth son, Geoffrey, on September 23, 1158. She had had five children in six years. After Geoffrey's birth she took a well-deserved respite from child-bearing for four years.

Henry's army meanwhile had assembled at Avranches. Conan's position was precarious at best, and he had no desire to meet Henry's forces in battle. At Michaelmas, before the King could start out, Conan came to Avranches and surrendered his claim to Nantes. Henry, in return, recognised him as Duke of Brittany and received Conan's homage as his overlord. He then took his army to Nantes to make sure of the city. The inhabitants received him as their lord, the rightful heir of his brother Geoffrey, and Henry placed the city in the charge of some of his trusted men.

At the beginning of the year Henry devised a plan, probably in consultation with his Queen, who had crossed over to Normandy in the preceding December, for increasing his territories

[1] Robert of Torigni, p. 197.

still further. The Dukes of Aquitaine from time to time had attempted to assert a claim to the County of Toulouse, to the southeast of their lands. Henry decided to revive that claim in his wife's name. He began by forming an alliance with Raymond, Count of Barcelona, who also held the Kingdom of Aragon in his wife's name. They met at Blaye in Gascony and sealed their alliance by agreeing to a marriage between Henry's second son, Richard, to whom he promised to cede the Duchy of Aquitaine in due time, and Raymond's daughter.[1]

With Toulouse thus cut off from the possibility of help from the south, Henry sent a formal summons to Count Raymond of Toulouse to surrender the County to him, which Raymond of course refused to do. He had married Constance, Louis's sister, after the death of her first husband, Eustace, King Stephen's son. He now notified Louis, his overlord and his brother-in-law, of the danger that was threatening him. Louis came to Tours and discussed the matter with Henry, but he could not put up a convincing argument about Henry's claim to Toulouse because he himself had, in 1141, asserted a right to that same territory on the same grounds as Henry was now demanding it. The Kings could come to no agreement and parted, but still on friendly terms.

Henry, on March 22, summoned his armies from England, Normandy, and Aquitaine to meet at Poitiers on Midsummer Day, June 24, for service till All Saints' Day, November 1. Since England was so far away, he demanded personal service only from his barons. Each knight, in lieu of service, was assessed two marks (£1 6s. 8d.), which would pay the wages of a substitute to fight in his place at eightpence a day for forty days, the normal term of military service. Henry levied the scutage, or monetary commutation of military service, 'not wishing to vex the agrarian knights',[2] which would indicate that the English country squire had already come into being.

The King also exacted an arbitrary 'gift' from the bishops, the religious houses, the towns, the sheriffs, who would of course pass the charge on to their counties, and the Jewish moneylenders, who were peculiarly at the King's mercy. There was a great outcry from the clergy at this act of sacrilege, as they termed the exaction of money from them, and they laid the blame for it at

[1] Ibid., p. 200. [2] Ibid., p. 202.

the Chancellor's feet. The 'gifts' of the clergy amounted to
£3,130, and the scutage proper brought in £2,440.[1]

Before setting out, Henry went to the Norman border for
another conference with Louis. Their parley, concerning both
the projected marriage of their children and Henry's designs on
Toulouse, lasted from June 6 to 8. Louis was torn between his
loyalty to his brother-in-law and his eagerness not to do anything
to imperil the marriage that was to strengthen still further the
bonds that existed, as he believed, between him and the King of
England. His feeble expostulations were of no avail. Henry
turned to the south.

His army, meanwhile, was gathering at Poitiers. The most
brilliant contingent was that of the Chancellor, who put seven
hundred knights in the field at his own expense. Henry joined
them on the appointed day, June 24, 1159, and the host set out for
Toulouse. Among the earls and barons who had crossed the
Channel to join the King's army was Henry's young cousin
Malcolm, King of Scots, who had succeeded his grandfather,
King David, in 1153. Just as King David had knighted Henry
in his youth, Henry now bestowed the belt of knighthood on
Malcolm as the army marched to the south.[2]

Louis had a last fruitless conference with Henry about July 6.
Henry pressed on and captured Cahors, and then the army encamped before Toulouse and laid siege to the city. Sieges were
usually long-drawn-out affairs, for the art of fortification was far
in advance of that of offence. A town or castle with stout stone
walls could usually resist the stone-throwers and catapults and
other crude engines almost indefinitely if its provisions held
out.

Sieges were extremely boring for both sides. The defenders
were imprisoned within their walls and soon reduced to short
commons. Often in a fit of boredom they would sally forth
and provoke the besiegers into a lively clash, merely to relieve
their pent-up spirits, and then take refuge again within the walls.
There was little for the besiegers to do beyond keeping a watch
to see that no food or help reached the besieged, while the
engineers worked the stone-throwers. Holding a large army together in a state of inactivity before the walls of Toulouse for

[1] J. H. Round: *Feudal England*, (London, 1909), p. 281.
[2] Robert of Torigni, pp. 202-3.

almost three months must have been difficult for Henry, and feeding this host would be an expensive business.

Boring though they no doubt were for his army, the months spent before Toulouse were busy ones for Henry, for Thomas, and for all the members of the King's household. Wherever he might be, Henry had to carry on the immensely detailed work of governing his various lands. Although he might delegate most of the routine business to his chief justiciars and seneschals, all matters of importance were decided by the King himself. These decisions were made known and put into force by a constant stream of written orders, prepared under the supervision of the Chancellor and authenticated by him with the Great Seal.

Whether he was before the walls of Toulouse or at the opposite end of his domains, in the northernmost part of England, his cares and responsibilities followed Henry wherever he went. A ceaseless procession of his subjects appeared before him, seeking favours or begging to be heard in matters beyond the competence of his subordinate officials. If a man was not satisfied with the verdict of a local court, his only recourse was to the King himself. If the King was in the most remote part of Aquitaine, the suitor had no choice but to follow him there. Worn out with pursuing the King all over England, Peter of Blois wrote to him, 'Solomon says that there are four things a man cannot know: the path of an eagle in the sky, the path of a ship in the sea, the path of a serpent on the ground, and the path of a man in his youth. And I can add a fifth: the path of the King in England.'[1]

Towards the middle of September, Louis, in a sudden and unwonted fit of decisiveness, entered Toulouse. He did not bring an army with him, probably because he thought that his moral support was all that Count Raymond needed. And, oddly enough, it was. When Henry learned that Louis was present in the city, 'out of foolish superstition and regard for the counsel of others',[2] and against the advice of the Chancellor, he called the whole business off and abandoned the siege.

The excuse he gave his troops, who were no doubt delighted to give up the boring task, was that he had too great a reverence for the person of his overlord, King Louis, to make war against him. This was nonsense, for Henry had not scrupled to make war,

[1] Peter of Blois, op. cit., col. 121.
[2] William Fitz Stephen, *Materials*, Vol. III, p. 33.

such as it was, against Louis in the past, and he continued doing so sporadically as long as Louis lived. The truth of the matter, as both the siege of Toulouse and the ineffectual expedition into North Wales indicated, was that Henry was not the fighter that either his father or his mother had been. With the resources of an empire that stretched from the Pyrenees to the borders of Scotland at his disposal, capturing a single city, no matter how well defended, should not have been an insuperable problem for a determined warrior.

Henry had neither his father's courage and daring in battle nor his mother's tenacity. Although he occasionally raised large armies, he used them only to intimidate and overawe his opponents. If the opponent refused to be intimidated, Henry simply gave up. The expedition to Toulouse had occupied his attention for the greater part of the year and had cost vast sums of money. All he had to show for it was Cahors and an alliance with the Count of Barcelona.

Henry ravaged all the country around Toulouse and withdrew to Cahors. After he had fortified this city he turned it and the surrounding region over to Thomas and to Henry of Essex, the Constable. He dismissed the contingents from Aquitaine and Anjou and started north with the remainder. While he had been occupied before Toulouse, Louis's brothers, Bishop Philip of Beauvais and Count Robert of Dreux, had been stirring up trouble along the Norman border. Henry hastened to the scene of the conflict and laid waste the territory about Beauvais.

The Chancellor, left in command of the Quercy, the region about Cahors, proved himself a stern and merciless governor. After the fruitless inaction before Toulouse, Thomas now armed himself in helmet and coat of mail and led his troops into battle as though he had been born to the sword rather than to the pen. He captured three castles that had hitherto been thought impregnable. To bring the region to subjection he levelled cities and towns to the ground and destroyed farms and crops with fire.[1]

With the Quercy thus devastated and terrified into submission, Thomas went to Normandy to join the King. In addition to the seven hundred knights of his household, he raised a force of twelve hundred knights and four thousand foot-soldiers to serve

[1] Edward Grim, *Materials*, Vol. II, p. 365; William Fitz Stephen, *Materials*, Vol. III, p. 34.

for forty days at his expense. He paid the knights 3s. a day and fed them all at his table. This contingent was the flower of Henry's army. It was always in the front; it always dared the bravest deeds; it always performed the most glorious feats. Thomas secured the finest trumpeters to be had, and their brazen voices sounded the assembly and the charge not only for the Chancellor's troops but for the whole army as well. Always in the front rank was Thomas the Chancellor, leading and exhorting his troops. Deacon though he was, he fought with a famous French knight, Engelram of Trie, unhorsed him, and led his charger away in triumph as a prize of war.[1]

This war, unlike the grim business in the Quercy, was a delightful sport for all concerned, in which no one was hurt except the wretched peasants whose fields were trampled by the resplendent knights. The object of the sport was to capture a knight from the opposing side and hold him for ransom. In addition to being an exhilarating adventure, war under these conditions could be quite profitable for a skilled fighter.

To match his Chancellor's prowess as a fighting man, Henry scored a diplomatic triumph that brought this series of raids to an end. He persuaded Simon of Montfort, Count of Evreux, to renounce his allegiance to Louis, do homage to Henry, and turn over three castles to him. Since these castles commanded the route between Paris and Orléans, Louis, cut off from the southern part of his domain, was forced to ask for a truce, unless he wanted to fight a long and costly war to regain them. In December the two Kings arranged a truce to last till May 22, 1160.[2]

Henry and Louis met at the expiration of the truce and agreed upon a treaty of peace, the terms of which were negotiated, as were all of Henry's treaties, by his Chancellor.[3] The arrangement for the marriage of the young Henry and Margaret was reaffirmed, and Louis repeated his promise to give her the Vexin as her dowry. To make sure that it remained neutral territory until the far distant day when the children should reach marriageable age, Louis consented to place it in the custody of the Knights Templars. It was agreed that Count Simon of Evreux should return to his allegiance to Louis without being punished for his defection and that he should keep all his castles. Finally, on behalf of his

[1] William Fitz Stephen, *Materials*, Vol. III, pp. 34-35.
[2] Robert of Torigni, p. 206.   [3] William of Newburgh, p. 159.

brother-in-law, Raymond of Toulouse, Louis agreed on a year's truce in that County, and Henry was allowed to keep what he had won, which was mainly the city of Cahors.

King Stephen's son William, Earl Warenne, had accompanied Henry to Toulouse and had died on the way back. The only one of Stephen's children then surviving was his daughter, Mary, who was Abbess of the convent at Romsey. William had inherited from his father the County of Boulogne, which it was vital for Henry to keep in friendly hands because of its proximity to England. Unless he acted quickly and with some show of legality, the County would revert to its overlord, King Louis.

Without consulting the wishes of the Abbess in the matter, Henry induced the Pope to dispense her from her solemn vows of religion and had her taken from her convent and married offhand to Matthew, the second son of his aunt Sibyl (Count Geoffrey's sister) and Count Thierry of Flanders. Thus Matthew became Count of Boulogne in his wife's right.

Thomas the Chancellor had his first serious difference with the King when he opposed this project and tried to persuade the Pope not to grant the dispensation. The new Pope, Alexander III, was in the midst of many difficulties and eager for the support of so powerful a ruler as Henry, and he therefore granted the dispensation in spite of Thomas's protests.[1]

Pope Adrian IV had died on September 1, 1159, while Henry was besieging Toulouse. Of the twenty-two Cardinals who were present at the election of his successor on September 7, eighteen voted for Cardinal Orlando Bandinelli, whose own vote is not recorded. The remaining three, all creatures of the Emperor Frederick Barbarossa, refused to concur in the election and chose one of their number, Cardinal Octavian, who took the name of Victor IV. To stifle the protests of the majority, the Count of Wittelsbach employed a mob to break up the conclave. Cardinal Orlando and his supporters fled to Nympha, where he was crowned as Alexander III on September 20.

The new Pope had taught canon law at Bologna and was one of the greatest canonists of his time. He had been Papal Chancellor under Eugene III and a trusted friend and adviser of Adrian IV, whom he had encouraged in his resistance to Frederick Bar-

---

[1] Herbert of Bosham, in *Materials*, Vol. III, p. 328.

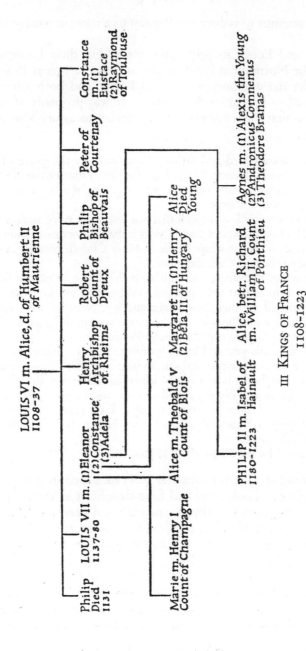

LOUIS VI m. Alice, d. of Humbert II of Maurienne
1108-37

Philip Died 1131

LOUIS VII m. (1)Eleanor (2)Constance (3)Adela
1137-80

Henry Archbishop of Rheims

Robert Count of Dreux

Philip Bishop of Beauvais

Peter of Courtenay

Constance m.(1) Eustace (2)Raymond of Toulouse

Marie m. Henry I Count of Champagne

Alice m.Theobald v Count of Blois

Margaret m.(1)Henry (2)Béla III of Hungary

Alice Died Young

PHILIP II m. Isabel of Hainault
1180-1223

Alice, betr. Richard m. William II, Count of Ponthieu

Agnes m. (1) Alexis the Young (2)Andronicus Comnenus (3) Theodore Branas

III Kings of France
1108-1223

67

barossa's attempt to reduce the Papacy to a mere appanage of the Empire.

Henry and Louis, in July 1160, assembled their bishops and barons, the Normans at Neufmarché and the French at Beauvais, to consider the question of the rival Popes, and both assemblies pronounced in favour of Alexander. It was probably after this conference that Henry wrote to Alexander to assure him of his allegiance.

> To his dearest lord and father, Alexander, by the grace of God Supreme Pontiff, Henry, King of the English, Duke of the Normans and Aquitainians, and Count of the Angevins, sends greetings and due submission in Christ.
>
> Your Discretion knows well that our ancestors were always faithful to the Holy Roman Church, which they on occasion showed in similar cases when, as schism arose in Holy Church because of sinful men, they followed Catholic unity.
>
> Approving, therefore, and imitating the devotion of my fathers, because I believe that your election is supported by the truth, I, together with all the men, both clerk and lay, committed to my rule by God, have with due solemnity received you, in the person of your legates, as the Supreme and Catholic Pontiff.
>
> I therefore ask you and in all humility beg you most mercifully to receive me as your spiritual son, to hear me, if it pleases you, and to receive kindly the bearer of this letter, in whose mouth I place my affairs to be more fully explained to you, and to give your consent to what he will tell you on my behalf. I am ready for your will, and I place myself and my affairs before you, to be fully submitted to your judgment.
>
> Witnessed by the Chancellor, at Rouen.[1]

In September Queen Constance of France died in giving birth to a daughter. Louis now had four daughters as the only issue of his two marriages. After Constance had been dead less than a month, he married Adela of Blois, the youngest sister of Count Henry of Champagne, who was betrothed to Marie, Louis's elder daughter by Eleanor, and of Count Theobald of Blois, who was betrothed to Alice, Marie's sister. Henry was not interested in the tangled relationships that would arise when Louis's brothers-in-law became also his sons-in-law, but he was gravely concerned that Louis should form so intimate an alliance with the house of

---

[1] Delisle-Berger, op. cit., Vol. I, p. 249.

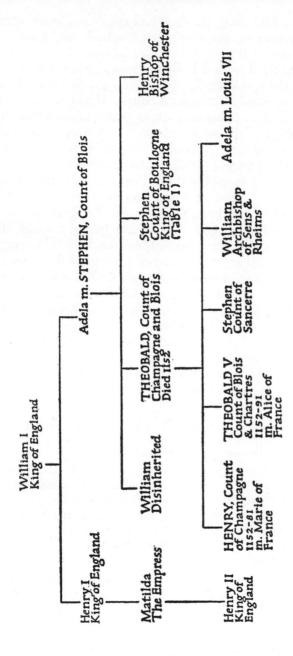

William I
King of England

Henry I
King of England

Adela m. STEPHEN, Count of Blois

Matilda
The Empress

William
Disinherited

THEOBALD, Count of
Champagne and Blois
Died 1152

Stephen
Count of Boulogne
King of England
(Table I)

Henry
Bishop of
Winchester

Henry II
King of England

HENRY, Count
of Champagne
1152–81
m. Marie of
France

THEOBALD V
Count of Blois
& Chartres
1152–91
m. Alice of
France

Stephen
Count of
Sancerre

William
Archbishop
of Sens &
Rheims

Adela m. Louis VII

IV THE HOUSE OF BLOIS

69

Blois, from which King Stephen had come and from which a possible pretender to the throne of England might some day again arise.

Henry countered with a brilliant move. The Pope had sent two legates, the Cardinals Henry of Pisa and William of Pavia, to his court to plead Alexander's cause. Henry induced them, probably as the price of his support, to grant a dispensation allowing the marriage of the young Henry, not yet six years old, and Margaret, less than three years old. The children were promptly married in the presence of the two Cardinals. Henry then claimed her dowry from the three Templars who were holding it in trust for her. Satisfied that the terms of the treaty between Louis and Henry had been fulfilled, the Templars turned the Vexin over to Henry, who thus at last gained control of the territory without which no Duke of Normandy could be content.

Henry proceeded at once to fortify Gisors and the other main castles of the Vexin. This looked to the baffled and exasperated Louis like a threat of war, and he and Count Theobald replied by fortifying Theobald's castle of Chaumont-sur-Loire as a threat to Henry's territory of Touraine. Henry hastened to the new scene of danger and put Louis and Theobald to flight. Thus a precarious peace was restored.[1]

The King's eldest son, already a married man, was now at a suitable age to begin his formal education, as the Archbishop of Rouen reminded the King:

> To his dearest lord, the illustrious Henry, etc., his servant Rotrou, by the divine permission Archbishop of Rouen, sends greetings in Him by Whom kings reign.
>
> Although other kings are of a rude and uncultivated character, yours, which was formed by literature, is prudent in the administration of great affairs, subtle in judgments, and circumspect in counsel. Wherefore all your bishops unanimously agree that Henry, your son and heir, should apply himself to letters, so that he whom we regard as your heir may be the successor to your wisdom as well as to your kingdom.[2]

Thomas the Chancellor already had a number of the sons of various nobles under his care, to be educated in knightly accomplishments. Henry added his son to the group, and the boy im-

---

[1] Robert of Torigni, pp. 208-9.
[2] Rotrou, Archbishop of Rouen: *Epistolae*, Migne, Vol. CCVII, col. 211.

mediately took to the Chancellor with the same affection that his father had.

Thomas was still Archdeacon of Canterbury as well as Chancellor. His long absence abroad, even though it was in the King's service, troubled the Archbishop. He more than once wrote to Thomas, asking him to return and give his attention at least for a time to the affairs of the archdiocese, for Theobald was old and becoming feeble. John of Salisbury, who had taken Thomas's place as the Archbishop's most trusted adviser, urged him to return to England before his old friend and patron died. At last the Archbishop wrote him as his spiritual father and ordered him to return as soon as he could get the King's permission.[1]

To all these letters the Chancellor replied that he would come as soon as he could obtain the King's leave, and the King declared that Thomas was indispensable to him and could not be spared at that particular time. Delay was added to delay, and the Archbishop died on April 18, 1161, with his Archdeacon still in Normandy.

Queen Eleanor gave birth to her second daughter and sixth child by Henry at Domfront in September 1161. The child was given her mother's name and baptised by Cardinal Henry of Pisa, to whom the Pope seems to have assigned the task of watching Henry to make sure that he did not, under the Emperor's prodding, transfer his allegiance to the anti-pope Victor.

Henry had already had his English barons swear to accept the young Henry as his heir. Now he again became concerned about the succession to the throne. In May 1162 he determined to exact once more an oath of fealty to his son. He ordered Thomas to take his young charge, his adopted son, as Thomas called him, back to England, to summon the Great Council in the King's name, and to require all the bishops and barons of the realm to swear fealty and do homage to the young Henry.

As Thomas was preparing to depart on this mission, the King told him of a second reason that required his presence in England. The See of Canterbury had now been vacant for over a year, and Henry determined that his dearest friend, his most valued counsellor, the man who was of one heart and mind with him, the Chancellor Thomas, should become Primate. With Henry as King and Thomas as Archbishop and Chancellor, State and

---

[1] *Materials*, Vol. V, pp. 11-12.

Church would be on such friendly terms as would be the wonder
and model of all Christendom. Not while they lived would
there be such strife and discord between King and Archbishop as
there had been between William Rufus and Anselm or between
Stephen and Theobald, with the Archbishop driven into exile
and the King threatened with excommunication and the realm
with interdict. Rather would they work together in all things
to the good both of the Church and of the kingdom, as had
William the Conqueror and Lanfranc.

Henry also had an ambition to cut a fine figure in the world by
having an archbishop as his chancellor, as the Emperor had.[1]

To Henry's amazement, Thomas vigorously resisted the plan.
He knew himself, and he knew the duties of an Archbishop of
Canterbury too well to think that they could enjoy such friendship and singleness of purpose as King and Archbishop as they
had experienced as King and Chancellor. Henry paid no attention to Thomas's objections. When the Chancellor persisted in
refusing the office, the King enlisted the support of the Papal
Legate, Cardinal Henry of Pisa. The King and the Cardinal
combined to overcome his refusal, and at last Thomas consented,
but still unwillingly.[2]

Thomas sailed to England with the young Henry early in May
1162.

[1] Ralph of Diceto: *Opera Historica*, ed. William Stubbs (Rolls Series, 2 vols.,
1867), Vol. I, pp. 307-8.
[2] Herbert of Bosham, in *Materials*, Vol. III, pp. 180-2.

V

THE KING AND THE ARCHBISHOP
1162 - 1163

THE Great Council of the bishops and barons met at the Chancellor's summons in London around May 23. They recognised the young Henry, then seven years old, as heir to the throne and swore fealty to him. That the boy received their homage in something approaching regal majesty is indicated by a charge in the Pipe Roll of £38 6s. 'for gold for preparing a crown and regalia for the King's son'.[1]

The King, meanwhile, had sent to Canterbury to order the monks of Christchurch to come to London and elect Thomas Archbishop of Canterbury. Since the See of Canterbury was of monastic origin and the archbishop was also abbot of the monastery, the monks of Christchurch, who also formed the cathedral chapter, had the right to elect the archbishop. Although every king on his accession swore to respect and preserve the freedom of the Church, which in practice meant the freedom of the cathedral chapters to elect their bishops, the election was usually made in the king's chamber and in his presence, and the man so elected was almost always the king's nominee.

The monks of Christchurch were loath to elect as archbishop a man who was neither a priest nor a monk. All but four of the successors of St. Augustine had been monks. The election of a mere secular deacon was unheard of. The monks had no choice, however; in obedience to the King, the Prior took some of the older monks with him to Westminster, and there they unanimously elected Thomas as Archbishop of Canterbury and announced their choice to the members of the Great Council.

The bishops and barons approved and confirmed the election. The only dissenting voice was that of Gilbert Foliot, Bishop of Hereford, who objected to the King's choice of a man of such worldly character for the highest ecclesiastical dignity in the land.

[1] Pipe Roll 8 Henry II, p. 43.

Gilbert said afterwards that the King had indeed done a marvellous thing when he turned a worldly man and a knight into an archbishop.[1]

Thomas immediately asked to be released from all secular obligations, that he be declared quit of all financial responsibilities that he might have incurred as Chancellor, and that he be allowed to take up his new duties without any necessity for accounting for the past. Since the affairs of the King and the Chancellor had been so inextricably involved that no amount of accounting could ever separate them, the young Henry, the Chief Justiciars, and the Great Council declared him quit of all obligations.

Thomas thereupon resigned the office of Chancellor and sent his seal to the King in Normandy. Henry fell into a fit of rage when he received it, for Thomas thus gave him clear warning, if his protests against his election had not already done so, that he had no intention of falling in with Henry's scheme to use the Archbishop of Canterbury as one of his servants.[2]

The Archbishop-elect was ordained priest by Bishop Walter of Rochester, his old friend and protector. On the following day, Sunday, June 3, 1162, the octave of Whitsunday, he was consecrated bishop by Henry of Winchester. In commemoration of the event, Thomas ordered that the first Sunday after Whitsunday be thenceforth celebrated throughout the Province of Canterbury as the Feast of the Most Holy Trinity, to Whom Canterbury Cathedral was dedicated.[3] Eventually Pope John XXII (1316-34) made it a feast of universal observance.

The new Archbishop entered on his duties with the same enthusiasm that he had shown as Chancellor. Just as he had formerly been outstanding for the magnificence of his life, now his household at Canterbury became the model of what a bishop's should be. As he had formerly been surrounded by the flower of English knighthood, he now, after his predecessor's example, made the wise and the holy welcome at his table. He began studying the Scriptures, with Herbert of Bosham as his teacher, and every day after dinner he discussed religious matters with his associates.

There is no evidence that Thomas underwent an emotional

---

[1] William Fitz Stephen, in *Materials*, Vol. III, p. 36.
[2] Ralph of Diceto, Vol. I, pp. 307-8.
[3] Gervase of Canterbury ,Vol. I, p. 171.

conversion such as has often led men to give up the pleasures of the world and turn to a religious life. He was guided largely by his strong sense of what was proper and fitting. He had not sought to be a bishop: the office had sought him. Doubtful though he was as to his own fitness for the office, Thomas had been overruled by the papal legate himself. He had been elected by the competent authority, and he had been validly consecrated to an office for which no man could be fully worthy. Conscious of his own shortcomings and of the incongruity of his past life with the demands of his present station, Thomas, in all humility, set to work to make himself at least less unfit to be a successor of the Apostles.

Although at table he took a few sips of wine and a few bites of meat so that his guests might not feel constrained to follow his austerity, his habitual drink was water in which fennel had been steeped, and he made his meal on bread alone. During the repast, which the knights of the household ate at the far end of the hall so that their cheerful chatter would not disturb the clergy, the Archbishop's cross-bearer, Alexander Llewelyn, read aloud from some edifying work. The second sons of nobles, between their arrival at puberty and their admittance to knighthood, were customarily educated in the Archbishop's household and served at his table. First in rank among these lads, of course, was the young Henry.

There was no distinctive clerical dress in those days, apart from the monastic habit, but Thomas laid away his gorgeous clothes and dressed in sober and sombre garments. He kept up all the charities of his predecessor and doubled the alms that Theobald had been accustomed to give. He fed the poor and vagrant; he clothed the poor of Canterbury; he visited his sick monks, and he set aside a tenth of his income for almsgiving. Every day he washed the feet of thirteen poor men in his private chamber, gave them a copious meal, and dismissed each one with a gift of four silver pennies.

It would be pointless to object that all these acts of piety were ostentatious; neither the Archbishop nor the King nor any other man of any degree save the lowest could have any privacy outside his bedchamber. Every action was carried out in public, before the gaze of a swarm of attendants and followers and companions and even idle onlookers. The halls of the great stood open to the

public, eager to note everything that passed.   The houses even of
the richest consisted only of a hall and a chamber.   The hall was
a large barn-like room with a wood fire burning in the middle of
the floor and the smoke finding its way out through a hole in the
roof.

All business was transacted in the hall.   The entire establishment ate there at wooden trestles, which were removed at the
end of the meal.   The lord and his friends ate at a separate table,
sometimes on a dais, at one end.   The kitchen was a separate
building in the larger establishments; in the smaller ones the
cooking was done over the fire in the hall.   At night the guests
and servants slept on the rushes of the floor, and the lord retired
to his chamber, which was also used as a withdrawing-room by
the lady of the house when she wanted to get away from the
throng that crowded the hall.   Under such conditions privacy
was almost impossible, and all a man's doings, whether good or
bad, might be called ostentatious, in the sense that they were
known to everyone.

Not everyone, however, could know of the harsh austerities
that Thomas imposed on himself in the relative privacy of his
chamber in an effort to subdue in himself those traits that stood
in the way of his spiritual growth.   Of the sins of the flesh, as
they are commonly understood, Thomas remained free throughout his life.   His most bitter enemies, in the days that lay ahead,
never uttered a single reflection on the purity of his personal life.
There remained, however, the more subtle temptations of spiritual pride, and these Thomas strove to overcome by methods that
have been followed by holy men of all times.

Only his most intimate associates could know that he received
the discipline on his bare shoulders daily till the blood ran down
his back.   Only at the end, when they stripped his body of its
blood-soaked garments, would they know that Thomas, who
once had worn only the most costly and splendid clothes, carried
next to his skin the harshest of penances, a shirt and drawers of
haircloth, so infested with vermin that, as Edward Grim, a witness to his murder, remarked, his martyrdom itself was light in
comparison with the torture the haircloth inflicted and his big
enemies hurt him less than those little ones.[1]

Pope Alexander, meanwhile, had fled from Italy as the Em-

1 Edward Grim, *Materials*, Vol. II, p. 442.

peror, after destroying Milan, advanced southward. He arrived at Montpellier in the spring of 1162, and Henry and Louis went to pay their respects to him and assure him of their support. The interview took place in September on the banks of the Loire, near Coucy. They received the Pope with fitting honour, one of them holding the bridle of his horse and the other his stirrups, and led him to the tent that had been prepared for him.

Alexander induced the two Kings, his principal supporters, to make peace and put an end, at least for a time, to the petty clashes that threatened sooner or later to break into open war. With Frederick Barbarossa ravaging Italy and bidding for the support of the English and French Kings in his attempt to foist an anti-pope on Christendom, Alexander was much concerned that Henry and Louis should be friends.[1]

Henry intended to keep Christmas in England, but when the royal party arrived at Barfleur there were such unfavourable winds that they could not sail. The King and Queen consequently held their Christmas court at Cherbourg. With a favourable wind, they sailed from Normandy and landed at Southampton on January 25, 1163. Thomas and the young Henry were waiting for them there. Herbert of Bosham[2] tells how the King and the Archbishop met with kisses and embraces and the greatest joy, the King exulting to see for the first time his former Chancellor as Archbishop. On the next day they set forth for London, Henry and Thomas riding apart, deep in friendly conversation.

Ralph of Diceto,[3] however, says that although they kissed, Henry had already begun to cool towards Thomas and forced him to resign the Archdeaconry of Canterbury, which he had continued to hold even after he became Archbishop. At Henry's request Thomas appointed to the post Geoffrey Ridel, one of the King's clerks.

Henry summoned the bishops and barons of the realm for his first meeting with the Great Council since he had left England four and a half years ago. The council assembled on March 3. The main subject for discussion was the See of London, which had been vacant since the death of Bishop Richard of Belmeis in the preceding May. Henry proposed that Bishop Gilbert Foliot be translated from Hereford to London, and the council unanimously agreed.

[1] Robert of Torigni, pp. 215-16.   [2] *Materials*, Vol. III, pp. 252-3.   [3] Vol. I, p. 308.

Gilbert Foliot was of a noble Norman family, which in itself would commend him to the King, his barons, and Gilbert's brother bishops. He was noted throughout both England and France for his learning, for the purity and austerity of his life, and for his eloquence. Henry had particular reason to be grateful to him for the way in which he had persuaded his kinsman, the Earl of Hereford, to abandon his defiant attitude at the beginning of the reign.

The approval of the Pope was necessary for the translation of a bishop from one see to another, for it was a most unusual step. No English bishop had been so translated since the Conquest, except to serve as Archbishop. Both the King and Thomas wrote to Pope Alexander, requesting him to approve of Gilbert's translation, on the ground that the See of London, the chief city of England, one much frequented by the King and all the great men of the realm, needed a bishop of exemplary character, of proven ability, and of great learning, and that Gilbert had amply shown all those qualities at Hereford. The Pope, on March 19, wrote a gracious letter to Gilbert, assuring him of his fitness for the post and ordering him to take it.[1]

Henry and Thomas also wrote to Gilbert, praising him for his virtues and urging him to accept the translation. In Thomas's letter there is no indication that he bore Gilbert any ill will for having opposed his election; Thomas's protests to the King when the matter was first broached showed that he shared Gilbert's views on his unworthiness.[2]

Gilbert accepted the translation, and on April 28 he was enthroned in St. Paul's Cathedral, with Archbishop Thomas presiding at the ceremony. Once he was enthroned, Gilbert immediately showed a less attractive side of his nature. Men were already whispering that the austere bishop's opposition to the election of Thomas proceeded, not from his doubts as to Thomas's fitness, but from his own ambitions to be Archbishop himself. Now he showed himself coldly ungrateful to the man who had procured his advancement. When he was requested to make the customary profession of obedience to the Archbishop of Canterbury as his metropolitan, Gilbert refused. He had already made such a profession to Thomas's predecessor when he was consecrated Bishop of Hereford, he maintained, and there was no

[1] *Materials*, Vol. V, pp. 27-28.   [2] *Materials*, Vol. V, pp. 24-26.

necessity for his repeating it when he was transferred to another see.[1]

At Windsor, on March 31, Robert of Montfort, before the King, accused the Constable, Henry of Essex, of cowardice and treason in North Wales in July 1157. Robert declared that Henry of Essex had cried out that the King was dead, that he had thrown the royal standard to the ground, and that he had fled from the battle. The Constable took up the challenge, which could be answered only by a trial by battle, a personal conflict between the accused and his accuser.

The issue was decided on an island in the Thames near Reading Abbey. Henry of Essex was conquered and fell, thus proving his guilt in the eyes of all men, although the King is said to have believed his assertion that the standard was knocked from his hand and that he let it fall by accident. The Constable was declared an outlaw, his estates were confiscated, and he was left for dead upon the field. His body was given to the monks of Reading to bury. They discovered that although he was grievously wounded he was not dead. When he recovered his health under their ministrations he became a monk at Reading; with lands and honour lost, there was nothing left for him in this world.[2]

At a meeting of the Great Council at Woodstock on July 1, the King brought up the question of the 'sheriff's aid', a payment of two shillings from each hide of land to the sheriff to recompense him for his labours in the administration of the county. (A hide of land varied from 48 to 120 acres; the latter figure seems to have been most common at this time.) Henry proposed that this aid, instead of being given to the sheriff, be paid directly into the Treasury as a regular tax.

> The Archbishop opposed him to his face, saying that they [the two shillings] should not be exacted as a tax. 'Nor as a tax,' he said, 'will we pay them, my Lord King, saving your pleasure. No matter how worthily the sheriffs serve us and uphold the servants or officials of the county and our men, we will never pay them as a tax.'
>
> The King, angered by the Archbishop's reply, said, 'By God's

[1] *Materials*, Vol. V, pp. 56-57, 60.
[2] Jocelin of Brakelond: *Chronicle*, ed. H. E. Butler (Nelson's Medieval Texts, 1949). pp. 68-71.

eyes, they shall be paid as a tax and entered in the King's books; nor is it fitting that you should oppose this, since no one wants to injure your possessions against your will.'

The Archbishop, foreseeing and taking precautions lest through his sufferance a new custom be introduced whereby later generations might be harmed, replied, 'Out of reverence for those same eyes by which you swore, my Lord King, they will not be paid in any of my land, and not a single penny from the land belonging by law to the Church.'[1]

Thomas, by raising the issue of preserving the ancient customs against innovations, the most potent of all arguments to the medieval mind, won his point. The King dropped the matter.

This incident, apart from the evidence it gives of Thomas's contradictory attitude to Henry, shows that the Great Council could reject a proposal made by the King. The purpose of the council was to advise the King, and bishops and barons valued highly their right to inform him of their views. At his summons they came from every part of England, not only to the ceremonial courts at Christmas, Easter, and Whitsuntide, but also to the meetings the King held at frequent intervals to discuss his plans. Not all the bishops and barons attended every meeting of the council, of course, but enough were present to give the assembly a representative character. It was never a mere inner circle of the King's friends and advisers.

Thomas's opposition to the King's plan for increasing his revenues added to Henry's ill will towards the Archbishop, which began when Thomas resigned his post as Chancellor. Thomas also opposed a plan that Henry devised to provide for his brother William by giving him the hand and the extensive estates of the Countess Warenne, the widow of King Stephen's son William. Since the two Williams were second cousins, Thomas forbade the one to marry the widow of the other on the ground of affinity.

Henry got around this difficulty by marrying the Countess, in the following year, to his bastard half-brother Hamelin, who now emerges from obscurity and henceforth appears as Earl Warenne. Since the relationship descended through the Empress and Hamelin was the son of an unknown woman and Count Geoffrey the Fair, he was not affected by it.

Stephen of Rouen says that after Thomas refused to allow

[1] Edward Grim, in *Materials*, Vol. II, p. 374.

William to marry the Countess his heart was broken. He went to Rouen and poured out his troubles to his mother. He also went to the monastery of Bec and told the monks of his great disappointment. Then he returned to Rouen and died of a broken heart on January 30, 1164. Stephen says that the King held Thomas responsible for his brother's death and that that was the principal reason for Henry's hatred for him.[1] It is obvious, however, that Henry's feelings towards Thomas had changed long before this.

Another source of friction between the King and the Archbishop arose from Thomas's energetic efforts to reclaim all the possessions of the archbishopric that had been alienated from it in one way or another. During the vacancy of the archbishopric, when its lands reverted to the king's custody until the next archbishop did homage for them, it was easy for the king to grant some of them to one of his favourites. Each archbishop in turn found it difficult to regain control of the lands that made up his temporal fief. Thomas was determined to recover all the lands that had ever belonged to his see. He held them as a sacred trust, he believed, and it was his duty to pass on to his successor all the lands that rightfully pertained to the archbishopric. These lands belonged not to Thomas or to any archbishop but to God and the See of Canterbury. It was as the steward of those lands that Thomas watched over them.

The chief offender, in his eyes, was the great and powerful Earl Roger of Clare, who had a most beautiful sister, whom Henry lusted after.[2] Thomas declared that Tonbridge Castle, which Earl Roger held, belonged to the See of Canterbury and demanded that Roger do homage to him for it. The Earl, on the other hand, maintained that he held the castle directly of the King. The matter was referred to the King, at Westminster, on July 22, and Henry declared in favour of the Earl.

Another dispute arose over the presentation to the church at Eynesford. When the living there fell vacant, Thomas gave it to Lawrence, one of his clerks. William, the lord of the manor, claimed that the presentation was his, and he expelled Lawrence and his servants by force. Thomas promptly excommunicated

[1] Stephen of Rouen: *Draco Normannicus*, ed. Richard Howlett, in *Chronicles of the Reigns of Stephen*, etc., Vol. II, p. 676.
[2] William Fitz Stephen, *Materials*, Vol. III, p. 43.

him for having laid violent hands on a cleric. When William complained to the King, Henry wrote to Thomas and ordered him to absolve William. Thomas replied that it was not for the King to tell him whom to absolve or whom to excommunicate. Henry then cited the ancient custom of the realm that forbade any cleric to excommunicate one of the King's tenants-in-chief without first consulting the King.

The reason for this ruling was not that the King was attempting to usurp the spiritual powers of the clergy but that an excommunicated man, cut off from the body of Christians, was of no use to the King in either council or war. The King therefore required that he be consulted before the drastic step was taken, in order that he might attempt to bring the offender to reason or, at the worst, that he might know that his tenant was under a sentence that forbade any Christian to have dealings with him.

Matters had now got to the point where the King would not speak to Thomas and dealt with him only through messengers. Thomas, to soften the King's wrath, absolved William of Eynesford. The King was not appeased. 'I am not grateful to him for this,' he said when he was told that Thomas had lifted the sentence.

The sorest point of all was the matter of 'criminous clerks', or people over whom the Church claimed jurisdiction and who had committed felonies against the law of the land. 'Clerks' embraced not only those in Holy Orders and those on whom the tonsure, the first step towards Holy Orders, had been conferred, but also those who had taken religious vows. Over all these the Church claimed sole jurisdiction and maintained that they could not be tried in civil courts, even for civil offences, but only in ecclesiastical courts. The courts Christian could not pronounce a sentence of blood, and their punishments, in comparison with those meted out by the civil courts, were ludicrously light, amounting at the worst to a severe penance, suspension from the exercise of the priestly functions, degradation from the clerical state, or confinement to a monastery for the rest of the offender's life.

After he had returned to England in January 1163, a series of crimes committed by clerks who went almost unpunished, to Henry's way of thinking, came to the King's attention. A cleric in Worcestershire was accused of having seduced a girl and then murdered her father. Archbishop Thomas had him given into the custody of the Bishop of Worcester, so that he could not be claimed by the King's officers. Another clerk stole a silver chalice from a church in London. Again, when the King ordered that he be tried before his judges, the Archbishop claimed jurisdiction over the offender. A priest in the diocese of Salisbury was accused of murder, and when he was unable to clear himself of the charge in the Bishop's court, Thomas ordered that he be deprived of his benefice and sent to a monastery to lead a life of penance.

Finally, one Philip of Brois, a canon of Bedford, was accused of having murdered a knight. He was tried before the Bishop of Lincoln and succeeded in clearing himself by compurgation, a method much used in the courts Christian. The secular courts relied upon the ordeals by battle, by water, and by fire to prove guilt or innocence. These ordeals assumed a direct intervention by God to show whether or not the one undergoing the test was guilty. The Church used a less crude method, that of compurgation. The accused solemnly swore that he was innocent, and his claim was supported by a number, usually twelve or more, of 'oath-helpers', who took the same solemn oath. This satisfied the Church, for the inference was that the whole matter was now removed into the hands of God, Who would punish those who swore a false oath far more effectively than any court could do.

Philip and his oath-helpers took the oath, and the Bishop thereupon released him. The relations of the slain knight then lodged an appeal before the King's justiciars. Philip refused to submit to the jurisdiction of the court and used vile and insulting language to Simon Fitz Peter, one of the justiciars. Simon complained to the King, and again Thomas claimed jurisdiction. He tried Philip in his own court and found him already proven innocent of the murder but guilty of having insulted the King's justiciar.

With an eye to the King, Thomas sentenced him to be deprived of his living and to be exiled for a year. This was an unusually heavy sentence for a court Christian, but the King was by no means satisfied. On the contrary, his anger was increased by the imposition of the sentence of exile, for he said that Thomas was assuming an unlawful power over the King's subjects and encroaching on the King's prerogatives.

Shortly after Michaelmas the King summoned the bishops to a meeting at Westminster. When they assembled, Henry spoke to them of the rapacity, greed, and dishonesty with which many archdeacons and rural deans were popularly credited. He then cited the growing scandal of the criminous clerks. In the nine years since he had come to the throne, he declared, over a hundred murders, in addition to such felonies as rape, theft, and extortion almost beyond number, had been committed by clerics who, because of their immunity from civil trial, had gone virtually unpunished.

William of Newburgh, himself a cleric but nevertheless an impartial observer, remarks:

> The bishops were more concerned with defending the liberties and dignities of the clergy than they were with correcting and restraining their vices, and they thought that they were doing a service to God and the Church if they protected from public punishment criminous clerks whom, because of their office, they either refused or neglected to restrain by the force of canonical censure.[1]

Even Herbert of Bosham, Thomas's most devoted follower, says that Henry was acting through a desire to secure the peace and good order of his realm.[2]

The whole evil, Henry declared, arose from the fact that the ecclesiastical courts claimed exclusive jurisdiction over all clerks and that their sentences were so light that they served neither as deterrents nor as punishments. If a priest were so wicked as to commit rape or murder, the mere degradation from his priesthood would appear a small matter to him, compared to the death sentence he might expect from a civil court.

The King now proposed to remedy the situation by returning to the customs of his grandfather, as he called them, although there is no record that any such procedure as he advocated had ever been carried out under Henry I. He asked the bishops to be more zealous in prosecuting clerical offenders, to agree to turn over criminous clerks, after they had been found guilty in the courts Christian and had been degraded from their clerical status, to the civil courts for punishment, and to cease infringing on the King's rights over his subjects by pronouncing such sentences as that of exile, which properly belonged to the civil power, in their courts.

[1] William of Newburgh, p. 141.   [2] *Materials*, Vol. III, p. 272.

Thomas and his bishops conferred together, and then Thomas, in the name of all of them, maintained that the reverence due to the priestly office prohibited that clerics should be judged by laymen in civil courts.

'It would be wicked and shameful indeed,' he said, 'for the royal mercy to appear so cruel and abominable that the hands consecrated to God, the hands that only shortly before had fashioned the image of the Crucified King, the Saviour of the world, should now, tied behind his back, proclaim the public thief, and that the head, anointed with the sacred chrism, before which only a short time ago the royal majesty had knelt, seeking grace and pardon, should now hang on a shameful gallows with a rope about its neck.'[1]

This was a moving defence of the sacred character of the priesthood, but it completely ignored the problem Henry was attempting to solve. The King demanded flatly that the bishops swear to observe the ancient customs. Although to the King the ancient customs meant the peace and good order that his grandfather had brought to the realm, to Thomas and his bishops they called up memories of the bitter struggles between Henry and Anselm in which the King had tried to reduce the Archbishop of Canterbury to complete subservience to him. Thomas, who had taken Anselm for his patron and model, now resisted Henry as stoutly as Anselm had stood up to the Red King and to Henry I. The Archbishop of Canterbury could be no mere creature of the King; there had been Archbishops of Canterbury long before there had ever been a King of England, and it was the See of Canterbury that had given England such unity and national spirit as it now possessed.

Conscious of the proud traditions of his office and of the long line of archbishops reaching back to St. Augustine, of whom he was now the successor, Thomas replied that he and his brother bishops would swear to observe the ancient customs, 'saving their order'.

By this reservation Thomas intended to make sure that none of the customs to which Henry was appealing should be contrary to their consciences and to their duties and obligations to the Church as bishops. Not all the customs of Henry's grandfather had been good customs, by any means. By shifting his ground from the

---

[1] Herbert of Bosham, in *Materials*, Vol. III, p. 269.

specific abuses under discussion to a general acceptance of what
he called the ancient customs, Henry forced the bishops to make
some reservation in order to protect themselves. Otherwise,
Henry could compel them to receive the ring and the staff, the
symbols of their spiritual office, from his hands; he could forbid
them to obey the summons of the Pope to a council; he could
intrude his own nominees into ecclesiastical offices at will; he
could leave bishoprics vacant indefinitely and appropriate the
revenues, as Henry I had done with the Archbishopric of Canterbury for five years after Anselm's death; he could force cathedral
chapters to purchase from him the right to elect their bishops, as
Stephen had done when he made the Chapter of London promise
him £500 for the privilege; and he could sell ecclesiastical offices
outright.

All these things had been done by his predecessors and, for all
the bishops knew, might be included by the King in what he now
called upon them to swear to observe. In short, an unconditional
acceptance of 'the ancient customs' might put the bishops entirely
at the King's mercy and make them wholly subservient to him.

In a rage, the King demanded of each bishop, singly and in turn,
that he swear to observe the ancient customs, and each bishop in
turn replied that he would so swear, 'saving his order'. Only
the time-serving Hilary of Chichester, in an effort to appease the
King, said that he would swear to observe the customs 'in good
faith'.

The King was not appeased by Bishop Hilary's feeble effort
and turned from him in scorn. Facing Thomas and the other
bishops, he demanded that they take the oath without any
reservation whatever.

The Archbishop replied that he had already sworn fealty to the
King 'in life and limb and earthly honour, saving his order', and
in that earthly honour were included all the customs of the kingdom. No oath that he could take now would be more binding
than that all-embracing one.

The whole day had passed, and now it was growing dark.
What might have been a friendly conference on a most difficult
problem—that of how best to deal with criminous clerks without
infringing on the rights of the Church over her clergy on the one
hand and the rights of the King over his subjects on the other—
had become a conflict between Church and State, with all the

bitter memories of the tyranny of the Red King, of Henry I and his struggle with Anselm, and of Stephen and his persecution of Theobald, that such a conflict stirred up.

It is a measure of how far apart Henry and Thomas had grown that Henry should see in Thomas's concern to preserve the rights of the Church a desire to shelter criminous clerks from justice and to deprive him of any jurisdiction over a large number of his subjects, and that Thomas should see in Henry's efforts to strengthen peace and good order in his realm an intention to encroach on that freedom from secular control that the Church had won only by many a bitter contest between king and archbishop in the past.

When Thomas refused to give up the reservation 'saving his order', the King turned abruptly and strode out of the hall without taking leave of any of the bishops.[1]

Early the next morning a messenger brought Thomas an order from the King, who had already left London secretly and before dawn, to surrender the castle of Berkhamstead and the Honour of Eye, which he had been holding since he was Chancellor. The King also withdrew the young Henry from Thomas's care.

Later in the autumn the King summoned Thomas to meet him at Northampton. They conferred in a field outside the town. Henry reproached Thomas for his ingratitude after all the favours he had showered upon him. The Archbishop protested that he was not ungrateful, but that when his duty to his King conflicted with his duty to his God, he had no choice but to obey the latter. He ended his defence by quoting, 'It is better to obey God than man.'

'I don't want you to preach sermons to me,' cried Henry. 'Aren't you the son of a peasant of mine?'

'It is true that I am not descended from a long line of kings,' Thomas replied, 'but then neither was Blessed Peter, the Prince of the Apostles, to whom the Lord gave the keys of the kingdom of Heaven and the rule of the whole Church.'

'That's true,' said the King, 'but he died for his Lord.'

'And I shall die for my Lord, when the time comes.'

Thomas again declined to omit the words 'saving my order' from his oath, and the King broke off the interview in anger.[2]

The dispute meanwhile was being reported to the Pope. It

---

[1] Herbert of Bosham, in *Materials*, Vol. III, p. 274.
[2] Anonymous I, in *Materials*, Vol. IV, pp. 27-29.

placed him in a most difficult position.   Henry's support was the
decisive factor in Alexander's struggle against the Emperor and
his anti-pope.   Alexander was grateful to Henry, and he feared
that if he lost the friendship of the King of England he would be
hard put to it to keep his throne.   On the other hand, he realised
that some of the things Henry was demanding might place the
Church in England wholly at the King's mercy.   The Pope's
problem was to mollify Henry so that he would not desert
him and turn to the anti-pope, and at the same time to assure
Thomas of his sympathy in his struggle to preserve the rights of
the Church.

In December Alexander sent three messengers to Thomas with
words of advice and also with letters from himself and some of his
Cardinals.   The tenor of both the letters and the advice was that
it was imperative to avoid a schism by any lawful means.   In his
vague references to the ancient customs, Henry had not explicitly
proposed anything directly contrary to the teachings of the
Church.   Rather than drive him into the arms of the Emperor
and his anti-pope, they all advised Thomas to submit to the King.
Henry had assured the Pope that he did not intend to force
Thomas to do anything derogatory to his order or against his will.
Thomas had humiliated the King by his open defiance, and it
would be harmful to the royal honour if it should appear that the
King was vanquished by the Archbishop.   Let Thomas simply
omit the words 'saving my order', and there would be peace both
in the kingdom and in the Church.   Once Thomas submitted,
Henry had assured the Pope, there would be no further mention
of the customs.   It was merely a question of salving the King's
wounded pride and dignity.

In the face of all this advice, Thomas said that he would do what
the Pope, the Cardinals, and their emissaries requested.   Thomas
and the messengers went to meet Henry at Woodstock.   The
Archbishop humbly made his submission to the King.   He swore
to Henry: 'I will observe the customs of the realm in good faith,
and, as is fitting and proper, I will obey you in everything else
that is good.'

Then Henry sprang his trap.

Since Thomas had openly and publicly defied him and the fact
was known all over the country, a mere act of submission in
private was not enough.   He required the Archbishop to make

his submission in the presence of the Great Council. Thomas could hardly refuse to say in public what he had already said in private. He therefore agreed to repeat his oath at the meeting that Henry proposed to call shortly after Christmas to witness the Archbishop's humiliation.[1]

[1] Anonymous I, in *Materials*, Vol. IV, pp. 31-33.

VI

THE KING AND THE TRAITOR
1164

THE Great Council met at Clarendon, near Salisbury, on January 25, 1164. Thomas meanwhile had been considering the act of submission that he would be expected to perform. He came to the conclusion that the Pope and his messengers had been misinformed both as to Henry's character and intentions and as to the nature of the ancient customs that Alexander had advised the Archbishop to swear to observe.

Thomas knew Henry more intimately than did anyone else. He realised the dogged tenacity of Henry's character. Once the King had made up his mind, he used every resource of persuasion, intimidation, threats, trickery, chicanery, and force to obtain his ends. The King might have succeeded in convincing the Pope that all he wanted was a mere verbal compliance from the Archbishop: Thomas knew better. He also knew that the ancient customs of Henry I included many things that he could not in good conscience accept.

The King and his eldest son, not yet nine years old, presided at the council. Thomas, as the first subject in the realm, sat in the place of honour on the King's right. The sinister figure of Roger of Pont l'Évêque, Archbishop of York, was on the King's left, waiting with hooded eyes for the public humiliation of the man he hated most in the world. Beyond the two Archbishops, in due order of precedence, sat the bishops, chief among whom were Gilbert Foliot, Bishop of London, coldly smug in the consciousness of his own virtues and austerities and thinking, no doubt, that if he had been made Archbishop he would certainly have managed things better than to arrive at such a pass that the bishops and barons of the whole kingdom should thus flock to witness his abasement; and the venerable Henry of Winchester, purged now of his ambitions and political pretensions, mellowed by the years, and suffering deeply for his Archbishop, whom his own hands had hallowed and whom he loved with all his generous heart.

In addition to the two Chief Justiciars, Earl Robert of Leicester and Richard of Luci, seven earls were sitting on the benches beyond the bishops: Reginald of Cornwall, the King's uncle; Roger of Clare, with whom Thomas had crossed swords concerning Tonbridge Castle; Geoffrey of Mandeville, Earl of Essex; Hugh of Chester, the son of Earl Rannulf, the notorious turncoat of Stephen's reign; William of Arundel, who had married the widow of Henry I; Earl Patrick of Salisbury, and William of Ferrars.

Filling the remainder of the benches and crowded into the rear of the hall were the officers of the King's household and a throng of barons and knights. Among these last was Richer of l'Aigle, an old man now, staring wide-eyed at the Archbishop of Canterbury, whom he had known as a bright young lad, a mere burgher's son, breathless at the joy and honour of riding beside a knight.

Henry opened the proceedings by calling upon the Archbishop to swear to observe the customs of the realm without any qualification whatever, as he had previously done at Woodstock. This was the moment they had all been waiting for: some with ill-concealed satisfaction that the Archbishop of Canterbury, who had been raised from nothing to be the first subject in the realm, whom everyone save the King greeted on bended knee, should now be publicly humiliated and brought low; others with deep sorrow that the only man amongst them who had the courage to stand up to the King and fight for the rights of the Church with all the courage of a Lanfranc or an Anselm should now be forced into a craven submission to what they knew in their hearts was wrong.

Thomas refused to take the oath.

The council was thrown into an uproar. 'The King's wrath was like the roaring of a lion.' As the angry discussion continued, Henry grew more and more furious.

Various persons tried to mediate between the King and the Archbishop. The Bishops of Salisbury and Norwich, who were already in the King's bad graces, begged Thomas to make his peace with the King, lest he put them all to death. Against their tearful entreaties Thomas stood firm and tried to quiet their fears. Then two of the most powerful earls of the kingdom, Robert of

Leicester and Reginald of Cornwall, came to the Archbishop and
spoke to him as his sincere friends. They warned him that the
King was in a fearful fit of rage 'and was ready to avenge the
insult with drawn sword'. They begged him, out of consideration for them, to make satisfaction to Henry, for otherwise the
King would force them to the dreadful shame and crime of laying
violent hands on their Archbishop. The bishops' talk of the
threats of death might be put down to their natural timidity, but
when such responsible men as the two earls spoke of the violent
measures that Henry was contemplating, it was enough to give
Thomas pause. He was not daunted, however, and told the earls
that he was ready to face death, if need be.

Last came Richard of Hastings, the Master of the Templars in
England, and one of his fellow knights, who were in great favour
with the King. They assured Thomas that all the King wanted
from him was a purely formal act of submission to satisfy his
injured honour. They swore on their soul's salvation that if
Thomas would make his submission the whole matter of the
customs would be dropped and the King would require nothing
of him in any way contrary to his will or to his order.

At this solemn assurance, Thomas called his bishops together
and told them what the Templars had sworn. Relying on that
oath, he informed his suffragans that he intended to submit to the
King. Thomas then, in the presence of the Great Council,
promised that he would obey the customs of the realm in good
faith.

The King turned to his barons. 'You have all heard,' he said,
'what the Archbishop of his courtesy has conceded to me. It
remains now for the bishops, at his order, to do the same thing.'

'It is my will,' said Thomas, 'that they satisfy your honour as I
have done.'

All the bishops then rose and took the oath.

Thomas, relying on the Templars' promise, thought that the
council was now at an end and stood waiting for the King to
dismiss them and leave.

Henry sprang his second trap.

'I believe,' he said, 'that it has come to the hearing of all of you
that the Archbishop and the bishops have conceded to me that
they will henceforth firmly keep and obey the laws and customs
of my realm. Now, lest any dispute or disagreement arise

between us on the subject, let the wisest and oldest of the nobles rise and go outside, and let them, with my clerks, recall the laws and customs of my grandfather, King Henry. Let them diligently write them down and bring them to me as soon as possible.'

The customs were duly remembered and written down. It seems probable that the document was prepared in advance, in the interval between Thomas's private submission at Woodstock and the meeting of the council, and that Henry had enlisted the help of Richard of Luci, his most experienced justiciar, in drawing it up. Certainly it was not the sort of code that could be prepared in the off-hand way that Henry's words suggest.

When the document was brought to the King, he had it read to the assembly. Thomas knew then that he had indeed been betrayed. The provisions went far beyond anything Henry had yet demanded or Thomas had feared. They not only perpetuated the worst abuses of the past; they were aimed at putting the Church in England directly under the royal control. The Church was to be made subordinate to the civil power and answerable to it, and civil law was to have precedence over canon law.

After the provisions had been read, Henry said: 'These customs have been conceded to belong to me. Therefore, lest any question should arise concerning them in the future or lest any new disputes should perchance come up, we will that the Archbishop put his seal to them.'

'By Almighty God,' cried Thomas, 'never, as long as I am alive, will my seal be put to them!'

From that refusal the King could not move him. Then Henry had his clerks draw up three copies of the Constitutions. One was given to Archbishop Roger of York, one was kept by the King, and the third was given to Thomas.

'I accept this,' he said, 'not, however, as consenting to it or approving it, but as a warning to the Church and in her defence, so that by it we may know what is planned against us. Now that we are aware of the snares and petty traps that are set for us, we shall be, God willing, more cautious.'

The Archbishop left in anger, without waiting for the King's dismissal.[1]

The Constitutions of Clarendon are a turning point and a land-

[1] Anonymous I, in *Materials*, Vol. IV, pp. 33-37.

mark in Henry's relationship with Thomas, in his conduct as
King, and in the history of English law.

Henry, by having the customs put in writing and then attempting to force Thomas to set his seal to them in the presence of the
Great Council, and Thomas, by refusing to seal them, brought
their quarrel to the point where no compromise was possible.
The Constitutions, taken as a whole, would have destroyed the
freedom of the Church in England and made it dependent upon
the civil power and subordinate to it.   By cutting off all appeals
to Rome and forbidding clerics to leave the realm without the
King's permission, they would have severed the relationship with
the Universal Church upon which the vitality of the Church in
England depended.

Henry thus put himself in the wrong and lost the advantage
that had hitherto been his.   Until he made his submission at
Woodstock, Thomas had been in the wrong or at least on dubious
ground at almost every point.   His defence of the criminous
clerks had been weak and contrary to common sense.   No
government, as Thomas must have known from his experience
as Chancellor, could tolerate the existence within itself of a
privileged group, no matter what their character, who were
officially recognised as being above the law of the land.   Although
Pope Alexander condemned the chapter of the Constitutions that
provided for the punishment of criminous clerks by the civil
courts after they had been degraded from the clerical state by the
courts Christian, his successor Innocent III (1198-1216) approved
that procedure as being eminently logical and just.

Apart from the principles involved in the dispute, Thomas
gives the impression of having gone out of his way time and
again to irritate and defy the King.   Granted that Henry's ambition to use the Archbishop as his Chancellor and as his tool was
wrong, a man who knew the King as well as Thomas did and
who was on terms of such intimacy with him surely could have
persuaded the King to abandon his design or at least explained
his refusal to further it in such a way as still to remain on terms
of affection and respect.   In spite of his violent temper and headstrong ways and occasional pigheadedness, Henry had a great
fund of hard common sense and a keen eye for the realities of a
situation, and it should not have been beyond Thomas's powers
to appeal to those qualities and to arrive at an understanding that

would leave him free to devote his talents to the task of being the best archbishop in the Church and a credit to the man who had made him what he was.

Once Henry reduced the customs to writing and included among them practices that had been violently opposed by the Church in the past and once he attempted to force the Archbishop to an explicit approval of them, he lost the sympathy and support of many of the bishops and barons, he forced the Pope to approve Thomas's stand, and he put himself irretrievably in the wrong. It was one thing for Thomas to give his verbal assent to 'the ancient customs of the realm'; it was quite another thing for him to set his seal to a group of provisions the whole effect of which was to perpetuate those abuses that had been tacitly tolerated in the past and to set them up as the model to which the Church in England would henceforth conform.

The Constitutions are a landmark in Henry's conduct as King because they are the first indication of his interest in the administration of the law and also the first indication of his genius as a legal administrator and reformer. During the first nine years of his reign he had shown no unusual abilities, as far as one can judge from the scanty records of those early years. Certainly he gave no promise of being as great a man as his grandfather or his great-grandfather had been.

The Constitutions, however, assuming that they are in the main Henry's work, show a remarkable grasp of legal realities. They are an attempt to establish the principle that in those border-line cases where both the civil and the ecclesiastical courts claimed jurisdiction, it was for the civil power to determine where the line of demarcation should lie. In formulating the Constitutions, Henry was no doubt helped by Richard of Luci and others of the 'noblest and oldest barons' who had had experience at the Exchequer and in the courts. The inspiration certainly came from Henry, and one may fairly attribute the Constitutions to him.

They stand out in the history of English law, both because they are the first rational code of laws in England, as opposed to either tribal custom or a rambling set of unrelated 'liberties', and because, although the Constitutions came to almost nothing, they contain the seeds of some of Henry's most important reforms and innovations. The use of the jury of accusation, for instance, for bringing to light offences that no-one dared denounce on his own responsibility, and the Assize *Utrum*, to determine whether land was held in alms and hence subject to ecclesiastical law or as a lay fief and thus under civil law, later became the foundation for the whole system of sworn inquests and assizes that marks Henry's most important contribution to English legal procedure.

The Pope wrote two letters to Thomas on February 27, 1164, from Sens, southeast of Paris, where he had taken up residence in the preceding September. In the first of the letters Alexander stumbled quite a bit in reminding Thomas that 'our dearest son in Christ, Henry, the illustrious King of the English', had 'a fervent disposition concerning the governing of his realm'. Because of that disposition, Henry had sent Arnulf, Bishop of Lisieux, and Richard of Ilchester, Archdeacon of Poitiers, to the Pope to ask him to make the Archbishop of York Papal Legate for all England and to order Thomas and all the bishops to keep the ancient customs and dignities of the realm. The Pope had given them an evasive answer.

These two messengers, the Pope reported, were followed by Geoffrey Ridel, Archdeacon of Canterbury, and John of Oxford. They had repeated Henry's demands much more insistently than had the previous two. The first embassy evidently was sent before the Council of Clarendon and the second one after it, for Geoffrey and John brought with them a copy of the Constitutions with Henry's request that the Pope 'confirm them with the authority of the Apostolic See to him and his successors'.

Faced with this document, Alexander could no longer fall back on evasions. To confirm it would be not only a repudiation of Thomas but also a renunciation of all that freedom of the Church from secular control for which Alexander's predecessors had fought so bitterly. To refuse to confirm it would be to risk Henry's displeasure and the possible loss of his support of Alexander's precarious position. Nevertheless, the Pope refused absolutely to confirm the Constitutions. To soften the blow, however, and to avoid provoking Henry into greater anger and bitterness against both Thomas and himself, Alexander sent the King letters of legation to be given to Thomas's most bitter enemy, the Archbishop of York.

The Pope closed this first letter with some pious observations on the necessity of bowing to the will of kings in all matters, 'saving the honour of the ecclesiastical order', and advised Thomas to work unceasingly to regain Henry's favour and love.

The second letter, written on the same day and apparently as an afterthought, told Thomas not to be cast down or in despair because the Pope had seemingly betrayed him and thrown him to his enemies by making Archbishop Roger Legate. Alexander told him that he had made the messengers swear that his commission would not be given to Roger without the Pope's knowledge and consent. Thomas and his Church of Canterbury were to be subject in ecclesiastical affairs to no-one except the Roman Pontiff, the Pope assured him, and if the King gave the letter to Roger without notifying the Pope, Alexander ordered Thomas to inform him of the fact immediately, so that he could exempt Thomas, his church, and the city of Canterbury from the Legate's jurisdiction.[1]

This conditional legation was not at all what Henry had in mind for the Archbishop of York. He wanted Roger to be given authority over Thomas so that he could bring him to submission. When the King learned of the limited nature of the powers the Pope was prepared to confer on Roger, he returned the letter with indignation.

When Thomas began to realise the depths of the chasm that had opened up between him and the King, whether through his fault or the King's it was immaterial, he sought an interview with Henry in a belated attempt to explain his position and the reasons that had forced him to adopt it. 'The Archbishop went to the King's private house, the enclosure of Woodstock, surrounded by a stone wall, where he heard the King was, to discuss matters with him, but he was turned away from the gate and went back to Canterbury.'[2]

Meanwhile, the anti-pope, Victor IV, died on April 22. With him the schism might have died, too, had it not been for the determination of the Emperor Frederick and his Chancellor, Reginald of Dassel, Archbishop of Cologne. All the other archbishops and bishops of the Empire wanted to recognise Alexander, but Archbishop Reginald insisted on prolonging the rupture. Without the faintest trace of legality, a new anti-pope, Guy of Crema, was elected and crowned under the name of Paschal III.

---

[1] *Materials*, Vol. V, pp. 85-88.
[2] William Fitz Stephen, in *Materials*, Vol. III, p. 49.

During the summer Thomas went again to the King at Woodstock and asked permission to go to see the Pope. Henry refused
to give him leave and closed the interview with the threat, 'I will
bring you low and put you back where you were when I found
you.'[1]

The Archbishop then retired to his manor at Romney. From
there he made two attempts to cross the Channel without the
King's leave. Once he was prevented by contrary winds; on the
second occasion the sailors recognised him and, fearing the King's
anger, refused to take him.

After this second attempt, Thomas returned to Canterbury
sick at heart. His household had all dispersed, and the Archbishop sat at the gate of his empty house like a beggar, alone in
the dark, and viewed the ruins of his life. How far he had come,
and now how far he had fallen! He had risen from humble and
obscure origins to be the intimate friend of a king and had shared
his sports and his labours, not only as his dearest friend but also
as his most trusted and capable helper. He had dazzled all eyes
and won all hearts with his charm, his generosity, his high good
spirits, and his great abilities. Then, from being second to the
King, he had gone on to another sphere in which he was second
only to the Pope and the spiritual father of the English nation.

And now how far he had fallen! Not only had he lost the
friendship and trust of the King; the man who once was of a
single heart and mind with him now bitterly hated him and
sought his humiliation, striving to bring him to heel as one
would an ill-trained dog. His bishops, of whom he was the
leader, were thrown into confusion and had deserted him. Even
the Pope, to whom alone on earth he could look for help, was
faint-hearted in his defence, fearful lest Henry desert him and turn
to the German schismatics.

The Archbishop of Canterbury huddled in a corner of the gate-
way, leaned his head against the wall, and wept.

One of his followers, meanwhile, bolder than the rest, had
come to Canterbury and made ready to spend the night in the
Archbishop's house. When it was time for bed, he told his page,
'Go and close the outer door of the hall, so that we may sleep
more safely.'

The boy took a light and opened the door to look out into the

---

[1] Anonymous I, in *Materials*, Vol. IV, p. 40.

darkness before he closed and bolted the heavy door. The Archbishop was huddled in a corner, sitting on the ground. He raised his head when he heard the boy, and the light shone on his face, wet with tears. The lad was terrified, thinking that he saw a ghost, and ran to tell his master.

The clerk would not believe him and went to see for himself. He brought the Archbishop into the hall and summoned some of the monks from the monastery. Thomas told them that it was not God's will that he should escape. Then he took a little supper and went to bed.

On the next morning some of the King's servants burst in. The news had spread that the Archbishop had escaped, and the King had sent them to confiscate all his goods. When they saw the Archbishop they retired in confusion.[1]

The King summoned Thomas to Woodstock, and when he came Henry greeted him with a joke. 'Isn't my kingdom big enough for the two of us, that you must try to flee from it?' The King then ordered that no one was to leave the country without his permission, and he had a strict watch kept at all the ports.

Later in the summer John the Marshal, a notorious oppressor of the clergy, laid claim to a part of the Archbishop's manor of Pagham. The King had recently published an ordinance to the effect that anyone who felt that he was not getting true justice in his lord's court could swear an oath to that effect and thus have his case transferred to the King's court. When John the Marshal's claim was heard in the Archbishop's court he took advantage of the new procedure, swore the required oath, and appealed to the King.

Being a prudent man, however, John had brought into court, hidden under his cloak, a troparium, or hymn-book, which he substituted for the copy of the Gospels when he took his oath. Then he reported to the King that he could get no justice from the Archbishop.

Henry summoned Thomas to appear on September 14 to answer John the Marshal's charges. On the appointed day the Archbishop did not appear. He sent in his place four knights and the Sheriff of Kent to testify that John's appeal to the King was invalid because of the defective oath he had sworn. The

---

[1] Alan of Tewkesbury, in *Materials*, Vol. II, pp. 325-6.

King was in a rage that Thomas had neither come in person nor offered any excuse for not doing so. He dismissed the knights and the Sheriff with insults and resolved to punish Thomas for this act of contempt, disobedience, and defiance.

The King called the Great Council to meet at Northampton on Tuesday, October 6, to consider Thomas's latest offence. Custom demanded that the Archbishop of Canterbury receive the first summons to a council, addressed to him personally as the first subject in the realm, but Henry refused to write to him because he did not want to give him a formal salutation. Instead, he ordered the Sheriff of Kent to cite the Archbishop to the council, as though he were the least of the King's tenants.

The Archbishop and his household went to Northampton on the appointed day to join the assemblage of bishops and barons. The King was out hawking. He spent the day along the River Nene at his favourite sport and did not return till evening.

On Wednesday morning the Archbishop rode with his clerks from their lodgings in St. Andrew's Priory to the castle. Northampton Castle was surrounded by a curtain wall, in which was the outer gate. In the courtyard stood the house in which the council was held, with the usual hall and chamber on the ground floor. Above the two rooms was a third, to which no special name was given. Adjoining the house was a chapel.

When the Archbishop arrived, the King was hearing Mass in the chapel. Thomas sat and waited for him. At the King's entrance, the Archbishop rose to greet him, ready to give and receive the kiss, the customary salutation among the English.[1] The King did not greet him.

The first matter to be taken up by the council was the matter of John the Marshal's suit and of the Archbishop's failure to answer the King's summons. Thomas referred to the fraudulent oath that John had taken on the troparium and enquired why he was not there to speak for himself. The King replied that he was in London on official business at the Exchequer and would come on the following day. Henry then dismissed the Archbishop from the council, telling him to return to his lodgings and that they would take up his case on the next day. Thomas withdrew, and there is no record of what the King and his council did after he left.

On Thursday the Archbishop was accused of 'an offence against

[1] William Fitz Stephen, in *Materials*, Vol. III, p. 50.

the majesty of the royal crown' because, when he was summoned by the King in the case of John the Marshal, he neither
came nor offered an excuse for not coming.   The King asked the
council for their verdict, and they unanimously found Thomas
guilty.[1]

The council then condemned him to the forfeiture of all his
movable property; in other words, he was to be stripped of everything except the lands belonging to the archbishopric.

Next Henry demanded £300 from him as the revenue from
the Honour of Eye and the castle of Berkhamstead, which the
King had given him when he made him Chancellor.

Thomas replied that he had been summoned to answer in the
case of John the Marshal, not for a financial accounting.   In any
case, he said, he had spent far more than that in repairing those
castles and the King's palace in London.   He said, however, that
he would give the sum demanded to the King, for he would not
allow any amount of money to be a cause for anger between
himself and his King.

Stung by this reference to his parsimony, Henry reminded the
Archbishop that he had just been deprived of all his movables and
asked him where he intended to find the money.   The King
demanded that he find sureties and told him roughly that he
would either find them or else remain there.   At this thinly
veiled threat of imprisoning the Archbishop, three laymen—the
Earl of Gloucester, John, Count of Eu and Lord of Hastings, and
William of Eynesford, the tenant whom Thomas had excommunicated in the dispute over advowsons—came forward and
stood sureties for him, each for £100.   This concluded the
business for Thursday.

On Friday the King demanded from the Archbishop 500 marks
that he said he had lent him during the Toulouse expedition and a
further 500 marks that he said Thomas had borrowed from the
Jews and for which the King had stood surety.   He followed this
up by demanding that the Archbishop give an accounting for the
revenues from the vacant bishoprics and abbeys that he had administered as Chancellor.   Herbert of Bosham says that the King
demanded 30,000 marks, a sum equivalent to the total revenues
of the Archbishopric of Canterbury for almost seventeen years,
as a final settlement.[2]

[1] Ibid., Vol. III, p. 52.   [2] *Materials*, Vol. III, p. 299.

(The mark was two-thirds of a pound, or 13s. 4d. Although sums of money were expressed in terms of shillings, marks, and pounds, these were mere units of accounting. The silver penny was the only coin minted. It represented a day's wages for the average working man.)

Whatever the sum demanded, it was now plain to all that the King would not stop till he had accomplished the Archbishop's ruin. More than that, his transparent reference to imprisonment on the previous day showed in what direction the matter was tending.

Thomas replied that it was impossible for him to give an accounting on no notice at all, but that he would do what was right at a time and place the King might name. Henry demanded that Thomas produce sureties for the money involved. The Archbishop asked to be allowed to take counsel with his suffragans and clerks. 'He left, and from that day the barons and other knights came no more to his lodging to see him, for they understood the King's intention.'[1]

On Saturday morning the bishops and abbots assembled at the Archbishop's lodging. Bishop Henry of Winchester, the most practical and the most fearless of them all, recalled that the young Henry, as a figurehead, and the Chief Justiciar, Richard of Luci, had in the presence of the Great Council given Thomas a release and quittance from all his secular obligations when he was elected. Bishop Henry had all the bishops who had been present at that occasion go with him to the King, and the venerable Bishop told Henry what had taken place.

Henry claimed that his son and the Chief Justiciar had acted without his knowledge and consent, and he refused to be bound by their actions. The Bishop, one of the richest men in England, then offered the King 2,000 marks to secure a quittance for the Archbishop. Henry refused. It was not money that he wanted, and all the bishops knew it.

They returned to Thomas and reported their failure. The Archbishop then called upon them for advice. Gilbert Foliot, Bishop of London, was the first to speak.

'If, Father, you recall how the Lord King has raised you up and what he has bestowed upon you, if you consider the evilness of the times and what ruin you are preparing to bring upon the

[1] William Fitz Stephen, in *Materials*, Vol. III, p. 54.

Catholic Church and upon all of us, you ought to resign the Archbishopric of Canterbury ten times over, if it were possible. And perhaps, if the King sees this humility in you, he will restore everything to you.'

Bishop Robert of Lincoln, 'a simple man and not very discreet', stated plainly what all were thinking.

'It seems to me that the King is after this man's life and blood, and he has to do one of two things: either give up the archbishopric or give up his life. And what good will the archbishopric do him if he is dead? That I cannot see.'

The remaining bishops gave such confused and contradictory advice that Thomas dismissed them.[1]

Sunday was passed in fruitless conferences and comings and goings. Thomas did not leave his lodging. During the night he was stricken with an illness, apparently renal colic,[2] so severe that he could not sit up in bed the next morning.

When this illness was reported to the King on Monday morning, Henry fell into a rage and swore 'by God's eyes' that he would not be deceived by any shams. He sent the Earls of Leicester and Cornwall to the Archbishop's lodging to find out if he were truly ill. When they had satisfied themselves, Thomas told them to inform the King that he would appear before the council on the next day, even if he had to be carried there on a litter.

In the course of the day two barons who were his faithful friends came to him secretly, through fear of the King, and warned him that if he came to the council he would either be thrown into prison with his tongue cut off and his eyes gouged out or be put speedily to death.

That evening the Archbishop sought the advice of his confessor, Robert, a canon of Merton, where Thomas had gone to school. Robert told him to say the votive Mass of St. Stephen on the next morning and then to go to the council with full confidence in God's mercy and the help of the Saints. 'This business is not yours, but God's, Who will be with you in all things,' he assured Thomas.[3]

Early on Tuesday morning, October 13, the distraught bishops

---

[1] Alan of Tewkesbury, in *Materials*, Vol. II, pp. 326-9.
[2] David Knowles: *The Episcopal Colleagues of Thomas Becket* (Cambridge, 1951), p. 168.　　　[3] Anonymous I, in *Materials*, Vol. IV, pp. 44-45.

H

came to Thomas and begged him to resign, for they had heard
that he was going to be condemned as a traitor. They were in a
difficult position. Most of them, with the notable exception of
Henry of Winchester, were in mortal terror of the King, whose
rage increased the more he was thwarted by Thomas. Many of
them, like Hilary of Chichester, were the King's creatures, and
their chief concern was to stay in his good graces. They had all,
at Thomas's order, taken the oath at Clarendon to obey 'the
ancient customs', and many of them, such as Gilbert Foliot, considered that oath still binding, in spite of the Archbishop's repudiation of it.

By this time it was apparent to everyone that the King would
not be content until he had accomplished the Archbishop's ruin.
The bishops had no desire to become involved in a struggle
between two such strong and obstinate men as Henry and
Thomas; when Thomas fell, as fall he must, they feared to be
dragged down with him. Thomas, on the other hand, believed
that as their archbishop he had the stronger claim to their loyalty,
especially since he was fighting for the rights of the Church. Far
from supporting him, the bishops had sat as members of the
council that had passed judgment on him. Thomas reproached
them with bitter words.

'Even if I were to keep silent, ages to come will tell how you
left me all alone in the struggle, how for two successive days you
have already sat twice in judgment on me, your Archbishop and
father, sinner though I am, and how you have become like nails
in my eyes and a lance in my side, you who should rise up with
me against the evil men and stand with me.'[1]

The Archbishop refused to resign.

As his confessor had advised him, Thomas celebrated the Mass
of St. Stephen, with its account of the stoning of the first Martyr,
at an altar dedicated to that Saint in the monastery church. As
soon as he began the Mass, men ran to tell the King that Thomas,
'like another Stephen the first Martyr, was celebrating that Mass
against the King and his wicked men, who were persecuting him.'[2]

Although he had about forty clerks with him, few would
accompany Thomas when he set out for the castle. When the
Archbishop and his little party left St. Andrew's a great crowd of

[1] Herbert of Bosham, in *Materials*, Vol. III, p. 303.
[2] William Fitz Stephen, in *Materials*, Vol. III, p. 56.

townspeople was waiting outside the monastery. They had heard that the King was going to have their Archbishop put to death that day. At the sight of him many burst into tears, and they all fell on their knees for his blessing. The crowd followed him to the castle.

At the Archbishop's approach the outer gate was quickly opened. It was even more quickly shut and locked after he and his clerks had passed through. They dismounted from their horses, and when they came to the door of the hall Thomas took the great cross that was carried before him from the bearer, Alexander Llewelyn, and carried it himself as he entered the hall. The bishops, barons, knights, and officials gaped in astonishment as the tall, gaunt figure of the Archbishop appeared in the doorway, carrying his cross in his own hands. Some of them ran to tell the King, who was in the upper room.

When Bishop Gilbert of London came forward to meet the Archbishop, Hugh of Nonant, one of Thomas's clerks, said to him, 'My Lord Bishop of London, why do you allow him to carry his cross himself?'

'My good man,' the Bishop snapped, 'he always was a fool, and he always will be.'[1]

The crowd made way for him, and Thomas, accompanied by his clerks, went into the inner chamber. The bishops were summoned to the meeting of the council. Thomas was left sitting in the chamber, holding his cross before him, with Herbert of Bosham beside him and William Fitz Stephen at his feet.

The bishops reported to the King that Thomas had forbidden them to sit in judgment on him and had appealed to the Pope. Henry sent some of his barons down to ask the Archbishop 'if he had indeed thus violated his oath, as the King's liege man, to observe the King's dignities in good faith, without evil will, and legitimately'. They also asked him if he was ready to give securities for the money he owed the King, to render an account of his financial transactions while he was Chancellor, and to stand trial on these matters in the King's court.

To these questions Thomas made a long reply. As for the homage and fealty he had sworn to the King, he considered himself bound by that oath, saving the obedience due to God, the dignity of the Church, and his honour as Archbishop. He

[1] Ibid., *Materials*, Vol. III, p. 57.

reminded the barons that he had been summoned to answer John the Marshal's complaint, and that alone. He had received many dignities from the King, whom he had served faithfully, both at home and abroad, and he had spent more in the King's service than he had received. Furthermore, as they all knew, before he had been consecrated he had received a full quittance from all secular obligations from the King's son and his Chief Justiciar in the presence of the Great Council. Why should he now be called upon to give an account of those matters? Finally, he declared that he placed himself and the Church of Canterbury under the protection of God and the Pope, and he forbade the bishops to sit in judgment on him.

Some of the barons returned to the King with Thomas's answer; others stayed in the chamber and talked loudly among themselves so that Thomas might hear them. One of them said:

'King William, who conquered England, knew how to tame his clerks. He took his own brother Odo, Bishop of Bayeux, prisoner when he rebelled against him. And Stigand, the Archbishop of Canterbury, he threw into a dark dungeon and sentenced to perpetual prison. And Geoffrey, Count of Anjou, the father of our lord the King, who subdued Normandy, had Arnulf, the Bishop-elect of Séez, and many of his clerks castrated, ... because without his consent Arnulf had had himself elected to the Church of Séez.'[1]

When the Archbishop's answer was brought to the King, he demanded that the bishops join the members of the Great Council in pronouncing sentence on Thomas. They attempted to excuse themselves by reminding him of the prohibition the Archbishop had laid on them. The King asserted that that prohibition was not binding because it was contrary to the oath Thomas had sworn at Clarendon.

Binding or not, the bishops replied, if they disobeyed it Thomas would excommunicate them all, to the great damage of the good name of the King and his realm. Then they made a bargain with Henry. If he would not force them to pass judgment on the Archbishop, they would appeal to the Pope against Thomas, accuse him of treason, and have him deposed from his office.

The bishops therefore sat apart from the barons while the King

[1] William Fitz Stephen, in *Materials*, Vol. III, p. 65.

demanded that sentence be passed against the Archbishop. The sentence was pronounced, and while the King waited in the upper room the members of the council, bishops and barons alike, went down to the Archbishop.

They found him sitting in the chamber, still holding his cross before him, with William and Herbert at his side. The Earl of Leicester, as Chief Justiciar, had the task of pronouncing the sentence. He began by reminding the Archbishop of how he had been admitted to the King's most friendly favour and of how much he had received from him. Never had they seen anyone so ungrateful, for Thomas had returned evil for good and hatred and ignominy for favour and glory. The Earl had been intimately associated with Thomas since his first days as Chancellor and had always loved him sincerely. He now stumbled miserably along and began to speak of Thomas's duty to hear the sentence.

'Sentence?' asked the Archbishop.

There could be no sentence without a trial, Thomas said, and a trial he had not had, for he had sat in the chamber all day and had never appeared before the court. He then forbade the Earl, 'by the authority and paternity that Holy Orders give me over you by the law of Christianity', to pronounce sentence against him.

The Earl turned with a sigh of relief to the Earl of Cornwall.

'You have heard silence imposed on me by archiepiscopal, indeed by divine, authority. Do you continue what is left and say what has been decided by the King.'

'I would not presume,' said the Earl of Cornwall, 'upon what has not been entrusted to me. If you want to say anything, say it, for in this affair I withdraw completely.'

Leicester turned despairingly to Thomas.

'I beg you, my lord, to wait while I report your answer.'

'Am I not a prisoner?' asked Thomas.

'No, my lord, by St. Lazarus.'

'Then I shall leave, for the hour is late.'

Thomas raised his cross and strode out of the chamber. At the sight of the Archbishop the crowd in the hall began to shout insults at him. Thomas walked through the midst of them, till he stumbled over a bundle of faggots for the fire in the middle of the hall, and almost fell.

Rannulf of Broc ran up to him and shouted 'Traitor!' in his ear. Thomas recovered himself and went on.

'Traitor!' shouted Hamelin, the King's bastard brother, now Earl Warenne.

The old fire flashed in the Archbishop's grey eyes.

'If I were a knight,' he said, 'with my own hand I would prove you a liar.'

Hamelin drew back.

The Archbishop and his clerks reached the door and mounted. They rode out of the gate, to be greeted by shouts of welcome from the townspeople waiting to see what the outcome would be. Thomas could hardly proceed for the people holding to his stirrups and his cloak, and all along the way the crowd knelt in the streets for his blessing. It was as a triumphal procession that they returned to St. Andrew's, between mid-afternoon and dark.[1]

Meanwhile the Archbishop of York and the Bishop of London advised the King to wait till after the council had been dismissed and the excitement had died down. Then he could have the Archbishop seized secretly and cast into prison without any witnesses.[2]

That night Thomas had a pallet laid in the church, behind the high altar, so that he might spend the night in prayer. Some of his clerks asked to be allowed to share his vigil with him, and he refused, saying that he did not want to disturb them. It was a night of high winds and torrential rain.

Bishop Henry of Winchester came to St. Andrew's early on the next morning to talk with the Archbishop. He asked Osbern, Thomas's chamberlain, what the Archbishop was doing.

'He is doing well,' Osbern replied. 'He left us last night, and we do not know where he went.'

'May he go with God's blessing!' said the Bishop, and he began to weep.

When the King learned that Thomas had escaped, he fell into such a rage that he could not speak. When he regained his breath he said, 'We have not finished with him yet!' He was resolved upon confiscating the revenues of the See of Canterbury immediately, but some of the bishops, fearing a general excommunication, persuaded him to wait till they had lodged their appeal with the Pope.[3]

[1] Anonymous I, *Materials*, Vol. IV. pp. 50-52.
[2] William of Canterbury, in *Materials*, Vol. I, p. 37.
[3] Anonymous I, in *Materials*, Vol. IV, pp. 54-55.

Henry felt certain that Thomas would again try to flee the country in order to lay his case before the Pope and perhaps the King of France. He gave orders that the coast be watched to prevent the Archbishop's escape. He also sent a letter to Louis to inform him of the situation:

To his lord and friend, Louis, the illustrious King of the French, Henry, King of the English and Duke of the Normans and Aquitanians and Count of the Angevins, sends greetings and affection.

Be it known to you that Thomas, who was Archbishop of Canterbury, has been publicly pronounced a culprit and a traitor to me and a perjurer in my court by the full council of the barons of my realm, and he wickedly withdrew under the open name of traitor.

Whence it is that I earnestly pray of you not to allow a man infamous for such crimes and treasons, or his men, into your kingdom or to allow such an enemy of mine, if you please, to receive any advice or help from you or yours, for I would not give any to any enemies of yours and of your realm, neither by me nor by my land, nor would I permit any to be given.

Furthermore, if you please, actively help me to avenge my shame upon such an enemy of mine, and look to my honour, as you would have me do for you if the occasion should arise.

Witnessed by Robert, Earl of Leicester.

At Northampton.[1]

The Great Council, with a collective sigh of relief that the troublesome matter of the Archbishop had been disposed of, at least for a time, turned to the consideration of affairs in Wales. Owain Gwynedd in the north and Rhys ap Gruffyd in the south and most of the princes in between them were pushing the English out of Wales to such good effect that only Basingwerk in the north and Cardigan in the south remained in English hands. Henry and the council determined to launch a great expedition against the Welsh in the spring and summer of the next year.

Henry had learned at least one thing from his previous encounters with the Welsh: he realised that the knights of the feudal levy, clad in their cumbersome armour and mounted on their great chargers, were of little use against the lightly armed and fleet-footed Welsh. He determined that the greater part of the army should be made up of foot-soldiers, and he accordingly sent letters to all his tenants-in-chief, informing them of the decisions that had been taken. With this the council was dismissed.

[1] *Materials*, Vol. V, p. 134.

Thomas, meanwhile, had made his escape and with three companions landed in Flanders on November 2. On the same day
an imposing delegation sailed from Dover. Henry sent the
Archbishop of York, four bishops, Earl William of Arundel,
Richard of Ilchester, John of Oxford, and a number of lesser men
to tell his side of the story to the King of France and the Pope.
They sailed in such a storm that, as William Fitz Stephen gleefully
records, the Bishop of London's cape and cowl were blown into
the sea.[1]

Thomas, dressed in a bedraggled monk's cloak, and his companions spent the first night after they landed in a barn. On the
next morning they set out for the Cistercian monastery near St-
Omer. As they were trudging along, footsore and weary, they
passed a couple of young men on the road. One of them had a
hawk on his wrist. Thomas shot a keen, appraising glance at the
bird.

'That man is the Archbishop of Canterbury!' exclaimed the
owner of the hawk.

'Don't be a fool,' his companion replied. 'What would the
Archbishop of Canterbury be doing, going around like that?'[2]

Many of Thomas's clerks, including Herbert of Bosham, who
had escaped to France ahead of him, joined him at St-Omer.
When the news of his presence got about, a crowd of French
ecclesiastics hastened to pay their respects to him. The most
influential of them was the Archbishop of Rheims, King Louis's
brother.

The English delegation meanwhile had an audience with Louis
at Compiègne and presented Henry's letters to him, in which
frequent reference was made to 'Thomas, the former Archbishop
of Canterbury,' as though the King had power to depose the
Archbishop.

'I am just as much a king as the King of the English is,' Louis
said, 'but I would not try to depose the most insignificant clerk
in my realm.'[3]

The English had no success with Louis. He assured them that
he would take Thomas under his protection and do all he could
to help him and to commend his cause most warmly to the Pope.

---

[1] *Materials*, Vol. III, p. 70.
[2] Alan of Tewkesbury, in *Materials*, Vol. II, p. 335.
[3] Herbert of Bosham, in *Materials*, Vol. III, p. 332.

Louis received Thomas at Soissons a few days later. The Archbishop's party had by now grown to forty, all well mounted and dressed. Louis received him with every mark of honour and favour and assured him that he would help him in every way he could. Louis was of course moved by a desire to embarrass Henry in thus receiving the man Henry had denounced as a traitor, but he also had a great admiration and respect for the Archbishop and was delighted to be of assistance to him.

Henry's ambassadors arrived at the papal court at Sens about November 25. In the presence of the Pope and his Cardinals, they began to set forth Henry's case. The Bishop of London spoke first and launched into an intemperate attack on Thomas as the cause of all the troubles between the King and the clergy.

'Be merciful, Brother,' the Pope admonished him.

'My lord, I am merciful to him.'

'I did not say, Brother, be merciful to him, but to yourself.'

Bishop Gilbert sat down in confusion. Bishop Hilary of Chichester, the noted preacher, then began an inflated discourse. He got himself tangled in a complicated ringing of changes on *oportuit . . . oportuebat . . . oportuerit* and made a howling error in grammar.

'You're having a hard time getting to port,' someone shouted, and the audience laughed him down.

The Archbishop of York then told the assembly that he knew the character and temperament of the Archbishop of Canterbury better than did anyone else. He was stubborn, said Archbishop Roger, and once he had taken up a position, right or wrong, he could not easily be moved from it. Only a severe punishment at the hands of the Pope himself would budge Thomas from his obstinacy.

Then Earl William of Arundel, who had been standing quietly among the knights, watching the bishops making fools of themselves by their venom and spite, asked to be heard.

'My lord,' he said, in his native Norman-French, 'we unlettered laymen do not know what the bishops have been saying. Therefore we must tell you, if we can, why we were sent here. We did not come here to argue or to make accusations against anyone, especially in the presence of a man before whose will and authority all the world rightly bows. But beyond any doubt we did come here to assure you, in your presence and in that of the whole

Roman court, of the devotion and love that our lord the King has always had for you and still has.'

Earl William went on to assure the Pope of the fidelity and good intentions of the King and of the foresight and discretion of the Archbishop, although some people, he added, thought that the Archbishop was not quite so clear-sighted as he might have been.

'And if it were not for the present falling out between the Lord King and the Lord Archbishop,' he concluded, 'the kingdom and the priesthood would rejoice together in peace and concord under a good prince and an excellent shepherd. This, therefore, is our prayer: that Your Grace do everything you can to heal this quarrel and to restore peace and love.'

After the speech had been translated to him, the Pope assured the Earl that he did indeed remember the many great favours that he had received from the King of England and that he was eager to return them.

'Since you ask for legates,' he said, 'you shall have legates.'

The ambassadors, who had distributed a great deal of money among the Cardinals, kissed the Pope's foot and withdrew, congratulating themselves on the success of their mission.[1]

The delegation was under strict orders to spend only three days at the papal court and then to return immediately to England. As they were preparing to leave, they saw a great procession approaching from across the River Yonne. The Archbishop of Canterbury, who had landed in rags in Flanders with three companions, now had an escort of over three hundred clerks and knights, drawn to him by his dazzling reputation and the remembrance of his exploits in France. As the mortified English delegation watched, the College of Cardinals, with their purses full of English gold, rode out to meet him.[2]

The Pope received Thomas with tears and embraces. Thomas recited the story of his quarrel with Henry before the Pope and the Cardinals. As the crowning argument, he produced his copy of the Constitutions of Clarendon and read them to the assembly. Even the Cardinals who were most favourable to Henry joined in condemning the Constitutions as contrary to the liberties of the Church.

[1] Alan of Tewkesbury, in *Materials*, Vol. II, pp. 337-41.
[2] William Fitz Stephen, in *Materials*, Vol. III, p. 74.

On the next day Thomas, kneeling before the Pope, took off his bishop's ring and placed it in Alexander's hands. He had not entered the sheepfold by the gate, he confessed; he had become Archbishop, not by a canonical election, but through the terror that the King had inspired in the monks of Canterbury. He therefore resigned his archbishopric into the Pope's hands. Although there was some dissension among the Cardinals, a few of whom saw in this a speedy and convenient solution to the problem, Alexander refused to accept the resignation and put the ring back on Thomas's finger.

The Pope then recommended that Thomas and a few of his followers go to the Cistercian abbey of Pontigny. There he would not be splendidly entertained, said Alexander, with a sly reference to Thomas's reputation and to the state in which he had arrived at Sens, but simply, as befitted an exile and a soldier of Christ.[1]

This arrangement was also pleasing to Louis. Pontigny was in Burgundy, and therefore Henry would not be able to accuse Louis of harbouring his enemies. At the same time, it was close enough for Louis to be able to make sure that no harm befell the Archbishop.

Thomas and a few of his clerks, among whom were Herbert of Bosham and Alexander Llewelyn, went to Pontigny and were welcomed by the community. The other clerks who had followed him into exile were scattered about in a number of French monasteries.

Henry's embassy returned to England and reported to him at Marlborough on Christmas Eve. The King held his Christmas court there, and on December 26 he informed the Great Council of the failure of his envoys. Far from deposing him, the Pope was favouring Thomas and sheltering him from the King's wrath.

Henry therefore confiscated the lands of the archbishopric and placed them in the custody of Rannulf of Broc, greatly to Rannulf's profit. He banished all the Archbishop's kindred. One of Thomas's sisters, Mary, a nun, found refuge in a French convent. Another, Matilda, was married, and she and her family were given shelter by the Abbot of Clair-Marais.

Some of Thomas's clerks fled overseas. Those who were unable to escape from England were hounded from place to

[1] Alan of Tewkesbury, in *Materials*, Vol. II, pp. 341-4.

place, a source of embarrassment and even of danger to their friends and kinsmen. William Fitz Stephen, however, composed a rhymed prayer for the King's use and presented it to him.[1] The King was so impressed by his abilities that he received him into his favour. Thus William was preserved, to write later the most impartial and the most readable of the biographies of Thomas of Canterbury.

[1] William Fitz Stephen, in *Materials*, Vol. III, pp. 78-81.

VII

THE ASSIZE OF CLARENDON
1165 - 1166

THOMAS, in his retreat at Pontigny, devoted himself to a life of penance, prayer, and study. It had troubled him that as Archbishop of Canterbury he was also the head of Christchurch Monastery, and yet he, unlike almost all his predecessors, was not a monk. He therefore asked the Pope to confer upon him the monastic habit. Alexander sent a habit that he himself had blessed, of the coarsest cloth and the crudest cut, with a cowl much too small for the Archbishop's head.

The Abbot of Pontigny privately clothed Thomas in the habit, which he thenceforth wore beneath his ordinary dress. Alexander Llewelyn could scarcely contain his mirth at the figure his master cut in the habit and aimed his jibes at the skimpy cowl.

'At least,' said the Archbishop, 'you can't laugh at me as you did yesterday.'

'How so?' Alexander asked.

'When I vested for Mass in an alb that was too big for me and that bunched up at the back when I tied the cincture, you wanted to know why my buttocks were so inflated. If the cowl were too big, you would accuse me of being hunchbacked. At least I am protected from such insults as that.'[1]

The Archbishop's education up to this time had been mainly in the law, although after his consecration he had begun to study the Scriptures. In the peace and solitude of Pontigny he took up the study of theology. He continued his readings in the Scriptures under the tutelage of Herbert of Bosham, who says that henceforth the Psalms and the Epistles were always in his hands. For a few days he tried to eat the coarse and tasteless food of the Cistercians, but his stomach rebelled and he became ill. Herbert told him to remember that he had been brought up on dainty food from his youth and that he could not at his age force

[1] Alan of Tewkesbury, *Materials*, Vol. II, pp. 345-6.

his stomach to accustom itself to such rude fare. Thomas thereupon moderated his austerities at table.[1]

The King crossed over to Normandy during Lent 1165 and had
an interview with Louis at Gisors on April 11. The chroniclers
do not tell what subjects the Kings discussed, but one may be
certain that the affair of the Archbishop of Canterbury was one
of the main topics. John of Salisbury wrote to Thomas in the
following month and told him that he found the King of France
much less enthusiastic in his defence than he had formerly been,
out of fear of what Henry might be driven to do by his anger.

John also expressed his uneasiness at learning that the Archbishop was studying canon law in his exile. John of Salisbury
was one of the greatest humanists of his age and a sound classical
scholar. He felt the fear, common in conservative circles, that
the new enthusiasm for the study of the law that was sweeping
the schools would lead to the neglect of the classics and that the
younger generation, though no doubt excellent lawyers, would
be lacking in any real knowledge and culture.

'Who arises from a reading of the laws or even the canons with
sorrow for his sins?' he asked. 'I will say more: the exercises of
the schools sometimes increase knowledge, so that tumults are
stirred up, but they rarely or never move to devotion. I should
prefer for you to meditate on the Psalms and turn over the Moral
Books of Blessed Gregory in your mind, rather than to philoso-
phise after the manner of the schools.'[2]

The greatest fear of both the Pope and the King of France was
that Henry would enter into an alliance with the Emperor
Frederick Barbarossa. Henry took a step in that direction by
receiving at Rouen an embassy headed by the Emperor's Chancellor, Reginald of Dassel, Archbishop of Cologne. They
agreed upon a marriage between Henry's eldest daughter, Matilda,
then eight years old, and Henry the Lion, Duke of Saxony and
Bavaria, the greatest of the Emperor's vassals and his cousin and
best friend. Henry the Lion, now thirty-six years old, had
brought the eastern part of Germany into subjection and had
almost a free hand in Germany while the Emperor was engaged
in Italy. The envoys also arranged a marriage between King
Henry's daughter Eleanor, then three years old, and the Emperor's

---

[1] Herbert of Bosham, *Materials*, Vol. III, pp. 376-9.
[2] *Materials*, Vol. V, pp. 161-5.

son Henry, a babe less than a year old.[1] While they were in Rouen, the Empress, in spite of her great liking for the Germans, refused to receive the ambassadors because they were schismatics.

Now that the ambition of her life was fulfilled and her son was King of England, Matilda lived quietly in Rouen and devoted herself to works of piety. Her memories of England were not happy ones, and her only recorded visit to that country after her son's crowning was at Michaelmas 1155.

The King then sent two of his most trusted clerks, John of Oxford and Richard of Ilchester, to the Emperor to treat further concerning the proposed marriages of the King's two daughters. His ambassadors were present at the Diet of Würzburg on May 23, 1165. Frederick had had a great deal of trouble in inducing his bishops to support his new anti-pope, Paschal III. At this council he forced them to swear never to recognise Alexander III as Pope. The two English clerics joined in taking the oath. In a letter to the Abbot of Stablo, Frederick boasted:

The honourable legates of our friend, the English King, whom he had sent to us, swore an oath on the relics of the Saints in the presence of all our court at Würzburg, on behalf of the English King and his barons, that the English King and all his realm would stand firmly on our side and cleave to the Lord Pope Paschal, to whom we cleave, and uphold our side; and that he would henceforth have no further dealings with the schismatic Roland [Alexander III].[2]

Either the legates exceeded their instructions or the Emperor misrepresented the extent of their oath, for Henry, although he lost no occasion to threaten to desert Alexander, did not recognise Paschal as the true Pope.

Henry returned to England about the middle of May, leaving Queen Eleanor at Angers. Her conduct there seems to have given rise to scandal. Bishop John of Poitiers, writing to his friend Thomas in the summer, told him that he could expect no help from the Queen, for she relied entirely upon the advice of Ralph of Faye, her uncle and an enemy of the Archbishop. Every day, said Bishop John, their boldness increased and lent truth to the other infamous things that had been said about them in the past.[3] The Bishop did not, however, specify what those things were.

---

[1] Robert of Torigni, p. 224. [2] *Materials*, Vol. V, pp. 183-8.
[3] *Materials*, Vol. V, pp. 196-8.

When he returned to England Henry made extensive and elaborate preparations for his Welsh campaign. He laid in vast supplies of grain, salt pork, and cheese and of shields, arrows, lances, pikes, and axes. In addition to the regular feudal levy of his earls and barons and their knights, he brought in troops from all his continental domains and hired a body of Flemish mercenaries.

By the end of July all was ready. The army with its cumbersome baggage trains set out from Shrewsbury and marched northwest to Oswestry. The main body of the Welsh, meanwhile, had assembled at Corwen, in the valley of the River Dee, to the northwest of Oswestry. Between the English and the Welsh lay the thickly wood Ceiriog Valley and then the Berwyn mountains, rising to a height of around two thousand feet.

As soon as the English entered the woods they were beset by the advance guard of the Welsh, employing the same tactics they had used in 1157. They harassed the English from the cover of the forest to such good effect that Henry halted the army and had a clear road cut through the trees. When at last they reached the bare slopes of the mountain, the ground under their feet was turned into a bog by torrents of rain. The horses floundered in the mud; the heavy wagons were mired down.

The fleet-footed Welsh, who thought nothing of the rain, kept up a steady volley of arrows and stones all the while. The English came to a halt and waited for the rain to stop. The wind and the rain redoubled their fury. Both men and horses had to be fed meanwhile. Their supplies dwindled while they remained motionless in the mud.[1]

Sick with rage, Henry led his army back to Shrewsbury. He had in his hands a number of Welsh hostages. Upon them he vented his wrath. He had twenty-five of them, including two young sons of Owain Gwynedd, savagely mutilated. The Welsh expedition was a complete failure. Henry had nothing whatever to show for ten months of planning and preparation and for the expenditure of a great sum of money.[2]

While Henry was thus engaged, Thomas was advising the Pope that only stern measures would be of any effect in dealing with the King, who had not hesitated to ally himself with the German schismatics. Apparently Thomas advocated the ex-

[1] Gerald of Wales: *Itinerarium Kambriae*, ed. J. F. Dimock, *Opera*, Vol. VI, p. 143.   [2] J. E. Lloyd: *History of Wales* (London, 1948), Vol. II, pp. 516-18.

treme penalties of excommunicating the King or of laying an interdict on England, or perhaps both. At any rate, Alexander wrote to Thomas in June 1165 and suggested that since the times were evil he would do well to act with great caution and forbearance and to do everything possible to regain the favour and good will of 'the illustrious King of the English'. In concluding the Pope forbade him to take any action against the King or the kingdom till after the following Easter.[1]

The cities of Lombardy were now beginning to unite against the Emperor and were offering such successful resistance to him that Alexander took fresh heart. He felt so confident of his position that he returned to Rome on November 23 and took up residence in the Lateran.

On August 22 King Louis's third wife, Adela of Champagne, gave birth to the long-awaited son, who was christened Philip, and in October Queen Eleanor gave birth to her third daughter, Joan, at Angers.

Henry convened the Great Council at Clarendon in January or February 1166. The principal subject for discussion was the necessity for improving the administration of justice.

At this time, thieves and robbers who were caught in the act or in possession of stolen goods were dealt with summarily by the lord of the manor, who usually had the cherished right of *infangenetheof*, or of hanging such thieves.

If a stranger was murdered and the men of the township in which the murder was committed could not produce the murderer in court, a murder-fine was levied on the township, on the supposition that the murderer was being sheltered from justice. The Pipe Roll of 1166 records 65 such murders, with a total of £171 13s. 4d. levied in murder-fines.

If the murderer was known and his victim was not a stranger, one of the kinsmen of the murdered man would ordinarily accuse or 'appeal' the murderer at the county court. If the accused denied the charge, the court would sentence him to ordeal by battle with the accuser. In many instances, however, the murderer would be too great and too powerful for anyone to dare to accuse him; in other cases the murdered man might not have any relations or his kinsmen might not be interested in risking their lives to avenge his death.

[1] *Materials*, Vol. V, pp. 179-80.

I

Because of this cumbersome machinery of appeals and of trial by battle, many murderers escaped justice, although their guilt was known to all the neighbourhood. Many thieves and robbers whose guilt was likewise known went unpunished because of the difficulty of convicting them if they were not caught in the act or with the stolen goods in their possession.

To remedy this situation, Henry and his council devised the method of procedure set forth in the Assize of Clarendon. The principal provision of the Assize is that the sworn jury of inquest or presentment is to be used to discover the names of those who are reported to be robbers, thieves, or murderers, or to have harboured them. The inquest is to go back to the beginning of Henry's reign. Twelve law-worthy men of each hundred, the administrative division between the township and the county, and four of each township are to take an oath that they will speak the truth. Then the justiciars or the sheriffs are to ask them if they know of anyone in the township who is commonly reputed to be guilty of those crimes.

The men so named are to be put to the ancient ordeal by water, that is, they are to be thrown, trussed, into a pool that has been blessed for this purpose. If they are innocent, the water will receive them and they will sink; if they are guilty, the water will reject them and they will float on the surface. The guilty men will presumably be punished by hanging. Even if they are proved innocent, however, if they have a bad reputation they are to abjure the realm and go out of the country (many of them took refuge in Scotland), and their chattels are to be forfeited to the King.

Shortly after this council, Richard of Luci, one of the two Chief Justiciars, and Geoffrey of Mandeville, Earl of Essex, went about the country putting the Assize into effect. They performed their judicial duties with great energy. By the following Michaelmas the Chief Justiciar, either alone or with Earl Geoffrey, had held the Assize in twenty-seven counties, and the sheriffs reported the results at their semi-annual audit at the Exchequer. The Sheriff of Lincolnshire, for example, 'renders account of the chattels of the fugitives and of those who failed in the judgment of water. He has paid £23 15s. 4d. into the Treasury on two tallies.' There follows a list of forty-one names, with amounts ranging from 12d. each from Hereward and Brunman to 71s. 10d. from Gilbert of Harbrough.[1]

In the twenty-seven counties, over 570 men were listed as fugitives who fled the country rather than face the ordeal or as having 'failed in the judgment of water'. Yorkshire, the most populous county, led the list with 129 names, and next came Norfolk and Suffolk, with 103 between them. Wiltshire, at the other end of the scale, had only three. The total amount collected was a little less than £400.

The second great enactment of this council was the Assize of Novel Disseisin, or recent dispossession. Although the text of this assize has not been preserved, it is attributed to this council because the action it permits is recorded for the first time in the Pipe Roll of this year: 'Thomas of Lufham owes 20s. for a disseisin against the King's assize.'[2]

By the provision of this assize, when a man claimed that he had been disseised, or dispossessed, of his land he might obtain from the King a writ ordering the King's justiciar to swear in a jury of twelve law-worthy men of the neighbourhood. The justiciar would then ask them: 'Did A. unjustly and without a judgment disseise B. of his land?' If the answer was 'Yes', the possession of the land would immediately be restored to B., and A. would in all probability be amerced, as was Thomas of Lufham. If the answer was 'No', then B. would probably be amerced for having brought a false accusation. (At this time, a distinction was made between a fine and an amercement. A fine was a supposedly voluntary payment made to the king to secure some privilege or even his good will; an amercement was what we now call a fine.)

This assize was of the greatest importance because it provided a quick and certain remedy for a common offence. It was the first of the possessory assizes that were among Henry's most important contributions to English legal development. Furthermore, it is one of the chief steps that Henry took to restrict the powers of the private courts of his barons and to transfer cases from their courts to his.

A suit concerning the possession of land would normally be heard in the court of the lord of whom the land was held. Since it was often the lord himself who attempted to dispossess a tenant, there were many times when a suitor could get no justice from his lord. By transferring the case to his court and making

[1] Pipe Roll 12 Henry II, pp. 5-6.   [2] Ibid., p. 65.

the verdict depend upon the oath of twelve men of good reputation, Henry made sure that his barons could not oppress their tenants in this way.

Henry's third act at this most important council was to order an investigation into exactly how many knights his tenants-in-chief had enfeoffed, or given land to. Up to this time, Domesday Book, compiled in 1086, was used as the source of information when aids or scutages were being levied on the basis of knights' fiefs. That book contained a list of the fiefs as they had been settled between William the Conqueror and his tenants. William had given a baron certain estates on condition that he furnish a stated number of knights for the king's army. There was no close correspondence between the size of an estate and the number of knights it owed. Sometimes a baron would enfeoff more knights than he was required to furnish, and the Exchequer would have no record of them.

The letter that the Archbishop of York sent to the King explains what Henry asked for and why:

> To his most dearly beloved lord, Henry, by the grace of God King of England, Duke of Normandy and Aquitaine, and Count of Anjou, his servant Roger, by the same grace Archbishop of York, and Legate of the Apostolic See, sends greetings.
>
> Your Majesty has ordered all your faithful subjects, both clerk and lay, who hold of you in chief in Yorkshire to inform you by their letters, under their seals, of how many knights each one has enfeoffed of the old enfeoffment of the time of King Henry your grandfather on the day and in the year when he was living and dead, and how many he has enfeoffed of the new enfeoffment after the death of your grandfather of happy memory, and how many knight's fiefs are not provided for in each one's demesne.
>
> And you have ordered that the names of all these, both of the new enfeoffment and of the old, be written in these letters, because you wish that if there are any who have not yet done liege homage to you and whose names are not written in your rolls, they do homage to you before the first Sunday in Lent.
>
> Obedient to your will in all things, I have with all diligence investigated in my holding, as far as the shortness of time allowed, and I send this information to you, my lord, in this present writing.[1]

The King had a practical reason for asking for the names of all

---

[1] *Liber Niger Scaccarii*, ed. Thomas Hearne (London, 1774), Vol. I, p. 303.

the knights. Henceforth he based his demands for aids and scutages on the number of knights a baron had actually enfeoffed, if that number was greater than the one the baron had owed under the 'old enfeoffment'. If a baron, for example, owed the services of forty knights and had enfeoffed fifty, he was assessed at the larger figure.

The letters were due by March 13. Those knights who had not sworn fealty to the King were required to take the oath in the presence of the King's justiciars at a meeting of the county court. The Pipe Roll for Lincolnshire records the amercement levied against one who failed to do so:

> Alan of Mumby owes 40s. because he was not present at the oath-swearing of the knights of the fief.[1]

The knights would have taken oaths of fealty to their lords when they were granted seisin of their fiefs. Henry's insistence that they now swear fealty to him as their lord paramount with a claim to their allegiance transcending all other fealties suggests that perhaps the King had got wind of or suspected dissatisfactions with his stern rule and possible disloyalties and rebellions, as yet unrecorded but due to burst into open revolt within a few years.

[1] Pipe Roll 12 Henry II, p. 8.

VIII

THE SUBJUGATION OF BRITTANY
1166 - 1168

JUST when Henry had matters in England well in hand, with a decisive step made toward strengthening the authority of his justiciars and toward putting down crime, he was forced to turn his attention to his Continental possessions. Queen Eleanor, whom he had left as his vicegerent in Maine, reported that some of the nobles, led by the Count of Séez, were in rebellion. Ralph of Fougères, one of the greatest of the Breton lords, was also organising his fellow barons against the hated rule of Duke Conan, Henry's vassal. And always there was the King of France, waiting for a chance to stir up trouble.

Henry crossed over to Normandy about the middle of March 1166. He went at once into Maine, seized the castles of the rebellious Count of Séez, and restored order in the province.[1]

Easter, meanwhile, was drawing near, the term set by the Pope for Thomas's efforts to bring Henry to reason by gentle means. Thomas twice wrote to the King to remonstrate against his treatment of the Church and of the Archbishop, but his letters had no effect.[2]

Shortly before Easter the Pope wrote to Thomas and authorised him to lay ecclesiastical censures on anyone who had done any violence or injury to Thomas, his followers, or the possessions of the See of Canterbury. Concerning the King the Pope gave Thomas no special orders, thus leaving him a free hand to deal with Henry as he saw best. On Easter Sunday Alexander followed this up by appointing the Archbishop Papal Legate to all of England except the Diocese of York, so that he might, with the Pope's authority, correct whatever needed to be corrected there.[3]

The first use that Thomas made of his powers was to lay an interdict on Bishop Jocelin of Salisbury for having disobeyed both

---

[1] Robert of Torigni, p. 227.   [2] *Materials*, Vol. V, pp. 266-78.
[3] Ibid., Vol. V, pp. 316-17, 328-9.

him and the Pope. Henry of Beaumont, Dean of Salisbury, had become Bishop of Bayeux in the preceding year. To fill the vacancy at Salisbury, the King ordered the Bishop and chapter to elect John of Oxford, one of Henry's favourite clerks, as Dean. John, however, had taken the notorious oath at the Diet of Würzburg never to acknowledge Alexander III as Pope. Both the Pope and Thomas therefore ordered Bishop Jocelin not to institute John as Dean. The Bishop was under a great deal of pressure from the King, and he felt that this was no time to bring down the royal wrath upon his head. He instituted John. Thomas thereupon put him under interdict, and the Pope, on May 27, 1166, confirmed the sentence. This was the first positive action the Pope had taken to indicate to Henry that he was not absolute master of the Church in England.[1]

Towards the end of May the King held a council at Chinon to discuss with his barons the measures to be taken against the revolt in Brittany. While the council was sitting, a barefoot monk named Gerard delivered a letter and a warning to the King from Thomas.

> With great longing I have longed to see your face and to talk with you; greatly for my own sake, but more greatly still for your sake. For my sake, so that at the sight of my face you might call to mind the devoted and faithful help that I rendered you when I was in your service, after my soul's conscience (thus may God help me at the Last Judgment, when all shall stand before His seat, to be rewarded as they have acted in the flesh, whether well or ill), and so that you might be moved to pity me, for I live by begging among strangers: and yet by God's grace we have enough to eat. . . .
>
> For your own sake, for three reasons: because you are my lord, because you are my king, and because you are my spiritual son. Because you are my lord, I owe you and I offer you my counsel and my service and whatever a bishop owes his lord, according to God's honour and Holy Church's. Because you are my king, I am bound to honour you and admonish you. Because you are my son, I am bound by my office to chastise and correct you. . . .
>
> [Thomas goes on to remind Henry that kings receive their power from the Church and admonishes him not to consort with schismatics or to persecute the Church.]
>
> Let us, if you please, go back to our see freely and peacefully and exercise our office freely, as we should and as reason demands that

[1] Ibid., Vol. V, p. 364.

we should.   And we are ready to serve you, as our dearest lord and
king, faithfully and devotedly, with all our strength, in whatever
things we can, saving the honour of God and of the Roman Church,
and saving our order.

Otherwise, you may be sure that you will feel the severity and
punishment of God.[1]

The monk Gerard amplified the threat with which the letter
closed and delivered the warning that Thomas was resolved to
resort to the extreme measures of an interdict on England and the
excommunication of the King if Henry did not renounce the evil
customs, restore the possessions of the See of Canterbury that he
had seized, and allow the Archbishop to return safely to England.

Henry burst into tears of rage and declared that Thomas was
trying to destroy him body and soul.   He turned to his bishops
and barons and shouted that they were all traitors, for they would
not rid him of the persecution of this one man.   He demanded
that they devise some means of averting the threatened sentences
of interdict and excommunication.

Bishop Arnulf of Lisieux said that there was only one remedy:
to appeal over Thomas's head to the Pope.   Henry therefore sent
Arnulf and Bishop Froger of Séez to notify Thomas of the appeal
and thus stay his hand.   When the bishops reached Pontigny,
however, they found that Thomas had set out on a pilgrimage to
Vézelay.

On his way, messengers reached Thomas from the King of
France to tell him that Henry had suddenly fallen gravely ill.
Henry had planned to have a conference with Louis, but he was
so ill that he was forced to ask the French King to excuse him.

Thomas reached Vézelay on Whitsun Eve, June 11, 1166.
The great abbey church, one of the glories of Romanesque archi-
tecture, was a noted place of pilgrimage, for the body of St. Mary
Magdalene was enshrined there.   Thomas wanted to do what he
was determined to do before a great crowd of people and not
almost secretly, as such an action would be if it were done at a
remote place like Pontigny.

The Archbishop celebrated the principal Mass of Whitsunday
at the request of the Abbot and preached to the congregation,
which filled the huge church.   At the conclusion of his discourse
he explained to his audience the causes of the discord between

[1] *Materials*, Vol. V, pp. 278-82.

him and the King of England, and the reasons for his exile amongst them.

Thomas then had candles lit and placed before him. As the great bell slowly tolled, the Archbishop, by the authority given him by the Roman Pontiff, pronounced the sentence of excommunication upon John of Oxford because he had associated with the German schismatics and sworn the oath at the Diet of Würzburg and because he had, contrary to the orders of the Pope and of the Archbishop, usurped the position of Dean of Salisbury.

Thomas excommunicated Richard of Ilchester, Archdeacon of Poitiers, because he also had associated with the schismatics and had taken the oath not to recognise Alexander III as Pope.

He excommunicated Richard of Luci, the King's Chief Justiciar, and Jocelin of Bailleul because they were the principal authors of the Constitutions of Clarendon and the prime movers of the King's assault on the liberties of the Church.

He excommunicated Rannulf of Broc, Hugh of St. Clare, and Thomas son of Bernard because they had laid violent hands on the property of the See of Canterbury.

As each sentence was pronounced, a candle was extinguished, to signify the spiritual death to which each man was doomed.

Thomas had intended to excommunicate the King also, as he later told his friends, but the news of Henry's illness led him to issue, instead, a denunciation of the King and a warning that unless he ceased his persecution of the Church he too would be excommunicated.

The Archbishop concluded by condemning the Constitutions of Clarendon and absolving the English bishops from their promise, taken at his direction, to obey the King's customs.[1]

The news of this drastic action reached Henry while he was still lying ill, probably at Chinon. He at once sent a messenger to Richard of Luci in England, ordering him to convene a council of the bishops and compel them to appeal to the Pope against Thomas's sentences. The bishops met at London on June 24 and obediently lodged the appeal. Alexander must have smiled when he read the beginning of their letter, in which they described Henry as 'most Christian in his faith, most honest in the purity of his conjugal relations, and incomparably active in preserving and propagating peace and justice'.[2]

---

[1] *Materials*, Vol. V, pp. 381, 385.   [2] Ibid., Vol. V, p. 403.

Henry meanwhile recovered from his illness and started out on his expedition to Brittany at the head of a large army. He was accompanied by William, King of Scots, who had succeeded his brother Malcolm in the previous December.

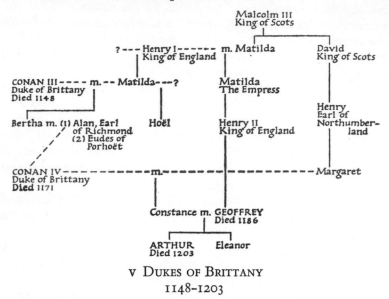

v DUKES OF BRITTANY
1148-1203

The whole of Brittany, under the leadership of Ralph of Fougères, was in revolt against Duke Conan IV, whom the Bretons considered little more than a puppet in the hands of the hated Normans. He was so ineffective a figure that the burden of ruling Brittany during Henry's stay in England had fallen on Queen Eleanor.

Brittany had been in a state of turmoil ever since the death of Duke Conan III in 1148. He had married Matilda, a bastard daughter of King Henry I. Matilda had borne two children: a son, Hoël, and a daughter, Bertha. Conan, however, had disclaimed Hoël and said that he was not his son. Bertha had married Alan, Earl of Richmond, and had a son, Conan, by him. When Earl Alan died in 1146 she had then married Eudes, Viscount of Porhoët. Upon the death of Conan III two years later, the Duchy was claimed by Hoël, by Viscount Eudes, and by the young Conan.

Ten years of civil war had followed, till Henry, claiming to be

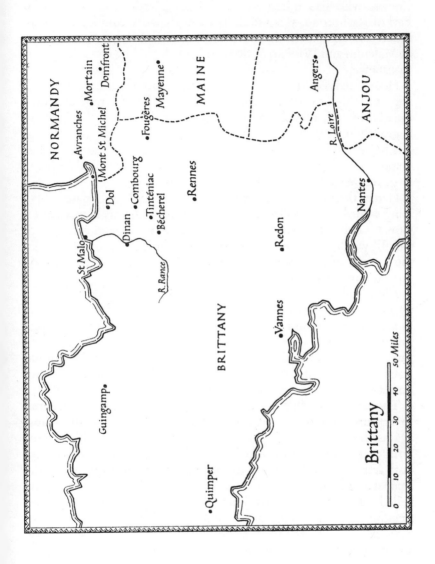

Brittany

0 10 20 30 40 50 Miles

overlord of Brittany, intervened and recognised Conan as Duke.
Conan, who had inherited his father's position in England as
Earl of Richmond, was much hated in Brittany, and his rule was
bitterly resented. In 1160 he had married Margaret, the sister
of Malcolm and William of Scotland, and by her he had a daughter
Constance.

Henry arrived at Fougères with an imposing army and laid
seige to Ralph's castle. This was warfare after the regular Continental model, played according to the rules that the Welsh so
flagrantly disregarded. When Ralph saw the futility of holding
out he surrendered on July 14, 1166, and Henry demolished his
castle. Ralph gave a number of hostages, including his daughter,
as guarantees of his future fidelity.

Henry then concluded a treaty with the hapless Conan. The
King's third son, Geoffrey, now eight years old, was betrothed to
Conan's daughter, Constance, who was five. Conan recognised
Geoffrey as his heir and surrendered the whole of Brittany, except
the County of Guingamp, to Henry, to hold in trust for Geoffrey
until the marriage should take place.

Almost all the barons of Brittany confirmed this arrangement
by doing homage to Henry. The King forced Viscount Eudes
to turn over his daughter, Conan's half-sister, to him as a hostage.
From Rennes, the chief city of Brittany, Henry went north
through Combourg to Dol, securing the submission of the Breton
nobles as he went, and then to Mont-St-Michel, where he no
doubt gave Abbot Robert the information here recorded.[1]

Thomas meanwhile wrote not only to the bishops in general
to reproach them for their conduct in appealing to the Pope
against him but also in particular to Gilbert Foliot, the author
both of the appeal and of a letter informing Thomas of it. In
both letters Thomas replied to the charges the bishops had made
against him. In his letter to Bishop Gilbert he made a thinly
veiled reference to the possibility that Gilbert's opposition to his
election and the Bishop's subsequent conduct were in part, at
least, due to Gilbert's own aspirations to the See of Canterbury
and to his jealousy of Thomas.[2]

Gilbert was stung to a reply that now fills twenty-three pages
of print. He vehemently denied that he had aspired to be Archbishop. Then he turned upon Thomas and declared that he had

---

[1] Robert of Torigni, p. 228.   [2] *Materials*, Vol. V, p. 517.

purchased the office of Chancellor 'for many thousands of marks' and that the gold he had acquired as Chancellor had obtained the See of Canterbury for him.   Gilbert went back to the scutage the King had levied on the Church for the expedition to Toulouse and declared that in exacting it Thomas had 'plunged a sword into the bowels of Holy Mother Church'.   He then reviewed the whole controversy between the King and the Archbishop and asserted that Thomas had destroyed the peace of the realm, violated his oath of fealty and his obligations to the King, betrayed his fellow bishops, and deserted his See of Canterbury.[1]

Henry had already made it known to the Cistercians that he was displeased that they were sheltering the Archbishop.   When the abbots of the order assembled at Cîteaux for a general chapter on September 14, he sent them a letter telling them that if they did not cease sheltering his enemy at Pontigny he would drive the Cistercians out of all his lands and confiscate their property.   The chapter took no action beyond reporting this to Thomas.   He, for the sake of his hosts, began casting about for another refuge.

King Louis then offered him asylum in the Ile de France.   The Archbishop moved to St. Columba's Abbey, near Sens, on November 11.   Louis provided him with a magnificent escort of three hundred men to show his joy at being able to welcome the persecuted Archbishop.

William, King of Scots, had joined Henry in Normandy, both in order to help him in his expedition into Brittany and in order to see his sister Margaret, Duke Conan's wife.   William had a heated discussion with Henry, probably over Henry's claim to homage from him and also over William's claim to the Earldom of Northumberland.   Whatever the cause may have been, Henry lost his temper and gave way to a spectacular exhibition of his wrath.

> One day when the King was at Caen and was discussing the matter of the King of Scotland, he broke forth in shameful words against Richard of Humez [Seneschal of Normandy], who seemed to be speaking somewhat in favour of the King of Scotland, and openly called him a traitor.   The King, burning then with his customary fury, threw the cap from his head, undid his belt, threw far from him the cloak and robes in which he was dressed, with his own hands tore the silken cover off the bed, and sitting down as though on a dung-heap began to chew the straw of the mattress.[2]

[1] Ibid., Vol. V, pp. 521-44.   [2] Ibid., Vol. VI, p. 72.

Henry was greatly annoyed that he had not yet received the help that he thought was due him from the Pope in his controversy with Thomas. He therefore sent an ill-tempered letter to Alexander:

> To his reverend lord and spiritual father, Alexander, by the grace of God Supreme Pontiff, Henry, by the same grace King of England, Duke of Normandy and Aquitaine, and Count of Anjou, sends greetings.
>
> I have received the letter that you sent me by Brother Geoffrey, and, having seen and understood it, I am greatly grieved and angered. I tell Your Excellency that I am surprised beyond belief that the Roman Curia should so openly work against me and my honour and my realm, which I entrust to no one save God alone. As is known to the whole world, you cherish and uphold traitors to me, who wickedly and treacherously work against me and whom you should rather destroy than protect. It is unheard of that the Roman Curia should protect traitors, and particularly traitors to me, which I have not deserved.
>
> What irritates me all the more is that this state of affairs has begun only in my time and concerning traitors to me. Furthermore, what moves me to even greater anger is the fact that not only does the Roman Curia uphold and protect traitors to me but also that there is no justice for me, although any low and miserable man may have it and although many clerks of the smallest importance have afterwards had it, as I have seen with my own eyes.[1]

Early in November Henry decided to send embassies to try to force the Pope to take some action against Thomas. His first ambassador was his most trusted John of Oxford, whom Thomas had excommunicated and deposed as Dean of Salisbury. John's mission was to secure his own absolution and restoration to the Deanery and to ask Alexander to grant a dispensation for the marriage of the King's son Geoffrey to Constance of Brittany. They were related in the fourth degree, with common ancestors in both Malcolm III of Scotland and Henry I of England. The second embassy was to make a general protest against the Pope's favouring of Thomas.

To the humiliation of Thomas and the rage and disgust of King Louis, when John of Oxford arrived in Rome Alexander absolved him from the sentence of excommunication and confirmed him in his office as Dean of Salisbury. Furthermore,

[1] *Materials.*, Vol. V, pp. 362-3.

when the King's second embassy arrived, they spoke to the Pope
to such good effect that immediately, on December 20, he despatched a letter to Henry that seemed to grant almost everything
he wanted except the deposition of Thomas.

> We have received the messengers of Your Magnificence, who are
> devoted to us and to the Church of God and most faithful, as we
> believe, to the Royal Sublimity in all things, and the letters that
> Your Excellency has sent us, with all the more benevolent mind and
> we have welcomed them with all the greater grace and honour in-
> asmuch as we know they have been sent by a magnificent prince
> and a most Christian king.

Alexander went on to tell Henry in the most obsequious terms
that he was sending legates who would have full power and
authority to hear, settle, and decide finally the case of Thomas,
the appeal of the bishops, and any other matters that might arise.
In the meantime he was going to forbid the Archbishop to pass
any sort of a sentence upon the King or any of his subjects.   If
Thomas should nevertheless pronounce any such sentence, the
Pope declared it in advance to be void.   He authorised Henry if
necessary to show this letter nullifying any sentence pronounced
by Thomas; otherwise the Pope requested that he keep it secret.
The legates would have power to absolve those whom Thomas
had excommunicated at Vézelay, and they should be on the road
in January.[1]

The letter that Alexander wrote to Thomas, however, gave,
as one might expect, a different version of his actions.

> Having received the letters and messengers of our dearest son in
> Christ, Henry, the illustrious King of the English, we have proposed
> to warn him again by our letter and our messenger and to soften his
> anger by our solicitous exhortations, so that he may be reconciled
> with you and receive you again into his favour and love.
>
> We trust and hope in the Lord that he will heed our exhortations
> and restore your church to you fully and peacefully.   Wherefore
> we ask, command, and advise Your Excellency, until we see the end
> and outcome of this affair, to bear with him patiently and in the
> meantime not to decree anything against him or any of his subjects
> that would hurt or damage him.
>
> However, if he does not care to accede to us by our messengers,
> if perchance we send any, we will not desert you, God willing, for

[1] Ibid., Vol. VI, pp. 84-86.

any reason, but we will take care to preserve the rights and honour
and dignity of you and your church, as far as the Divine Grace permits.
Nor will you be lacking in authority at last, if otherwise the King
cannot be recalled, to exercise your office freely.

We wish, however, for you to keep this secret.[1]

Worse was yet to come to Thomas. Alexander appointed as
his legates Cardinal William of Pavia, who had been Thomas's

WILLIAM, 1153-6

HENRY, 1155-83 'The Young King'	*m.*	Margaret of France (*see* Table IV)
MATILDA, *b.* 1156	*m.*	Henry the Lion, Duke of Saxony
RICHARD, 1157-99 Duke of Aquitaine King of England	 *m.*	betrothed to Alice of France (*see* Table IV) Berengaria of Navarre
GEOFFREY, 1158-86 Duke of Brittany	*m.*	Constance of Brittany (*see* Table VI)
ELEANOR, *b.* 1162	*m.*	Alfonso VIII, King of Castile
JOAN, *b.* 1165	*m.*	William II, King of Sicily
JOHN, 1166/7-1216 King of England	*m.*	(1) Hadwisa of Gloucester (2) Isabella of Angoulême

VI CHILDREN OF HENRY II AND ELEANOR

most energetic detractor and enemy at the papal court, and Cardinal Otto. On top of this, Thomas learned that John of Oxford
had returned to England boasting that he had been absolved by
the Pope himself and restored to the Deanery of Salisbury. He
further declared that he could get anything he wanted from the
Pope, that he had persuaded Alexander to exempt the King from
any sentence passed by any bishop except the Pope himself, and
that he had letters from the Pope ordering the English bishops not

[1] *Materials*, Vol. VI, p. 86.

to obey Thomas in any way whatever. When the Bishop of
London, Gilbert Foliot, saw those letters he declared: 'Henceforth Thomas is no longer my archbishop!'

'Beyond any doubt,' cried Thomas in his anguish, 'the Lord
Pope has smothered and strangled not only me but himself and
all the clergy of England and France as well!'[1]

Now that her husband apparently had Brittany well under control, Queen Eleanor returned to England in the autumn. On
Christmas Eve, 1166, according to Ralph of Diceto, she gave
birth to John, her fifth son and eighth child by Henry, at Oxford.
However, Robert of Torigni, the only other strictly contemporary chronicler who mentions John's birth, places it a year
later, in 1167[2]

Pope Alexander, meanwhile, had been receiving the vehement
and bitter reproaches of both Archbishop Thomas and King
Louis for his complete surrender to Henry. John of Salisbury,
who had been an intimate friend of Alexander's predecessor,
wrote a letter of dignified rebuke, reminding the Pope that not
even St. Peter himself could absolve a man who persevered in
wickedness and in his intention to sin and warning him that the
only way he could enjoy Henry's favour was to let him have his
way in all things.[3] Alexander had also been receiving reports of
the loud boasts that the English envoys had been making since
their visit to him.

Moved by these protests and by the realisation that he had
made a fool of himself in the eyes of others by his spineless surrender to the English King, Alexander, on May 7, 1167, sent a fresh
set of instructions to his legates, the Cardinals Otto and William,
who were making a leisurely progress across Provence. Instead
of ordering them to England with full power to settle all matters,
as he had promised Henry, he now told them that their primary
object was to remove all bitterness and suspicions from the Archbishop's mind, to reconcile him with the King, and to make a full
peace between them. The Cardinals were not to go to England
or to do anything of any importance in any of Henry's lands until
the King and the Archbishop were fully reconciled.[4]

Late in the summer the envoys of Henry the Lion arrived in

[1] Ibid., Vol. VI, pp. 150-3.
[2] Ralph of Diceto, Vol. I, p. 325; Robert of Torigni, p. 233.
[3] *Materials*, Vol. VI, pp. 176-9.   [4] Ibid., Vol. VI, pp. 200-2.

England to escort Matilda to Germany. As the King's eldest daughter she was provided with a magnificent outfit. The Pipe Roll records the purchase of '20 pairs of bags and 20 pairs of chests' (they came in pairs so that they could be slung over the backs of pack horses), '7 saddles gilded and covered with scarlet and 7 pairs of gilded reins', 34 pack horses, 'clothes for the King's daughter when she was sent to Saxony' to the value of £63 13s. 7d., and '2 large silken cloths and 2 tapestries and 1 cloth of samite and 12 sable-skins'.[1]

The King recouped himself for these expenses and made a handsome profit besides by collecting an aid for his daughter's marriage. A lord had the right to exact an aid from his tenants on three occasions: for the ransom of his body, if he were captured by the enemy; for the knighting of his eldest son; and at the first marriage of his eldest daughter.

The assessment for this aid was based on the returns the barons had made in 1164. The barons took the view that as long as they furnished the King with the number of knights that was due from their holdings, it was their concern alone whether they kept the whole number as household knights and enfeoffed none of them, or whether they enfeoffed exactly the number they were bound to furnish, or whether, if they had land enough, they enfeoffed more than they were required to furnish. In keeping with this attitude, both the bishops and the barons paid at least an instalment on the amount based on the knight-service that they owed according to the old enfeoffment, but not one of them made any payment on the additional knights of the new enfeoffment, if they had any such. The barons simply did not pay; the bishops also entered the protest that they did not admit that they owed anything on the new enfeoffment.

In addition to this aid, which was a recognised obligation, the King extracted money for his daughter's marriage from the cities, towns, and even the smallest villages. The largest sum was, of course, demanded of London, which was assessed £617 16s. 8d.[2] The aid realised the sum of almost £4,500 paid in by Michaelmas 1168, out of a total revenue of £21,000 for the year.[3]

---

[1] Pipe Roll 13 Henry II, pp. 2-3.   [2] Pipe Roll 14 Henry II, p. 3.
[3] J. H. Ramsay: *History of the Revenues of the Kings of England, 1066-1399* (Oxford, 2 vols., 1925), Vol. I, pp. 98, 100.

In September 1167 Henry had to go back to Brittany, where a fresh rebellion had broken out against his vassal Conan, under the leadership of Eudes, Viscount of Porhoët. After the death of his wife, Bertha, through whom he laid claim to Brittany, Eudes had married the daughter of Hervey, Viscount of Léhon. He now enlisted the support of his brother-in-law, Guiomar, and stirred up the Bretons once more against the hated Normans.

Henry acted with great decisiveness, stung by the refusal of the Breton nobles to abide by their oaths of fealty. When Guiomar saw his castle, which he had most amply supplied and put into a state of defence, captured and burned, and many others either captured or surrendered, he was overcome with terror. Realising the futility of further resistance, he submitted to the King and gave hostages to him.[1]

While Henry was still in Brittany he received the news of his mother's death on September 10, at Rouen. She died, 'worn out by old age and fevers',[2] and was buried at the Abbey of Bec. Henry distributed her great wealth among various churches, monasteries, leper hospitals, and the poor. She left a large sum of money to continue the building of the stone bridge across the Seine at Rouen, a work of piety that she had begun.[3]

The Papal Legates, who had been proceeding through France at a snail's pace on the theory, firmly held by the Roman Curia, that the longer they could postpone an action the easier it would be, had a conference with Henry at Caen towards the end of October. The King repeated his accusations against the Archbishop with further embellishments. Thomas, he said, had incited King Louis to make war on him. Furthermore, he had gone to the King's cousin, Count Philip of Flanders, with whom Henry had always been on the most friendly terms, and tried to stir up war between them. The King now asserted that Thomas owed him 44,000 marks and had fled the kingdom in order to escape paying them. The Pope was entirely misinformed about the ancient customs of the realm, over which there had been such an uproar, and Henry offered to submit them to the Cardinals for their approval.

When the Legates showed the King the Pope's letter of instructions, making a reconciliation between Thomas and the King the

---

[1] Robert of Torigni, p. 232.   [2] Stephen of Rouen, p. 712.
[3] Robert of Torigni, p. 233.

condition upon which their going to England depended, Henry fell into a rage that brought the interview to a close.

Having signally failed to reconcile the King, the Legates then summoned Thomas to a meeting in Normandy. The Archbishop refused to go anywhere where he might be at the mercy of the English King, even under the Legates' safe-conduct. He objected, furthermore, to the expense of a long journey when he was living on King Louis's charity, and he said that he could not undertake one on such short notice as the Legates had given him.

After a further exchange of letters, the Cardinals and the Archbishop met on November 18 on the French side of the Norman border, between Gisors and Trie. The Legates opened the conference by reminding Thomas of the Pope's concern over the quarrel, of the Legates' labours and the perils of the nine-months' journey they had made from Rome to Normandy in order to settle the dispute, of the greatness of the King and of the necessities of the Church, of the evils of the time, of the love and honour and benefits that Henry had showered on Thomas, and of the harm and injury that Thomas had done to the King, especially in inciting the King of France to make war on him. How, they asked him, could the King's indignation be appeased, unless Thomas was willing to show great humility and moderation and concern for the King's honour?

Thomas replied that he was willing to show all the humility and honour and reverence for the King that he possibly could, 'saving God's honour and the freedom of the Church and my own honesty and the possessions of the Church'.

The Legates asked him if he would be willing in their presence to swear to observe the constitutions that his predecessors had always observed, and thus put an end to all quarrels and be restored to the King's favour and to his see and to peace for himself and his followers.

None of his predecessors, Thomas said, had ever been forced to swear to keep the customs. They were contrary to the law of God, they had been condemned by the Pope at Sens, and they destroyed the freedom of the Church.

The Legates then asked Thomas if, since he would not approve the customs, he would at least tolerate them and, without any further mention of them, go back to his see. Thomas had been caught in this trap once before. He refused to be taken in by such a transparent manoeuvre to place him again in the King's power.

Since they could move neither Henry nor Thomas, the Cardinals then had an interview with King Louis. He indignantly denied that Thomas had been inciting him to war against Henry; on the contrary, he swore that the Archbishop had repeatedly advised him to preserve the peace.[1]

The Legates went back to Henry and found him at Argentan on Sunday, November 26. The King went two leagues to meet them, welcomed them with much effusiveness, and accompanied them to their lodgings. On Monday morning they conferred with him for two hours. At the end, the King went to the door of the hall with the Legates and shouted after them, as they hurried back to their lodgings: 'I hope I never lay eyes on a Cardinal again!'

The King went back into the hall, and the council of bishops and barons sat with him almost till dark. Then the bishops, with worried faces, went to the Cardinals' lodgings. On Tuesday the council sat till mid-afternoon, and then the bishops scurried from the King to the Cardinals, from the Cardinals to the King, and back to the Cardinals again.

Henry, his patience exhausted, got up early Wednesday morning and went hawking. The clergy met with the Cardinals, and Bishop Gilbert Foliot summed up the complaints of the King and the bishops against the Archbishop. In the course of his speech he referred to the 44,000 marks that Henry was claiming from Thomas. The Archbishop apparently believed, Gilbert said, that just as baptism freed one from all sins, so the episcopal consecration freed one from all debts. This witticism was greatly appreciated. Bishop Gilbert concluded by renewing, in the name of all the bishops of England, their appeal to the Pope against the Archbishop and named the following November as the term of their appeal, thus giving everyone a year's respite.

The Cardinals left Argentan on Tuesday, December 5. At their parting Henry burst into tears and begged them to intercede with the Pope for him so that he might be wholly freed from the troublesome Archbishop. Cardinal William of Pavia likewise burst into tears. Cardinal Otto, however, could hardly restrain

---

[1] *Materials*, Vol. VI, pp. 256-60.

his sniggers at this lachrymose spectacle. Henry at once despatched
two messengers to the Pope to renew his demands.[1]

The two Cardinals informed Thomas on December 9 of the
outcome of the conference at Argentan. They ordered him not
to lay any sentence of excommunication or of interdict on anyone
in England without the Pope's express permission. They also
sent a report to the Pope of their failure to effect a reconciliation,
of the bishops' appeal, and of the restraining orders they had laid
on the Archbishop.[2]

Thus Alexander, by his duplicity and indecisiveness, succeeded
merely in making a bad situation worse. By first promising
Henry almost everything he wanted and then dashing down his
hopes, he had driven the King into an attitude of stubborn
defiance. By seeming to favour the Archbishop and then tying
his hands so that he could not use his spiritual powers, the only
powers left him, he cast Thomas into dejection and made him
despair of ever receiving any help from the head of the Church
for whose freedom he was fighting. Finally, he earned the contempt of King Louis and other interested observers and made
them more resolved than ever to do all in their power to help
the Archbishop, whom the Pope had apparently repudiated.

A revolt in the South, however, left Henry little time to deal
with either Pope or Archbishop. In January 1168 almost the
whole of Poitou and Aquitaine broke into rebellion. The Dukes
of Aquitaine had never been able to exercise much control over
their nobles, for the nobles were not bound to their duke by anything more substantial than the oath of fealty, an oath the Southerners took lightly indeed. Now that their duke was a hated
foreigner who was far away across the Loire most of the time, the
men of Aquitaine tried to cast off his yoke. The Count of La
Marche, the Count of Angoulême, Aimeric of Lusignan, the
brothers Robert and Hugh of Silly, and many others stirred all
the land south of the Loire into open rebellion.

Henry collected an army and hastened to Poitou. He captured
the rebels' stronghold of Lusignan and laid waste all the country
around it. He placed strong garrisons in all his castles and saw
to it that they had ample supplies. Robert of Silly surrendered
to him and renewed his oath of fealty. Henry, however, would
not give him the customary kiss of peace as an assurance that he

[1] *Materials*, Vol. VI, pp. 269–74.   [2] Ibid., Vol. VI, pp. 280–5.

held no enmity against him. Shortly afterwards he had Robert imprisoned and kept on so meagre an allowance of bread and water that he perished.

Henry then had to hurry back to Normandy, for his truce with Louis, with whom he had been conducting sporadic hostilities ever since his return from England in 1166, was due to expire at Easter, and he anticipated further trouble with him. It occurred to him that the Southerners might be more likely to respect and obey their Duchess, who was of their own blood, than himself. He accordingly left Eleanor, who had rejoined him before Christmas, as his regent. Her son Richard, then ten years old and already her favourite son and designated successor to Aquitaine, was with her.[1] To help her in her difficult task Henry chose Earl Patrick of Salisbury, an experienced soldier who had been unfailingly faithful to the Empress and to him.

Meanwhile the Counts of Flanders and of Champagne had been treating with Louis concerning the terms of a peace with Henry. Louis was increasingly jealous of the magnitude of Henry's holdings in France. He realised, however, from Henry's negotiations to secure Brittany for his son Geoffrey, that as his sons grew up Henry might have to divide some of his lands among them and be content with the title of King of England and, perhaps, Duke of Normandy.

Therein, so he thought, lay Louis's opportunity. He proposed, as the price of peace, that Henry publicly renew his oath of fealty to him for the Duchy of Normandy. The second condition was that he should cede the Counties of Anjou and Maine to the young Henry, Louis's son-in-law, and that the young Henry should then do homage for them and swear fealty directly to Louis, with no intermediate obligations to his father. Lastly, Louis proposed that Henry cede the Duchy of Aquitaine to Richard on the same conditions, and he offered to give Richard the hand of Alice, his daughter by Adela of Champagne, but without any dowry. This was, of course, a thinly veiled attempt to split up Henry's empire.

Henry came to Pacy-sur-Eure, in Normandy, and the Count of Champagne brought Louis's conditions to him. In the midst of the preliminary negotiations Henry learned that the rebels in Poitou had seized the castle of Lusignan from Eleanor and Earl

[1] Delisle-Berger, op. cit., Vol. I, p. 425.

Patrick and were stocking it in preparation for another outbreak. He hastily appointed Archbishop Rotrou of Rouen; Richard of Humez, Constable of Normandy; and Richard of Luci to continue the negotiations on his behalf while he hurried back to Poitou.

This interruption convinced Louis that Henry was not sincere in seeking to arrange a peace with him. Some Poitevin nobles came and complained to him, as Henry's overlord, that Henry was depriving them of all their liberties. Louis and the nobles agreed that neither would make peace with Henry without the knowledge and consent of the other.

Henry returned to Normandy, after once more reducing Lusignan, and on April 7 had a conference with the Counts of Flanders and of Champagne and a number of French nobles. They reported that Louis would not meet Henry until he had agreed to restore peace in Poitou and give back to the nobles what he had taken from them, presumably their castles. Louis also renewed his former conditions.

Neither side trusted the other, and Henry was not willing to make any concessions to the rebellious Poitevins. Instead of a peace, a truce was agreed upon to last till the following July.[1] As soon as the agreement was made, Henry learned that the Poitevins had killed Earl Patrick in an ambush on March 27 and had gravely wounded and captured the Earl's young nephew, William Marshal, the second son of John the Marshal, whose charges against the Archbishop of Canterbury had led to the summoning of Thomas before the King's court. Queen Eleanor, 'who was very valiant and courteous', ransomed the handsome young knight and gave him horses, arms, money, and rich clothes.[2]

Even before the truce with Louis was agreed upon, Henry had summoned Viscount Eudes of Porhoët and the other Breton nobles to serve in his army against the Poitevins. Eudes refused, and the other Breton nobles joined him. Eudes was especially bitter against Henry because the King had seduced his daughter, whom he had given as a hostage to Henry and who was now pregnant by him.[3] The whole of Brittany was once more up in

[1] Robert of Torigni, pp. 235-6.
[2] *Histoire de Guillaume le Maréchal*, ed. Paul Meyer (Paris, 3 Vols., 1891-1901), lines 1869-88.   [3] John of Salisbury, in *Materials*, Vol. VI, p. 456.

arms against Henry. Eudes and his allies had aroused the nationalistic feelings of the Bretons by circulating stories that they had appealed to King Arthur and that the great Breton hero had promised to help them.

The Arthurian legends were immensely popular in the twelfth century. Geoffrey of Monmouth had collected the Welsh folk tales about Arthur, joined them to some dubious history, and set them in an atmosphere of knights and chivalry and tournaments. He dedicated his *History of the Kings of Britain* to Robert of Gloucester around 1135, and it quickly became the most widely read work of its time. Wace, across the Channel, used Geoffrey's history as the basis for his *Roman de Brut*, a metrical version in Norman French, which he dedicated to Queen Eleanor in 1155.

True to his promise, King Arthur sent a letter to Henry in which he reproached him for having attacked the Bretons without a proper declaration of war, as the rules of chivalry demanded, and warned him that if he did not give up the Breton castles and cease annoying his people, King Arthur would return and make war on Henry.

When Henry read this letter, 'he laughed and was not afraid'. He answered it, however, lest Arthur should think that he was lacking in respect for him, and proposed that he should hold Brittany under Arthur's 'rule and peace' as his vassal.[1]

With this correspondence attended to, Henry set out for Brittany to subdue Eudes and his allies once and for all, leaving Eleanor to handle the rebels in Poitou. Eudes's county of Porhoët occupied most of central Brittany, with its chief town at Vannes, on the south coast of the peninsula. Henry spread fire, destruction, and terror throughout the country. He destroyed Eudes's castles and took the whole county of Porhoët and half of Cornouaille away from him.

Then he marched from Vannes across the peninsula to St-Malo, taking Bécherel and Tinténiac, two strong castles between Dinan and Rennes, on the way. Roland of Dinan, one of the leading rebels, had a castle at Léhon, immediately south of Dinan. Henry did not have time to lay siege to the castle, for it was now late in June and his truce with the King of France expired at the end of the month, but he destroyed the town and devastated the countryside. He then crossed the River Rance and 'delivered

1 Stephen of Rouen, pp. 696-706.

Roland's land to rapine and the flames'.[1]   Henry did such a thorough job of subduing the Bretons that he felt confident it would be a long time before they would attempt to rebel again.

At the beginning of July the two Kings took up their quarters for the conference, Henry at La Ferté-Bernard and Louis at Chartres.   Henry had in his party Cardinal William of Pavia, and he also had a letter from the Pope, about which he boasted greatly, for it suspended the authority of the Archbishop of Canterbury until he should become reconciled with the King.

Fresh from his triumphs in Brittany and convinced that he had the Pope under his thumb, Henry was in no mood to make concessions to anyone.   He refused to come to Louis at his bidding, although Louis waited for him at the appointed place all day. With the failure of the Kings to come to any terms, the series of pointless raids that passed for war was resumed, although neither side gained any lasting advantage.

Late in the summer the Emperor Frederick Barbarossa sent Henry the Lion, Duke of Saxony, on an embassy to the English King, to assure him that the Emperor was eager to help him in every way possible against the French King and was willing to provide an army for his assistance.   Henry declined this offer gracefully, saying that his own army was quite capable of keeping the French in check.   Henry had his hands full already in trying to keep Aquitaine and Brittany under control, and he had no desire to embark on a full-scale war of conquest such as the Emperor was now proposing.

The second proposition advanced by the Duke was that the English should desert Alexander III, join the Germans in their schism, and recognise Paschal III as Pope.   Now that Henry had Alexander's letter suspending the authority of the Archbishop of Canterbury, his feelings towards the Pope were less bitter than they had been.   Largely for the salutary effect it might have on Alexander, however, he caused the clergy to meet in London and demanded that they swear to receive Paschal as Pope.   The English bishops were unanimous in refusing to take such an oath, and their firm attitude caused Henry to give up the idea.

Although the King could not agree to either of their proposals, he treated the envoys with great honour and sent them back with rich gifts.   He wrung 5,000 marks from the Jews of England as a

[1] Robert of Torigni, pp. 236-7.

gift to Duke Henry and the Emperor.[1]   This offer of an alliance
with the Emperor tremendously increased Henry's self-impor-
tance, already greatly inflated by his success in Brittany and
Aquitaine and by the subservient attitude of the Pope.

The anti-pope died on September 20, and Abbot John of
Struma was elected, with, if possible, even less show of legality
than Paschal had been, in his stead.   He took the name of
Calixtus III, and thus the schism continued.

Henry's boasts about the letter that Alexander had sent him,
whereby Archbishop Thomas was suspended from any authority
over the King and the Church in England, had horrified the pious
King Louis.   He wrote to the Pope complaining that although
he had never wavered in his allegiance to Alexander and although
he had frequently implored him, without mingling any threats
with his requests, to help Thomas, Alexander had done everything
he could to help not Thomas but Henry, who was now exhibiting
the Pope's letter on all sides and boasting that Thomas had no
power in his realm.[2]

Queen Adela added her voice to her husband's:

> To her most holy lord and dearest father, Alexander, by the grace
> of God Supreme Pontiff, his humble and devoted daughter Adela,
> Queen of the French, sends greetings and faithful service with a
> sincere heart.
>
> I speak to you as to my father and lord, whose honour my lord
> the King and I and all our realm cherish as our own.   Your honour
> is our honour, and your confusion (may God ward it off!) is our
> confusion.   We have received you as our father and lord, and for
> God's sake and yours we despise the enmity of kings who go raving
> round our borders, seeking your life.   Please hear your daughter,
> and in what I am about to say do not condemn my female sex, but
> listen to the voice of my love.
>
> Last year John of Oxford, who won such an easy victory over
> Rome by his perjury, caused a very grave scandal in the French
> Church.   Then some Cardinals followed him.   If they did any
> good, we have not heard of it in our land, and I wish that the evil
> they did could be covered up.   And thus the scandals were multiplied.
>
> Now the King of England, by his latest messengers, has obtained
> an open letter by which (if indeed it has not been tampered with)
> you have decreed that the Archbishop of Canterbury, whom he has

[1] Gervase of Canterbury, Vol. I, pp. 205, 207.
[2] *Materials*, Vol. VI, pp. 460-1.

already kept in exile for justice's sake for four years, cannot lay any sentence on him or his land or punish any person in his land, until he has been received back into the King's favour.

From this letter, Father, would it not look as though he had authority to sin without being punished and to keep the Archbishop in exile forever, since it is for him to decide whether or not he will receive the Archbishop back into his favour? The whole Church here is so scandalised that it could not be any more upset, for a bad example has been given to all princes. My lord the King, in whose care you placed the Archbishop, is most upset, for if you persist an innocent man will be strangled between his [Henry's] hands.

Our whole realm grieves because our enemies have prevailed with you. My lord the King is waiting for the fulfilment of your promise, and unless it is quickly fulfilled he and his children will learn from that what they may expect from the Roman Church.

Farewell, most holy and dearest Father, and please help the Archbishop of Canterbury.[1]

Alexander wrote to both Thomas and Louis in his usual vein, saying that his letter to Henry did not really mean what it said; he was merely treating the King with patience and gentleness in order to recall him to the right path. The fervour of his charity and love for Thomas had not grown cold but was becoming greater from day to day. He promised that when the appointed time came he would give Thomas full faculties to exercise his power without any appeals.[2]

Meanwhile the inconclusive war between Henry and Louis was continuing with sporadic forays along the Norman border. Hostilities were suspended at the beginning of Advent, and the two Kings, shortly before Christmas, agreed to hold a conference on the feast of the Epiphany, January 6, 1169, and to try to arrange a lasting treaty of peace.

[1] *Materials*, Vol. VI, pp. 461-2, 485-6.   [2] Ibid., Vol. VI, pp. 468-9.

IX

'THE KING, THE KING'S SON'
1169 - 1170

BEFORE the two Kings met for their conference, Henry's cousin, Count Theobald of Blois, came to him and explained the terms that Louis was offering, including the acts of homage to be performed by Henry's sons. Perhaps Count Theobald pointed out to him the difficulties that had attended Henry's succession to the throne and urged upon him the necessity for making arrangements so that his sons should not be placed under the need to fight for their inheritances as Henry had done. The surest way of providing for an orderly succession upon his death would be to have the King of France, by receiving in advance the homage of his heirs, guarantee that no interloper could take their lands in France away from them. At any rate, Henry readily agreed to the terms.

Three monks, sent by the Pope to effect a reconciliation between Henry and Thomas, also had an interview with the King before the conference. Henry tried an entirely new approach with them. He told them that he was most eager to arrange an honourable peace with the Archbishop, for he was waiting only for that before he took the Cross and set out for the Holy Land. This was the first time Henry mentioned his desire to become a crusader, but henceforth he used it to extricate himself from many a tight spot. The monks, dazzled by the prospect of being able to arrange matters so that the great King might go on Crusade, summoned Thomas to come to the conference with King Louis.

Henry and Louis met at Montmirail, not far from La Ferté-Bernard, on the border of Maine, on January 6, 1169. In allusion to its being the feast of the Epiphany, Henry greeted Louis with a pretty speech: 'On this day, my lord King, on which the Three Kings offered gifts to the King of Kings, I commend myself, my sons, and my land to your keeping.'

Henry then did homage to Louis and renewed his oath of fealty to him, promising to 'render him such aid and service as the Duke of the Normans owes to the King of the French'. The two Kings shook hands and kissed, as a sign of their reconciliation. Louis surrendered to Henry a number of Breton and Poitevin noblemen who had taken refuge with him because they were afraid that they might meet with the same fate that befell Robert of Silly. Henry promised to return to them all the castles and lands he had taken away from them, to keep the peace with them, and to make compensation for the burnings and killings that had been committed.[1]

On the following day the young Henry, not quite fourteen years old, did homage directly to Louis, his father-in-law, for Anjou, Maine, and Brittany. He had already done homage for Normandy in October 1160. Richard, then eleven years old, did homage to Louis for the Duchy of Aquitaine, and he and Alice, Louis's daughter, were betrothed.[2] Alice, as her sister Margaret had been, was turned over to Henry to be brought up in his household. The assignment of Henry's lands in France to his three eldest sons was made complete when Geoffrey, later in the year, did homage to the young Henry for Brittany.

Louis was generally considered to be rather simple-minded, whereas Henry was credited with great astuteness. By this day's doings, however, Louis scored a triumph that eventually, after many a tortured year, secured Henry's downfall more thoroughly than Louis could ever have imagined. He could not attempt to break up Henry's empire by force, but he hit upon a much more effective, though slower, way of vanquishing the English King. By having Henry's sons do homage directly to him for Henry's various French fiefs, Louis laid the groundwork for Henry's ultimate defeat, and Henry, for all his vaunted astuteness, acquiesced gladly in the arrangement that made that defeat possible.

When these matters were finished, Archbishop Thomas came before the King in the presence of the bishops and nobles of both parties, knelt before him, and said: 'Be merciful to me, my lord, for I place myself in God's hands and yours, for God's honour and yours.'

In the four years since they had last met, Thomas, for the first

---

[1] John of Salisbury, in *Materials*, Vol. VI, pp. 506-7.
[2] Gervase of Canterbury, Vol. I, p. 208.

time in his adult life, had lived almost in solitude, far from the excitement of the court and the attention of great men. He had passed those years in prayer, in study, in harsh penances to bring his proud body into subjection to his will, and in meditation upon his duty to God and the Church. He had received scant help or encouragement from the Pope or from his fellow bishops in England, but his long pondering had strengthened his conviction that the only right course of action was to resist with all his might Henry's efforts to make him swear to do what he knew was wrong. Even though the Pope, blinded by his anxiety to rule as the temporal prince of a petty Italian state as well as the Vicar of Christ, affected not to see it, Thomas knew that if he gave in to Henry and swore unreservedly to obey the Constitutions, he would be abdicating his responsibilities as Archbishop of Canterbury and delivering the Church in England, bound hand and foot, to the absolute rule of the King. Come what might, Thomas was resolved to insist on the reservation that would make it clear that his first duty was to God.

As the envoys reported to the Pope:

> The King said that he wanted nothing more from the Archbishop than that he, as a priest and a bishop, should promise before them all in true words that he would without any guile obey the customs that the holy Archbishops of Canterbury had obeyed toward their kings and that the Archbishop himself, in another place, had promised to him.
>
> The Archbishop replied that he had done fealty to the King when he had sworn to obey him in life and limb and earthly honour, saving his order, and that he was ready to keep his oath most faithfully, and that more than that had not been required of any of his predecessors.
>
> When the King insisted upon this article, the Lord of Canterbury added that although none of his predecessors had done or promised this and he himself should not rightfully do it, nevertheless he said that for the sake of the peace of the Church and for his favour he would promise to obey all those customs that his holy predecessors had kept to their kings, saving his order, as far as he could, according to God, and he would do whatever he could to regain his love, saving God's honour, asserting that he had never served him more gladly than he would now, if it pleased him.
>
> But the King would not accept this, unless he would promise him, precisely and absolutely, under oath, to keep the customs, for he asked nothing more of him. Because the Archbishop would not

do this, although many persons urged him to, the King left without having made peace.[1]

Neither Henry nor Thomas had budged an inch in the last five years; the situation was exactly as it had been at the close of the Council of Clarendon. Even some of Thomas's companions in exile blamed him for not having made the concession that would have allowed them to return to England. As they were riding back to Sens, one of the party, Henry of Houghton, had trouble with his horse. 'Hey,' shouted Henry, making sure that the Archbishop would hear him, 'get along, saving God's honour and Holy Church's and my order!'

Henry, meanwhile, was boasting to the Pope's envoys that nowhere else in all the world did the Church enjoy such freedom as in England and nowhere else did it enjoy such peace. Nowhere else were the clergy treated with such honour, Henry declared, although the English clergy were filthy and savage, being for the greater part sacrilegious, adulterous, robbers, thieves, seducers of virgins, incendiaries, and murderers.[2]

When he returned to Sens, Thomas wrote to Henry to make his position clear:

> To his most serene lord Henry, by the grace of God the illustrious King of the English, Duke of the Normans and Aquitanians, and Count of the Angevins, Thomas, the humble servant of the holy Church of Canterbury, sends his greetings and devoted service, with all due respect and love.
>
> Your Royal Nobility may remember that I told you, in the presence of the Lord King of the French and of many who were there, that I was ready, for God's honour and yours, to put myself entirely on God's mercy and yours, so that I might thus deserve your peace and favour. That form of words, my lord, did not please you, unless I would promise to observe the customs that our predecessors observed to yours.
>
> I therefore concede, my lord, that I will observe them, as far as I can, saving my order, and if I knew in the Lord how to promise anything more fully or more clearly, I was ready then and I am ready now to do so, in order to regain your favour. I have never served you as gladly as I am ready to serve you now.
>
> And because it has not yet pleased you to receive my service, I beg Your Majesty to remember my past services and the benefits you conferred on me, for I remember that I am bound by oath to

---

[1] *Materials*, Vol. VI, pp. 488-9.   [2] Ibid., Vol. VI, p. 509.

serve you in life and limb and earthly honour, and whatever I can
do for you, under God, I am ready to do, as for my dearest lord.
And God knows that I have never served you as gladly as I am ready
to do, if it should please you.

May my lord fare ever well.[1]

The Pope's envoys continued to urge Henry to make peace
with Thomas, but they found him as slippery as an eel.

He told us: 'I did not expel the Lord of Canterbury from the
realm, and yet, out of reverence for the Lord Pope, if he will do
what he ought to do and obey me in those matters in which his
predecessors obeyed mine and which he himself promised, he may
go back to England and have peace there.'

Then, after a variety of answers, he said that he was going to
summon the English bishops and ask their advice, but he would not
set a day. We cannot report that he has done anything to make us
feel sure of peace for the Lord of Canterbury and of the execution of
your orders.

Because he changed his answers so often, we asked him if he
would allow the Archbishop to return to his see and enjoy his peace.
He replied that the Archbishop could never enter his land until he
did what he ought to do and promised to obey what others obeyed
and what he had promised to obey.

Then we asked him to have his answer written down in an open
letter and sealed with his seal, so that we could give you some
definite information, which we had not yet had, since he changed
his answers so often. He, however, did not want to do this.

When we reported this to the Archbishop, he said that he was
ready to do whatever he ought to do and to obey whatever his predecessors had obeyed, insofar as he could, saving his order, but that
it would be unlawful for him, without the authority of the Lord
Pope, to undertake any new obligations that his predecessors had
not been bound to and to promise anything in that way, except
saving his order, because you had forbidden anyone to promise
anything along those lines except with the reservation, saving God's
honour and his order.[2]

Those perpetual rebels, Count Adalbert of La Marche and
Count William of Angoulême, were again causing trouble in
Aquitaine, and Eleanor could not reduce them to order. In
March Henry went to deal with them. He began with Count
Adalbert, whose land lay midway between Poitiers and Angou-

[1] *Materials*, Vol. VI, pp. 513-14.   [2] Ibid., Vol. VI, p. 517.

L

lême, and destroyed his castle. Then he marched south and over-
came Count William. He destroyed all the castles of the rebels,
and they once again swore to keep the peace. Henry was forced
to spend the spring and summer in Aquitaine, going into Gascony,
at the extreme southern part of the Duchy, to bring that region,
which he had not hitherto visited extensively, under his firm rule.

The King turned northward in the early part of August. On
his way to Normandy, he stopped in Anjou to have work begun
on one of his most lasting memorials. His predecessors had built
churches and abbeys; Henry caused a great series of embankments,
thirty miles long, to be built along the Loire to keep the river
from flooding the fields and meadows.[1]

Pope Alexander, meanwhile, in an effort to postpone still
further the necessity for making any decision, had sent two more
envoys, the Subdeacon Gratian, his notary, and Master Vivian, to
effect a reconciliation between Henry and Thomas. They had
arrived in France in July, while Henry, with his army, was still
in 'the remote parts of Gascony'. When they heard that the
King had returned to Normandy they went to Domfront on
August 23, 1169, to see him.

The King was out hunting when they arrived and did not return
till late in the day. He went directly to the envoy's hospice and
greeted them 'with great honour and reverence and humility'.
While he was talking with them, the young Henry rode up to the
gate with a troop of lads, all blowing their horns 'as is done when
a stag is taken'. The young Henry, full of the gaiety and charm
that captivated everyone who met him, paid his respects to the
envoys and gave them the stag for their dinner.

On the next day they began a series of conferences that lasted
till September 16. Henry dragged them all over Normandy,
shifting his grounds as often as he changed his lodgings. First he
insisted that as a preliminary to any further negotiations the envoys
should absolve all those whom Thomas had excommunicated, a
list that now included the Bishops of London and Salisbury. The
envoys refused to do so until Henry had first made peace with the
Archbishop. Henry complained angrily that the Pope paid no
heed to him in anything and revived his threats of joining the
German schism.

'By God's eyes,' he shouted, 'I will go elsewhere!'

[1] Robert of Torigni, p. 242.

'Don't threaten us, my lord,' Gratian replied. 'We fear no threat, for we come from a court that is accustomed to giving orders to emperors and kings.'

When the envoys stood firm in their refusal to make any concessions to him and mentioned the possibility that he might be excommunicated if he continued in his defiant attitude, Henry cried: 'Do as you will. I don't care an egg for you or your excommunications.'

Some of his bishops remonstrated with him over his treatment of the envoys.

'I know, I know,' said Henry impatiently; 'they are going to lay an interdict on my land. But cannot I, who can seize the strongest castle any day I choose, cannot I seize one clerk if he lays an interdict on my land?'

At last, after almost a month of haggling, Henry agreed to a formula of peace with the Archbishop. He would allow Thomas and all his clerks to return freely to England; he would restore all the confiscated possessions of the archbishopric; and he would submit to the Pope in all things and do whatever he ordered. Then, at the last moment, when everyone was rejoicing that the dreary business had been brought to an end, Henry insisted that the formula contain the provision, 'saving the dignity of his realm'. This was a clear announcement that he intended to enforce the Constitutions of Clarendon, and no one could budge the King from that stand. The envoys gave up their task in despair.[1]

Henry wrote to the Pope to express his disappointment at the obstinate stand taken by the legates. He asked Alexander to lift the sentences of excommunication imposed by 'that perfidious traitor', Thomas, and to prohibit him from pouring forth the venom of his excommunications upon any others. Unless Alexander complied with his requests, 'despairing of your good will, we shall be forced to look elsewhere for our safety and honour'.

Thomas saw clearly, as he reported to the Pope, that by Henry's insistence upon 'the dignity of his realm' he meant nothing other than the Constitutions, which he was accustomed to refer to as his 'royal dignities' and which had been condemned by Alexander himself in one of the rare moments when he had been compelled to take a definite stand.[2]

---

[1] *Materials*, Vol. VII, pp. 70–75, 78–82.   [2] Ibid., Vol. VII, pp. 118–23.

A sentence of interdict, prohibiting all divine services, was what Henry most dreaded and what all his delaying tactics were intended to avert. He feared now that he might so far have exhausted the patience of both the Pope and the Archbishop that one or the other of them might launch the sentence. He could not prevent them from passing such a sentence, but he could take every precaution against its being published in England.

He accordingly sent to his justiciars in England, to be published all over the country, a stringent set of orders, known as the Ten Ordinances. They provided that if anyone was found with letters from the Pope or the Archbishop imposing an interdict, he was to be treated as a traitor to the King and the realm. Strict rules were laid down governing the movement of clerks across the Channel.

A friend wrote Thomas to tell him of the punishments that had been proclaimed against anyone who violated the Ordinances. If a monk brought the letters of interdict into England, his feet were to be chopped off; if a secular priest, he was to be blinded and castrated; if a layman, he was to be hanged; and if a leper, he was to be burned. If any bishop wished to leave England through fear of an interdict, he could take nothing with him save his bishop's staff. All English students were recalled from foreign schools, and if they did not obey they were to be sentenced to perpetual exile. Priests 'who did not want to sing', that is, who might obey an interdict and refuse to celebrate Mass, were to be castrated.[1]

Louis and Henry met at St-Denis, just outside Paris, on November 16, 1169. They agreed that Count Raymond of Toulouse was to answer to the young Richard, as Duke of Aquitaine, for his fief of Toulouse. Henry also agreed to put Richard in Louis's hands to be brought up and trained to knighthood. For a lad to be educated in the household of his future lord was a common arrangement at that time. In this case the fact that Richard was betrothed to Louis's daughter Alice, who was being brought up in Henry's household, made such an arrangement especially fitting.

After this agreement had been reached, King Louis, Archbishop Rotrou of Rouen, the envoy Vivian, and Count Theobald of Blois united in urging Henry to make peace with Thomas, who

---

[1] *Materials*, Vol. VII, p. 146.

had come to Paris at Vivian's bidding and was waiting for a summons from the King. Henry went to Montmartre on the following day for a further conference concerning Thomas. Apparently Henry and Thomas did not meet; the negotiations seem to have been conducted by intermediaries.

The Archbishop begged Henry, for the love of God and of the Pope, to give back to him and his fellow exiles his favour, his peace, their safety, their possessions, and all that had been taken from them. He offered to submit to him in all matters in which an archbishop should submit to his king.

Henry replied that he would gladly forget all injuries and lay aside all accusations, if he had any, against Thomas, and he declared that if Thomas had any complaints and accusations against him he was ready to answer them in the court of his lord the King of the French or before the judgment of the French Church or of the schools of Paris.

Thomas answered that he would submit to the judgment of the court of the French King or of the French Church if Henry wanted him to, but that he would rather discuss the matter with him in a friendly fashion than take part in a formal suit. He asked that Henry give back to him his church and his possessions and everything that had been taken away from him and give him the kiss of peace as a sign that he had received him back into his grace and peace and as an assurance of his safety.

Henry replied to this in a speech so involved that although to the simple it might seem that he was granting all that Thomas asked, to the cautious it was full of impossible conditions. Both simple and cautious, however, agreed that Henry flatly refused to give Thomas the kiss of peace. This was no empty gesture, but a solemn pledge that the giver had cast all enmity out of his heart and intended no harm to the recipient. It was regarded as even more binding than an oath, both because the kiss of peace was one of the ceremonies of the Mass and because a man who betrayed another to whom he had given the kiss thus put himself on a level with Judas, who betrayed his Lord with a kiss.

The participants were all disgusted that at this point, after having led them along so far, Henry should openly avow that all his talk of granting peace and safety to Thomas was a sham. King Louis told Thomas that he would not, for any amount of gold, advise him to go back to England unless Henry would first

give him the kiss of peace in public, and Count Theobald counselled him likewise.   Many of those present recalled vividly what
had happened to Robert of Silly after Henry had refused to give
him the kiss of peace.

The conference broke up, and Louis rode with Henry as far as
Pacy in the expectation that Henry would entrust Richard to him,
as they had agreed.   Henry, after making a number of excuses,
at last said that he would fulfil his promise at a meeting at Tours at
some unspecified time.   Louis realised that he had been tricked,
and the two Kings parted on less friendly terms than they had met.

Henry, later in the month, sent a messenger to Vivian with
twenty marks and the request that he try again to make peace
between him and the Archbishop.   Even Vivian was disgusted,
and he sent back the money with a letter warning the King that
unless he granted the requests Thomas had made at Montmartre,
confirmed them by a written charter, and gave Thomas the kiss
of peace, his land would be laid under interdict.[1]

After this conference, Henry and his son Geoffrey went to
Brittany, and Henry held his Christmas court at Nantes.   He
then visited all the castles in Brittany, receiving the homage and
oaths of fealty of all the 'counts and barons and free men of
Brittany' who had not yet sworn their oaths to the King and their
intended Duke.[2]

Word had got about that the only reason Henry was willing to
go through the outward forms, at least, of making peace with
Thomas was that he might induce him to return to England and
crown his son Henry, a project that the King had been contemplating at intervals for the past eight years.   By ancient custom only
the Archbishop of Canterbury might crown the king, and as long
as Thomas remained in exile the ceremony could not be performed.

Henry had, however, during the winter,[3] extorted briefs from
the Pope authorising the coronation and empowering the Archbishop of York to perform the ceremony.   As soon as he received the briefs Henry acted quickly, for he knew Alexander's
devious ways too well to give him time to follow up his letters
with orders countermanding them.

[1] *Materials*, Vol. VII, pp. 161-71.
[2] *Gesta Regis Henrici Secundi*, ed. William Stubbs (Rolls Series, 2 Vols., 1867),
Vol. I, p. 3.   (Hereafter referred to as *Gesta*.)
[3] *Materials*, Vol. VII, p. 227.

Just as Henry expected, Alexander wrote to the Archbishop of
York and all the bishops of England on February 26, 1170, telling
them that it had come to his hearing from many people that the
right to crown and anoint the King of England belonged by
ancient custom to the Archbishop of Canterbury. He therefore
ordered them not to presume to attempt such a thing or to allow
anyone else to do so, under peril of their offices and their episcopal orders.[1] The damage had already been done when Alexander
had granted permission for the coronation, however, and these
letters cancelling, as was Alexander's custom, what he had already
done, could neither reach Henry in time to prevent his acting on
the previous briefs nor be delivered easily in England, as the Pope
must have known.

Once Henry received the briefs he sailed for England and
landed at Portsmouth on March 3, 1170, after an absence of four
years. He was immediately met on all sides by complaints of the
exactions, injustices, and oppressions of the sheriffs. Although
the justiciars occasionally visited the counties, the sheriffs had
charge of all the legal and financial administration, except in those
cases where the offence was expressly reserved to the King's court.
Since the justiciars were in each county for only a few days and
the sheriff resided there permanently, the authority of the sheriffs
was little curtailed by that of the justiciars. Furthermore, in
almost every case the sheriffs were local magnates and large landholders. It is not surprising, then, that these men should be
charged with having abused the great powers of their offices,
particularly during a time when the King was long absent from
the country.

After Easter, which Henry kept at Windsor, the King and his
court went to London, where he held a meeting of the Great
Council. They discussed the intended crowning of the young
Henry, the statutes of the realm, and the complaints against the
sheriffs. The King suspended almost all the sheriffs and appointed commissions of reliable men to go over the whole country to
conduct a searching investigation into their behaviour. The
instructions for conducting this investigation, which was to be
completed by June 14, were set forth in the Inquest of Sheriffs.

Henry meanwhile made elaborate preparations for his son's
crowning. He spent 34s. 9d. 'for gold for gilding the vessels of

[1] Ibid., Vol. VII, p. 217.

the King, the King's son, and for repairing the swords for the King's coronation'.[1]

The young Henry and his wife were waiting at Caen with Queen Eleanor. When his preparations were complete, Henry sent Richard of Ilchester to bring the lad to England. When Richard reached Caen he told Margaret, Henry's wife, to stay with Queen Eleanor for a few more days and to be ready to come to England as soon as the King sent for her.

Bishop Roger of Worcester, a younger son of Earl Robert of Gloucester, whom Thomas had consecrated Bishop in 1164, was waiting in Normandy in an effort to get a passage to England. He had letters from the Pope and from Thomas to the Archbishop of York, forbidding him to crown the young Henry. Bishop Roger had also received a summons to attend the council that the King had called to meet in London on June 11. Queen Eleanor and Richard of Humez, Seneschal of Normandy, forbade him to cross, and when he tried to get a ship on his own initiative he found that all the sailors had been warned not to give him passage.

The young Henry, with Bishop Froger of Séez, Bishop Henry of Bayeux, and Richard of Ilchester, sailed for England on June 5, leaving Margaret behind with her mother-in-law.

The King held a meeting of the Great Council in London on June 11. The commissioners to investigate the conduct of the sheriffs made their report, and they told such a sorry tale of corruption, favouritism, malfeasance, and misappropriation of funds that the King discharged twenty-two of the twenty-nine sheriffs, whom he had already suspended from office until the investigation was completed.[2] By drawing on his court and the Exchequer for the new sheriffs, the King gained the double advantage of putting in these most important posts men who had had technical training in the law and in finance and of replacing the local magnates, with all their local interests, ties, and loyalties, by servants whose loyalty was to the King and who would be directly under his control.

Thomas, meanwhile, had learned that the coronation was to be performed on June 14 by Archbishop Roger of York. Although some of Thomas's messengers had succeeded in smuggling his orders and the Pope's, forbidding the coronation, into England,

---

[1] Pipe Roll 16 Henry II, p. 16.   [2] *Gesta*, Vol. I, pp. 4-5.

no notice had been taken of them, and they had necessarily been delivered in such a clandestine manner that the recipients could easily claim not to have received them at all.

Thomas had hoped that Bishop Roger of Worcester would be able to deliver his prohibition, which could not then be ignored, but since Roger was not allowed to leave Normandy the Archbishop was forced to find another messenger. The ports were watched so strictly that any man who reached England would probably be stripped and searched. He therefore gave a nun, Idonea, a letter to the Archbishop of York and asked her to deliver it. Idonea succeeded in her task and placed the letter in Roger's hands on Saturday, June 13.[1]

Archbishop Roger of Pont l'Évêque, in spite of the prohibition of the Pope and of Thomas, anointed and crowned the young Henry, then fifteen years old, as King of the English in Westminster Abbey on Sunday, June 14, 1170. The Archbishop was assisted by four English bishops, Hugh of Durham, Gilbert Foliot of London, Jocelin of Salisbury, and Walter of Rochester, and two Norman bishops, Henry of Bayeux and Froger of Séez. William, King of Scots, and many of the English earls and barons were present at the ceremony.

'The King, the King's son', as the young Henry was henceforth called, inherited the good looks of his grandfather, Count Geoffrey the Fair, united to a singularly attractive and sunny disposition. He was 'the most handsome prince in all the world, whether Saracen or Christian'.[2]

This crowning of the king's intended successor while the king was still living was without precedent in England, although Stephen had attempted it and had been forbidden to do so by the Pope. It was, however, the usual practice in France. Henry considered himself at least the equal of the King of France, and if the heir to the French throne could be anointed and crowned in advance, so most certainly could the English heir. Henry's principal concern was to make sure of the orderly division of his lands and the undisputed succession of his eldest son to the throne of England when he himself should die. He was thirty-seven at this time, well into middle age by medieval standards, and life was uncertain at its best.

---

[1] *Materials*, Vol. III, p. 103; Vol. VII, pp. 307-9.
[2] *Histoire de Guillaume le Maréchal*, lines 1956-8.

To make sure that the succession should be peaceful and orderly, on the day after the coronation Henry had all his earls and barons and tenants in chief, including the King of Scots and his brother, David, 'become the men of the new King, his son, and he made them swear, on the relics of the Saints, allegiance and fealty to him against all men, saving their fealty to him.[1]   The young Henry was not only his father's designated successor; by virtue of his anointing and crowning he was truly King of the English, and the English nation, in the person of its leading men, recognised him as such.   Thus Henry, all unwittingly, took a step that was to further Louis's plan beyond the French King's greatest hopes.

[1] *Gesta*, Vol. I, p. 6.

X

THE KING AND THE MARTYR
1170

THE news of the young Henry's crowning quickly reached the ears of King Louis. He was enraged that his daughter Margaret was not crowned with her husband, and he saw in this omission an indication that Henry perhaps intended to have his son repudiate the marriage. Louis started the usual raids along the Norman border and threatened to seize the Vexin, Margaret's dowry. Henry hastened back to Normandy to meet the threat and landed at Barfleur around June 24.[1]

When Bishop Roger of Worcester heard of his cousin's approach he went out from Falaise and met the King about three miles outside the town. As soon as Henry saw him he began pouring reproaches on him.

'Now it is clear that you are a traitor! I myself told you to come to my son's crowning, and I told you the day. But you would not come, and thus you showed plainly that you care neither for me nor for my son's advancement. And it is also clear that you favour my enemy and hate me and mine. But you shall no longer enjoy the income from your bishopric. I will take it away from you, for you have shown that you are un-worthy of it and of any other benefice. Indeed, you are no son of the good Earl Robert, my uncle, who brought you and me up in his castle and had us taught our first lessons in manners and letters together!'

Bishop Roger in a gentlemanly fashion excused himself by saying that when he had reached the port he had received a letter forbidding him to cross to England.

'The Queen is there in the castle at Falaise,' Henry said, 'and Richard of Humez either is there or will be there soon. Now do you say that they were the authors of that letter?'

'I do not say that the Queen was the author, for if she hides the

[1] *Gesta*, Vol. I, p. 6.

truth through respect or love for you, you will be all the more angry with me; if she confesses the truth, you will rave disrespectfully against that noble lady, and not for all the world would I have her hear one bitter word from you. The wrong was done when you ordered me to be present at the crowning, for it was unlawful and an offence to God; not because of who was crowned, but because of who did the crowning. If I had been there, I would not have allowed him to crown your son.

'You say that I am not the son of Earl Robert. But you have not shown by any fitting return that my father, that same Earl Robert, was your uncle, who brought you up with due honour, who fought King Stephen for sixteen years for your sake, and who bore the assaults of the enemy till he was captured in battle for your sake.

'One of my younger brothers, a stout knight, you kept in a state so poor and unfitting to his abilities that for very poverty he gave up his knighthood and his station in life, bound himself to perpetual servitude to the Hospitallers of Jerusalem, and took their habit and dress. That is the way you make your close servants and familiar friends happy; that is the way you reward their merits.'

A knight from Aquitaine, who did not know Bishop Roger, was riding with the party and heard his words to the King.

'Who is this man who is talking so boldly?' he asked.

When he was told that he was a bishop, the knight replied: 'It is a good thing for the King that he is a priest. If he were a knight, I don't think he would leave two acres of land to the King.'

Someone else in the party, hearing the King berating the Bishop, thought that he would gain favour with the King by speaking harshly to the Bishop, too. Henry turned on him in a fury.

'You miserable wretch!' he shouted. 'Do you think that just because I discuss things with my kinsman and my bishop, you or anyone else can revile him or threaten him? I can hardly keep my hands away from your eyes; it will be death for you or anyone else to bark at the Bishop!'

When they arrived at the castle, Henry and his cousin had dinner together and chatted amiably.[1]

---

[1] William Fitz Stephen, in *Materials*, Vol. III, pp. 104-6.

Archbishop Rotrou of Rouen and Bishop Bernard of Nevers
came to the King as soon as they heard that he had returned to
Normandy.   They showed him a letter from the Pope, ordering
them to make peace between him and Thomas, and warned him
that unless he agreed to the reconciliation on the terms the Pope
proposed they would have no choice but to pronounce the long-
dreaded interdict.   The King, now that his object was attained
and his son was safely crowned, consented to the terms, and the
two commissioners then went to Thomas to tell him of the
agreement.

On July 6 Henry met Count Theobald of Blois, who was acting
as Louis's representative, at La Ferté-Bernard to discuss the terms
of peace with the French King.   Henry readily agreed to send
Margaret to England and to have her crowned with her husband,
thus removing Louis's chief grievance.

A fortnight later Henry and Louis met at Fréteval, on the
River Loir, about thirty-five miles west of Orléans, in Louis's
territory.   During the two days of their conference the Kings
composed their differences.   As Henry was taking leave of Louis
he said: 'Tomorrow that thief of yours shall have his peace, and
a good one at that.'

'What thief are you talking about, by the Saints of France?'
Louis asked.

'That Archbishop of Canterbury of yours.'

'I wish mine were like yours,' Louis said.   'You will have great
honour in the eyes of God and men if you make a good peace
with him, and we shall be grateful to you.'[1]

On the following day, Wednesday, August 22, 1170, the feast
of St. Mary Magdalene, Henry and Thomas met in the Traitors'
Meadow, outside Fréteval.   Henry was accompanied by the
Archbishop of Rouen, all the bishops of Normandy, Bishop
Roger of Worcester, and his nobles.   William of Champagne,
Archbishop of Sens, came with Thomas, and many French
bishops and nobles were there.   Louis, at Henry's request, did
not come, but he was represented by Count Theobald.

When Henry saw the two Archbishops approaching he doffed
his cap and rode to meet them.   After he had greeted them he
drew Thomas aside, and they rode out of earshot of the party.
Thomas wrote to the Pope later that he reproached Henry for

[1] Ibid., Vol. III, p. 108.

having the Archbishop of York crown his son, in violation of the rights of Canterbury. After some discussion, Henry admitted that he had done wrong. When Thomas mentioned his love for the young Henry, the King's face brightened, and he said:

'If you love my son, you will have a double reason for doing what you should, for I gave him to you as a son, and you, you will remember, received him from my hand. And he loves you with such affection that he cannot bear the sight of any of your enemies. He would break them into bits if it were not for his reverence and fear of my name.'

Moved by this reference to happier days, Thomas dismounted and knelt at Henry's feet. To the joy of the watching crowd, the King leaped from the saddle and threw his arms around the Archbishop. He held the stirrup and forced him to mount again.

'My lord Archbishop,' he said, 'let us go back to our old love for each other, and let each of us do all the good he can to the other and forget utterly the hatred that has gone before.'

They then turned back to where the courtiers were waiting, and Henry announced the reconciliation. He agreed to all the terms about which there had been such long dispute. He promised to take Thomas back into his favour, to give his peace and security to him and his followers, to give back to him the See of Canterbury and all its possessions, and to make amends for having had his son crowned by the Archbishop of York.[1]

Someone, probably the Archbishop of Rouen, then asked the King to give Thomas the kiss of peace.

'In my own land,' said Henry, 'I will kiss his mouth and his hands and his feet a hundred times; I will hear his Mass a hundred times; but let it be put off for a little while. I am not speaking captiously. It pertains to my honour that he should be seen to defer to me in something; in my land it will seem that he is giving the kiss through grace and kindness, whereas here it would seem to be through necessity.'[2]

Henry asked Thomas to accompany him into Normandy to show that their reconciliation was complete, but the Archbishop, put on his guard by the King's refusal to give him the kiss of peace, declined. He was a guest of the King of France, he said, to whom he was under great obligations, and he could not honourably

---

[1] *Materials*, Vol. VII, pp. 327-34.
[2] William Fitz Stephen, in *Materials*, Vol. III, p. 111.

leave France without first paying his respects to Louis. Henry then told Thomas to send one of his clerks to him later on. The King would give him letters to his son and the justiciars, and the clerk could then cross to England and take possession of the Archbishop's property and that of the other exiles.

Henry knelt and asked the Archbishop for his blessing; Thomas gave it; and the conference broke up at sunset.[1]

Although this was considered a reconciliation and a peace, and many of the bystanders knelt and gave thanks to God and St. Mary Magdalene when the King received Thomas in such friendly fashion, neither one of them had made any concessions to the other. Henry had not signed a 'form of peace' with the Archbishop, and he had not given him the kiss of peace. Indeed, Henry's new insistence that he would give Thomas the kiss only when he was in his own land and his invitation to him to leave France, where he was under Louis's protection, and go with him to Normandy, had a sinister sound in Thomas's ears, as he showed by promptly declining the invitation.

Soon after Henry returned to Normandy, about August 10, he fell so gravely ill of a tertian fever that it was widely reported that he had died. In preparation for his death, Henry divided his lands among his sons. The young Henry was to receive the lands that his father had held by inheritance, that is, England, Normandy, Anjou, and Maine; Richard was to receive Aquitaine, which he was to hold of the King of France; and Geoffrey was to have Brittany, which he likewise was to hold of King Louis. No provision was made for John, the youngest son, beyond that he was to be brought up and provided for by his eldest brother.

Henry then ordered that if he should die his body should be taken to the monastery at Grandmont and buried at the chapel door, at the feet of Stephen of Muret, the founder of the order. The Good Men of Grandmont were a penitential order whose lives were of such rigorous austerity and poverty that the Cistercians appeared sybarites in comparison with them. His bishops and barons protested that such a poverty-stricken church was not a royal burying place and that it would be against the dignity of the realm for him to be buried there. The King insisted, nevertheless, and showed them an agreement he had made with the Good Men to that effect.[2]

---

[1] *Materials*, Vol. VII, p. 342.   [2] *Gesta*, Vol. I, pp. 6–7.

Henry recovered from his illness, and at Michaelmas he made a pilgrimage of thanksgiving to the shrine of Our Lady at Rocamadour, in the Quercy, about forty miles north of Cahors.[1]

Pope Alexander, on September 10, wrote to Thomas in an attempt to justify his own actions with regard to him. If he had seemed remiss on his behalf, it was because he believed it necessary to use patience in order that good might come from evil. He then informed Thomas that he was suspending from their office all the bishops who had taken part in the crowning of the young Henry.

On September 16 the Pope wrote to notify the Archbishop of York and the Bishops of Durham, London, Salisbury, and Rochester of the sentences he had passed upon them because they had crowned the young Henry in defiance of the rights of Canterbury and of the orders of the Pope and of Archbishop Thomas. In his letter to Archbishop Roger the Pope also accused him of having omitted from the coronation ceremony the customary oath binding the King to preserve the liberties of the Church and of having added one to uphold the customs of his ancestors.[2] These letters the Pope sent to Thomas, since they could not be delivered in England.

In the course of this year Eleanor, the King's second daughter, was taken to Castile and married to Alfonso VIII. She was now nine years old. Her husband, three years her senior, had become King of Castile when he was less than two years old.

Henry meanwhile had given some of Thomas's clerks the promised letters ordering his son to restore the possessions of the Archbishop of Canterbury. When the clerks presented the letters to 'the King, the King's son', at Westminster on October 5, the young Henry told them that he would have to take counsel. When they were recalled, Geoffrey Ridel, Archdeacon of Canterbury, speaking for the young King, told them that since Rannulf of Broc and the others had taken possession of the belongings of the archbishopric at the King's orders, they would first have to be informed of the new commands. He therefore directed them to come back on October 15.

The messengers succeeded in speaking more privately with the young Henry when he was on his way from London to Windsor, and he greeted them much more affably than he had when was

[1] Robert of Torigni, p. 248.   [2] Materials, Vol. VII, pp. 357-68.

surrounded by his counsellors. The envoys nevertheless warned the Archbishop not to come back to England until he was more fully restored to the King's favour and good will, for everyone in England was convinced that there could be no peace between the King and the Archbishop, and no one would dare be seen talking with the messengers.[1]

Thomas, when he received their report, wrote to the King to protest against the delay in fulfilling his promise of restitution. Why, he asked, was it necessary for his son to consult Rannulf of Broc before obeying the King's commands?

> In the meantime the aforesaid Rannulf is wasting the goods of the Church and openly heaping up our crops in Saltwood Castle and boasting to many people (as we have learned from men who are ready, if you will, to prove it), that we shall not eat a whole loaf of bread in England before he, as he threatens, will take our life. You know, most serene lord, that a man shares in the guilt of a sin that he can correct but does not do so. And what can Rannulf do, unless he is upheld by your will and armed with your authority?[2]

When the King received this letter, he invited Thomas to meet him for another conference. They met at Amboise, about fifteen miles up the Loire from Tours, on October 12. Both Count Theobald and Archbishop William of Sens accompanied Thomas to make sure that he came to no harm. Henry promised again to make full restitution to the Archbishop and to direct his son to see that it was done. He further promised that an investigation would be made concerning Saltwood Castle, which belonged to the archbishopric and where Rannulf of Broc had established himself with a host of kinsmen and retainers, and that the Archbishop should have what rightfully belonged to him.

The two parties met again early the next morning at Chaumont, about ten miles further up the Loire. The King had his chaplain celebrate a Mass for the dead, at which the kiss of peace is not given, for fear that Thomas might stand near him and thus force him into a position where he would have to give him the kiss.[3]

When the conference was resumed that morning, Henry repeated his promises of peace and restitution, and it was agreed that the King and the Archbishop would meet at Rouen on November 1 and set out for England together.

---

[1] *Materials*, Vol. VII, pp. 389-93.   [2] Ibid., Vol. VII, pp. 393-5.
[3] Herbert of Bosham, in *Materials*, Vol. III, p. 469.

At their parting Henry said: 'Go in peace; I will follow you, and I will see you in Rouen or in England as soon as I can.'

'My lord,' Thomas answered, 'I feel in leaving you that you will never see me again in this life.'

'Do you take me for a traitor?'

'God forbid, my lord,' said the Archbishop.[1]

Thomas and his clerks went back to Sens to prepare for their return to England. He knew that he had done all he could do in exile. He had called the attention of the Pope and of the whole Christian world to his plight. Henry, for his part, had made it clear, by his insistence on his 'royal customs', that the root of the whole difficulty was his attempt to usurp the rule of the Church in England. All that now remained to Thomas was to go back to England and meet whatever the King had in store for him.

He sent John of Salisbury ahead of him to England, where John arrived on November 18. He inspected the manors of the archbishopric and found the houses empty, the barns torn down, the land stripped bare, and all the rents collected up till Christmas. Next he went to the young King and met with a cold reception. Finally, he visited his mother, whom he had not seen for some seven years, for he had been driven into exile even before Thomas left England.

In his letter reporting all this, John said that Archbishop Roger of York, Bishop Gilbert of London, and their accomplices were preparing to go to the King, together with a few canons from each of the five sees then vacant, and there, outside the kingdom, elect bishops for the vacancies according to the King's will. John anticipated that this would place the Archbishop in a difficult position, for if he consecrated the men elected in such a flagrantly uncanonical manner he would offend God, and if he refused to consecrate them he would offend the King.[2]

Thomas meanwhile took leave of his friends. The French provided him and all his clerks with horses, clothes, and every-thing necessary for their journey. When he thanked King Louis for sheltering him and took his leave, Thomas said: 'We are going to England to fight for our lives.'

'So it seems to me,' Louis replied. 'Furthermore, my lord Archbishop, since he has not given you the kiss of peace, if you

[1] William Fitz Stephen, in *Materials*, Vol. III, p. 116.
[2] *Materials*, Vol. VII, pp. 407-9.

listen to me you will not trust your King. Stay here; as long as King Louis lives you will not want for wine and food and all the riches of Gaul.'

'God's will be done,' said Thomas, as they parted in tears.

When he kissed Maurice of Sully, Bishop of Paris, he said: 'I am going to England to die.'[1]

Thomas went to Rouen to meet Henry. When he arrived he found waiting for him, not Henry, as the King had promised, but the detested John of Oxford, with a letter from the King:

> Be it known to you that I could not come to meet you at Rouen at the time that was agreed upon between us, for my friends in France let me know that the King of the French was getting ready to go into the Auvergne against my men, to do harm to them and to my land. These men of the Auvergne also told me the same thing and begged me to come to their help.
>
> Therefore I could not come to you at Rouen at the time that was agreed upon between us, but I am sending to you John, Dean of Salisbury, a clerk of my household, to go with you to England, and by him I am sending word to Henry, the King of the English, my son, to let you have all that is yours well and peacefully and honourably and also to set aright anything that might have been done concerning your affairs that was less than fitting.
>
> And because many things have been reported to me and to my son concerning your delay, which perhaps are not true, it would behove you, I think, no longer to put off your going to England.
>
> At Loches.[2]

Henry was by no means the injured party, as his letter asserted, nor did the Auvergne seem to be in any danger from Louis. Henry, driven by that insatiable lust for further territory that had so alarmed King Louis, was now laying claim to Berri as a part of the Duchy of Aquitaine. He led a large army from Loches, about twenty miles southeast of Tours, by a roundabout way to Bourges, the city under dispute. When he arrived he found Louis already there with an equally large army, ready to contest his claim. Henry had not anticipated any opposition. He therefore asked for a truce and went back to Normandy.[3]

Escorted by John of Oxford, Thomas and his party went to Witsand, in Flanders. When they arrived, Miles, Dean of

---

[1] William Fitz Stephen, in *Materials*, Vol. III, p. 113.   [2] *Materials*, Vol. VII, p. 400.
[3] *Gesta*, Vol. I, pp. 10-11.

Boulogne, brought a message from Count Matthew. 'Take care,' warned the Count; 'those who seek your life are ready. They have besieged the ports, so that when you land they will seize you and either kill you or put you in chains.'[1]

While they were waiting, a ship landed from England. The pilot sought out the Archbishop and told him that he was going to his death, for he himself had seen the armed guards waiting for him at the port.[2]   Thomas also learned that the Archbishop of York and the Bishops of London and Salisbury were waiting at Dover for a ship to take them to Normandy.   In obedience to the King's summons, they were going to conduct, in Henry's presence, a travesty of an election of bishops to the vacant sees of Bath, Chichester, Ely, Hereford, and Lincoln.   Furthermore, the guards at the ports had been ordered to search Thomas, his house-hold, and his baggage as soon as their ship landed and to confiscate any letters they might find from the Pope.

Thomas therefore sent a lad ahead of him bearing the Pope's letters suspending Roger of York and excommunicating Gilbert of London and Jocelin of Salisbury.[3]   The boy succeeded in placing the letters in the hands of the prelates in the presence of witnesses and then in fleeing from the guards.[4]

The Archbishop's clerks, meanwhile, were growing impatient at the delay. 'Look, my lord,' they said; 'we can already see England.   The sails of many ships are billowing in the crossing. Why do we not go aboard?   Are we to be like Moses, who saw the Promised Land but never reached it?'

'Why are you in such a hurry?' Thomas asked.   'In less than forty days after you return, you will want to be anywhere in the world rather than in England.'[5]

The Archbishop and his party sailed from Witsand the day after he had despatched the lad to Dover, and as he neared the English coast Thomas had his great processional cross raised in the prow of the ship.   They landed at Sandwich, a port that belonged to the archbishopric, on Tuesday, December 1. Rannulf of Broc and Gervase of Cornhill, the Sheriff of Kent, were waiting with a body of armed men.   They immediately

---

[1] William of Canterbury, in *Materials*, Vol. I, p. 86.
[2] Herbert of Bosham, in *Materials*, Vol. III, p. 472.
[3] *Materials*, Vol. VII, p. 403.
[4] William of Canterbury, in *Materials*, Vol. I, pp. 89, 95.
[5] William Fitz Stephen, in *Materials*, Vol. III, p. 117.

attempted to seize the Archbishop, but John of Oxford intervened. He showed them the King's letter granting the company peace and safe conduct and ordered them, 'lest it redound to the King's infamy', not to molest the clerks.[1]

The Archbishop and his clerks made a triumphal progress to Canterbury on the following day. The whole population of Kent turned out to line the ten miles of road between the port and the city, and as Thomas passed through each village the parish priest with his cross and his choir fell in ahead of their Archbishop. In Canterbury the bells pealed in deafening crashes all over the city, the cathedral was hung with rich fabrics, and the great organ, with seventy men pumping for all they were worth, sent forth mighty blasts of sound that shook the building.

The Primate prostrated himself before the high altar and then seated himself on the Throne of St. Augustine. After six years of exile, the Archbishop of Canterbury was back in his cathedral. He gave the kiss of peace to each monk of Christchurch and then preached a sermon on the text: 'We have an everlasting city, but not here; our goal is the city that is one day to be.'[2]

On Thursday messengers from the young King came to demand that Thomas lift the sentences of suspension and of excommunication that had been laid upon the Archbishop of York and the two Bishops. Thomas replied that he could not lift the suspension of the Archbishop of York, both because Roger was not under his jurisdiction and because the Pope had expressly reserved that sentence to himself. Although it was not fitting for an inferior to remove a sentence laid by his superior, he would nevertheless venture to absolve the Bishops of London and Salisbury, who were under his jurisdiction, for the sake of peace in the Church and out of respect for the King, if they would swear to obey whatever commands the Pope might lay upon them.

The two Bishops were inclined to accept this condition in order to be freed from the sentence, but Archbishop Roger dissuaded them. He convinced them that it would be better to go on to Normandy, as they had been ordered to do, and report the matter to the King. In the meantime he sent Geoffrey Ridel to the young King to warn him that Thomas was plotting to have him deposed.[3]

---

[1] *Materials*, Vol. VII, pp. 403-4.   [2] Hebrews xiii, 14.
[3] *Materials*, Vol. VII, pp. 405-6.

After Thomas had been at Canterbury a week, he sent messengers to Winchester to tell the young Henry that he was coming to see him, his king and his lord. Thomas had brought three horses as a gift for the young King, the most suitable present he could find for a young man being trained to knighthood. In describing them, William Fitz Stephen, who had rejoined the Archbishop when he returned, shows that he shared his master's eye for horseflesh:

> He had brought with him three costly chargers, of wondrous speed, elegant in stature, beautiful in form, high-stepping, their delicate flanks rippling as they walked, their nostrils quivering, their members trembling, too high-strung to stand still, their housings worked with flowers in various colours, which he intended to give as a new gift to his new lord.[1]

While the messengers were on their way to Winchester, Thomas set out for London. When he drew near the city, an enormous crowd met him. Three miles outside the city the poor scholars and all the clergy of London burst into the *Te Deum*, and, singing and weeping for joy, they led the Archbishop through the kneeling throng. Thomas rode with his head bowed to hide his tears.

The great procession arrived at the Church of St. Mary in Southwark, and while the canons greeted Thomas the crowd sang the *Benedictus Dominus Deus Israel*. Through the mighty roar penetrated the shrill voice of a madwoman, Matilda, crying: 'Archbishop, beware the blade! Beware the blade!'

Thomas spent the night in the hospice of the Bishop of Winchester, in Southwark. On the next day came a messenger from the young King. He forbade Thomas to come to him or to visit any town or city in the kingdom, and he ordered him to return to Canterbury immediately and not to leave that city.

The Archbishop started back for his cathedral. Five of his knights, fearing for his safety, rode with shield and lance to protect the party. Word was immediately sent to the King, in Normandy, that Thomas had raised a large army and was going about the kingdom in coat of mail and helmet to attack his cities and depose his son.[2]

The Archbishop of York and the Bishops of London and Salisbury meanwhile had arrived in Normandy and found the King

[1] *Materials*, Vol. III, p. 122.   [2] Ibid., pp. 122-4.

at his hunting lodge at Bures, near Bayeux. They laid their complaints before him, and these, together with the garbled reports he had been receiving of Thomas's conduct in England, drove him almost mad with rage. He sent a letter of bitter reproach to the Pope, telling him that 'my most dangerous enemy, to live with whom is death for me', was spreading confusion throughout his realm and plotting against him. He asked Alexander to lift the sentences imposed on his subjects and to examine fairly the complaints that had been laid against them.[1]

On Christmas Day, which fell on Friday, Thomas celebrated both the Midnight Mass and the High Mass of the Day in his cathedral. Before the High Mass he preached on the text: 'Peace on earth to men of good will.'[2] He reminded his audience of the long line of Archbishops of Canterbury, some of whom had been canonised as confessors and one of whom, St. Alphege, was venerated as a martyr. It was possible, said Thomas, that they might soon have another martyr.[3]

The King held his Christmas court at Bures, and most of his time was spent in raging against Thomas. 'Over and over again, burning with wrath, in a dreadful voice he cursed all those whom he had nourished, who were beholden to him for the grace of his friendship and the bestowal of benefits, because they would not avenge him on that one priest, who thus disturbed him and his realm and who sought to dismiss him from his dignities and disinherit him.'[4]

Four knights of the King's household, Reginald Fitz Urse, William of Tracy, Hugh of Morville, and Richard the Breton, slipped away from the court on Christmas night and started for England.

Thomas celebrated High Mass on the great feasts of St. Stephen and St. John on the two days immediately following Christmas. On the 27th he sent Herbert of Bosham and Alexander Llewelyn to report to the King of France and the Archbishop of Sens on the difficulties he was undergoing in England, and he sent a messenger to Rome to tell the Pope that the peace that Henry had promised him was no peace.

The four knights, who had taken different roads in order to

---

[1] *Materials*, Vol. VII, pp. 418-20.   [2] Luke ii, 14.
[3] William Fitz Stephen, in *Materials*, Vol. III, p. 130.
[4] Herbert of Bosham, in *Materials*, Vol. III, p. 487.

avoid spreading an alarm, met at Saltwood Castle on Monday and were welcomed by Rannulf of Broc and his family.

On Tuesday morning, December 29, 1170, the Archbishop said Mass, made his confession, and went about his daily round. The four knights, accompanied by Robert of Broc, Rannulf's brother, and a dozen knights from Saltwood Castle, rode to Canterbury. The four conspirators and Robert of Broc went directly to the Archbishop's house, while the remainder of the group rode through the town, ordering the people to stay in their houses, no matter what they heard or saw. They could have hit on no more effective way of arousing the people, and the town was soon in an uproar.

When they arrived at the Archbishop's house the four conspirators and Robert entered the hall. It was then a little past mid-afternoon. The Archbishop and his clerks had just finished dinner, and the servants were eating in the hall. When the knights entered, the servants offered them food and drink, which they refused. They went on into the chamber, where Thomas was talking with some of his clerks and monks. They sat sullenly on the floor till at last Thomas turned to them and saluted them.

'The King has sent us to you from across the sea,' Reginald Fitz Urse said, 'to order you to absolve the bishops you excommunicated when you returned to England, to restore those who have been suspended by your authority, and afterwards to go to Winchester to his son the King whose crown you are trying to take away, to make satisfaction for such outrages and to submit to the judgment of his court.'

Thomas patiently explained to them that it was not he but the Pope who had laid the sentences on the bishops; that he had no jurisdiction over the Archbishop of York and could not release him from the Pope's sentence; and that he would absolve the two Bishops from their excommunication if they would swear to submit to the judgment of the Church. He also explained that he had no intention whatever of trying to take away the young King's crown; his only complaint on that score was, not that he had been crowned, but that the one who crowned him did so in violation of the rights and dignities of the See of Canterbury.[1]

The knights broke out in loud threats against him. 'This is the

[1] William Fitz Stephen, in *Materials*, Vol. III, pp. 129-34.

King's order,' they told him: 'that you and all of yours get out of the realm and the land that is under his rule. There will be no peace for you or any of yours from this day henceforth, for you have broken your peace with him.'[1]

'You are wasting your time threatening me,' said the Archbishop. 'If all the swords in England were hanging over my head, you could not sway me from keeping God's justice and obeying the Lord Pope. Foot to foot you will find me in the Lord's battle. I went away once, because I was a timid priest; now I have come back, on the Pope's advice and in obedience to him, to my church. Never again will I leave it. If I can exercise my priesthood in peace, it will be well for me; if not, may God's will be done for me. Moreover, you know what there is between you and me; wherefore I am the more astonished that you should dare to threaten the Archbishop in his own house.' Thomas said this to remind Reginald, William, and Hugh that they had done homage and sworn fealty to him when he was Chancellor and that they were therefore his men.

The loud voices of the knights had drawn all the Archbishop's household into the chamber. Reginald turned to them and said: 'We order you to guard this man so that he cannot get away.'

'I am easily guarded,' said Thomas. 'I will not go away.'

The knights rushed into the courtyard and armed under a mulberry tree. The Archbishop's servants, meanwhile, shut the doors of the hall and bolted them, while the clerks stood about Thomas and debated what they should do. From the cathedral came the cries of the weeping and terrified townspeople, who had taken refuge there when they saw the knights enter the Archbishop's house and the gate close behind them. When the four knights tried to re-enter the hall and found the doors bolted, Robert of Broc, whose family had taken over the Archbishop's house during his exile, showed them where some work was being done on the wall. The carpenters and masons had left their tools there, and with them Robert and the knights started to break through the wall.

The monks urged Thomas to take refuge in the cathedral, but he refused, lest the knights think that he was afraid of them and was running away from them. He had told them that he would not go away, and he intended to wait for them in his chamber.

[1] Edward Grim, in *Materials*, Vol. II, p. 432.

The shouts of the knights could be heard as they tried to force their way, and the monks were filled with terror. They attempted to carry or drag the Archbishop towards the shelter of the cathedral, but he stoutly resisted. Then they told him that the community had already begun Vespers and that his place was in the cathedral, taking part in the Divine Office. At that appeal to his dignity, Thomas yielded. He would not give the impression of running away to hide, however. He called for his cross-bearer, so that they might go in seemly fashion. Alexander Llewelyn had been sent abroad, and Henry of Auxerre was acting in his place.

With his cross duly carried before him and with his terrified monks and clerks leading the way, the Archbishop started for the cathedral. Since the courtyard was full of shouting knights, they went through a little-used door into the monastery cloister, which lay between the Archbishop's house and the cathedral.

They entered into or near the north transept. The monks in the choir, who had already begun Vespers, stopped their chant and hurried to meet the Archbishop, for word was beginning to spread that he had been killed. They could see the knights coming across the cloister, and they wanted to close and bolt the door.

'God forbid,' said Thomas, 'that we should make His house into a fortress! Let everyone who wants to come into God's church come in. May God's will be done!'[1] Then he started for his usual place in the choir and went up a few steps from the north transept into the choir.

Reginald Fitz Urse rushed into the cathedral, shouting: 'Follow me, King's men!' Hard on his heels came the other three. They were all armed in coat of mail and helmet, with their visors down and their eyes gleaming through the slits. Only by the devices on their shields could they be distinguished. They carried drawn swords in their hands. Behind them were the armed knights from Saltwood Castle and a renegade subdeacon, Hugh of Horsea, known as Hugh Evil-Clerk.

At the sight of them, John of Salisbury and most of the monks and clerks fled, some to hide in the crypt, others behind the altars, and some in the roof. 'Thinking that I too would be struck by the sword,' confesses William of Canterbury,[2] 'aware of my sins

---

[1] William Fitz Stephen, in *Materials*, Vol. III, pp. 134-9.
[2] In *Materials*, Vol. I, pp. 133-4.

and not fit for martyrdom, in a quick denial I climbed the stairs, beating my hands together.'

William Fitz Stephen, Robert of Merton, the Archbishop's aged confessor, Edward Grim, an English priest from Cambridge who had come to see the Archbishop, and a few monks stood beside Thomas. The Archbishop took his stand against a pillar in the southeastern corner of the north transept, near St. Benedict's altar, and waited.

'Where is that traitor?' cried one of the knights in the gathering darkness of the cathedral. The long winter night had already begun, and only the flickering candles and lamps lighted the great building.

Thomas stood in silence.

'Where is the Archbishop?' shouted another.

'Here am I,' cried Thomas, 'no traitor, but a priest of God. And I am amazed that you come into God's church in such guise. What do you want?'

'Your death, for it is unbearable that you should live any longer,' said one of the knights, as they ran up to the Archbishop.

'And I embrace death,' Thomas said, 'in the name of the Lord, and I commend my soul and the cause of the Church to God and Blessed Mary and the patron Saints of this church. God forbid that I should flee from your swords, but by God's authority I forbid you to touch any of my men!'[1]

Then they tried to lay hands on him and drag him outside the cathedral, but Thomas would not be moved. He seized Reginald, all unwieldy in his coat of mail, and hurled him staggering.

'You pander!' cried the Archbishop. 'Do not touch me, Reginald, for you lawfully owe me fealty and obedience. You are mad to come here with your accomplices!'

As the other knights tried to drag him outside, for fear that the townspeople gathered in the cathedral would attempt to rescue him, the few remaining monks and Edward Grim held firmly to him.

'I owe you no fealty or obedience against my fealty to my lord the King,' Reginald said, as he recovered his balance. Then he raised his sword, and at the sight of the instrument of death the Archbishop bowed his head and murmured the names of God and St. Mary and the blessed martyr Denis. Edward Grim lifted

[1] William Fitz Stephen, in *Materials*, Vol. III, pp. 140-1.

his arm to protect the Archbishop, and the sword cut his arm almost to the bone.   The blow knocked off the Archbishop's cap, cut off a part of the crown of his head, and glanced off his left shoulder, cutting his clothes down to his flesh.

When they saw the sword gleaming in the darkness, the few remaining monks fled.   Only William Fitz Stephen, Robert of Merton, and Edward Grim, with his arm almost severed, stood with the Archbishop.   Thomas raised his arm and with his sleeve wiped away the blood that was flowing into his eyes from the wound in his head.

Then William of Tracy dealt the Archbishop two mighty blows on the head with his sword, and Thomas fell forward on his hands and knees.   Edward Grim heard him murmur: 'For the name of Jesus and the safety of the Church, I am ready to embrace death.'[1]

As the Archbishop sank to the pavement, Richard the Breton struck him such a blow that he cut off the top of his head and broke the sword against the stone floor.   All four blows of the murderers were aimed at the crown of the Archbishop's head, which had been anointed with the sacred chrism at his consecration.

'Take that,' Richard cried, 'for the love of my lord William, the King's brother!' Richard had been the man of Henry's younger brother, William.[2]

The fourth knight, Hugh of Morville, had been keeping at bay with his bare sword the townspeople, who watched in speechless horror as their Archbishop was being murdered.   Hugh of Horsea, the Evil Clerk, now leapt on the prostrate body, put his foot on the neck, and dug into the skull with his sword, scattering the Archbishop's brains and blood over the pavement.

'Let's get away from here, knights!' he cried.   'This fellow won't get up again!'[3]

The knights rushed out of the cathedral, crying: 'The King's men!   The King's men!' They plundered the Archbishop's house and stripped it of everything of any value.   They took the horses from the stables and loaded them with plate and vestments and books.   They took all the money they could find, and they

---

[1] Edward Grim, in *Materials*, Vol. II, pp. 436-7.
[2] William Fitz Stephen, in *Materials*. Vol. III, p. 142.
[3] Edward Grim, in *Materials*, Vol. II, p. 438.

collected every scrap of writing and sent it across the Channel to the King.[1]

The news of the murder reached Henry at Argentan on New Year's Day. He lost no time in writing to the Pope:

To Alexander, by the grace of God Supreme Pontiff, Henry, King of the English, Duke of the Normans and Aquitainians, and Count of the Angevins, sends greetings and due devotion.

Out of reverence for the Roman Church and love for you, which, as God is my witness, I have faithfully sought and always kept till this present time, I granted peace and the full restitution of his possessions, according to your order, to Thomas, Archbishop of Canterbury, and allowed him to cross over to England with a fitting retinue.

He, however, on his coming brought not the joy of peace but fire and the sword, when he made accusations against me concerning the realm and the crown. Furthermore, he attacked my servants indiscriminately and excommunicated them without cause.

Not being able to bear such effrontery from the man, those he had excommunicated and other men from England rushed in upon him and, what I cannot say without sorrow, killed him.

Wherefore I am gravely concerned, as God is my witness, for I fear that the anger I had formerly conceived against him may be accounted as the cause for this evil deed.

And because in this deed I fear more for my reputation than for my conscience, I beg Your Serenity to encourage me with the healthful medicine of your advice in this matter.[2]

[1] William Fitz Stephen, in *Materials*, Vol. III, p. 144.
[2] *Materials*, Vol. VII, p. 440.

PART II

THE KING AND HIS SONS

XI

THE ACQUISITION OF IRELAND
1171 - 1172

THE murder of the Archbishop of Canterbury profoundly shocked the whole of Christendom; many men said that it was the most dreadful thing that had happened since the Crucifixion. Bishops and even Popes had been murdered by pagans, but for an archbishop to be hacked to death in the consecrated precincts of his cathedral in the sight of a large crowd of people, by men acting if not on the direct orders certainly at the instigation of a Christian king, was regarded with universal horror.

That Henry was guilty of the murder of Archbishop Thomas no one doubted. Archbishop William of Sens, in reporting the crime to the Pope, wrote that Henry 'admitted to us by a certain Carthusian whom he sent to us that he had been the cause of his death and that he had killed him'. Even the envoys whom the King sent to Alexander immediately after the murder were forced to admit that Henry had been the cause of Thomas's death and that 'something he had said had supplied the murderers with the occasion for killing him'.

The Pope was so moved by the accounts of Thomas's death that he determined to inflict upon Henry, the real cause of it, a punishment of appalling severity. Shortly after Easter Alexander announced that he was going to send legates to the King 'to observe his humility' before they would absolve him of complicity in the murder.[1]

Henry meanwhile was busy making sure of his new acquisition of Brittany. After Duke Conan died, on February 20, 1171, the King took an army into the Duchy and demanded the submission of the Breton nobles. Viscount Eudes of Perhoët refused to do homage to him, and Henry promptly drove him out of Brittany. Viscount Guiomar of Léhon, when he saw the size of Henry's army and the severity with which he treated Eudes, came to the

[1] *Materials*, Vol. VII, pp. 443, 476-8.

King on Whitsunday, May 16, and surrendered himself and his castles to him. Acting in his son Geoffrey's name, Henry thus made himself the ruler of Brittany.

During this spring, Count Humbert III of Maurienne sent an envoy to the King to propose a marriage between his eldest daughter, Alice, and Henry's youngest son, John. Humbert's territory of Maurienne, corresponding to the modern Savoy, was of great strategic importance, for it commanded the principal Alpine passes between France and Italy. He had no sons and proposed to settle his County on Alice. Henry was greatly pleased at the bright prospects this offered his youngest son, for whom no adequate provision had yet been made, and he sent the envoy back with an encouraging answer.[1]

Ever since the beginning of his reign, Henry, in his ceaseless quest for further lands to add to his empire, had had a half-formed intention of going to Ireland and asserting his authority over that country. In 1155 he had put away for future use a bull from the Pope authorising him to bring Ireland under subjection, and recent events there led him to believe that this was the proper time to put his plans into effect.

Dermot McMurrough, King of Leinster, had been driven out of Ireland by Rory O'Conor, High King of Ireland, and Tiernan O'Rourke, Lord of Meath, in 1166. Dermot had gone to Henry in Aquitaine to ask for his help in regaining his kingdom. Although Henry had been too busy at the time with his efforts to subdue the rebels in Aquitaine to give him any assistance, he had received Dermot's fealty and authorised him to enlist the help of any of his subjects who might be willing to embark on such an adventure.

Richard of Clare, Earl of Pembroke, known as 'Strongbow', was the most powerful man to respond to Dermot's invitation. He had great holdings in South Wales and was able to raise a large army there. Dermot promised him both the hand of his daughter, Eva, and the succession to the Kingdom of Leinster in return for his help. Strongbow landed in Ireland with over a thousand soldiers in August 1170. Dermot meanwhile with the help of other English and Welsh adventurers had regained his kingdom. With the arrival of Strongbow he aspired to even greater things, and the allies captured Waterford and Dublin. True to

[1] Robert of Torigni, pp. 249-50.

his promise, Dermot gave Strongbow his daughter, and when he died, in May 1171, Strongbow succeeded to his title and lands.

Henry now became alarmed that one of his subjects should be setting himself up as a king in a land upon which Henry had designs, and he ordered Strongbow to come and give an accounting of his actions and intentions. The Earl sent word that he had gone to Ireland with Henry's permission and that he was ready to do homage and swear fealty to him for his Irish lands. Henry then determined to go to Ireland and investigate the state of affairs for himself.

He held a council of his barons at Argentan in July 1171 and announced his intentions to them. An added reason for his expedition to Ireland was that two papal legates were said to have reached France and to be even now on their way 'to observe his humility'. When the King heard this rumour he made his plans to cross the Channel without delay.

After giving strict orders that no-one and especially no clerks or pilgrims were to be permitted to cross the Channel without first giving securities that they intended no evil or harm to the King or the realm, Henry sailed for England on August 1 and landed at Portsmouth on the 3rd. His first act was to order that any bearer of papal letters who succeeded in landing was to be seized as a public enemy. Henry was taking no chances on allowing the legates to follow him to England.

From Portsmouth the King went to Winchester to visit Bishop Henry, who was on his deathbed. The gallant old Bishop had been blind for some time. He bitterly reproached the King for having caused Thomas's death. He died, 'old and full of days', on August 8, having been Bishop of Winchester for forty-two years.[1] He left his vast wealth to be divided between the Church and the poor, and he gave his great treasure of vestments and gold and silver vessels and illuminated books to his cathedral.[2] Under his direction and inspiration, the monks of St. Swithun's Priory at Winchester had produced some of the most beautiful manuscripts that have ever been made. His Psalter, now in the British Museum, and the great Bible in three volumes, still to be seen in the Chapter Library at Winchester, show a delicacy and richness that made them outstanding examples of British book illumination.

[1] Ralph of Diceto, Vol. I, p. 347.   [2] Robert of Torigni, p.252.

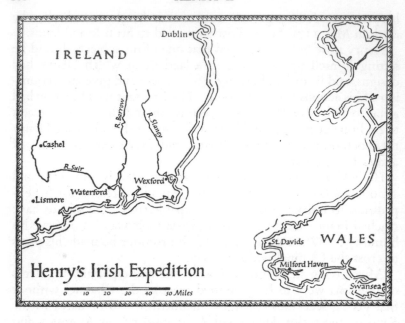

Henry's Irish Expedition

The King spent the month of August in preparing for his expedition to Ireland. At the beginning of September he assembled his army in Gloucestershire on the edge of the Forest of Dean, whence they were to march to Milford Haven and meet the ships collecting there. While Henry was at Newnham, Rhys ap Gruffydd came to him and made a treaty of peace. After the death of Owain Gwynedd in the previous November, Rhys had become the undisputed leader of the Welsh. He had attained this position the more easily because Earl Richard of Pembroke and many of the more adventurous of the Anglo-Normans in South Wales had gone off to Ireland and left him with no rivals of importance. Rhys promised to turn over twenty-four hostages to Henry as pledges of his loyalty, and he undertook to furnish three hundred horses and four thousand head of cattle for the army.

When he heard that Henry was preparing to go to Ireland, Strongbow, now glorying in the title of Earl of Leinster, hastened to meet him. He came to the King at Newnham around September 8 and made an abject submission to him. He agreed to surrender Dublin and the adjacent territory and all the towns and castles along the coast, and he promised that he and his heirs would hold the rest of Leinster as a fief of Henry and his heirs.[1]

Accompanied by Strongbow and Rhys ap Gruffydd, Henry and his army marched across South Wales to Milford Haven, where they were detained for almost a month by unfavourable winds.   They sailed at last on Saturday, October 16, 1171, with a fleet of four hundred ships, carrying an army of around four thousand men, of whom five hundred were knights.   They landed at Croch, eight miles from Waterford, on the following day.   On Monday the King entered Waterford.   The officials whom he had sent over ahead of him received him with great honour.   Ragnald, chief of the men of Waterford, made his submission to the King, and Strongbow did formal homage and surrendered to the King the territories they had agreed upon at Newnham.

As the news of the King's arrival spread, the Irish chieftains of their own accord came to make their submission.   The first was Dermot McCarthy, King of Cork, who swore an oath of fealty to Henry, gave hostages for his fidelity, and promised to pay a yearly tribute.   After staying a fortnight at Waterford, the King went on to Lismore and then to Cashel.   Donell O'Brien, King of Limerick, came to him and made his act of submission, as did the lesser chieftains of Munster.   Within this short time, thanks to his fame, to his imposing army, and to the strife of the Irish amongst themselves, Henry secured the whole of southern Ireland at no effort beyond that of showing himself there.[2]

The King went on to Dublin about November 11.   All the remaining leaders of the Irish, except the King of Connaught, came to him, did homage to him for their lands, and swore fealty to him.   Roderick, King of Connaught, declared that he himself was the rightful King and lord of all Ireland, and he refused to submit to Henry.   The King could not conduct a military operation against him that winter 'because of the inundation of the water and the steepness of the mountains and the wilderness of lands that were between them'.[3]

Henry's new Irish subjects built a palace for him outside the walls of Dublin, wondrously constructed of wattles, after the fashion of their land.[4]   There he held his Christmas court with

---

[1] Gerald of Wales: *Expugnatio Hibernica*, p. 273.   [2] Ibid., pp. 276-8.
[3] *Gesta*, Vol. I, pp. 25-26.   [4] Ibid., Vol. I, pp. 28-29.

the kings and richer men of Ireland.   At the enormous dinner of the day, roast cranes, which the Irish had hitherto abhorred, were served, and Henry induced his guests to eat crane for the first time.[1]

While Henry was celebrating Christmas in Ireland, his eldest son was in Normandy.

> Henry, the young King, was at Bures, near Bayeux, at Christmas, and because he was holding his first court in Normandy, he wanted to have the festival celebrated in a magnificent fashion.   Bishops, abbots, counts, and barons were there, and many gifts were given to many men.   And to show what a multitude was present, when William of St. John, the Procurator of Normandy, and William son of Hamon, the Seneschal of Brittany, who had come with Geoffrey, Duke of Brittany, his lord, were eating in a certain room, they forbade any knight whose name was not William to eat in the same room.   When they put the others out of the room, there remained a hundred and ten knights who were all named William, in addition to many others of the same name who ate in the hall with the King.[2]

The bishops of Ireland, assembled at Cashel immediately after Christmas, received Henry as their king and lord, swore fealty to him against all men, and sent him letters confirming to him and his heirs the kingdom of Ireland.   Then they passed a number of constitutions to bring the usages of the Church in Ireland into conformity with those of the Universal Church.   Having secured the fealty and allegiance of the kings and bishops of Ireland, Henry lacked only the Pope's approval to make his title unassailable. He therefore sent the decrees of the council and the bishops' letters of submission to Alexander, with the request that he confirm Henry and his heirs in their possession of the kingdom of Ireland.[3]

The winter was one of such violent storms and such a prevailing westerly wind that no ship could cross from England and Henry was cut off from all his other lands.   He stayed in Dublin till Candlemas Day, February 2, 1172, and then went on a leisurely progress to Wexford, arriving on March 1.   He remained there a month, still cut off from England by the bad weather and unable for the same reason to proceed against the King of Connaught, the only chieftain who had refused to submit to him.

Towards the end of March the first ships landed from England

[1] Gerald of Wales, op. cit., pp. 279–80.   [2] Robert of Torigni, p. 253.
[3] *Gesta*, Vol. I, p. 28.

since the beginning of the year. They brought the news that the Cardinals Albert and Theodwine were waiting for Henry in Normandy and that they were threatening to lay all his lands under interdict if he did not come to them immediately. By now the whole Christian world was ringing with accounts of the miracles that were being wrought at Thomas's tomb at Canterbury. These reports, which would indicate that Thomas was indeed a saint, influenced the Cardinals to adopt a more peremptory tone to the King than any other legates had heretofore used. They also changed Henry's attitude. Instead of ignoring the legates and closing both his ports and his ears to their messengers, the King now hastened to comply with their orders.

Henry abandoned his plans for remaining in Ireland till he could conquer Connaught and set about making provision for the government of the country after his departure. He gave the whole of Meath to Hugh of Lacy, put him in command of the city of Dublin, with a garrison of twenty knights, and ordered him to build a castle there.[1] Finally, he made him Justiciar of Ireland, a position equivalent to that of viceroy.[2] Earl Richard of Clare was permitted to keep what was left of his County of Leinster.

These measures established Anglo-Norman garrisons in Ireland and introduced feudal tenures after the English model. Henry's most important act was to provide for the colonisation of Dublin by English settlers from Bristol.

> Henry, King of the English, Duke of the Normans and Aquitainians, and Count of the Angevins, to the archbishops, bishops, abbots, earls, barons, justiciars, officials, and all his faithful men, French and English and Irish, in all his land: greetings.
>
> Be it known to you that I have given and granted and by this present charter confirmed to my men of Bristol my city of Dublin, to be inhabited by them.
>
> Wherefore I will and firmly command that they inhabit it and hold it of me and my heirs well and in peace, freely and quietly, wholly and fully and honourably, with all the liberties and free customs that the men of Bristol have at Bristol and through all my land.[3]

[1] *Gesta*, Vol. I, p. 30; Gerald of Wales, op. cit., p. 286.
[2] Roger of Hoveden: *Chronicle*, ed. William Stubbs (Rolls Series, 4 vols., 1868-71), Vol. II, p. 34.
[3] *Historic and Municipal Documents of Ireland*, ed. J. T. Gilbert (Rolls Series, 1870), p. 1.

The King sailed from Wexford early in the morning on April 17, 1172, and landed at Port Stinan, near St. David's, in time to hear Mass at St. David's Cathedral and then to eat the dinner that had been saved for one of the clerks of the church.[1]

The King spent about a fortnight in England on his way to Normandy. It was probably at this time that he gave orders that a scutage was to be collected from all his tenants-in-chief who had neither gone with him to Ireland nor sent knights or money to him. No attempt was made to collect the usual 'gift' or 'aid' from the towns. The bishops and abbots again were assessed on the basis of the returns they had made in 1166 of the old and the new enfeoffments, and again they refused to pay a penny on the new enfeoffments. Little attempt was made, apparently, to assess the lay barons on the new basis. Even so, the sheriffs had great difficulty in collecting from them. The barons offered a great variety of excuses for not paying, and some of them simply could not be found.

The amount collected in this scutage was £2,144, out of a total revenue for the year of £21,000. A substantial part of the revenue came from the vacant bishoprics, which realised over £6,000. Winchester, the richest see in England, brought in over £1,500, and Canterbury around £1,300.[2]

Although there is no record of such discussions, Henry must have conferred with Richard of Luci, his sole Chief Justiciar since the death of Earl Robert of Leicester in 1168, on a growing spirit of disaffection that had begun to manifest itself during the King's long absence. The chief evidence for that disaffection is the fact that large sums of money were spent in strengthening and re-building the royal castles, mainly in East Anglia and the Midlands, and along the Scottish border. Most of the work consisted in replacing the primitive wooden castles that had been built by William the Conqueror with more substantial structures of stone. This work was undertaken on such a scale that one can hardly escape the conclusion that it was intended to meet the possibility of a rebellion of some sort.

Rumours were beginning to circulate, also, concerning the young King's dissatisfaction with the role his father had assigned to him. Now seventeen years old, he had returned to England

---

[1] Gerald of Wales, op. cit., p. 288.
[2] Ramsay, op. cit., Vol. I., pp. 111-13.

shortly after Christmas. Although he had the title of King and had been duly anointed and crowned, his father allowed him no authority whatever. England was ruled, during Henry's absence, by Richard of Luci. Ralph of Diceto[1] says that while the King was in Ireland Ralph of Faye, Queen Eleanor's uncle, and Hugh of St-Maure, a treacherous baron of Anjou, at Eleanor's suggestion tried to turn the young Henry against his father by harping on the anomaly of his position.

Whether or not he had heard these rumours, Henry at any rate took his son to Normandy with him. They sailed from Portsmouth around the middle of May and landed at Barfleur. The King sent messengers at once to the two legates to ask them where it would be convenient for them to meet him. They named the monastery at Savigny, a few miles east of Avranches, 'so that we might be helped by the prayers of religious men', as they explained in a letter to Archbishop William of Sens. They needed the prayers, for when the conference began, on May 17, Henry was as stubborn and as ill-tempered as ever.

The legates made it plain that they did not intend to bargain over the conditions and that they would lay all of Henry's lands under interdict if he did not meet them. The King would not agree to the conditions, and at last he stormed out of the conference and declared that he was going back to England. His Norman bishops explained the gravity of the situation to him and persuaded him that he had no choice but to submit.

The legates met the King and his bishops at Avranches on Sunday, May 21, 1172, and Henry made his compurgation of any complicity in the murder of the Archbishop of Canterbury. As the legates reported, 'First, touching the Holy Gospels, not at our demand but of his own free will he purged his conscience concerning the death of Thomas of holy memory, formerly Archbishop of Canterbury, swearing that he neither ordered it nor willed it, and that when he heard of it he was greatly grieved.'[2]

In his report of his submission Henry omitted any reference to the murder, but even he could not conceal the fact that Thomas, from his tomb, had utterly vanquished the King.

Henry, King of the English, and Duke of the Normans and Aquitainians, and Count of the Angevins, to his dear and faithful Bartholomew, Bishop of Exeter: greetings.

[1] Vol. I, p. 350.   [2] *Materials*, Vol. VII, pp. 520-2.

Be it known to you that by God's grace I landed in Normandy after a favourable voyage and found all my lands across the sea established by God's favour in all peace and tranquillity and my men and faithful subjects, as was fitting, filled with the greatest joy at my coming.

Then I went to my lords the legates, and although at first I found them hard and apparently unyielding, nevertheless, beyond the hope of all and contrary to the opinion of many, the sought-for peace, to the honour of God and the Church and of me and my realm, was restored between us, as you may learn more fully from the following.

These, then, are the conditions I promised, at their instance, to observe: that from the Feast of Pentecost next, for a year, I will give as much money as, in the judgment of the Templars, will support two hundred knights for the defence of the land of Jerusalem for a year, and that I will allow appeals to be made freely to my lord the Pope, with the provision that those of whom I am suspicious will swear before they leave the kingdom that in their journey they will seek neither evil to me nor harm to my realm; and that I will forgo the customs that have been introduced in my time against the churches of my land, which, however, I think are few or none; and that if any possessions of the See of Canterbury have been taken away I will restore them fully, as they were a year before the Archbishop left England. Moreover, I will restore my peace and their possessions to clerks and to lay people of either sex who were dispossessed on account of the aforesaid Archbishop. And this they enjoined on me to observe on the part of my lord the Pope for the remission of all sins.

Now that peace has been restored, I would come to England immediately, if it were not that my lords the legates are to have a conference at Caen on the Tuesday next after the Lord's Ascension. But when I do return, do not delay to come to me immediately.[1]

All this had been done more or less privately, and the Cardinals insisted that Henry repeat his promises in as public a manner as possible. A council of all the Norman bishops and barons had been summoned to meet at Caen on Tuesday, May 30, as Henry had informed Bishop Bartholomew. In the presence of these dignitaries the King once again made the required promises. In addition, he freed the English bishops from their oath to observe the Constitutions of Clarendon and promised not to exact such an oath in the future. His son joined with him in renouncing the Constitutions.[2]

[1] *Materials*, Vol. VII, p. 518.   [2] Ibid., Vol. VII, pp. 522-3.

Richard, Henry's second son, was now in his fifteenth year. Inasmuch as his eldest son had been crowned King of England when he was fifteen, Henry determined that Richard should be formally recognised as Duke of Aquitaine. Richard seems always to have been Eleanor's favourite son, and it was at her request and prompting that Henry made this decision. On Sunday, June 11, 1172, Richard was solemnly enthroned in the abbot's seat at St. Hilary's Abbey at Poitiers. Archbishop Bertrand of Bordeaux and Bishop John of Poitiers gave him the lance with the banner of the Dukes of Aquitaine flying from it.

Then the party, which no doubt included Queen Eleanor, went to Limoges and was received with a great procession. The prelates put on Richard's finger the ring of St. Valerie, the sacred insigne of the Dukes of Aquitaine, saying:

> Receive the ring of dignity and by this know that it is in you the seal of the Catholic Faith; for you are today instituted Duke and Prince of Aquitaine, so that, happy in your deeds and abounding in faith, you may rejoice with the Lord of Hosts, to Whom is honour and glory.[1]

Richard was then proclaimed Duke of Aquitaine by all the people. Just as in the coronation of the young Henry, there was nothing provisional about the ceremony. Richard was not only the acknowledged heir to the Duchy; he was now Duke of Aquitaine.

Now that he had made his peace with the Church, the King, on the advice of the legates, met Louis, who was accusing him of having broken his promise, made two years previously, to have Margaret crowned with her husband. Henry agreed to have the ceremony performed immediately. He sent the young couple to England, escorted by Archbishop Rotrou of Rouen and Bishops Roger of Worcester and Giles of Evreux. On August 27 Archbishop Rotrou anointed and crowned Margaret as Queen of England and crowned Henry in St. Swithun's Cathedral at Winchester, with Bishops Roger and Giles assisting him. This most unusual step of having a foreign archbishop crown the Queen of England was taken because Louis, out of love and respect for the memory of Archbishop Thomas and also because

---

[1] *Ordo ad benedicendum Ducem Aquitaniae*, in *Rerum Gallicarum Scriptores* (Paris, 1781), Vol. XII, p. 451.

they were personally loathsome to him, insisted that Archbishop Roger of York and the Bishops of London and Salisbury be forbidden even to attend the ceremony.[1]

On September 20 Pope Alexander wrote letters to Henry, to the bishops, and to 'the kings and princes of Ireland', confirming Henry's title to the island and ordering the Irish, about whom he had been receiving some shocking reports, to obey the King with all due submission. To the bishops he wrote:

It is known to us from your letters and it has come to the notice of the Apostolic See from the trustworthy accounts of others with what enormities of vices the Irish people are infected and how, since they have neglected the fear of God and the religion of the Christian faith, those things have followed that bring peril to their souls.

We understand from your letters that our dearest son in Christ, Henry, the illustrious King of the English, moved by the divine inspiration and bringing together his forces, has subjected to his rule those barbarous and uncivilised people, ignorant of the Divine Law, and that they have begun to desist from those things that were being done unlawfully in your land.

Wherefore we are filled with joy and give hearty thanks to Him Who conferred such a victory and triumph upon the aforesaid King. And we pray that through the vigilance and care of that same King, with your careful help, those undisciplined and wild people may learn the service of the Divine Law and the religion of the Christian faith, through all things and in all things, and that you and the other men of the Church may enjoy due honour and tranquillity.[2]

At the beginning of November the King ordered the young Henry and his wife to cross over to Normandy and join him. The young King much preferred the independence of his own court and household in England, and he came most unwillingly. Since King Louis had expressed a desire to see his daughter, Henry sent the young couple to visit him.

Louis received them 'with great honour and joy', and they stayed several days with him. Henry complained to his father-in-law that although he had been crowned King of the English and had done homage to Louis for Normandy, his father would allow him no power or authority in either country. In addition, the King complained constantly of his son's extravagance and kept him on an absurdly small allowance.

[1] Ralph of Diceto, Vol. I, pp. 352-3.
[2] *Liber Niger Scaccarii*, Vol. I, pp. 42-43.

Louis heard these complaints most sympathetically. He advised the young man, when he went back to Normandy, to demand that his father give him complete control over either England or Normandy, so that he could settle down with his wife and gain some experience in governing the lands that were already his in name. If his father would not do this, Louis told the young Henry to come back with his wife to France. Louis was both his father-in-law and his lord, to whom he had done homage and sworn fealty, and the King of France would see to it that his liege man received justice from his vassal, the King of England.[1]

[1] *Gesta*, Vol. I, p. 34.

XII

'THE ENGLISH DO NOT KNOW HOW TO FIGHT'
1173

KING Henry and Queen Eleanor held their Christmas court
of 1172 at Chinon, in Anjou. It is to be hoped that
Eleanor enjoyed the feasting and the pageantry, for this
was to be the last time that she presided as Queen of England as
long as her husband lived. She was drawn into the web that
Louis was weaving for Henry's downfall, and thus she accomplished her own undoing. The immediate occasion for the up-
heaval that threatened to disrupt Henry's empire and that left
Eleanor behind prison bars was a treaty for the marriage of her
youngest son, John.

Count Humbert III of Maurienne, who two years earlier had
proposed a match between his daughter Alice and the young
John, sent messengers to Henry to invite him to come to a con-
ference and make the formal betrothal of the children. The
King summoned his eldest son from Normandy, where the young
Henry and his wife, after their visit to King Louis, had spent their
Christmas at Bonneville, and father and son went together to
Montferrand in the Auvergne. Around Candlemas, February 2,
1173, Count Humbert arrived with his daughter, and the contract
was drawn up.

Henry promised to pay Count Humbert five thousand marks
in three instalments, the last to be paid when John and Alice were
married. Humbert for his part agreed to make John his heir to
the County of Maurienne. When the contract was sealed and
witnessed, Count Humbert gave his infant daughter to King
Henry to be brought up in his family.

The party then went to Limoges, arriving there about February 21. Now that the betrothal contract had been sealed and
Alice delivered to Henry, her father began to fear that he had
made a poor bargain. His prospective son-in-law, although he
was a son of the King of England, had no land and no prospects

of any, since his father had already divided his lands amongst his three eldest sons.   Count Humbert therefore asked Henry what and how much of his lands he intended to give John, to match the magnificent dowry his daughter was bringing.

Henry replied that he would give John the castles of Chinon, Loudon, and Mirebeau.   These castles were all in Anjou, and Anjou had already been assigned to the young Henry.   The young King, bursting with his grievances, flatly refused to relinquish the castles to his brother, either then or at any time in the future.   Futhermore, he renewed his demand that his father free him from the leading-strings in which he was kept, allot him a definite portion of the lands to which he had nominal title, and allow him to exercise an independent authority there.   He did this 'at the counsel of the King of France and at the counsel of the earls and barons of England and of Normandy, who hated his father'.[1]   A further grievance was that Henry had dismissed from his son's retinue some knights, including one Asculf of St-Hilaire, whom he considered to have a bad influence over him.[2] Father and son quarrelled so violently that no-one could make peace between them.

When the council at Limoges was dismissed, on February 28, Henry took his discontented son with him and started for Normandy as quickly as possible.   They reached Chinon on the evening of March 5, and Henry made ready to spend the night there.   During the night his son slipped away with a few of his friends and followers and rode as far as Alençon the next day. By the 7th the young Henry had reached Argentan, and his father, having lost a night's ride, arrived at Alençon.   The young Henry rode all night, crossed the French border, and by cockcrow of the 8th reached the King of France, at Chartres.[3]

When Henry found out where his son had taken refuge, he sent envoys to Louis to ask him to send the young man back to him, and he promised that if there had been anything amiss in his treatment of his son he would take the advice of his council and set it right.

'Who sends me such orders?' asked Louis.

'The King of the English,' the envoys replied.

'That is not true.   The King of the English is here present, and

[1] *Gesta*, Vol. I, p. 41.   [2] Robert of Torigni, pp. 255-6.
[3] *Gesta*, Vol. I, pp. 41-42.

he sends me no orders by you.   But if you call his father, who
was formerly King of the English, King now, let it be known to
you that that King is dead, for he resigned his realm to his son, as
everyone knows.'[1]

Henry distrusted Louis at all times and especially now that he
was posing as the champion of his son.   He therefore hastened to
Normandy to make an inspection of the castles along the French
border, where trouble might first be expected.   He went first to
Gisors, his chief fortress in the Vexin, and saw to it that it was
well stocked with supplies and its garrison alerted to possible
trouble.   Then he went all over the Duchy, making sure that the
castles were in a good state of defence.   He also sent orders to the
keepers of his castles in England, Aquitaine, and Brittany to warn
them to be on the alert.

Pope Alexander III, meanwhile, on February 21, 1173, canonised Thomas of Canterbury, whom he had done so little to help
while he was living.   In a letter to the clergy and people of
England, the Pope wrote:

> England is filled with the fragrance and power of the miracles
> and signs that Almighty God is working through the merits of that
> holy and reverend man, Thomas, formerly Archbishop of Canter-
> bury, and the whole body of faithful Christians everywhere rejoices
> that He Who is wonderful and glorious in His saints has made
> illustrious after his death His holy one, whose praiseworthy life
> shone with great glory and merits and was consummated by a
> glorious martyrdom.
>
> Although no-one who gives thought to his life and his praise-
> worthy conversation and considers his glorious passion can doubt
> his sanctity, nevertheless our Saviour and Redeemer has willed that
> the signs of his sanctity should be illuminated after his death by
> splendid miracles, so that all may recognise that he who for Christ's
> sake with the constancy of unshakable virtue bore trials and perils
> has received the reward for his labours and struggles in everlasting
> happiness.
>
> We therefore . . . in the presence of a great gathering of clergy
> and people, at the beginning of Lent, with the mature counsel of
> our brethren, solemnly canonised the aforesaid Archbishop in the
> Church and decreed that his name be written in the catalogue of
> saints.
>
> Wherefore we admonish you and by the authority vested in us

[1] William of Newburgh, p. 170.

strictly order you solemnly to celebrate every year the birthday of the aforesaid glorious Martyr on the day of his passion and beg him with your prayers to obtain forgiveness of our sins, so that he who in life bore exile for Christ's sake and in death the martyrdom of suffering with steadfast strength, moved by the prayers of the faithful, may intercede for us before God.

Given at Segni on March 12.[1]

The flight of the young Henry, far from being a mere piece of childish petulance, as Henry was at first inclined to think, began to turn into an affair of great seriousness. Shortly after Christmas, apparently, Eleanor had quarrelled resoundingly with Henry and then had fled to her Duchy of Aquitaine, taking Richard and Geoffrey with her. Archbishop Rotrou of Rouen wrote her a long letter, placing the blame squarely on her. He concluded:

> Before matters come to a worse end, return with your sons to your husband, whom you are bound to obey and with whom you are forced to live; return lest he mistrust you or your sons. Most surely we know that he will in every way possible show you his love and grant you the assurance of perfect safety. Bid your sons, we beg you, to be obedient and devoted to their father, who for their sakes has undergone so many difficulties, run so many dangers, and undertaken so many labours.
>
> Lest with thoughtless ease what has been acquired with such painful labour be destroyed and dispersed, we say these things to you, most noble queen, for the love of God and in true charity, for you are our parishioner, as is your husband.
>
> We cannot flout justice. Either go back to your husband, or by canon law we shall be compelled and forced to lay the censure of the Church on you. Although we say it unwillingly, unless you return to your senses we shall do this with grief and tears. Farewell.[2]

Eleanor paid no attention to this letter. She sent Richard and Geoffrey to join their elder brother. She then attempted to follow them, disguised as a man, and was captured by Henry's agents. The King, who had long ago ceased to feel any affection for her, if indeed he had ever loved her rather than the rich lands she brought him, had her put in close confinement. Gervase of Canterbury says that the whole affair of the flight of her sons was of her devising and that everything had been planned by her

---

[1] *Materials*, Vol. VII, pp. 547-8.
[2] Peter of Blois: *Epistolae*, in Migne's *Patrologia*, Vol. CCVII, cols. 448-9.

advice. Eleanor, he adds, 'was a very clever woman, born of noble stock, but flighty'. The author of the *Gesta Henrici* says that 'the authors of this heinous treachery were Louis, King of France, and, as some say, that same Eleanor, Queen of England, and Ralph of Faye', her uncle.[1]

Louis's part in the affair was quite clear. In encouraging Henry's sons to rebel against him, Louis may have felt that he was acting entirely within his rights, for the young Henry and Richard had done homage and sworn fealty directly to him for the Duchies of Normandy and Aquitaine. No word was said then about any overriding claims that Henry might have on those duchies and on the fealty of his sons. In the same way, Geoffrey held his Duchy of Brittany of his eldest brother, to whom he had done homage, and not of his father.

Louis, therefore, in furthering this plot for his rival's downfall, could claim to be, as indeed he was, the liege lord of the three lads, and he could also claim that in assisting them in their revolt he was merely doing his duty to his vassals and helping them to gain what was rightfully theirs. Furthermore, his son-in-law had been lawfully anointed and crowned King of England, and his coronation oath had made no reference to any provisional abeyance of his rights while his father was still living.

Louis held a council at Paris during the spring and no doubt presented his arguments along the foregoing lines. He then swore that he would help the young Henry and his brothers with all his power in their war against their father and in gaining the kingdom of England. Count Philip of Flanders, Count Matthew of Boulogne, and Count Theobald of Blois did homage and swore fealty to the young Henry, and he rewarded them with promises of lands in the countries he had set out to conquer. Either at this council or shortly afterwards, a great number of discontented Norman, Breton, and Poitevin nobles joined the cause of the rebels in an effort to free themselves from Henry's oppressive rule.[2]

While his sons and their allies were organising their conspiracy, Henry was occupied with the affairs of the Church. The Legates Albert and Theodwine ordered that the vacant bishoprics in England, as well as the Archbishopric of Canterbury, be filled

[1] Gervase of Canterbury, Vol. I, p. 242; *Gesta*, Vol. I, p. 42.
[2] *Gesta*, Vol. I, pp. 43-49.

immediately.   Six dioceses were vacant, and both Bath and Lincoln had been without a bishop for seven years.   Since Henry
was diverting into his treasury over £6,000 a year from the vacant
sees, he would have been content to let the vacancies continue indefinitely, but the Cardinals were peremptory in their demand.

Henry accordingly wrote to the Pope to assure him not only
that the vacancies would be filled but also that they would be
filled by free elections, in order to remove any suspicion that he
was having his favourites promoted.[1]

The King then ordered the various cathedral chapters to proceed
with their free elections.   To the chapter at Winchester he wrote:

> Henry, King of the English, and Duke of the Normans and Aqui-
> tainians, and Count of the Angevins, to his faithful monks of the
> Church of Winchester: greetings.
> I order you to hold a free election, and I forbid you, however, to
> accept anyone save Richard my clerk, Archdeacon of Poitiers.[2]

The bishops and other clergy met in London at the end of
April and proceeded with the free elections.   The plum of the
vacant sees, Winchester, went to Richard of Ilchester, as Henry
had ordered.   Lincoln, the next in riches and importance, was
given to Geoffrey, the King's bastard son, who was now about
twenty years old.   Geoffrey Ridel, Archdeacon of Canterbury,
was rewarded with Ely.   Reginald, Archdeacon of Salisbury,
the son of Bishop Jocelin, was elected to Bath.   Chichester went
to John, Dean of that diocese, and Hereford to Robert Foliot, a
near kinsman of Bishop Gilbert of London.

Not one of these men was distinguished either for sanctity or
for learning, and several of them were notorious for quite the
contrary.   Their elections, which were of course mere confirma-
tions of their appointments by the King, showed a spirit of obstinate defiance on Henry's part.   Four of the six were either open
enemies of Thomas or closely related to his enemies; not one of
them had supported the Archbishop.   None of Thomas's friends,
on the other hand, was even considered, although John of Salisbury was one of the most able men in England.

Then the clergy turned to the vexing question of a successor to
St. Thomas.   After much discussion, the assembly decided to
refer the matter to the King, who had not yet made his wishes

---

[1] *Materials*, Vol. VII, pp. 553-4.   [2] Delisle-Berger, Vol. I, p. 587.

known. They sent two monks, one of whom was Richard,
Prior of the convent at Dover, to Normandy to find out the
King's pleasure. Bishop Gilbert at the same time wrote to the
King to assure him that he had no aspirations to be Archbishop of
Canterbury, although there is no indication that anyone had pro-
posed his name.[1]

In order to appease the monks of Canterbury, the King allowed
them to elect a monk as their next archbishop. They named
Prior Richard, who had been educated at Canterbury but who
had taken no part in the quarrel between Henry and Thomas.
He was therefore the least objectionable choice the monks could
have made, from the King's point of view.

On Saturday, June 9, all the bishops and bishops-elect accompanied Prior Richard to Canterbury, where the people received
them with a great procession. All the preparations were made
to consecrate Richard on the next day. That evening a messenger arrived with the following letter:

> Henry, by the grace of God King of England and Duke of Nor-
> mandy and Count of Anjou, the son of King Henry, to his dear and
> faithful Odo, Prior of the Church of Canterbury, and to the whole
> convent: greetings and love.
>
> From the account of certain trustworthy men we have learned
> that my father is attempting to institute certain unfitting persons
> into your church and also into the churches of the Province.
>
> And because this cannot be done without our consent, for by
> reason of our kingly anointing we have received the realm and the
> care of the whole realm, we have appealed this matter to the Roman
> See in the presence of many men, and we have, by letter and by our
> envoy, notified our venerable fathers and friends, the Cardinals
> Albert and Theodwine, the Legates of the Apostolic See, that we
> have made this appeal, and they, like prudent men, have deferred
> to the appeal.
>
> We have also notified our faithful Bishops of London, Exeter,
> and Worcester by letter of this appeal. And in the same manner
> that we have appealed, we appeal again under your testimony.[2]

This appeal put a stop to the consecration not only of Prior
Richard but also of the six bishops-elect. That the young
Henry's statement that he had 'received the realm and the care of
the whole realm' was received without question and his injunc-

---

[1] *Materials*, Vol. VII, pp. 555-7.   [2] Gervase of Canterbury, Vol. I, p. 245.

tion obeyed is evidence that his conspiracy, no matter how far it may have advanced on the Continent, was not yet taken seriously in England.

Even Henry seemed as yet undisturbed by the flight of his sons and the reports that must have been reaching him of the preparations under way in France. Ralph of Diceto says that he spent this time in Rouen, hunting even more than usual, showing a cheerful face to all comers, and replying patiently to his petitioners. It was not till many of those whom he had brought up from childhood, whom he had knighted, and whom he had made his constant companions and friends began to desert him that he realised the seriousness of the revolt.[1]

From plotting the young Henry and his supporters now proceeded to action. Towards the end of June Count Philip of Flanders invaded Normandy with a large army and laid siege to Aumâle. It was easily captured, for Count William the Fat, whom Henry had deprived of his title of Earl of York in the first year of his reign, merely put up a token resistance. Never an enthusiastic supporter of King Henry, he was now, through old age and bulk, little inclined to resist the Flemings. He and his knights surrendered, and Philip held them for ransom.

About a week later the young Henry and his brothers joined Count Philip and his brother, Count Matthew, and besieged the castle of Driencourt, at Neufchâtel. It was probably in preparation for this taste of war that the young Henry was knighted. Someone suggested to him that his friends would fight more boldly if they were led by him as a knight. The young man agreed readily and said: 'Truly, the best knight that ever was or ever will be, who has done and will do the most, shall gird me with the sword, God willing.'

When a sword was brought to him, Henry, ignoring the counts and barons, went to his friend William Marshal, a landless knight, held out the sword to him, and said: 'From God and from you, gentle sir, I would have this honour.'

William girded the sword about his young master's waist and kissed him, and thus the young King became a knight.[2]

King Louis, as his sovereign lord, knighted Richard during this year,[3] perhaps at the same time that his elder brother was knighted.

---

[1] Vol. I, pp. 373-4.   [2] *Histoire de Guillaume le Maréchal*, lines 2069-92.
[3] *Gesta*, Vol. I, p. 63.

The siege of Driencourt lasted a fortnight.   In the course of the fighting Count Matthew was gravely wounded.   Shortly after the castle was taken, he died of his wounds.   His wife Mary, the daughter of King Stephen, who had been taken out of her convent by King Henry and married to him, had borne him two daughters. In 1170 she retired to a convent at Montreuil, and her husband, by what juggling of dispensations it is not stated, then married Eleanor, the widow of the Count of Nevers.   She was a daughter

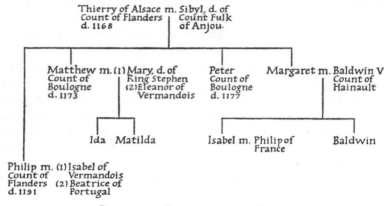

VII COUNTS OF FLANDERS AND BOULOGNE

of Count Ralph of Vermandois and Queen Eleanor's sister, Petronilla, and her sister, Isabel, was married to Matthew's brother Philip.[1]   Since Matthew had no sons, upon his death his brother Peter, who had been elected Bishop of Cambrai but had not yet been consecrated, renounced his bishopric, had himself knighted, and became Count of Boulogne.   Philip, after the fall of Driencourt, returned to Flanders by way of Eu, for Count John of Eu had already joined the young King and turned his County over to him.[2]

Count Philip's return to Flanders just as Louis was beginning extensive operations in Normandy led Henry and his officials in England to suspect that Philip might be planning to invade England.   They therefore sent out an extensive fleet 'to guard the sea' during the summer.[3]

[1] Robert of Torigni, p. 246.
[2] *Gesta*, Vol. I, p. 49; Ralph of Diceto, Vol. I, p. 373.
[3] Pipe Roll 19 Henry II, pp. 2, 13, 43, 117.

At the same time that the young Henry was getting his first taste of warfare at Driencourt, King Louis presented a much more serious threat to Normandy by laying siege with a large army to Verneuil. He was well equipped with stone-throwers and other siege engines, but Verneuil was one of Henry's strongest fortifications along the border. In addition to the well fortified castle, the town was divided into three wards, each surrounded by a moat and a strong wall. Hugh of Lacy, whom the King had recalled from Ireland to help him, and Hugh of Beauchamp were in command, and they put up a stout resistance.

It was probably in the latter part of June, when the full gravity of the situation became evident, that Henry made a quick trip to England to discuss the matter with his Chief Justiciar. No chronicler mentions it, and we have no certain knowledge of Henry's whereabouts from Easter, when he held his court at Alençon, till early in August, when he started to the relief of Verneuil, beyond the statement of Ralph of Diceto that he spent the time at Rouen. This trip is referred to only in the Pipe Roll:

[Southampton]: For the expenses of the Esnecca [the King's ship] when it crossed to Normandy to meet the King, £7 10s.

For hiring a cart to carry the King's bags to Winchester, 9d.

[Northamptonshire]: For the King's maintenance at Northampton for 4 days, £32 6s. 5d.

And for the Sheriff's expenses, £72 11s. 9d., for robes that he bought for the King.[1]

At about this same time Earl Robert of Leicester and William of Tancarville, the Chamberlain, collected all the money they could find and went to the justiciars in London to ask leave to cross over to Normandy. They swore the required oath of fealty to the King, but when they reached Normandy they joined the young Henry. The Earl of Leicester was the first of the English barons to desert to the young King, and his defection is the more surprising in view of the fact that he was the son of the man who had been Henry's Chief Justiciar and one of his most faithful supporters. No chronicler assigns any reason for his action. He went to his castle at Breteuil and prepared to resist the King. Henry had his vast estates in England confiscated, his stock sold, and his men heavily fined, and the land of William of Tancarville was likewise confiscated.[2]

[1] Ibid., pp. 33-34, 55.　　　　　　　　　　[2] Ibid., pp. 102-4, 196.

When Earl Robert's treachery became known in England, the Chief Justiciar and the King's uncle, Earl Reginald of Cornwall, summoned 'the army of England', the national levy of all free men, as contrasted to the feudal levy of the barons and their knights. On July 3 they laid siege to the city of Leicester, where the Earl's followers had gathered in the strongly fortified castle. An enormous army was raised, and vast preparations were made for this 'war of Leicester'.

Even with their great host of soldiers and array of siege engines the army could not take the castle. After more than three weeks of siege the attackers set fire to the city on July 28, and the citizens sued for peace. They were amerced three hundred marks and allowed to go wherever they pleased, with their chattels, till peace should be restored. When the town had been evacuated, the attackers tore down the gates and demolished the walls. The knights of the impregnable castle then agreed to a truce till Michaelmas.[1]

To help pay the expenses of the 'war of Leicester', the Chief Justiciar laid a tallage on the boroughs and the royal demesne and collected around £2,500.[2]

While Richard of Luci was besieging Leicester and King Louis was besieging Verneuil, Henry was busy suppressing a rebellion on the borders of Brittany. He had summoned the Breton barons to renew their oaths of fealty to him, to make sure that they did not join his son, and Ralph of Fougères refused to come. Instead, he set to work rebuilding his castle at Fougères, which Henry had previously demolished. Earl Hugh of Chester, the son of the most accomplished turncoat and traitor of King Stephen's reign, had been on a pilgrimage to St. James of Compostella when the revolt broke out, and on his way back he joined Ralph. Asculf of St-Hilaire, whom the King had dismissed from his son's entourage, and a number of other discontented and rebellious knights came to him also.

In anticipation of trouble, Henry had hired a great army of mercenary soldiers, the notorious Brabantines, who were reputed to fear neither God nor man. He sent a detachment of them to devastate Ralph's lands, an assignment after their own hearts, in which they were notably successful. Some of Ralph's men ambushed a large party of them as they were hauling supplies for the

---

[1] Ralph of Diceto, Vol. I, p. 376.　　[2] Ramsay, op. cit., Vol. I, p. 114.

army, and since the Brabantines 'had neither leader nor protector' they were all killed. Ralph, emboldened by this success, then burned the castles of St-James and Tilleul.

The situation was rapidly getting out of hand, and Henry went to take command of the army. Ralph, hearing of his approach, warned all his men to take their horses and arms and cattle and hide in the forest. Before they could reach the safety of the woods, however, Henry's army surprised them and captured a vast quantity of booty. Ralph and his allies succeeded in escaping into the forest.[1] With the rebels thus dispersed but not vanquished, Henry returned to Rouen and learned then of the serious situation at Verneuil.

King Louis had been battering away at the walls of that town for almost a month without any success. By the end of July, however, the inhabitants were facing starvation. They asked for a truce from Louis and offered to surrender on August 9 if they were not relieved by then. Louis agreed to allow them to send messengers to Henry to ask for help, provided they would give him hostages, and he swore that if they surrendered the town to him on the appointed day he would return their hostages and neither do the citizens any harm nor allow anyone else to harm them.

When he received news of their plight, Henry at once set out to relieve Verneuil. In addition to such forces as he could levy in Normandy or bring over from England, he had over ten thousand mercenary soldiers. He arrived at Conches, twenty-five miles north of Verneuil, on August 6 and spent the next day there, waiting for his army to catch up with him. On the 8th they marched to Breteuil, the Earl of Leicester's castle, half-way to Verneuil. When the Earl heard of the King's approach he fled to join Count Philip and left his castle undefended.

As Henry and his captains were drawing up the army in battle array to march against the French, Archbishop William of Sens and the Counts Robert of Dreux, Henry of Champagne, and Theobald of Blois came to him on Louis's behalf to propose that they declare a truce and have a conference concerning the possibility of peace. Henry accordingly granted a truce during the following day and agreed to meet Louis on the morrow to discuss the terms. He then returned with his army to Conches, probably because their supplies were there.

[1] Robert of Torigni, p. 259.

On the following day, August 9, Henry and his army returned to Breteuil to meet the French. This was the third time in two days that the weary foot-soldiers had covered the stretch of road between Conches and Breteuil under the burning summer sun, and there was much grumbling. The army waited till the middle of the afternoon, and the French still did not appear. Then, to the south, in the direction of Verneuil, they saw a great cloud of smoke and flames. Henry and his army dashed to Verneuil as fast as they could and found the town in flames. Louis, when the truce with the citizens had expired, had set fire to the town, sacked it, and carried the inhabitants away as prisoners.

Henry and his forces set out in pursuit and succeeded in capturing or killing a great many stragglers, but Louis and the main body of his army got safely away. Henry returned to Verneuil and spent the night camped outside the smouldering town. He gave orders that the walls were to be rebuilt immediately. On the following day the army took the castle of Damville, a few miles to the east of Breteuil, to give it the feeling that all the marching had not been entirely in vain, and then returned to Rouen.[1]

No sooner had Henry arrived there than he learned of a fresh outbreak in Brittany. Ralph of Fougères and his allies had bribed the castellans of Combourg and of Dol and were using those towns as their headquarters while they devastated the countryside. Henry once more sent his Brabantines to deal with Ralph. They succeeded in putting the Breton knights to flight and in killing many of the foot-soldiers. They captured Asculf of St-Hilaire and several other knights, who were then imprisoned at Pontorson.

Ralph of Fougères, the Earl of Chester, and sixty knights were cut off and took refuge in the castle of Dol. The Brabantines, the King's knights, and the populace of the district, who had suffered cruelly from the raids, besieged the castle on August 20. Henry, at Rouen, 145 miles away as the crow flies, received the news of this latest development on the evening of the 21st and arrived at Dol at mid-morning on the 23rd to take charge of operations. He had his stone-throwers set up and put to work battering the castle into submission. The garrison surrendered on Sunday, the 26th. Henry sent Earl Hugh of Chester to be

[1] *Gesta*, Vol. I, pp. 50-56.

imprisoned at Falaise. Ralph of Fougères gave his two sons, Juhel and William, as hostages for his good behaviour. In spite of this, he refused to submit to the King and escaped to the forest. Henry had his Brabantines demolish Ralph's castles and devastate his lands.[1]

This crushing defeat marked the end of the revolt in Brittany. Henry went to Le Mans in high good humour and held his court there on Our Lady's birthday, September 8. When he returned to Normandy a week later, his success in Brittany had so impressed King Louis that he sent messengers to ask Henry to meet him to discuss the possibility of peace.

The two Kings met at their traditional conference place, Gisors, on September 25, 1173. The young Henry, Richard, and Geoffrey accompanied their overlord, the King of France. Henry showed the greatest eagerness to win his sons back to him. He offered to give his oldest son half the revenues of the royal demesnes in England and four castles there, or, if the young man preferred to live in Normandy, half the revenues of the Duchy, all the revenues from his estates there, and three castles. To Richard he offered half the revenues of Aquitaine and four castles. He offered Brittany to Geoffrey, who had just turned fifteen, provided he could obtain the Pope's permission for his marriage to Constance.

Henry offered to submit the whole matter to the arbitration of Archbishop Peter of Tarantaise, a Cistercian with a great reputation for sanctity, and to the papal legates, and to give his sons any further revenues that the arbitrators might deem fair. However, in all these lands he was offering his sons he reserved to himself the powers of justice and of royal government.

It was his insistence that although his sons might have titles and revenues they should have no authority that had led them to break away in the first place, and they were not willing to return to the state of tutelage in which he apparently proposed to keep them indefinitely. The conference was continued on the following day, but the sons refused to accept their father's terms.[2] Although the chroniclers blame Louis for their refusal, it is obvious that the sons, at the outset of their revolt, had determined to force their father to delegate some of his powers to them,

---

[1] Robert of Torigni, pp. 260-1.
[2] *Gesta*, Vol. I, pp. 59-60.

and while Louis encouraged them in this attitude he can hardly be held wholly responsible for it.

Late in the summer William, King of Scots, who had never relinquished his claim to Northumberland, collected an army and invaded England. It is difficult to see any evidence of co-ordination between the rebellions on the Continent and King William's invasion of England. It seems more likely that he simply took advantage of the situation to strike out on his own and snatch what he could while the King of England was occupied elsewhere.

William had 'an infinite multitude of the men of Galloway, nimble, naked, their heads shaven, girded on the left side with knives, armed with anything that would inspire terror, carrying in their hands spears that they could throw accurately for a great distance, and waving long lances as ensigns when they went to war'.[1]

Bishop Hugh of Durham, who had no love for King Henry, allowed this savage horde to pass unopposed through his County. When they reached Yorkshire they set to work, ravaging the country. 'The King of Scotland began to depopulate England, to burn manors, to collect vast booty, to lead mere women away as captives, and to tear the children half-alive out of the bellies of pregnant women.'

At the news of this invasion, Richard of Luci and Humphrey of Bohun, Constable of England, raised an army and marched north to meet the Scots. King William retreated before them, and they pursued him into Lothian. They burned Berwick and devastated the country so thoroughly that William, sickened by his own medicine, asked for a truce. The English leaders were more than willing to suspend hostilities, for they had just received the news of an invasion of East Anglia that threatened more serious perils to the country than any the Scots had inflicted. The Chief Justiciar agreed to a truce till mid-winter, and then the English army hastened south to meet the new danger.

Earl Robert of Leicester, after his flight from Breteuil, had gone to Flanders and, no doubt with the help of Count Philip, raised an army there. He was accompanied on this expedition by his wife, Petronilla, the heiress of the great Norman house of Grantmesnil, and by a number of French and Norman knights.

[1] Ralph of Diceto, Vol. I, p. 376.

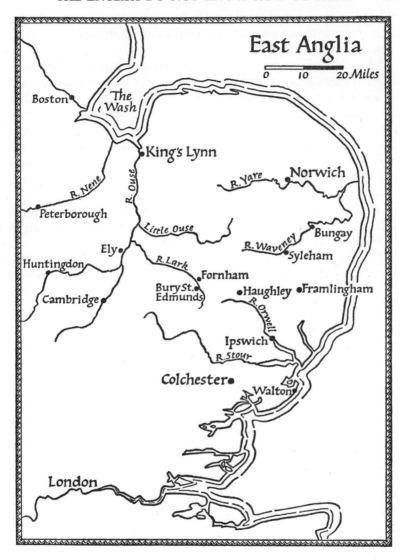

Earl Robert and his army sailed from Wissant and landed at Walton on Michaelmas Day, September 29, 1173. He was joined by Earl Hugh of Norfolk, who had already imported a large number of Flemings to garrison his castles.

The two Earls went to Haughley, a castle that had been en-

trusted to Rannulf of Broc, and laid siege to it.   On October 13
they captured and burned the castle and took thirty knights,
whom they held to ransom.

From Haughley they went to Earl Hugh's castle at Framlingham.   There was some dissension there between them and probably between their wives as well, for 'his stay there appeared to
be burdensome to Hugh Bigod, the lord of the castle, and
especially displeasing to Hugh's wife'.[1]   Earl Hugh was an old
man, and he had no designs outside East Anglia, where he was
almost absolute master.   His dream was to return to the good
old days of gentle King Stephen and to rid East Anglia of the
meddlesome officials of the Angevin upstart, a troublesome crew
of low-born Treasury clerks and self-inflated justiciars who had
picked up a smattering of law when they hung about the fringes
of the court at Westminster.

The Earl and Countess of Leicester, seeing that they were un-
welcome, decided to go to the relief of the garrison at Leicester.
When the Earl asked the advice of his companions on this step,
Petronilla replied:

> May the Lord God, who is rightful King, forbid
> That you should give up this journey for Humphrey of Bohun,
> Or for the Earl of Arundel or for his fair speaking!
> The English are good boasters, but they do not know how to fight.
> They are better at drinking and gorging themselves.[2]

The Countess Petronilla, carrying shield and lance, rode with
her husband at the head of their troop of Flemings.   At every
halt, the Flemings would dance and sing in their native tongue:

> Hoppe, hoppe, Wilekin, hoppe, Wilekin,
> Engelond is min ant tin.[3]

Jordan Fantosme represents them as saying:

> We have not come to this country to dwell,
> But to destroy King Henry, the old warrior,
> And to have his wool, for which we long.
> My lords, that is the truth: most of them were weavers
> And did not know how to bear arms like knights.

[1] Ralph of Diceto, Vol. I, p. 377.

[2] *Chronique de Jordan Fantosme*, ed. Richard Howlett, in Vol. III of *Chronicles
of the Reigns of Stephen, etc.*, lines 981-5.

[3] Matthew Paris: *Historia Anglorum*, ed. Sir Frederic Madden (Rolls Series,
3 vols., 1866-9), Vol. I, p. 381.

But they had come for this, to have gain and war,
For there is no richer land than St. Edmund's on earth.[1]

Humphrey of Bohun, meanwhile, hastened to Bury St. Edmunds to block Earl Robert's path to Leicester.   The Constable
was joined by Earl Reginald of Cornwall, Earl William of
Gloucester, and Earl William of Arundel.   Leicester swung to
the north to avoid the English army.   The invaders were now
on St. Edmund's land, and when the English, numbering three
hundred, marched to meet them they carried the banner of the
martyred King of East Anglia.   All the men of the district
accompanied them.

The armies met at Fornham St. Genevieve, a few miles north
of Bury St. Edmunds, on October 17.   'In a moment, in the
twinkling of an eye', the English put the Flemish weavers to rout.
The soldiers had little work to do; the enraged peasants fell on the
invaders and slaughtered them.

There was in the country neither serf nor hind
Who did not go to kill Flemings with fork and flail.
The armed knights had nothing to do
But to knock them down, and the peasants killed them.[2]

The Countess Petronilla, in attempting to flee, fell into a ditch,
lost her rings, and almost drowned.   The Earl and Countess and
all their knights were captured, and the Flemings were either
killed by the peasants or drowned in the ditches.   Earl Robert
and his wife were sent to Falaise to be imprisoned there with the
Earl of Chester.[3]

With the Earl of Leicester thus disposed of, the Constable
turned his attention to the Earl of Norfolk and his Flemings.   He
assembled an army and stationed it at Bury St. Edmunds, at
Ipswich, and at Colchester 'to curb the arrogance of Earl Hugh'.
Hugh had so many Flemings that the English were afraid to risk
a direct attack upon them, but they hoped by confining them to
their castles to starve them into surrender.

The Earl was too wily a fox to be caught in such a trap.   He
bribed the English magnates and obtained a truce until a week
from the following Whitsunday.   One of the terms he exacted
was that his Flemings, to the number of fourteen thousand, should

---

[1] Jordan Fantosme, lines 999-1005.   [2] Ibid., lines 1086-9.
[3] *Gesta*, Vol. I, p. 62.

have safe conduct through Essex and Kent to Dover and ships ready to take them across to Flanders.[1]

The news of the defeat of the Earl of Leicester was a serious blow to King Louis and the young Henry, who had placed high hopes on the Earl's being able to prepare the way for the young King to follow him and lay claim to all England. While they were grieving over this disappointment, the elder Henry, around Martinmas, November 11, marched his Brabantines into Touraine where some of the nobles were taking advantage of the general confusion to rebel against him. He quickly suppressed the disorders there, which were on a limited scale, and seized the castles of the rebels.[2]

With his rebellious subjects thus checked, at least for the time being, Henry returned to Normandy and held his Christmas court at Caen. It must have been a cheerless occasion for him, with his wife under close custody, with three of his sons in rebellion against him, sheltered and encouraged by his rival, the King of France, and with his barons in England, Normandy, and Aquitaine plotting treason, as he well knew, at that very moment.

[1] Ralph of Diceto, Vol. I, p. 378.   [2] *Gesta*, Vol. I, pp. 62-63.

XIII

'ST. THOMAS, GUARD MY REALM FOR ME!'
1174

THE truce that Bishop Hugh of Durham had arranged with the King of Scots expired at the middle of January. Bishop Hugh met King William and induced him to extend the truce till the end of March by promising him three hundred marks from the revenues of the barons of Northumberland.[1] The Bishop had been for so long a power unto himself in his County Palatine of Durham, almost an independent principality, that it was characteristic of him to act thus on his own initiative, as one independent ruler treating with another. And as an independent ruler he fortified his castle at Durham and built another one at Northallerton.[2]

Roger of Mowbray took advantage of the truce to build a castle at Kinnardferry in the Isle of Axholme, a marshy stretch of land along the River Trent in the extreme northwest of Lincolnshire. Further north he fortified his castles at Thirsk and Kirkby Malzeard, which blocked the way through Yorkshire, either to the Scots coming down from the north or to the English on their way to the defence of Northumberland.[3]

Although neither Roger nor Bishop Hugh made an open alliance with the King of Scots, it was obvious, since they were making all these preparations of their own accord, that they did not have King Henry's interests in mind. Roger of Mowbray was one of the most powerful barons in England, with extensive lands in Warwickshire, Leicestershire, and Yorkshire. He had taken little part in public affairs; most of his energy up till this time had been devoted to managing his great estates and to founding religious houses, of which he was a notable benefactor.

At the beginning of April, when his truce with Bishop Hugh expired, the King of Scots first prudently collected the three

---

[1] *Gesta*, Vol. I, p. 64.   [2] Roger of Hoveden, Vol. II, p. 57.
[3] *Gesta*, Vol. I, p. 64.

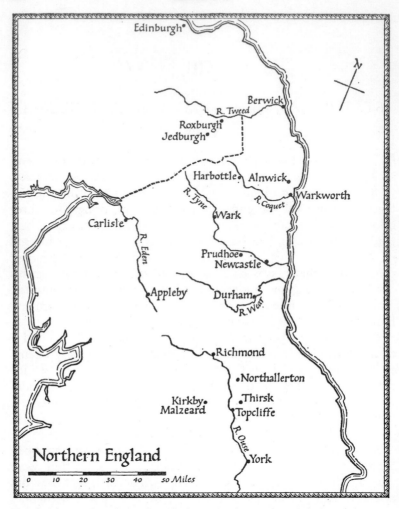

Northern England

hundred marks that the Bishop had promised him and then
marched his army into Northumberland.   He sent his brother,
David, Earl of Huntingdon, to Leicester, where the rebel garrison
had invited him to join them.   While David and his retinue
marched southward 'with hauberks and helmets and beautiful
painted shields',[1] King William began his operations by laying
siege to the castle at Wark, in the upper valley of the Tyne.   This
fortress was held by Roger of Stuteville, Sheriff of Northumber-

[1] Jordan Fantosme, line 1114.

land, who had stocked it during the winter with 48 chalders (a Scottish measure equal to 12 quarters or 96 bushels) of oatmeal and 63 chalders of malt for the garrison of ten knights and forty soldiers 'dwelling in Wark Castle'.[1]

Roger and his men, fortified by their heroic diet of oatcakes and beer, 'thought not an alderberry of their siege'[2] and put up a fierce resistance. King William had a stone-thrower brought up and assembled, but it cast the first stone into the midst of the Scots and knocked down one of their own knights. Then William ordered his men to set fire to the castle, but the wind suddenly changed and gave the Scots a good scorching. Remarking, 'Indeed, this performance seems very costly to me,'[3] King William abandoned the siege.

> King William, with his great assembled army, goes away
> Towards Carlisle the beautiful, the city strong and garrisoned.
> Lord Roger of Mowbray and his chivalry
> And Lord Adam of Port join his Borderers.
> The earls of Scotland lead the hated host
> Who never had pity about doing devilry.
> They so went their ways . . .
> That they could see Carlisle, filled with beauty;
> The sun lights up the walls and the turrets.
> Whoever has a gay banner gladly displays it,
> And the trumpets sound from every rank.[4]

Carlisle, under the command of Robert of Vaus, was as stoutly defended as Wark. William left part of his army there to starve the city into submission, while he led the remainder southeast into Westmorland.

> The King had very soon the castle of Appleby;
> There were no people there, so that it was all unguarded.
> Cospatric son of Orm, an old grey-haired Englishman,
> Was the constable; he soon cried mercy.[5]

The Scots then went back into Northumberland and captured Warkworth, on the east coast. From there King William turned west again, captured Harbottle, and returned to Carlisle. By this time the townspeople and the garrison were facing starvation. Robert of Vaus asked for a truce till Michaelmas and agreed that

---

[1] Pipe Roll 20 Henry II, p. 105.   [2] Jordan Fantosme, line 1204.
[3] Ibid., line 1257.   [4] Ibid., lines 1344-54.   [5] Ibid., lines 1465-8.

if King Henry had not sent him help by that date he would surrender the city and the castle. William took hostages to assure himself of Robert's good faith and granted the truce.[1]

The King then took his army once more into Northumberland. He was afraid to attack Newcastle-upon-Tyne, the strongest fortress in the North of England. He laid siege instead to Prudhoe, eleven miles up the Tyne. Odinel of Umframville, the castellan, when he saw the danger threatening his castle, mounted 'good brown Bauçant'[2] and rode south for help while the garrison held the Scots at bay. By riding all day and night, Odinel reached York, eighty miles away, and told Robert of Stuteville, the Sheriff of Yorkshire, of the great danger threatening from the north. Robert immediately called out the fyrd, the levy of all the men of the county.

Hearing of the approach of this army, William abandoned the siege of Prudhoe and fled northward. When he reached Alnwick, safe, as he thought, from his pursuers, he laid siege to the castle there with only a small group of his household knights and sent most of his army to ravage and plunder the countryside.[3]

King William had invaded the North early in April and laid siege to Alnwick at the beginning of July, apparently. We now leave him before the walls of Alnwick, with his army ravaging Northumberland, and turn our attention to the course of affairs farther south during those three months. Since during this crucial time there was fighting from Northumberland to Poitou, it is perhaps easier to follow a geographical rather than a chronological order in dealing with these events.

Geoffrey, King Henry's bastard son, had been elected Bishop of Lincoln in the spring of the previous year. Although his qualifications for that position were as yet unknown, except that he had attended the schools at Northampton, a famous centre of learning, for six months in 1170-1,[4] he now proceeded to show that he had the makings, if not of a good bishop, at any rate of a good fighter. When Roger of Mowbray had joined the King of Scots, he had left his castle of Kinnardferry in the charge of his younger son, Robert. On May 5, 1174, Geoffrey called out the fyrd of Lincolnshire and laid siege to that castle. Robert of Mowbray, caught by surprise, attempted to escape to Leicester

[1] *Gesta*, Vol. I, pp. 64-65.   [2] Jordan Fantosme, line 1671.
[3] *Gesta*, Vol. I, p. 66.   [4] Pipe Roll 16 Henry II, p. 20.

and summon help and was captured on the way. Geoffrey seized the castle and had it demolished.

Exhilarated by this success, the fledgling fighter marched north to York and invited the Archbishop to join him. Roger of Pont l'Évêque summoned his knights, and the combined forces laid siege to Mowbray's castle at Kirkby Malzeard. Within a few days they captured the castle and its garrison. Geoffrey turned the fortress over to Archbishop Roger and strengthened the one at Topcliffe, a few miles from the Mowbray castle at Thirsk, to make sure that the approaches from the north were well guarded. This, Geoffrey might well feel, was not at all a bad beginning for his career; at least he could boast of far greater success in war than could any of his legitimate brothers.

At the beginning of King William's foray he had sent his brother, David, to join the garrison at Leicester, as we have seen. Although Richard of Luci and Earl Reginald of Cornwall had burned the town during the preceding summer, the garrison in the castle had not surrendered, and after the expiration of the truce at Michaelmas they had continued to hold out, under the command of the constable, Asketill Mallory, and of Earl William Ferrers.

Shortly after the close of Whitsun Week, May 19, 1174, Asketill Mallory led the knights of Leicester to Northampton. The castle there was under the command of Robert son of Sawin, the Sheriff of Northamptonshire, who had had a garrison of ten knights since the preceding autumn.[1] The Sheriff, his knights, and the townspeople went out to meet the rebels and were soundly defeated. The knights fled back into the castle. Over two hundred burgesses were captured, in addition to those wounded. The rebels then returned triumphantly to Leicester with a great store of plunder.

Encouraged by this success, Earl Robert Ferrers, early one morning about a month later, led his forces out of Leicester and attacked Nottingham. The King had spent enormous sums on Nottingham Castle, which was both the strongest fortress in the Midlands and the key to the defence of that area. Nevertheless, the rebels took the town without the slightest difficulty. Some of the inhabitants they slaughtered, and others they took prisoners. They plundered the town and set fire to it, and then they

[1] Pipe Roll 20 Henry II, p. 51.

returned unharmed to Leicester with their prisoners and their booty.

The rebels, with their headquarters at Leicester, now had control of the Midlands, and Richard of Luci was powerless to reduce their stronghold. The Chief Justiciar, instead of making another frontal attack on them, summoned an army, around June 24, and went to Huntingdon, where Earl David had installed himself. When Richard laid siege to Huntingdon Castle, Earl David's knights sallied forth, burned the town lest it furnish shelter for the besiegers, and then went back into the castle. The Chief Justiciar then built a 'castle' in front of the gates of Huntingdon Castle, so that no one could enter or leave it.[1]

With the garrison thus bottled up, Richard went to deal with a grave situation in London. The general spirit of revolt and lawlessness had spread to that city. Gangs of young men, many of them of good birth, were roaming the streets by night, killing those they encountered and breaking into houses and stealing whatever they could find. There was of course no such thing as a police force, and the justiciars were powerless to cope with these depredations. Richard of Luci was forced to go to London in an effort to restore order.

While the Scots were ravaging Northumberland, the English rebels were raiding the Midlands, and London was undergoing a reign of terror from lawless gangs, further trouble developed in East Anglia. Count Philip of Flanders, after almost a year of inaction, swore in the presence of King Louis and his nobles that within a fortnight from Midsummer Day he would invade England and conquer it for the young Henry. On May 15, 1174, he sent an advance party of 318 chosen knights, who landed at the mouth of the River Orwell. The truce that Earl Hugh of Norfolk had agreed to when he dismissed his mercenaries was due to expire on the 19th. Gladly and with a clear conscience he welcomed the new arrivals and lodged them in his castles of Bungay and Framlingham.

On June 18, under Earl Hugh's leadership, the Flemish knights rode to Norwich. Norwich Castle, of which the great Norman keep survives, was a strong fortress and should have been able to hold out indefinitely. The Flemings, however, took it without any difficulty, carried off a great treasure, and held many of the richer burgesses for ransom.[2] Jordan Fantosme says: 'A

---

[1] *Gesta*, Vol. I, pp. 68-71.   [2] Ralph of Diceto, Vol. I, p. 381.

Lorraine traitor betrayed it, therefore it was surprised,'[1] which seems the most reasonable explanation for the ease with which it was taken.

While his kingdom was thus being beset on every side, Henry was making a leisurely progress through his Continental domains. On April 30 he left Normandy and went into Maine, his home-land, where the population turned out to pledge their fealty to him. When he reached the borders of Anjou he dismissed the entourage of nobles who had accompanied him through Maine, and their place was taken by the Angevins, who greeted him with even more enthusiasm.

Henry kept the Whitsun feast at Poitiers on May 12. While he was there, he heard that some of Richard's forces had occupied Saintes. He hastened southeastwards with an army of faithful Poitevins and arrived at Saintes so unexpectedly that the garrison, taken by surprise, fled from their fortifications and took refuge in the principal church. Henry had them dragged out of their shelter and captured sixty knights and four hundred bowmen. After putting trustworthy men in charge of Aquitaine he turned north.[2]

The King summoned a council of his Norman bishops and barons to meet at Bonneville-sur-Toques on Midsummer Day. King Louis, meanwhile, had held the council, around Easter, at which Count Philip had sworn his oath to conquer England for the young Henry. For the first time, concerted action seems to have been agreed upon. Some of the French nobles, including Count Theobald of Blois, swore to accompany Count Philip to England, and the others agreed to attack Normandy at the same time, seize whatever castles they could, devastate the land, and lay siege to Rouen if it were practicable to do so.[3] Henry had a number of French nobles in his pay, and they reported all these designs to him. The King occupied himself between his arrival in Normandy and the meeting of the council in making sure that his castles near the French border were well stocked and in the care of men on whom he could rely.

The justiciars in England meanwhile sent messenger after messenger to the King to tell him of the perilous state of affairs in his island realm. When Henry made no reply, they sent one of

[1] Line 897.   [2] Ralph of Diceto, Vol. I, pp. 379-80.
[3] Robert of Torigni, p. 263.

their own number, Richard of Ilchester, Bishop-elect of Winchester, in whom the King had the utmost confidence. Richard
found him at Bonneville on June 24, holding his council.

The Normans had of course noted the arrival of the string of
messengers from England. When Richard came, they said:
'Since the English have already sent so many messengers and now
send this one, what more can they do to persuade the King to
return, unless they send over the Tower of London itself?'[1]

When Henry heard of the state of affairs in England:

'St. Thomas,' said the King, 'guard my realm for me!
To you I declare myself guilty of that for which others have the
    blame.'[2]

Henry continued to consult with his Norman barons and gave
them instructions about guarding the frontier, apparently in-
different to the disturbing news from England, till he learned,
around July 6, that his eldest son and the Count of Flanders had
already assembled an army and a fleet at Gravelines and were
waiting for a favourable wind to cross to England. Then he
acted quickly.[3]

He did not dare to leave his prisoners behind to be rescued,
perhaps, by King Louis or to escape through some treachery of
the Normans. He sent the Earl of Chester, the Earl and Countess
of Leicester, and a number of others in chains to Barfleur to be
shipped across the Channel. He took with him his only faithful
son, the boy John; his daughter Joan; his Queen, under close
guard; Queen Margaret, the young Henry's wife; and the three
girls betrothed to his sons, Alice of France, Constance of Brittany,
and Alice of Maurienne. With these members of his family and
with his captives he sailed from Barfleur on Monday morning,
July 8, 1174, while his army of Brabantines sailed from Ouistre-
ham. The same wind that was delaying the young Henry and
Count Philip was blowing strongly on the Norman coast, too,
but the King, to the terror of his sailors and still more to that of
his entourage, ordered his fleet to set sail.

Henry landed at Portsmouth on the same evening. His first
concern was to put his prisoners into safe keeping. Eleanor was
sent to Salisbury Castle to be closely confined. Margaret and the

---

[1] Ralph of Diceto, Vol. I, pp. 381-2.   [2] Jordan Fantosme, lines 1605-6.
[3] *Gesta*, Vol. I, p. 72.

other young girls were sent to Devizes.   The Earl of Leicester
and some of the remaining prisoners were taken in chains to
Porchester, while the less dangerous ones were kept at Winchester.

Although Henry had declared over and over again that he was
innocent of any complicity in the murder of St. Thomas and had
sworn many oaths to that effect, his conscience nevertheless told
him that he was responsible for the death of the man who had in
happier days been his dearest friend and most trusted associate.
The flood of miracles at Canterbury deflated his pride and convinced him that in the struggle with the Archbishop he had been
in the wrong, since God was choosing thus to make manifest the
true character of 'that traitor, Thomas', as the King had formerly
called him.   He saw in the perils that now beset him, with his
sons in revolt, his nobles rebelling against him, and his enemies
attacking him on every side, God's punishment for his guilt.

On Friday morning, July 12, he set out from Southampton
and rode to Canterbury, breaking his fast with only bread and
water and wearing the coarse woollen gown of a pilgrim.   At
St. Dunstan's Church, outside the city, he dismounted and walked
barefoot to the cathedral, leaving a trail of blood on the sharp
stones of the roadway.   Entering the crypt, he prostrated himself
with outstretched arms before the Martyr's tomb.   As he lay
there, Bishop Gilbert of London, speaking for him to the great
crowd that had gathered to witness the spectacle, declared that
'he neither ordered nor willed the death of the Archbishop nor
sought it by any artifice.   But because the murderers had taken
occasion from some words of his, dropped without sufficient cir-
cumspection, he begged absolution from the bishops who were
there present.'[1]

A crowd of the clergy had either accompanied him or met him
at the cathedral.   The bishops absolved him from his guilt.
Henry stripped off his pilgrim's gown.   As he lay naked before
the tomb, the bishops, abbots, and all the monks of Christchurch
in due order scourged him, each one giving him three lashes and
some of them five.

'He remained there in prayer before the holy Martyr all that
day and night; he took no drink, nor did he go out for the needs
of nature.   As he came, so did he stay, nor would he allow a

[1] Ralph of Diceto, Vol. I, pp. 382-3.

carpet or anything else to be put under him.'[1]   At daybreak the
next morning, Saturday, July 13, he heard Mass at St. Thomas's
tomb.   Then, still fasting, the King rode to London.
  On Wednesday night, July 17:

> The King was leaning on his elbow and slept a little,
> A servant at his feet was gently rubbing them;
> There was no noise or cry, or anyone who spoke,
> No harp or viol sounded there at that hour,
> When the messenger came to the door and softly called.
> And the chamberlain said: 'Who are you there?'
> 'I am a messenger, friend; now come closer.' . . .
> While they are speaking, the King has awakened,
> And he hears a cry at the door: 'Open!   Open!' . . .
> The messenger entered, who was very well bred,
> And saluted the King, as you may shortly hear:
> 'Sir King, God save you Who dwells in Trinity,
> Your body first and then all your intimate friends!'
> 'Brien,' said the King, 'what news do you bring?' . . .
> 'Sir,' thus said the messenger, 'hear me a little.
> Your barons of the North are right good people.
> On behalf of my lord [Rannulf of Glanville], kindly hear me.
> He sends you by me greetings and friendship,
> And my lady much more, whom you know well.
> He sends you by me word not to be disturbed.
> The King of Scotland is taken and all his barons.' . . .
> 'Then,' says King Henry, 'God be thanked for it,
> And St. Thomas Martyr and all God's Saints!'
> Then the messenger went to his hostel,
> He has plenty to eat and to drink;
> And the King is so merry that night and so joyful
> That he went to the knights and woke them all up:
> 'Barons, wake up!   This has been a good night for you!
> Such a thing have I heard as will make you joyful:
> Taken is the King of Scotland, so it has been told me for truth.
> Just now the news came to me, when I should have been in bed.'[2]

  King William, when he reached Alnwick, had thought that
he was safe from pursuit and had sent most of his army out to
ravage the countryside, while he and only a small group of his
knights continued the siege of Alnwick.   The Yorkshire army,
summoned by Odinel of Umframville, reached Prudhoe on the

[1] Gervase of Canterbury, Vol. I, p. 248.
[2] Jordan Fantosme, lines 1962-2026.

Tyne by a forced march and found that the Scots had retreated to the north. The mounted knights had ridden ahead of the foot-soldiers in their eagerness to check the invaders, and they were worn out from their long journey.

When they held a council to decide on the next step, the more cautious pointed out that they were only four hundred horsemen and that it would be madness for them to attack an army that they estimated at over eighty thousand. The bolder knights, however, declared that a foe who had behaved as vilely as the Scots should be fought in every way possible and that since their cause was just they should not despair of victory; which, being translated from the language of the clerical chronicler into that of the knights, meant that they were spoiling for a good fight and intended to have one.

The bolder knights prevailed. After a few hours of sleep they set out early in the morning on Saturday, July 13, and rode twenty-four miles by five o'clock. Then a thick mist closed in on them, so that they could scarcely see where they were going. They stopped for another conference. Bernard of Baliol declared: 'Turn back who will! I am going forward, even if no-one follows me. I will not brand myself with perpetual disgrace!'

They rode on, and when the mist suddenly lifted they saw Alnwick Castle before them, with King William and sixty of his knights playing before the castle, safe and fearing nothing. When William caught sight of them he thought at first that they were a party of his own knights, returning from a foraging expedition. The English unfurled their banners, and the Scots realised their mistake.

William seized his arms, leaped upon his horse, and led his little band against the English, crying: 'Soon we shall see who are the true knights!' His horse was killed and fell on him, and Rannulf of Glanville took the King prisoner. It was a matter of only a few moments to capture the remaining Scottish knights.

The brief engagement was over at almost exactly the same time that King Henry was completing his penance at Canterbury. This coincidence convinced the King that the English victory at Alnwick was a miracle wrought on his behalf at the intercession of St. Thomas as an indication of his forgiveness. Henry firmly believed henceforth that he and Thomas were even dearer and closer friends than they had ever been during the Martyr's lifetime

and that St. Thomas was his special patron, interceding for him
in Heaven and watching over his realm.   In the future, whenever
the King returned to England from his numerous visits across the
Channel, his first act was always to go straightway to St. Thomas's
tomb and perform his devotions there.

Roger of Mowbray fled to Scotland, the marauding bands of
Scots hastened north of the Tweed as soon as they learned of the
capture of their King, and the rebellion in the North collapsed
almost immediately.   Rannulf of Glanville put his royal captive
in prison at Richmond to await King Henry's pleasure.[1]

On the morning after he received the news of the victory at
Alnwick, King Henry, radiating strength and confidence, went
to Huntingdon, where the siege was dragging along interminably.
The King's bastard son, Geoffrey, came from Lincoln with seven
hundred knights to help him.   When they met, Henry exclaimed:
'My other sons have proved themselves bastards; this one alone is
my true and legitimate son!'[2]   Henry took charge of operations
and prosecuted the siege so vigorously that the garrison surrendered on July 21.[3]

The King went next into East Anglia, where Earl Hugh had
five hundred knights and a multitude of Flemings, sent over by
the young Henry and Count Philip, strongly ensconced in his
castles at Framlingham and Bungay.   From Bury St. Edmunds
Henry took his army to Syleham, on the River Waveney, and
began his preparations for laying siege to Hugh's castles.   In the
excitement of these operations a horse belonging to a Templar
kicked the King in the thigh and hurt him badly.[4]

Although Earl Hugh had a sizable army and two exceedingly
strong castles, the capture of King William, the collapse of the
rebellion in the North, and Henry's success at Huntingdon dis-
couraged him from further resistance.   He came to treat for
peace and received such generous terms that he surrendered on
July 25.   'He did homage to the King, swore fealty, and returned
again to his allegiance.'   He gave hostages for his future fidelity
and paid a thousand marks as an amend.   The army of Flemings
that Count Philip had sent over were allowed to return, after

    [1] William of Newburgh, pp. 183-5.
    [2] Gerald of Wales: *De Vita Galfridi Archiepiscopi Eboracensis*, ed. J. S. Brewer.
Opera, Vol. IV, p. 368.   [3] *Gesta*, Vol. I, pp. 72-73.
    [4] Roger of Heveden, Vol. II, p. 64.

swearing that they would never again come to England with hostile intent. The young King's mercenaries were allowed to go back with all their arms and baggage. In an access of generosity, the King even ordered that the payments of the customary 'third penny', a third of the receipts from the amercements levied at the county courts, be resumed to Earl Hugh.[1]

The King then went to Northampton and held a triumphal court on July 31 to receive the submission of the rebels. William, King of Scots, was brought from his prison at Richmond with his feet tied together under his horse's belly, and Henry kept him in custody. Bishop Hugh of Durham, who had been too cautious to join the rebels but who, on the other hand, had done nothing to check them, surrendered his castles of Durham and Northallerton. Roger of Mowbray came from Scotland and surrendered Thirsk; Earl Ferrers surrendered his castles, and Asketill Mallory, the constable of the Earl of Leicester, surrendered Leicester Castle.[2]

Henry was surprisingly lenient in dealing with the rebels. Since they had made war upon their king, they might have expected death or banishment and the confiscation of their lands. Earl Hugh of Norfolk was let off with a fine and the others with the surrender of their castles. Henry and his contemporaries seem to have taken the view that a king had to expect a bit of rebellion now and then from his high-spirited barons as he steadily tightened the screws on them by curbing their powers and depriving them of their old jurisdictions. Unnoticed by the chroniclers of the time but apparent in every page of the Pipe Rolls were the continually increasing power of the royal government, the steadily expanding sphere in which the royal courts operated, to the detriment of the jurisdictions claimed by the barons for their courts, and the relentless extraction of money from men of every degree on every possible pretext, from the vast sums demanded from the barons as 'reliefs' (payments to secure their inheritances) or simply to gain the King's good will, to the crushing amercements laid on the lowest for offences against the tyrannical forest laws.

As the King's power steadily increased, his deputies for the exercise of it were no longer the earls and great barons but,

[1] Pipe Roll 20 Henry II, p. 36.
[2] Roger of Hoveden, Vol. II, pp. 64-65.

rather, a new class of professional officials and judges, men of modest origins who had received their training at the Exchequer or in the courts and who were wholly dependent upon the King. As they saw these men supplanting them and exercising many of the powers that had formerly belonged to the baronage, it was but natural that the earls and barons should give vent to their resentment in an occasional outburst of defiance. The King took a remarkably calm view of their offences. Only when they rebelled repeatedly, as did the barons of Brittany, did Henry resort to savage measures of revenge.

With the rebellion in England crushed, the rebel forces dispersed, their castles surrendered, and the King of Scots a prisoner, Henry sailed from Portsmouth on August 8, taking with him his Brabantines, a thousand Welshmen under the command of the Lord Rhys, and his prisoners, including King William and the Earls of Chester and Leicester.[1] While he had been occupied in England, his eldest son and Count Philip, realising that their projected invasion had no chance of success, had joined forces with King Louis and laid siege to Rouen on July 22. The besieging army worked in shifts through the day and night, so that the defenders were hard pressed and could scarcely catch their breath.

While King Henry was making his way along the coast from Barfleur, Louis proclaimed a truce on August 10, the feast of St. Lawrence, for whom he had a special reverence. The people of Rouen seized on the occasion with gladness and had a great holiday. Either through joy or in order to irritate their enemies, they went singing loudly through the streets, and the knights of the garrison staged a tournament outside the city walls in a meadow by the river, in full view of the enemy.

Count Philip came to King Louis and pointed out to him that while the people within the city were dancing and singing and the knights without were having their sport, the city lay open to them. He proposed that they arm in silence and launch a surprise attack. Louis at first refused because it would be to his shame if they violated the truce he had proclaimed in honour of St. Lawrence. Philip and some others so taunted him with softness, however, that he agreed. The French began stealthily to prepare for the attack.

Some clerks, meanwhile, had climbed a church tower within

[1] *Gesta*, Vol. I, p. 74.

the city and were admiring the view of the Seine valley. They noticed the unusual activity behind the French lines and sounded the alarm on Ruvello, 'an exceedingly old but wondrously loud bell'. The knights ceased their tilting and galloped back into the city, the gates were slammed in the faces of the French, and the soldiers mounted the ramparts and fought off the enemy, who had brought up scaling ladders and were pouring over the walls.[1]

King Henry, with his Brabantine mercenaries and his thousand Welshmen, reached Rouen on the next day. On the 12th, early in the morning, he sent the Welshmen out on the sort of work at which they excelled. They disappeared into the woods, reached the rear of the French army, and surprised a train of forty wagons loaded with food and wine. They captured or killed the drivers, unhitched the horses, broke up the wagons, and, if the author of the *Gesta Henrici* is to be believed, poured out all the wine.

The English forces meanwhile were busy filling in a ditch that lay between them and the French and making a level stretch over which two hundred knights could ride abreast. Seeing that it was no longer a question of a siege but rather of a pitched battle, Louis had his stone-throwers and other siege engines burned and ordered his knights to arm.

'And the knights and armed soldiers came out of their tents and impetuously met the knights of the King of England, and some of them were captured and some were wounded; many horses, however, were killed there.'[2] Among the gravely wounded was Philip's brother Peter, who had renounced the Bishopric of Cambrai in order to become Count of Boulogne.

On the next morning, August 13, Archbishop William of Sens and his brother Count Theobald of Blois came to Henry on Louis's behalf and asked for a truce, so that he might withdraw his forces to Malaunay. They swore solemnly that if he would grant the truce, Louis would come to him for a conference on the following day. When Henry agreed, the French withdrew to Malaunay and pitched their tents; then, under cover of night, they fled and did not stop till they were safely back in France. The two envoys returned to Henry and arranged for a conference to be held at Gisors on September 8.

When Louis and Henry met they were unable to come to terms. They agreed, however, to an extension of the truce till Michael-

[1] William of Newburgh, pp. 190-4.   [2] *Gesta*, Vol. I, p. 75.

mas. Richard, meanwhile, acting on his own, was attacking his father's castles in Poitou and doing his best to make himself master of his Duchy. It was characteristic of Richard that already, at the age of fifteen, while his elder brother and his allies were engaging in one abortive project after another, he struck out on his own and fought as best he knew how. As a condition of the truce, Louis promised Henry that neither he nor his ally, the young King, would help Richard in any way.

The lad, however, was no match for his father with his great army of mercenaries. When Henry led them into Poitou, Richard did not dare meet him in a pitched battle. He fled from place to place as his father advanced to the south. At last he learned that Louis and the young Henry had sued for peace and that he was fighting alone. 'He came weeping and fell on his face prone on the earth before the foot of the King his father, begging forgiveness of him.' Henry raised him up and kissed him, 'and thus the King finished his war in Poitou'. On his father's advice Richard went to Louis and his elder brother and told them that he had given up the struggle.[1]

The King met his three rebel sons at a conference at Mont Louis, between Tours and Amboise, on September 29, and on the following day they agreed to the terms of peace. Henry, Richard, and Geoffrey 'returned to their father and to his service, as to their lord, free from all oaths and undertakings they had made among themselves or with others, against him or his men'. Both the King and his sons forgave all their enemies and promised to harbour no malice. The King of Scotland, the Earls of Chester and Leicester, Ralph of Fougères, and their hostages, however, were excluded from the general amnesty.

Henry then proceeded to define the positions of his sons and to strip them of their claims to rule any territory independently of him. The young Henry was to have two castles in Normandy, chosen by his father, and an income of £3,750 sterling a year. Richard was to have two castles in Poitou 'from whence no harm could come to the King' and half the revenues of Poitou. Geoffrey was to have half the income from the marriage portion of Constance, Conan's daughter, and the whole of it after his marriage.

The young Henry formally consented to the grants that his

[1] *Gesta*, Vol. I, pp. 76-77.

father now made to John.   Instead of the three castles that Henry had originally promised him, the King gave him a much richer portion.   He was to have a thousand pounds a year from the revenues of the royal demesne in England and the castles of Nottingham and Marlborough.   In Normandy he was to have £250 sterling and two castles at his father's will; he was to have a further £250 sterling yearly from the revenues of Anjou; and he was to have a castle in Anjou, one in Touraine, and one in Maine.

'Furthermore, King Henry, the son of the Lord King, and his brothers gave assurance that they would never demand anything more of the Lord King their father, beyond the prescribed and determined settlement, against the will and pleasure of the Lord King their father, and that they would withdraw neither themselves nor their service from their father.   Richard and Geoffrey, the King's sons, became his men for what he had given and granted them.   Although his son Henry wanted to do homage to him, the Lord King would not receive it, because he was a king, but he took securities from him.'[1]

King William had been kept in prison at Falaise ever since Henry had brought him to Normandy in July.   The leading men of his kingdom were allowed to visit him freely, and at their advice, early in December, he made a complete and abject submission to the English King.

> This is the agreement and fine that William, King of Scotland, made with his lord Henry, King of England, the son of Matilda the Empress.   William, King of Scotland, became the liege man of the Lord King against all men, for Scotland and for all his other lands, and did fealty to him as his liege lord, as his other men are wont to do to him.   He likewise did homage to King Henry, his son, and fealty, saving his faith to the Lord King his father. . . .
>
> The earls and barons and other men of the land of the King of Scotland from whom the Lord King may wish to have it shall do homage to him against all men and fealty as their liege lord, as his other men are wont to do, and to King Henry, his son, and his heirs, saving their faith to the Lord King his father.   Likewise, the heirs of the King of Scotland and of his barons and his men shall do homage and allegiance to the heirs of the Lord King against all men.

Finally, as a pledge of his good faith and as the price of his release, William promised to turn over to Henry the castles of

[1] Ibid., Vol. I, pp. 77-79.

Q

Roxburgh, Berwick, Jedburgh, Edinburgh, and Stirling, which would give Henry effective control over the country.[1]

The treaty with the King of Scots was ratified at Valognes on December 8, and on the 11th, after William had left hostages, including his brother David, with the King, Henry sent him to arrange for the surrender of the five castles.[2]   Finally, the Earls of Chester and Leicester were released and their lands were restored to them.

The King held his Christmas court at Argentan, and probably all four of his sons were with him.   The three elder ones had lost their gamble and were reduced to a state of dependence more abject than they had been in before.   Louis's plans had failed for the time being, but he had planted the seeds well, and they would spring up again.

While her husband and sons were feasting on 'the meat of four score deer sent to the King beyond the sea',[3] Eleanor kept her Christmas with scant cheer in her prison in Salisbury Castle.

[1] *Gesta*, Vol. I, pp. 96-99.   [2] Pipe Roll 21 Henry II, p. 16.
[3] Ralph of Diceto, Vol. I, pp. 396, 398.

XIV

'HE BROUGHT CHIVALRY BACK TO LIFE'
1175 - 1176

SHORTLY after the beginning of the year 1175, Henry went
to Anjou to make sure that his castles there were in the hands
of reliable men. He sent Richard to Poitou to see to it that
his barons in that unruly province were keeping the peace and
that the castles the rebels had built or fortified were reduced to
the state they had been in at the beginning of the rebellion. As
an indication of his confidence in his son, he ordered his bailiffs
in Poitou to provide for all his needs and to place the Poitevin
army at his disposal.

Towards the end of March the King went to Caen and sent
word to the young Henry, at Rouen, to join him and go across
to England with him. The young Henry meanwhile had been
in correspondence with his father-in-law, and Louis had succeeded
in convincing him that once his father took him to England,
where he would be beyond any help from Louis, the King would
imprison him, as he had Queen Eleanor. Louis shrewdly pointed
out that his father had refused to accept his homage at the general
peace-making, as he had that of the younger sons, and that such a
refusal indicated that the King had evil designs on him. Louis
may well have reminded him of what had happened to Archbishop Thomas after the King had declined to give him the kiss
of peace.

The young Henry then refused to go with his father. The
King sent many messengers to plead with him, and at last the
young man came to his father at Bures on April 1. 'He fell flat
on the earth at the feet of the Lord King his father, begging him
with tears to receive homage and allegiance from him, as he had
done from his brothers, and he added that if the King refused to
accept his homage he would not believe that he loved him.'

Henry accepted his son's homage and then, to prove his confidence in him and to show how groundless were his fears, sent

him to visit Louis and to tell him what he had done.   While his
eldest son was on this visit, the King sent Geoffrey into Brittany
to tear down the castles the rebels had built during the war.

The young Henry returned to Normandy and joined his father
at Cherbourg on Holy Saturday, April 12.   They celebrated the
Easter festival together.   On the 22nd Count Philip of Flanders,
who had taken the Cross on Good Friday and vowed to go to
Jerusalem in the following summer, visited them at Caen.   He
made peace with his cousin, and he and the young Henry released
each other from the promises they had exchanged during the
rebellion.   Philip had brought with him the charter the young
Henry had given him two years earlier, granting him the earldom
of Kent, with Dover and Rochester Castles.   This charter, a
pathetic reminder of the young Henry's pretensions, Philip gave
to the King in exchange for one granting him the resumption of
his regular subsidy of a thousand marks a year.   Philip and the
two Henrys parted on the best of terms.

The King, his son, and Queen Margaret crossed from Barfleur
and landed at Portsmouth on Friday, May 9, 1175.[1]   Henry and
his son were now such friends that 'every day at the stated hour
for meals they ate at the same table'.[2]

The two Kings found that Archbishop Richard of Canterbury,
whom the Pope had consecrated in April 1174, had summoned
the English bishops for a council, which, with the King's permission, was held on Sunday, May 18, at Westminster.   While
the bishops were in London, Henry summoned his earls and
barons to join them.   In their presence, on May 20, he turned
his son's insistence on doing homage and fealty to him into a
public humiliation of the young Henry that must have rankled
bitterly in that lad's proud heart.   While he and his son sat before
the assembly, the King had the following letter read:

Henry the King, the father of the King, to his faithful subjects:
greetings.

I give thanks to Almighty God and to the Saints, Whose grace,
although not because of my merits, has visited and gladdened me
beyond belief.

My son, King Henry, came to me at Bures, and on the Tuesday
next before Palm Sunday, . . . with great shedding of tears and
many sobs, he prostrated himself before my feet, humbly begging

[1] *Gesta*, Vol. I, pp. 81-84.   [2] Ralph of Diceto, Vol. I, p. 399.

for mercy and that I would, with fatherly love, grant him forgiveness for what he did to me before the war and during the war and
after the war.

He also begged with all humility and as much devotion as he
could that I, as his lord and father, would accept his homage and
allegiance, asserting that he would never believe that I had given up
my indignation against him unless I would do to him what I had
done to his brothers, at the importunity of their patience and
humility.

I therefore, moved by pity and believing that he spoke from his
heart and that he was remorseful and humbled before me, put away
my anger and indignation against him and wholly took him into my
fatherly favour, having received homage from him and an oath upon
the holy relics placed before him that he would bear me faith against
all men and abide by my counsel henceforth in all his doings and that
as long as he lived he would seek no harm to either my men or his
who had served me in this war, but that he would honour and advance them as my faithful subjects and his, and that he would order
all his household and all his state by my advice and henceforth do
likewise in all things.[1]

After having thus made a public spectacle of his son's humiliation and submission, the King took him to Canterbury, accompanied by Archbishop Richard, to give thanks to God and St.
Thomas 'for the peace so gloriously restored to him'.[2] The
choir of the cathedral had been destroyed by fire in the previous
September. The work of rebuilding it was under the direction
of William of Sens, the first architect of an English cathedral
whose name has come down to us.

While the young Henry was thus being led about by his father,
Richard was engaged in reducing the castles of the rebels in
Aquitaine. These rebels had not been his allies during the revolt;
they had turned against all authority, either his father's or his own,
and it was as much to his advantage, as prospective Duke of
Aquitaine, as it was to his father's, for him to bring them under
control.

Around Midsummer Day he laid siege to a castle in the
Agenais, lying about half-way between Bordeaux and Toulouse,
which Arnald of Bonville had fortified against him. Richard
brought up his siege engines and within two months captured the
castle and its garrison of thirty knights. Geoffrey was engaged

---

[1] Ibid., Vol. I, pp. 399-401.   [2] Gervase of Canterbury, Vol. I, p. 256.

in a similar task in Brittany, and 'he inflicted many evils on the men of that country who had held out against his father in the time of war'.[1]

The King's uncle, Earl Reginald of Cornwall, died on July 1, 1175, and was buried in Reading Abbey, where his father lay. Although the Earl had three daughters, the King kept his lands with the intention of giving them to John, who seems by now to have been firmly established in his position as Henry's favourite son.[2]

Archbishop Richard, during the previous autumn, had consecrated all the bishops-elect except Geoffrey, the King's bastard son, who needed a dispensation from the Pope, both because of his illegitimacy and because of his being under the canonical age of thirty. While the King was holding a council at Woodstock, a mandate was received from the Pope on July 9, dispensing Geoffrey from those impediments. Archbishop Richard thereupon confirmed his election. He was received with a solemn procession at Lincoln on August 1. He was so ill fitted for his post, however, because of his youth and inexperience, that his father sent him to Tours to study 'until he should be worthy of the dignity of such an honour'.

At this same council the King decreed, as a measure of protection for his person, that none of his late enemies should come to his court except at his order and that no-one should come to court before sunrise or remain after sunset. He also ordered that no-one east of the Severn was to wear arms, either bow and arrow or a pointed knife.[3]

These orders were observed only for a short time. Henry's ways were so informal and so lacking in kingly pomp that he soon returned to his old habit of being readily accessible to anyone who wanted to see him.

From Woodstock the King and his son went to Lichfield, and there Henry ordered that four knights and their companions, who had killed one of his foresters, should be hanged. This year marks the beginning of the King's practice of having in his train as he travelled about the country some of the royal justiciars, who heard cases in his presence. These hearings were distinct from those conducted by the itinerant justiciars, who made a circuit of

¹ *Gesta*, Vol. I, p. 101.   ² Robert of Torigni, p. 268.
                            ³ *Gesta*, Vol. I, p. 93.

the country in the course of the year.   The Pipe Roll for this
year for the first time carries a separate group of entries for the
counties the King visited, under the heading: 'Pleas and Agree-
ments by William son of Ralph and Bertran (of Verdun) and
William Basset in the King's Court.'

These can hardly be called judicial hearings, for the majority
of them resulted in fines offered 'to have the King's good will'.
They marked the beginning, however, of Henry's active partici-
pation in the work of the King's Court, and although that work
can scarcely be distinguished from the extortion of bribes, it led
to a further concentration of power in his hands, for he asserted
his right to override both his sheriffs and his itinerant justiciars
and to settle all cases that were brought before him.

When they reached Nottingham, on August 1, the King accused
the barons and knights of that part of the country, one of the
chief centres of disaffection, of breaches of the forest law.   He
later extended this accusation to include a great host of barons,
knights, clerks, and villeins alike.   He began laying heavy amercements, a work that was continued by his forest justiciars and that
bore fruit in the Pipe Roll of the following year.

Richard of Luci, the Chief Justiciar, protested vigorously
against these forest amercements.   He showed the King his own
letters ordering Richard to open the forests and fishponds during
the war and to permit all who wanted to hunt and fish therein.
Richard felt that his own honour was at stake, since it was with
his permission that those whom the King was now prosecuting
had acted.   Henry paid no attention to his protests.

The two Henrys met the King of Scots at York on August 10
for a formal ratification of the treaty they had agreed upon at
Falaise as the price of William's release.   The King of Scots was
accompanied by his brother David and by all his bishops, earls,
barons, knights, and freeholders, 'from the greatest down to the
least'.   They assembled in the cathedral, and all the Scots, beginning with their King, did homage and swore allegiance to
King Henry and then to Henry, his son, 'saving their faith to his
father'.[1]

With the Scots reduced to abject submission, the King then
accused 'the earls and barons and even the clerks of Yorkshire
and even the clerks of the Church of St. Peter of York' of offences

[1] Ibid., Vol. I, pp. 94-96.

against the forest laws. In addition to these charges, he had the sheriff, Robert of Stuteville, lay heavy amercements on a great many people for their offences during the rebellion, although the men of Yorkshire, from the accounts of the chroniclers, acted with courage and loyalty in defeating the Scots. These amercements seem especially unfair in view of the fact that Yorkshire had borne the brunt of King William's depredations in 1172. While the lesser folk were heavily punished, the leaders of the rebellion, the Earls of Leicester and Chester and Earl Ferrers, were restored to their lands and honours, and even Earl Hugh of Norfolk was amerced only a thousand marks.

In addition to these exactions, the itinerant justiciars, Hugh of Cressy and Rannulf of Glanville, punished the people still further for their offences. Finally, in his new role as fount of justice, the King heard nine cases in the City of York, of which eight resulted in fines ranging from ten to six hundred marks 'to have the King's good will'.[1]

Count Philip of Flanders, meanwhile, was prevented from fulfilling his vow and setting out for the Holy Land by trouble that arose in connection with his wife, Isabel of Vermandois, the daughter of Queen Eleanor's sister, Petronilla, whom he had married in 1155, and who brought him the Counties of Amiens and Vermandois as her dowry. Isabel had fallen in love with one Walter of Les Fontaines, 'who shone amongst his fellow knights like Lucifer amongst the smaller stars by reason of his noble birth and the brilliance of his uprightness and wisdom', and took him as her lover. Count Philip found out about it and three times forbade Walter to set foot within his house.

When they were at St-Omer around the middle of August, Philip left one day amidst loud talk of being gone for several days. Isabel at once sent for her lover and received him in her bedchamber. Philip, who was waiting at no great distance, was notified by a servant detailed for that task, rushed back, and surprised the lovers.

Walter, in his uprightness and wisdom, tried to hide behind the excuse that the Countess had sent for him. Philip had him tied hand and foot, beaten almost to death, and then hung by his heels over a noisome cesspool, 'where he most miserably finished his life'. Walter's kinsmen then stocked their castles and re-

[1] Pipe Roll 21 Henry II, pp. 182-3.

belled against Philip, who was delayed from his pilgrimage by the necessity for putting down the rebellion.[1]

Rory O'Connor, King of Connaught, who had refused to submit to Henry when he was in Ireland, had been sorely pressed, since the King's departure, both by Strongbow and Strongbow's brother-in-law, Raymond the Fat, and by the petty kings who were nominally subject to him. In order to secure Henry's recognition and support, Rory sent three envoys to the King. Henry called a meeting of the Great Council to discuss their proposals, and a treaty was agreed upon.

> This is the settlement and agreement that was made at Windsor on the octave-day of St. Michael, in the year of Our Lord 1175, between the Lord King of England, Henry, the son of the Empress Matilda, and Rory, King of Connaught: . . .
>
> To wit, that Henry, King of England, granted to the aforesaid Rory, his liege man, King of Connaught, as long as he faithfully serves him, that he may be king under him, ready for his service as his man; and that he may hold his land as well and in peace as he held it before the Lord King of England entered Ireland, by paying him tribute; and that he may have every other land and its inhabitants under him and exercise justice, so that they may pay full tribute to the King of England, and he may keep them for himself by his hand and his law.

Henry promised that if Rory needed help in governing his kingdom the King's Constable and his other servants in Ireland would give it him. In return for his recognition as High King, Rory agreed to pay one hide 'pleasing to the merchants' for every ten head of cattle in Ireland. The treaty specified, however, that the cities of Dublin, Wexford, and Waterford and the Counties of Meath and Leinster were to remain under Henry's direct control, so that only the purely Irish areas were to be subject to Rory.[2]

At the end of October Cardinal Hugh Pierleoni landed in England and went to Winchester to see the King. Henry and his son, accompanied by their court, went to meet him and received him with every mark of honour. Gervase of Canterbury says that the King was trying to get a divorce from Eleanor, who was still imprisoned in Salisbury Castle, and that he had summoned the Legate for that purpose. Gerald of Wales adds that

---

[1] *Gesta*, Vol. I, pp. 99-101.   [2] Ibid., Vol. I, pp. 101-3.

he did this with the intention of marrying Alice of France, who was in his keeping and who was betrothed to Richard.[1]

Henry loaded the Cardinal with gifts and fair words, and there can be little doubt that even without those bribes he could have secured an annulment of his marriage if he had so desired, since Eleanor was as closely related to him as she was to her previous husband, Louis of France. Before he took any steps to rid himself of her, however, Henry had second thoughts about the matter. In giving up Eleanor he would also give up her Duchy of Aquitaine. Not only would he thus lose half his continental domains at one stroke; he would also be forced to surrender it to Eleanor as Duchess and Richard as Duke of Aquitaine, with Louis as their overlord. It would invite trouble, of a surety, thus to place weapons in the hands of a woman who hated him and of a son who had already rebelled against him.

Henry consoled himself by taking as his regular mistress one Rosamund Clifford, the 'Fair Rosamund' of later ballads and legends. Gerald of Wales was undoubtedly referring to her when he wrote: 'The King, who before this [the rebellion of his sons] had been a secret adulterer, now became a notorious one, consorting openly and shamelessly, not with the Rose of the World [*Rosa Mundi*], as she was falsely and most frivolously styled, but, more truly, with the Rose of an impure man [*Rosa immundi*].'[2]

Although Henry had summoned the clergy to meet at Woodstock in the preceding July to elect a Bishop of Norwich, no action had been taken at that time. At Eynsham, on November 26, 'by the agreement of the monks of Norwich, by the King's consent, by the Archbishop's connivance, and by the Cardinal's authority', John of Oxford, Dean of Salisbury, was elected Bishop of Norwich.[3] No-one embroiled in the controversy over St. Thomas had earned such hatred and contempt from the Archbishop's friends as had this time-serving clerk who had taken the schismatical oath never to recognise Alexander III as Pope. It is significant that Henry made no attempt to advance him till after the arrival of Cardinal Hugh Pierleoni, whom Gervase of Canterbury[4] accuses of having gone all over England taking

---

[1] Gervase of Canterbury, Vol. I, pp. 256-7; Gerald of Wales: *De Principis Instructione*, p. 232.   [2] Gerald of Wales, op. cit., pp. 165-6.
[3] Ralph of Diceto, Vol. I, p. 403.   [4] Vol. I, p. 257.

money right and left to put in his own coffers. Archbishop
Richard consecrated John 'Bishop of the East Angles' at Lambeth
on December 14.

The King and his son kept Christmas at Windsor, and the King
paid all the young Henry's debts that he had run up 'for eating
and drinking' in Normandy, Maine, and Anjou during the last
three years.[1] In the course of this year the young Henry's friend,
Asculf of St-Hilaire, set out for Jerusalem and died on the way.[2]

During this year a plague raged in England, 'so that on many
days seven or eight bodies of the dead were carried out to be
buried', presumably from the same church.[3] The plague was
followed by a dire famine. The winter was so severe that everything was covered with snow and ice from Christmas till Candlemas.[4] What with the devastation resulting from the war, the
crushing fines levied by the King for forest offences and for having
given aid to his enemies, the plague, the famine, and the severe
winter, the year could hardly have been a happy one in England.

The new year brought the promulgation of a new and stricter
set of laws. At a meeting of the Great Council at Northampton
on January 25, 1176, the King instituted a new assize to supersede
the one published at Clarendon ten years earlier. He began by
dividing the country into six judicial districts and appointing
three justiciars for each district. All of them had had previous
experience as justiciars, as sheriffs, or as clerks at the Exchequer.
These men, called 'itinerant justiciars' for the first time in the
Pipe Roll of this year, swore, with their hands on the Gospels,
that they would obey the assize and make all the men of the kingdom keep it. The King then had the assize, or instructions to the
justiciars, read to the assembly.

The Assize of Northampton added three crimes, forgery, arson,
and treason, to the offences to be enquired into by the justiciars.
It omitted any mention of the sheriffs, which would indicate that
Henry wanted his new justiciars to take over some of the judicial
functions formerly exercised by the sheriffs in the county courts.
Those who failed the judgment of water, in addition to being
exiled, were to have their right foot lopped off.

The principal innovation was the introduction of the proceeding later known as the Assize of Mort d'Ancestor. The earlier

[1] Ralph of Diceto, Vol. I, p. 404.   [2] Robert of Torigni, p. 272.
[3] *Gesta*, Vol. I, p. 104.   [4] Robert of Torigni, p. 270.

Assize of Novel Disseisin provided a remedy in the King's courts for those who had been unjustly deprived of their land. No provision had been made, however, for a rightful heir who was unable to gain possession of his inheritance in the first place. As long as his only recourse was to the court of the lord who was denying him his inheritance, he had little hope of obtaining justice.

This assize provided that if the lord of the fief denied possession to the heir, the justiciars were to summon a sworn inquest, as in the earlier proceeding, of twelve law-worthy men, who would then state on oath what lands the dead man was possessed of at the time of his death. When they had given their verdict, the justiciars were to see to it that the heir was given possession of those lands.

This procedure marked an important step in the King's steady curtailment of the power of his barons by taking legal jurisdictions away from them, even though their own lands were concerned, and making his courts supreme over theirs. The lands in question belonged to the barons, to be sure, but they held them of the King, whose ownership of all the land of England was at this time no mere legal fiction but a real possession, as Henry took pains to impress upon his barons, both by asserting his over-riding right to jurisdiction over it and by confiscating the lands of those who incurred his displeasure.

The itinerant justiciars set out on their circuits and covered most of England before the Michaelmas following. Each sheriff accounted then 'for the chattels of the fugitives and outlaws and those who failed the judgment of water by the Assize of Northampton' and gave a list of their names, as directed by the closing chapter of the Assize. The total came to around 570 men, and their confiscated chattels brought in the sum of £274 7s. 4d.

At the King's advice, Cardinal Hugh Pierleoni summoned all the bishops and abbots of England to a council at Westminster 'to hear the orders and precepts of the Supreme Pontiff'. The clergy met on Laetare Sunday, March 14. When the prelates took their seats, Archbishop Richard of Canterbury sat at the Legate's right, in the position of honour. Archbishop Roger of York was not content to sit at the Cardinal's left, in the second place. He claimed precedence over the Archbishop of Canterbury, and, when Richard would not yield his seat to him, he plumped himself down in the Archbishop's lap.

At this insult to their Archbishop, his servants, some of the bishops, and the monks of Canterbury threw Roger to the floor, kicked and beat him unmercifully, and tore his clothes to shreds. When he was rescued from his assailants and set on his feet again, he went away sniffling, to exhibit his wounds and his tattered robes to the King. As he left, many of the members of the council shouted after him: 'Go on, you betrayer of St. Thomas! Your hands still stink with blood!'

The Legate, unable to quell the riot and seeing his authority scorned, dismissed the council.[1]

The young Henry had now been constantly with his father for over a year. The King had taken him with him wherever he went, explained the administration of the country to him, had him beside him at all his councils, and done everything in his power to win his love and fidelity: everything, that is, except the one thing the young man wanted. His father still would not grant him any territory of his own, over which he might exercise independent authority. No doubt the elder Henry thought that he was training his son for his future station in life. To the younger Henry, however, it seemed that he was little better than a prisoner, dragged about over the country, separated from his friends, and pinched in purse.

Even the most sober of the chroniclers throw aside all restraint in praising his beauty and charm. 'He was handsome beyond all others in body and in face, most blessed with eloquence and affability, most happy in men's love and grace and favour, so moving in persuasion that he led almost all his father's subjects to rise up against him,' says Walter Map. 'So rich, so generous, so lovable, so eloquent, so handsome, so vigorous, so gracious in all things, so little lower than the angels: yet he turned it all to evil.' 'A most fair fountain of evil' and 'a most lovely palace of sin' are some of the epithets Walter applies to him.[2]

The young Henry determined to get away from his father's supervision and conceived the idea of going on a pilgrimage to the shrine of St. James at Compostella. Henry saw through the scheme immediately as proceeding not from any religious feeling

[1] *Gesta*, Vol. I, pp. 112-14; Gervase of Canterbury, Vol. I, pp. 258-9; Ralph of Diceto, Vol. I, pp. 405-6.　　　　[2] *De Nugis Curialium*, pp. 139-40.

'but from the evil counsel of his flatterers, who sought to free him from the gentleness of his fatherly castigation'. The King refused his permission. After repeated requests failed to move his father, the young Henry then asked leave to go at least to Normandy. The King agreed. The young Henry and his wife and their household went to Porchester, but a contrary wind delayed their departure.

The King went to Winchester to hold his Easter court, and since the young Henry was still waiting at Porchester the King invited his son to join him. Richard and Geoffrey landed at Southampton on Good Friday, April 2, and went to Winchester on the following day. Henry held a great court and celebrated the festival with his three sons.[1] His bear was brought from Nottingham, and an entry in the Pipe Roll suggests that Queen Eleanor was present at the feast or at least that she was permitted to leave her prison and come to see her sons:

> To Robert Mald, 56s., for paying for the Queen's maintenance at Winchester, by the King's writ.[2]

Richard had come to England to report to his father on his difficulties in Aquitaine and to ask for help. After his initial success in the preceding summer, a great conspiracy of the Aquitanian nobles had sprung up over the winter. Such trouble threatened that Richard was afraid that he would not be able to cope with it alone.

He got scant help from his father. Henry persuaded his eldest son to go to Poitou with Richard and help him put down the rebellion. This was at least a temporary solution for the problem of how to keep the young Henry occupied and out of trouble, but it helped Richard not at all. The young King and his wife sailed from Southampton on April 19, and Richard sailed in a separate fleet. As soon as Henry and Margaret landed at Barfleur they hastened to France to see King Louis. Richard, with characteristic independence and self-reliance, went on to Poitou, raised an army, and marched to Limoges, where Viscount Aymar was raising the standard of rebellion. Richard first captured Aymar's castle at Aixe, a few miles west of Limoges, and took forty knights prisoner. Then he laid seige to Limoges. Within a few days he captured the city and its fortifications. With the

---

[1] *Gesta*, Vol. I, pp. 114–15.   [2] Pipe Roll 22 Henry, II pp. 90–91.

Northern Aquitaine

rebels thus checked, he returned to Poitiers towards the end of
June.

His elder brother then joined him, and Richard called a council
of his Poitevin barons.   They advised him to proceed against
Viscount Vulgrin, the son of the Count of Angoulême and the
chief promoter of the revolt.   Henry, Richard, and his Poitevins
accordingly laid siege to Vulgrin's castle at Château-neuf-sur-
Charente and took it within a fortnight.

With the campaign barely begun, the fickle young Henry left

his brother and went back to Poitiers. While Richard continued his expedition into the Angoumois, Henry used Poitiers as
his headquarters for rallying round him many of the French and
Norman knights who had sided with him during the rebellion.
Soon the young King had gathered a band of companions of
such dubious character that his Vice-Chancellor, Adam of
Churchdown, was gravely alarmed and feared that his young
master was preparing for a second rebellion. Adam therefore
wrote to King Henry to warn him of the state of affairs. His
letter was intercepted and brought to the young Henry.

'Take him out,' the young King ordered, 'and tie his hands
behind his back and whip him naked through the streets of the
city, proclaiming, so that all may know, that he is a traitor to me.
And take him to Normandy, and whenever you come to a city
whip him naked through the streets, and imprison him at Argentan.'[1]

During this summer, whether before or after his excursion to
Poitou there is little indication, the young Henry was introduced
to the joys and excitement of the tournament. The author of
the *Gesta Henrici* says that immediately after his landing in April
Henry went to visit Louis and does not mention him again till he
joined Richard at the end of June. The biographer of William
Marshal,[2] who can hardly be relied upon for exactitude concerning events that happened about fifty years before he wrote his
poem, says that Henry and his suite, which included William
Marshal, landed in Flanders and met Count Philip. Philip
greeted his young cousin, an erstwhile ally, warmly and took
him to a great tournament. The young Henry, fresh from his
father's leading-strings and furnished with clothes and horses
after the King's parsimonious fashion, expressed a wistful desire
to join in the tournament, if only he had arms and horses. Count
Philip, who rejoiced in his reputation for splendid generosity,
fitted him out magnificently, and Henry took part in the game.

From that day, the young King threw his whole heart and soul
into tournaments. He gathered about him a band of young men
of similar tastes, probably the same knights that he recruited at
Poitiers, and they went from tournament to tournament. ' The
young King, who was good and beautiful and courteous, did so

[1] *Gesta*, Vol. I, pp. 115, 120-3.
[2] *Histoire de Guillaume le Maréchal*, lines 2436-96.

well in his life that he brought chivalry back to life, which at that time was near to death. . . . He brought joy and laughter back into the world.'[1]

The tournaments of the Twelfth Century were by no means the beautiful and romantic spectacles that later writers made of them. They differed little from actual warfare, except that they were held at a time and place advertised well in advance; hostilities ceased by general agreement at a given hour and were followed by a truce devoted to drinking, boasting, visiting, and, for the less fortunate, the repairing of armour and the dressing of wounds; and at the end of the tournament the leading men of each side met and awarded the prize to the best fighter.

Otherwise, these combats were indistinguishable from real wars. Men fought with naked weapons, but few knights were seriously injured because of the protection afforded by their almost impenetrable coats of chain mail. Some men led bands of foot-soldiers, armed with pikes, onto the field, and they could inflict great damage on each other. The knights did not hesitate to gang up on a single man of the opposing side if they could cut him off from his fellows. The biographer of William Marshal tells, with great approval of his master's cleverness, how William, sitting at table, saw a knight fall from his horse and break a limb outside the hostel. William ran out, captured the defenceless knight, lugged him into the house, and told his companions: 'Here, this will pay your debts.'[2]

The young Henry consistently lost, until he picked up a trick from his cousin Philip. The Count of Flanders, who enjoyed the highest reputation for chivalry, would wait with his troop of knights on the side lines till the others were exhausted and in disorder. Then the gallant Count would charge into the encounter and capture knights right and left.[3]

In addition to the excitement and joy of the battle and the satisfaction of sharing in the roughest sport known in those days, the tournament offered rich rewards to the skilful. The object, as in real warfare, was to capture as many of the opposing knights as possible and hold them to ransom. A good and experienced fighter like William Marshal could not only support himself thus but also amass a small fortune. An inexperienced fighter like the

[1] Ibid., lines 2637-41, 2693-5.   [2] Ibid., lines 7209-32.
[3] Ibid., lines 2713-72.

R

young Henry, on the other hand, who brought onto the field as many as a hundred knights in his entourage, could lose large sums indeed.[1]

Tournaments were not held in England till the reign of King Richard. From the time of the Conquest, the assembling of large bodies of armed knights in such warlike exercises would have held the threat of revolt, and neither Henry nor his predecessors would tolerate them. They flourished in France and Normandy on a great scale. In Aquitaine, however, their place was taken by serious and almost constant warfare amongst the nobles or between the nobles and the ducal power.

It was this rebellious warfare that Richard was determined to stamp out. Young as he was, for Richard was not yet nineteen, he set about with a grim earnestness in utter contrast to the frivolous irresponsibility displayed by his elder brother. Later in his life Richard showed a passionate interest in poetry and music, but in his youth we can see, from the scanty references of the chroniclers, only a serious young man, gifted with great strength, long legs, and good looks, golden-haired and blue-eyed, relentlessly hammering away at the rebellious Southern nobles till they should acknowledge and respect his rule.

After his brother left him in the lurch, Richard pushed south and laid siege to Angoulême, where in the castle were gathered the leading rebels of the Angoumois and the Limousin: William Taillefer, Count of Angoulême; Viscount Vulgrin, his son; Viscount Aymar of Limoges; and the Viscounts of Ventadour and Chabenais. Their rebellion was fanned by the troubadour, Bertrand of Born, lord of Hautefort, who had composed a poem, *Un sirventes on motz non falh*, to stir them up against Richard.[2]

Even though they were thus inspired, the rebels were no match for Richard and his army, and they surrendered after a week's siege. Count William delivered up his city of Angoulême and five of his most important castles to Richard. The young victor sent the rebels to his father, in England, for their punishment, but Henry sent them back to await his return to Normandy.[3]

Early in September Henry sent his youngest daughter, Joan, to Sicily to be married to King William II. Her father provided

[1] *Histoire de Guillaume le Maréchal*, Introduction, pp. xxxvi–xxxix.

[2] F. J. M. Raynouard: *Choix des poésies originales des troubadours* (Paris, 6 vols., 1819-20), Vol. IV, p. 141.   [3] *Gesta*, Vol. I, p. 121.

her with a splendid outfit, including a robe, presumably her wedding dress, that cost the stupendous sum of £114 5s. 5d., by far the most costly garment mentioned in the Pipe Rolls.[1] Women wore a robe reaching from their neck to their feet, with ample sleeves to the wrists. It was fastened at the throat or shoulders by brooches and gathered at the waist by a girdle. Robes were made of wool, of linen, or of silk, depending upon the wealth of the wearer. For the upper classes they were richly embroidered with the needlework for which England was famous. One may surmise, from its cost, that Joan's was not only heavily embroidered but encrusted with jewels as well.

The King held a council at Windsor at Michaelmas and announced his decision to take all the castles of the country into his own hands in order to forestall the possibility of another rebellion. Even the most faithful of his barons were forced to surrender their castles, into which the King put his own trusted men; even the Chief Justiciar, Richard of Luci, whose loyalty no-one had ever questioned, had to surrender his castle of Ongar, in Essex.

In addition to the heavy amercements levied for offences against the forest laws, the King had his justiciars amerce many of those who took part in the rebellion, who gave aid to his enemies, or who were suspected of disloyalty. Cospatric, son of Orm, 'the old grey-haired Englishman', was amerced five hundred marks 'because he surrendered Appleby Castle to the King of Scots'. Twenty-three of his friends and advisers, including 'William, the clerk of Appleby', were included in the sentence.[2] These amercements brought the total paid in or accounted for by the sheriffs at the Exchequer for the year to over £22,600, including £4,600 from the forest amercements.[3]

At the council at Windsor the King's cousin, Earl William of Gloucester, named the young John as heir to his vast estates in the west of England. William had three daughters, of whom the two oldest were already married, and no sons. The King now declared that in exchange for these lands John should marry the youngest daughter, known as Hadwisa, Isabel, or Avice, if the Pope would dispense them from the impediment of consanguinity. John's previous betrothed, Alice of Maurienne, had died some time before this; no chronicler took the trouble to

[1] Pipe Roll 22 Henry II, pp. 12-13.   [2] Ibid., p. 119.
[3] Ramsay, op. cit., Vol. I, pp. 125-6.

record the child's death.　As a sop to the two elder daughters, who were thus being disinherited, Henry promised to pay each of them a hundred pounds a year.[1]

The King kept his Christmas at Nottingham, and his sons Geoffrey and John were with him.　Queen Eleanor was still presumably confined in Salisbury Castle.　The young Henry and his wife held their court at Argentan in Normandy, and Richard was at Bordeaux.[2]

[1] *Gesta*, Vol. I, pp. 124-5.　　　　　　　　　　[2] Ibid., Vol. I, p. 131.

XV

'OUR PEACE-LOVING KING'
1177 - 1179

ALTHOUGH Richard had, for the time being, subdued the northern part of his Duchy, Gascony, in the south, began to show signs of revolt. Immediately after Christmas the young Duke marched south to Dax, where Viscount Peter of Dax and his friend Count Centulle of Bigorre had fortified the castle and were preparing to defy him. Richard captured the castle and moved southwest to Bayonne, against Viscount Ernald Bertram, who surrendered within ten days. He then went on to Ciboure and captured the castle of St-Pierre on January 9. He destroyed the castle, and after this display of his strength he forced the Basques and Navarrese to swear to forego their evil customs and particularly their habit of preying on the pilgrims to Compostella. He returned triumphantly to Poitou at Candlemas and sent messengers to his father to announce his successes.[1]

The King, meanwhile, held a meeting of the Great Council at Northampton around the middle of January. Count Philip of Flanders sent two ambassadors to tell him that King Louis was demanding his nieces, the two daughters of Count Matthew of Boulogne, the heiresses to that County now that both their father and their uncle Peter, who had died in the previous year, were dead. Louis proposed to marry Ida, the elder, to his son, Philip, and thus secure Boulogne for the French crown; the younger, Matilda, he planned to marry to the son of Count Theobald of Blois.

After thus displaying the weapon that Count Philip could use against Henry if he were so minded, his envoys told Henry that Philip would be grateful if the King would send him the money he had promised to hire knights for the defence of Jerusalem, a gesture that Henry had promised to make for the repose of the soul of Count Matthew.

[1] *Gesta*, Vol. I, p. 132.

Henry realised the threat implicit in this message. Boulogne in French hands would be a constant menace to England. He therefore assured the Count that he would fulfil his promise 'more fully and more perfectly even than he had promised', if Philip would agree not to dispose of his nieces without the King's consent.[1]

At this council the King took the first step toward fulfilling a vow he had made, 'for the remission of his sins', to build a house for the Austin Canons in honour of St. Thomas, who had been educated at an Austin house at Merton. Henry had obtained permission from the Pope to delay setting out on the crusade, which he had promised to do within three years after his absolution at Avranches in 1172, by undertaking to build three monasteries.[2] With characteristic niggardliness, Henry ousted the secular canons from the church at Waltham that King Harold had built and endowed and where the last Old English king was buried. Henry enlarged the church and installed a group of Austin Canons, to live on the endowment that Harold had provided.

His second foundation, begun at this same time, was at Amesbury, in Wiltshire. The nuns of the convent there had acquired a reputation for loose living, and their abbess, the Lady Beatrice, was said to have had three children since she had become a nun. The Pope therefore ordered that she be deposed. Henry sent Bishops Bartholomew of Exeter and Roger of Worcester to Amesbury to turn out the wretched Beatrice, to whom the King gave a pension of ten marks a year 'lest she die of hunger and want', and to disperse the nuns, except those who were willing to remain and submit to the new discipline that Henry proposed to introduce.

The King sent to the Abbess of Fontevrault, a great house in the Loire valley ten miles west of Chinon, and asked her to provide a group of nuns to take over the house at Amesbury. The nuns at Fontevrault, the mother house of a contemplative order that had spread widely through Anjou and Poitou, had a reputation for great sanctity and enjoyed the particular favour of the Counts of Anjou. Henry's aunt Matilda, the widow of William the Atheling, had been Abbess there. By paying the expenses of the nuns' journey and making some repairs to the

[1] *Gesta.*, Vol. I, pp. 133, 136.
[2] Gerald of Wales: *De Principis Instructione*, p. 170.

buildings, Henry counted Amesbury in fulfilment of his vow.[1]

The King kept Palm Sunday, April 17, 1177, at Reading. While he was there, messengers came from Count Philip to tell him that the Count was preparing to come to England to confer with him and to make a pilrimage to the shrine of St. Thomas. Philip landed at Dover on the 20th and went straightway to Canterbury. The King hastened to meet him on the next day, and the cousins made their devotions together. Philip asked and received the King's permission to set out on his long-deferred pilgrimage to the Holy Land, and Henry gave him five hundred marks to help pay his expenses. The Count set out around May 1, accompanied by many French knights and by an English contingent headed by William of Mandeville, Earl of Essex, the King's best friend.[2]

At a meeting of the Great Council at Oxford in May, the King announced his new plans for the governing of Ireland and for the advancement of his son John. He had secured from Pope Alexander permission to crown whichever of his sons he chose as King of Ireland. Henry now revealed that he intended to confer that honour on John, who was ten years old at the time. Until such time as his son should be able to rule in his own person, Henry sent Hugh of Lacy back to Ireland to act as his vicegerent.[3] Betrothed to one of the richest heiresses in England and with the prospect of being King of Ireland, John's fortunes looked fair indeed.

King Louis, meanwhile, had been insisting that the marriage contract between Richard and his daughter Alice be fulfilled. They had been betrothed at Montmirail in January 1169, and Alice had been turned over to Henry. She was now sixteen, and Richard was almost twenty. It may be that Henry was unwilling, in view of Louis's support and encouragement of his sons during their rebellion, for Richard to come still further under the influence of the King of France by marrying his daughter. A more discreditable explanation is that Henry was already unduly attracted to the young Alice. As early as October 1175 he was said to be contemplating divorcing Eleanor and marrying Alice. In later years he was accused of having made her his mistress and of having had several children by her.

[1] *Gesta*, Vol. I, pp. 134-6.   [2] Ibid., Vol. I, pp. 158-9.
[3] Ibid., Vol. I, pp. 161-5.

Whether or not such a relationship existed at this time, Henry at any rate displayed great reluctance to have her married to Richard. Richard, for his part, showed not the slightest interest in the matter.

A letter from Pope Alexander states that Louis had already referred the question to him in the preceding year:

> Alexander the Bishop, the servant of the servants of God, to his beloved sons, Peter, Priest of St. Chrysogonus, and Hugh [Pierleoni], Deacon of San Angelo, Cardinals and Legates of the Apostolic See: greetings.
>
> Inasmuch as the daughter of our dearest son in Christ, Louis, the illustrious King of the French, whom Henry, the illustrious King of the English, received long ago to unite in marriage to his son Richard, Duke of Aquitaine, is said to have reached an age fitting for marriage: the same King of the French complains seriously concerning us, because with our sufferance, as he asserts, that same daughter has neither been returned to him nor turned over to the aforesaid Duke, as she should be.
>
> Because, therefore, the same King of the French insists upon one or the other, and we would not, as we should not, fail to help him in this matter, for it would be disgraceful, unseemly, and absurd that the daughter of this same King should any longer be detained in such a manner: we order you by this Apostolic letter to strive jointly and singly on our part and yours, by solicitous admonitions and exhortations, to induce the aforesaid King of the English either to have the aforementioned daughter of this same King turned over to the aforenamed Duke within two months, in magnificent fashion, as befits both Kings, or to return her to the aforesaid King without delay.
>
> If, however, he does neither of these at your bidding within the prescribed period, by our authority we forbid the celebration of all divine offices, except the baptism of babes and the shriving of the dying, in the whole Province of Canterbury, without the remedy of appeal, until he does one or the other. And if he is not brought to reason by this, then do you lay the whole County of Poitou under like sentence. Furthermore, if one of you should not want or should not be able to concern himself with following this matter through, then let the other one of you nevertheless follow through with it.
>
> Given at Anagni, on May 21 [1176].[1]

The two Cardinals, in view of the weak ending of this letter,

---

[1] *Rerum Gallicarum Scriptores* (Paris, 1808), Vol. XV, pp. 954-5.

failed to take any punitive measures against Henry. They warned him of the Pope's attitude, however, and Henry strove to place the blame on Louis. On April 30, 1177, the Pope wrote a much stronger letter to Cardinal Peter alone, giving him definite orders to pronounce an interdict on all of Henry's lands if he did not either return Alice to her father or have her married to Richard within forty days.[1]

At the news of this latest threat, Henry sent a group of envoys to King Louis to charge him with failing to abide by his treaties. Although Henry had acquired the Norman Vexin, Margaret's dowry, by a bit of sharp practice, he now claimed that Louis had also promised him the French Vexin, lying between Gisors and Pontoise. Furthermore, by the terms of the marriage contract made at Montmirail, Louis had agreed to give the city of Bourges to Alice as her dowry. Henry demanded that Louis give him both those territories before Alice and Richard were married. Finally, he insisted that Louis send his daughter Margaret, who was pregnant and had gone to visit her father without Henry's leave, back to Normandy. In the meantime, about June 19, Queen Margaret gave birth, in Paris, to a son. The child lived long enough to be christened William and died when he was three days old.[2]

A messenger from his envoys brought Henry the news, on July 12, that Cardinal Peter, who had meanwhile been elected Bishop of Meaux and was taking a much keener interest in King Louis's affairs, had at last decided to obey the Pope's orders. The Cardinal had paid no attention to Henry's demands on Louis and had announced that unless Henry immediately permitted Richard to marry Alice or else returned her to her father, he would lay his dominions on both sides of the Channel under interdict.

At the receipt of this news, Henry consulted Archbishop Richard 'and other wise men of his realm who were there present'. They advised the usual recourse in such circumstances, an appeal to Rome. The prelates then 'placed the King, themselves, and the whole realm of England under the protection of the Lord Pope and appealed to him'.[3] An appeal to Rome could be counted on to introduce at least a year's delay into the matter, to give Henry time to think up further expedients.

[1] Ibid., Vol. XV, pp. 955-6. [2] *Gesta*, Vol. I, pp. 168-9, 177.
[3] Ibid., Vol. I, pp. 180-1.

While the King was thus engaged, the Pope and the Emperor Frederick Barbarossa were concluding a treaty of peace and putting an end to the schism. After he was defeated by the Lombard League at the Battle of Legnano, on May 29, 1176, Frederick sued for peace. The long negotiations were concluded at Venice on July 24, 1177. The Pope's envoys absolved the Emperor from his excommunication; Frederick and his bishops abjured the schism, renounced their adherence to the anti-pope Calixtus, and accepted Alexander III as the true Pope.[1]

Henry, accompanied by his son Geoffrey, sailed for Normandy on August 17. As soon as he landed, he sent Geoffrey 'to make war on his enemies of Brittany'. The young Henry and Richard met their father 'with great joy and honour'[2] and went with him to Rouen. Henry met Louis at Nonancourt on September 21, in the presence of Cardinal Peter and many barons and bishops, amongst whom was John of Salisbury, who had been elected Bishop of Chartres in the preceding year. Henry astonished them all by agreeing without any difficulty to the marriage of Richard and Alice, but he astutely omitted to set any date for it. By what arguments he swayed the credulous Louis we do not know; at any rate, he completely confused the issue by inducing Louis to agree to set out on the Crusade with him.

Let all men, both present and to come, know that I, Louis, by the grace of God King of the French, and I, Henry, by the same grace King of England, wish it to come to the knowledge of all men, both present and to come, that we, by God's inspiration, have promised and sworn that we will go together in the service of Christianity and that we will take the Cross and go to Jerusalem, as it is contained in the writing concerning the taking of the Cross that was made between us.

We will that all men know that we are thus and wish henceforth to be friends and that each of us will guard the other in life and limb and earthly honour, against all men, to the utmost of his power. And if anyone shall try to do harm to either of us, I, Henry, will help Louis, King of France, my lord, against all men to the utmost of my power. And I, Louis, will help Henry, King of England, against all men to the utmost of my power, as my man and faithful liege; saving the faith we owe to our men, as long as they shall keep faith with us. And neither of us henceforth will shelter any enemy of the other in his land from the time when he is demanded thence.[3]

[1] *Gesta*, Vol. I, pp. 189-90.   [2] Robert of Torigni, p. 273.
[3] *Gesta*, Vol. I, pp. 190-4.

This treaty was a masterpiece of duplicity on Henry's part, for it satisfied Louis and the Papal Legate concerning Alice's marriage without committing Henry to a definite date for giving up the young woman.

In the course of this year, Peter of Blois, Archdeacon of Bath, wrote a description of how Henry appeared to those about him. The King, he says, is somewhat red-headed, for 'venerable age and approaching greyness have somewhat changed' his originally golden-red hair. (Henry was forty-four at the time this was written.) He is already beginning to grow bald, but his hair is so arranged as to conceal the fact. He is of medium height. His head is spherical and well proportioned to his body. His face is square. His eyes are round and shoot fire when he is aroused. 'The well-arched feet, the legs of a horseman, the deep chest, and the arms of a boxer denote a man strong, agile, and audacious.' His hands are rough and unkept; he never wears gloves, except when he is hawking.

'Every day, at Mass, in council, and in other public affairs of the government, he always stands on his feet from morning till night. And, although his legs are greatly scarred and livid from the frequent kicks of unruly horses, he never sits, except only when he is riding or eating. If need be, he can make four or five days' journey in one.' He wears leggings without any cross-wrappings; his caps have no elegance; and he wears the first clothes that come to hand. 'A vehement lover of the forest, when he ceases from war he exercises himself with birds and hounds.'

The King gives himself up to such ceaseless activity, Peter explains, because 'his flesh would enormously burden him with its mass of fat if he did not dominate the insolence of his belly by fasts and exercise. . . . For he does not lie in his palace like other kings, but he traverses the provinces and looks into the deeds of all men and judges most severely those whom he has placed as judges over others.

'No one is more subtle in counsel, more fluent in eloquence, more fearless in danger, more modest in prosperity, more steadfast in adversity. When he once loves a man, he is constant in his friendship; when he once takes a dislike to a man, on the other hand, he restores him with difficulty to the grace of his friendship.

'Bows, swords, hunting spears, and arrows are always in his hands, unless he is in Council or at his books. Whenever he can take a rest from his cares and worries, he busies himself with reading in solitude or tries to solve some knotty question with a group of clerks. . . . With the Lord King of the English, his daily school is the constant conversation of the most learned men and the discussion of questions. No King is more honest in speech, more polished at table, more moderate in drinking, more magnificent in his household than is our King. . . .

'Our peace-loving King, victorious in war and glorious in peace, strives for peace above all the good things of this world and brings peace to his people. All his thoughts and words and deeds are directed towards the peace of his people. . . . In walls, in towers, in fortifications, in moats, in enclosures for wild beasts and fishes, and in the building of palaces, no one more knowing or more magnificent could be found anywhere.'

As might be expected of a friend of Bishop Reginald of Bath, to whom Peter owed his advancement, Peter declares that Henry was entirely innocent of the death of St. Thomas. On the contrary, 'the Lord King has the glorious Martyr as his principal patron in all his difficulties. . . . You may be most certain that neither death nor the sword have destroyed that love with which the King and the Martyr loved each other in former days.'[1]

Shortly after Martinmas, November 11, Henry met Louis at Graçay to settle the disputed ownership of the Auvergne. Henry wanted to solve the question by means of a sworn inquest such as was used in England, but Louis would have no part in such a novel procedure. He insisted that Henry adhere to the method they had agreed upon in the treaty of the preceding September, whereby each King appointed three bishops and three barons to a commission. The commission was duly named, and its verdict was accepted by both Kings.[2] What the verdict was, however, the chroniclers do not state. That it was unfavourable to Louis and that there was an element of fraud about the business is evident from the remarks that Louis, old and sick, made to Henry on this occasion.

'You have done me many injuries, King, from the very beginning of your reign and even before, scorning the reverence you owe to your fealty and homage to me. I shall not speak of the other injuries, but only of the lands that you have occupied

---

[1] Peter of Blois: *Epistola LXVI*, in Migne's *Patrologia*, Vol. CCVII, cols. 195–210.   [2] *Gesta*, Vol. I, p. 196

against all law and justice. And of all the injuries you have done me, this one concerning the Auvergne is by far the greatest and the most flagrant, for you dare thus shamelessly to keep it against all law and against the rights of the Crown of France.

'Although I cannot, because of my advancing age, regain this or the other lands by strength of arms, nevertheless I do not give up my claims and my complaints against you. Rather do I, before God and these barons of the realm and our faithful subjects, publicly proclaim the rights of the Crown to the Auvergne especially, to Berri and Châteauroux, and to Gisors and the Norman Vexin.

'Although because of my sins He has not granted it to me to regain the rights of the Crown, I beg the King of Kings, Who has given me an heir, at least to allow him to do so. Therefore I commit the defence of my realm henceforth to God and to my heir and to the barons of the Crown.'

When he had said this, Louis burst into tears and turned away from the man who had taken his wife, corrupted his daughter, and stolen his lands.[1]

The King returned to England on July 15, 1178, and went straightway to St. Thomas's tomb. On August 6, at Woodstock, he knighted his son Geoffrey, who was almost twenty years old. This was the first time that Henry had been able to knight one of his sons, for the eldest had been knighted by William Marshal, and the King of France had knighted Richard. As soon as he was girded with his belt and sword, Geoffrey went to Normandy and followed tournaments with the same enthusiasm as did his eldest brother.[2]

Richard, meanwhile, resumed his never-ending task of bringing his rebellious nobles of Aquitaine to order. Although he had apparently subdued the rebels in the southwestern part of his Duchy in the early months of 1177, he now found that fresh trouble was breaking out in that area. He raised an army in Poitou and went to Gascony. When he reached Dax, he learned that the citizens of that town, for some unstated reason, had seized the Count of Bigorre and imprisoned him. Since Centulle had aided and encouraged Viscount Peter in his rebellion of the previous year, Richard was delighted to find him thus subdued.

[1] Gerald of Wales: *De Principis Instructione*, pp. 226-7.
[2] *Gesta*, Vol. I, pp. 206-7; Ralph of Diceto, Vol. I, p. 426.

'But Alfonso, King of the Aragonese, grieving that his friend
the Count of Bigorre was held in chains, came to the aforesaid
Duke and, solicitous that his friend should be released from the
aforesaid Duke's prison, stood surety for him before the Duke
that the Count would do the will of the Duke and of his father,
the King of England.' Richard exacted a heavy ransom from
Count Centulle and then released him.[1]

During the autumn the King held a meeting of the Great
Council and revised the system of judicial circuits that he had
instituted at the Council of Northampton in 1176.

> The King enquired concerning the justiciars whom he had
> appointed in England, if they had treated the men of the realm well
> and wisely; and when he learned that the land and the men of the
> land had been gravely oppressed by such a multitude of justiciars,
> for they were eighteen in number, by the counsel of the wise men
> of his realm he selected five only, two clerks and three laymen, who
> were all of his private household.   And he ordered that those five
> should hear all the complaints of the realm and do right, and that
> they should not depart from the King's court but should remain
> there to hear the complaints of men, so that if any question came be-
> fore them that they could not settle, it should be presented in the
> King's hearing and settled as it pleased him and the wiser men of the
> realm.[2]

The complaints against the justiciars are not stated, but the confession of Rannulf of Glanville, noted in the Pipe Roll of the
previous year, is an indication of how they might have acted.
Rannulf, the victor of Alnwick, now Sheriff of Yorkshire and one
of the King's justiciars, admitted that he and his servants took
'£1,644 16s. 4d. and 2 silver dishes and 4 gold rings and 2 chargers
and 16 palfreys and 3 greyhounds and 36 horses and 6 falcons and
7 mewed hawks and 75 cattle and 8 pigs and 120 sheep and 49
seams of oats and 140 cartloads of timber' as booty 'both from the
county and from the land of Everard of Ros'.   In exchange for
two Norwegian falcons, the King issued a writ allowing him to
keep his loot.[3]   The cash alone was more than the annual income
of the richest subject of the realm.   Even more astonishing than
the magnitude of Rannulf's thievery is the fact that the King not
only forgave him but marked him for further advancement.

[1] *Gesta*, Vol. I, pp. 212-13.   [2] Ibid., Vol. I, pp. 207-8.
[3] Pipe Roll 23 Henry II, pp. 81-82.

The King kept Christmas at Winchester, with his sons Geoffrey and John. Eleanor, in her prison, was bravely decked for the holidays:

> For 2 cloaks of scarlet and 2 capes of scarlet and 2 grey furs and 1 embroidered coverlet for the use of the Queen and her servant-girl, £28 13s. 7d., by the King's writ.[1]

The young Henry was still in Normandy. Richard was at Saintes, where he had been called by the threat of a rebellion amongst the nobles of the Saintonge. Immediately after Christmas he summoned the Poitevin army and laid siege to Pons, a castle belonging to Geoffrey of Rancogne, one of the most powerful barons of the Saintonge and the leader of the rebellion.[2] Richard settled down for a long siege.

Now that the schism was ended, Pope Alexander summoned a General Council to meet in March 1179. Four English bishops attended it. One of the decrees of this council, the Third Lateran, forbade tournaments:

> Following in the footsteps of our predecessors of happy memory. Popes Innocent [II, 1130-42] and Eugene [III, 1145-53], we prohibit to be held those detestable markets or fairs, called tournaments in the vulgar tongue, in which knights, so it is said, are wont to assemble and rashly fight together to show off their strength and daring, whence come death and peril to their souls. If any of them should die there, although he is not to be denied the Sacrament of Penance, he may not have ecclesiastical burial.[3]

This decree had little effect on the holding of tournaments. When William Marshal was on his deathbed, in 1219, his good friend Henry Fitz Gerald reminded him: 'Clerks tell us and give us to understand that no one can be saved if he does not give back what he has taken.'

'Henry, listen to me a little,' the Marshal replied. 'These clerks are too hard on us; they try to shave us too close. I have taken five hundred knights and kept their arms and horses and all their trappings. If the Kingdom of God is forbidden to me on that account, I can't do anything about it, for I can't give it all back.'[4]

[1] Pipe Roll 24 Henry II, p. 128.   [2] *Gesta*, Vol. I, pp. 213, 221.
[3] Ibid., Vol. I, pp. 222-38.
[4] *Histoire de Guillaume le Maréchal*, lines 18476-88.

The young Henry, meanwhile, had spent three years and all the money he could lay his hands on in going from one of 'those detestable markets or fairs' to another along the French and Norman border.   He went so far in debt that his word was no longer good, and William Marshal had to stand surety for him.

> Truly, the young King, in castles and in cities and wherever he went, lived at such great expense that when it came time to leave he did not know how to get away from his debts.   And when he went to settle his bill, then came his creditors for horses and robes and food and drink.
> 'This one has a tally for three hundred pounds, this one for a hundred, and th's one for two hundred: that amounts to six hundred,' said the writers.
> 'Who will take this debt in hand?' cried the middlemen.
> 'My lord does not have any money here, but you will have it in a month,' [William Marshal said.]
> 'My faith,' said the townsmen, 'if the Marshal takes the debt in hand, we are not worried in the least, for it is as good as paid.'[1]

Perhaps because he had exhausted both his money and his credit, the young Henry returned to England on February 26. He and his father kept Easter, April 1, at Winchester.   Immediately after the feast, Richard of Luci obtained the King's reluctant permission to resign his position and retire to the monastery he had founded at Westwood.   He had been Chief Justiciar jointly with the Earl of Leicester from the beginning of Henry's reign till Leicester's death in 1168 and then sole Chief Justiciar.   Henry was most devoted to this faithful, loyal, and capable man, and only his advanced age secured his release from the King's service.   He took the habit of an Austin Canon and lived in the monastery till his death, in the following July.

Duke Richard, meanwhile, had been besieging Pons for three months with no success.   Shortly after Easter he started on an expedition that left his contemporaries gaping with astonishment and admiration.   Until this time, the young Duke had shown remarkable tenacity, determination, courage, and serious application to the task of subduing his almost anarchic Duchy, but, perhaps because of his youth and inexperience, he had demonstrated no outstanding gifts as a military leader.

---

[1] *Histoire de Guillaume le Maréchal*, lines 5073-94.

After a stalemate of three months, he left his constables in command of a part of his army and with the remainder made a series of lightning raids into the territory of Geoffrey of Rancogne. Within three days he took Richemont. By this time he had had his fill of taking castles and receiving the submission of the defeated lords, only to have them rebel all over again as soon as his back was turned. He utterly demolished Richemont. In rapid succession he captured four more castles and had them all razed to the ground.[1]

With these minor strongholds demolished, on May 1, 1179, Richard advanced on Taillebourg, Geoffrey's chief and strongest fortress, 'a most desperate undertaking, a work that no-one before him had ever dared to attempt', the sort of feat that Richard was henceforth to glory in. Taillebourg was considered completely impregnable. It was protected by three moats and then by triple walls, amply supplied with great stones for the ramparts. The castle was abundantly stocked with all sorts of supplies and 'crammed with a thousand men fit for fighting'. When Richard drew near with his army, Geoffrey and his knights merely laughed at him from their impregnable fortress.

Richard, in grim earnest, reduced the surrounding countryside to a desert. After removing everything of any value, his army burned all the buildings, chopped down the vines and trees, and laid the fields waste. Then they pitched their tents close to the walls, and Richard ordered the siege engines to be assembled and began hurling great stones against the walls.

The garrison, full of pride in their own strength and eager to punish the presumptuous young man who dared to attack a castle that everyone knew was impregnable, sallied forth from the town on May 8 in an effort to catch Richard by surprise. The young Duke was not to be caught by surprise, however. He fought the assailants with such fury that they turned and fled back into the town. Richard and his men pursued them so closely that attackers and defenders poured into the town together, and thus the garrison, with the enemy in their midst, lost all the advantage of their three moats and their triple walls. Those who were lucky enough to reach it took refuge in the keep. Richard then pillaged and burned the town. When he set his stone-throwers to work on the tower at close range, Geoffrey and his

[1] *Gesta*, Vol. I, p. 213.

men surrendered, on May 10. Richard immediately had all the walls demolished and the town torn down.[1]

Geoffrey, completely at Richard's mercy surrendered Pons, and Richard had the castle demolished. Vulgrin, who had recently succeeded his father as Count of Angoulême, was so impressed by the utter defeat of his friend and ally that he came to Richard shortly after Whitsunday, May 20, and surrendered Angoulême and Montignac. The young Duke had both castles reduced to rubble.[2] He was no longer playing the knightly game as practised by the nobles of Aquitaine, who rebelled and fought and surrendered and then restocked their castles and rebelled again. He was intent on cowing these rebel vassals into a permanent submission.

'With all things completed according to his will, the Duke of Aquitaine crossed over to England and was received by his father with the greatest honour.'[3]

[1] Ralph of Diceto, Vol. I, pp. 431-2.
[2] *Gesta*, Vol. I, p. 213.
[3] Ralph of Diceto, Vol. I, p. 432.

XVI

'A SOLDIER IN MY FATHER'S SERVICE'
1179 - 1181

WITH the retirement of Richard of Luci, the Chief Justiciar, the King found it necessary to reorganise the judicial system, of which Richard had been the head. At a meeting of the Great Council at Windsor on April 10, 1179, Henry proposed a new scheme. The earlier division of the country into six judicial circuits had led to too great a delegation of authority; the succeeding plan of using only five judges was inadequate to handle the multitude of cases.

Henry therefore divided the country into four circuits, with five judges assigned to each of three of them and six to the fourth. Three of the groups were headed by bishops who had long experience in the King's service. Bishop Richard of Winchester was assigned to the Southwest; Bishop Geoffrey of Ely to the Midlands; and Bishop John of Norwich to East Anglia and the Southeast. Rannulf of Glanville and five other justiciars were assigned to the North and also to serve as 'justiciars appointed to the King's court to hear the cries of the people'.[1]

That bishops should serve as justiciars was in open violation of the law of the Church. It had been specifically forbidden by Canon XXV of the Third Lateran Council (1179), to name only the most recent of the prohibitions against the holding of secular offices by clerics, which provided that those who did so should be deprived of their ecclesiastical offices because of their neglect of their spiritual duties. These men, however, were bishops only by accident, as it were; they were efficient and loyal civil servants who were rewarded for their services by the most fitting gifts in the King's hand.

Ralph of Diceto[2] tells of the difficulties Henry encountered in trying to find honest and efficient judges. The King did not change his aims, Ralph says, but many times he changed the

[1] *Gesta*, Vol. I, pp. 238-9.   [2] Vol. I, pp. 434-6.

persons by whom he hoped to accomplish them.   He tried using abbots, earls, military men, members of his own household, and his most intimate friends as judges, and he found them all wanting. They oppressed the poor, favoured the rich, and allowed their decisions to be swayed by gifts.

Ralph, a zealous supporter of the King, tries to shift the blame for the many oppressions from the King's shoulders to those of his judges.   That many of them were corrupt and venal is undeniable.   It is also undeniable, from the account of Rannulf of Glanville's pillaging in Yorkshire in 1177, that the King condoned such conduct in his favourites.   Mercenary though the justiciars often were, they were only following the example set them by their royal master.   As long as the courts were used as a means of raising money, gross injustices were inevitable.

Even though the judicial processes were often corrupt and inefficient, one must not lose sight of the permanent value of the great reforms instituted by Henry II in the legal procedure of England.   Although their immediate aim was usually to remove the administration of justice from the hands of the barons and place it in those of the King's justiciars in order to curb the independence of the barons, their lasting effect was to introduce a uniform system of courts and legal procedure throughout the country and to make all men subject to the same laws.   The justice dispensed by the royal officials was far from perfect, but even so it was greatly superior to that meted out in the local courts.   The regular use of travelling judges or itinerant justiciars, going all over the kingdom to hear cases, ensured that a uniform system of law was administered.

Henry also tried to lessen the importance of the primitive judicial ordeals and to substitute for them a more rational procedure.   Although men were still put to the ordeal by water, it was only after the accusations against them had been made by trustworthy and reliable men, supported by the considered voices of their neighbours.   Even though men succeeded in coming clean from the ordeal, its importance was further diminished by their being condemned to exile if they had been accused of grave crimes by the common report of the neighbourhood.   Furthermore, Henry removed a whole class of civil actions pertaining to the possession of land both from the jurisdiction of the barons' courts and from the verdicts of ordeal by battle by instituting the possessory assizes of Novel Disseisin and Mort d'Ancestor.

Henry had founded, in his own parsimonious fashion, two religious houses in fulfilment of his vow. He now began the third, in an even more niggardly way. He induced the monks of the Grande Chartreuse, in Burgundy, to send a small group to found the first Carthusian house in England, which they did with some misgivings. Theirs was a small order, much more concerned that each house should be a centre of holiness than that their numbers should increase. Each house was limited to thirteen professed monks, each one living a life of prayer and contemplation in his own little house and garden, grouped around the cloister, and a like number of lay brothers.

When the small band arrived, Henry gave them the manor of Witham, on the edge of Selwood Forest, on the border of Somerset and Wiltshire, and left them to fend for themselves. The bewildered monks found themselves in a wild and remote region, unable to communicate with the inhabitants, and without a roof over their heads, for the manor was populated by its peasants. They made crude huts for themselves and tried to begin at least a semblance of monastic life. The King promised over and over again to help them, but he did nothing. At last the Prior, in despair, went back to the Chartreuse to report on the situation.

At this juncture, when the few remaining monks were on the point of going back to Burgundy, the King heard of the fame of Hugh of Avalon, the Procurator of the Grande Chartreuse, and despatched Bishop Reginald of Bath to the mother-house with instructions to use every effort to have Hugh sent to take charge of the community at Witham.[1]

Hugh was a strange combination of great sanctity and hard-headed common sense. He cared nothing for the things of this world, and he had greater respect and love for the most loathsome and disfigured leper than for any king. Although he dwelt more in the next world than in this, when his duty compelled him to deal with mundane affairs he displayed a shrewdness that, joined with his fearlessness, made him more than a match even for the wily Henry.

When he arrived in England, Hugh began by having the in-

---

[1] *Magna Vita Sancti Hugonis Episcopi Lincolniensis*, ed. J. F. Dimock (Rolls Series, 1864), pp. 52–55.

habitants of the manor moved elsewhere, and he insisted that the King recompense them for any losses they might have suffered in the removal. As the result of some plain speaking on the part of the monks, Henry began to keep his promises. Hugh was thus able to begin building a priory after the Carthusian pattern at Witham.[1]   The Pipe Roll for 1180 shows the first expenditures for the new foundation.   The King gave £40 'for the work of the Carthusian brothers dwelling at Witham', and £13 6s. 8d. to buy clothes for them.[2]

The coinage under Henry II had become increasingly debased, through counterfeiting, through clipping and paring, by which the weight of the penny was steadily decreased as it passed through successive hands, and through the dishonesty of the moneyers, who introduced more alloy than the permitted 18 dwt. to each 11 oz. 2 dwt. of silver.   Mints were operated by moneyers, private individuals who bought their dies from the king's goldsmith and who made their profits from the difference between the price they paid the king for the silver bullion and the value of the metal when minted into pennies.   The king in turn got the bullion from the mines, mostly in Cornwall, which were a royal monopoly.

In 1180 Henry issued a new coinage, the 'short-cross' penny, a design that was used unchanged, even to the superscription, from 1180 to 1247, through the reigns of four kings.   This is probably the ugliest coin ever issued in England, childishly crude and poorly stamped.   The obverse shows the King's head, crowned, within the inner circle, and the inscription HENRICUS REX and the King's hand, holding a sceptre, in the outer circle. The reverse has a short cross, from which this issue takes its name, in the inner circle, with four groups of four pellets each between the arms of the cross.   In the outer circle are the name of the city where the coin was minted and the abbreviation of the moneyer's name.[3]

When the new money was put into circulation, the old, debased coins were called in.   Martinmas, November 11, 1180, was set as the last day when the old coinage could be exchanged for the new.[4]   This operation was oppressive to the poor, for the

---

[1] *Magna Vita*, pp. 67-75.   [2] Pipe Roll 26 Henry II, pp. 96, 131.
[3] G. C. Brooke: *English Coins* (London, 1950), pp. 82, 103-4; photograph on Plate XXII.   [4] Gervase of Canterbury, Vol. I, p. 295.

money was not exchanged on the basis of a new penny for an old, but by weight. The coinage had become so debased that it took, on an average, ten old pennies to buy nine new ones.[1]

King Louis, who was now about sixty years old, was beginning to feel the weight of his years. He therefore determined to have his only son, Philip, anointed and crowned King of the French. He issued a summons to his bishops, counts, and barons to assemble at Rheims on the feast of Our Lady's Assumption, August 15, 1179, for the coronation of the lad, who would then lack only six days of being fifteen years old.[2]

Before the appointed day, however, Philip fell gravely ill. While he was hunting in a forest he became separated from his companions and lost his way. He wandered all night through the forest and was found the next morning by a charcoal burner, who led him to the court. Philip, who evidently did not have a strong constitution, fell ill from fright and exposure, and his life was despaired of.[3]

Louis was almost beside himself with worry and anxiety for his heir. 'The King, the lad's father, would rather give his own life than see his son thus tortured.' One night he had a dream in which Archbishop Thomas came to him and said: 'Our Lord Jesus Christ has sent me, His servant, Thomas of Canterbury, the Martyr, to you so that you may know that if you believe and with a contrite heart go to His servant Thomas of Canterbury, the Martyr, your son will recover from his illness.'

Louis told his dream to his counsellors and asked their advice about going to England to ask the Martyr's prayers. They advised against it, 'because it would be perilous for him to cross over to another's kingdom and fall into the hands of a strong man'. After the Saint appeared to him in the next night and again in the third, Louis determined to make the pilgrimage, regardless of the dangers.

Accompanied by Count Philip of Flanders, who had returned from the Holy Land during the previous year, and only a few noblemen, the King of France landed at Dover on Wednesday, August 22, 1179. 'Assuming now the name and dress of a pilgrim, he most devoutly visited England, which neither he nor any of his predecessors had ever visited, either with hostile intent

---

[1] Pipe Roll 29 Henry II, pp. 153-4.   [2] *Gesta*, Vol. I, p. 240.
[3] Robert of Torigni, pp. 282-3.

or as a peaceful comer.' Henry met him at the harbour with a great crowd of clergy and people and received his old rival, now care-worn and racked by grief, with the greatest honour.

Early the next morning the two Kings went to Canterbury. Louis hastened to the Martyr's shrine in the crypt and prostrated himself at his friend's tomb. He lay there in prayer, fasting, all through the day and night. On the 26th Henry accompanied him back to Dover, and Louis returned to France.

When he reached Paris the anxious father found that his son had completely recovered. Louis issued orders for Philip's coronation on November 1 and then went to St-Denis to give thanks for his recovery. On the way to the abbey he was stricken with paralysis and lost the use of his right side.[1]

On All Saints' Day, November 1, 1179, at Rheims, Philip was anointed and crowned King of the French by his uncle, the Cardinal William, Archbishop of Rheims. His god-father, Count Philip of Flanders, bore the golden sword of state in the procession. The young Henry, as a gesture of friendship, carried the golden crown before the young King, whom he called his brother. When the crown proved too heavy for the frail Philip, Henry held it over his head throughout the ceremony.[2] King Louis was not present at the coronation, which he had eagerly longed to see; he was lying paralysed in Paris.

Philip of Flanders immediately set to work to supplant Queen Adela and her brothers in the lad's affections and counsels. The Count was a brilliant, open-handed, and dashing man, much renowned for his valour in tournaments, and precisely the sort of figure to dazzle the sickly young Philip. The Count succeeded so well that soon he had completely turned the lad against his mother and his uncles. Philip drove his uncles from the court and quarrelled so bitterly with his mother, whom he attempted to deprive of her dower lands, that she was forced to take refuge with her brothers. To make sure that he was undisputed master, Philip stole his father's seal from him as he lay paralysed.[3]

He made such threats against Queen Adela and her brothers that they turned in despair to the young Henry and asked him to use his influence with his father to persuade him to help them. Although the young Henry had always been on the most friendly

[1] *Gesta*, Vol. I, pp. 240-3.   [2] Ralph of Diceto, Vol. I, pp. 438-9.
[3] *Gesta*, Vol. I, p. 244; Ralph of Diceto, Vol. II, p. 6.

terms with Philip of Flanders, he had a genuine affection for his father-in-law, now disabled and at his son's mercy. For his sake the young Henry crossed over to England around the end of March 1180 and laid the situation before his father. Henry had already heard alarming reports of Philip's conduct and feared that he might be planning an invasion of Normandy. He had therefore sent an embassy to King Louis, but they had found him so helpless in his illness that they could accomplish nothing.[1]

Louis, when a similar situation had arisen between Henry and his son, had encouraged the son and given him all the help in his power. It is greatly to Henry's credit that he now dropped all his affairs and crossed over to Normandy to try to bring the rebellious young Philip to reason. Before he left, he appointed Rannulf of Glanville Chief Justiciar, to govern the kingdom in his absence.[2]

The two Henrys crossed over to Normandy around April 15, 1180. Queen Adela, two of her brothers, Counts Theobald of Blois and Stephen of Sancerre, and many of the French nobles whom Philip was oppressing came to them and begged their help. The King promised to do all in his power for them and summoned an army, with the intention of invading France after Easter. Philip, when he learned of this, called on his army to make ready for war.

Immediately after Easter, however, Philip so effectively alienated his nobles that he did not dare trust them to assemble in the field for him. He went to Flanders and, against the advice of all his counsellors, who greatly distrusted the growing influence of the Count of Flanders upon their young master, married Isabel of Hainault, Count Philip's niece, then ten years old. The Count, who was childless, promised to make the young King his heir both to Flanders and to Vermandois, his wife's marriage portion.

King Philip issued a summons to his bishops and nobles to the coronation of his Queen at Sens on Whitsunday, June 8. When the time drew near, Count Philip began to fear that the French nobles, who were bitterly opposed to the match, would contrive to prevent the coronation. He advised the young King to anticipate the date. Philip and Isabel were therefore crowned at sunrise on the feast of the Ascension, May 29, in the Abbey of St-

[1] Roger of Hoveden, Vol. II, p. 196; *Gesta*, Vol. I, p. 245; Ralph of Diceto, Vol. II, p. 4.   [2] Roger of Hoveden, Vol. II, p. 215.

Denis, by Guy of Noyers, who had succeeded Cardinal William as Archbishop of Sens.

Immediately such a storm of protest arose as had followed the crowning of the young Henry by the Archbishop of York. The French nobles, already angered by the marriage, were indignant that the ceremony had been performed almost in secret. Their anger, however, was as nothing compared to that of the young King's uncle, Cardinal William, who as Archbishop of Rheims alone had the right to crown the Kings and Queens of France. He at once sent messengers to the Pope to complain of the outrage and to demand the immediate punishment of all concerned in it.

Henry met the two Philips at Gisors on June 28 and attempted to make them see reason. 'Now with gentle words, now with harsh', he pleaded with the lad to make peace with his mother and uncles. Against the passionate protests of the Count of Flanders, Philip at last agreed to receive them into his favour. Henry and the young King then sealed a treaty that incorporated most of the terms of the settlement made between Henry and Louis in September 1177. Henry turned next to his cousin of Flanders. Now that he was defeated for the nonce, Count Philip renewed his homage to Henry for the lands that he held of him in England, and Henry agreed to continue his yearly subsidy of a thousand marks.[1]

King Louis, after giving 'whatever gold or silver, whatever gems or rings, whatever precious vestments or regal ornaments he had to the poor', died at Paris on September 18. 'He was a man of warm devotion to God and of great gentleness to his subjects and of notable reverence for the clergy, but he was rather more simple-minded than is becoming to a prince.'[2]

Although King Henry's bastard son Geoffrey had been elected Bishop of Lincoln, he had not yet been consecrated. Still only a deacon, he enjoyed the revenues of the see, but the diocese had been without a bishop for fifteen years. The Pope therefore ordered Archbishop Richard to see to it that Geoffrey either received the episcopal consecration and began to fulfil his duties or resigned without delay. After his martial exploits in 1173, Geoffrey had been much in the company of his father, who made him his Chancellor, and he seems honestly to have doubted his

---

[1] *Gesta*, Vol. I, pp. 245-9.
[2] Ralph of Diceto, Vol. II, p. 7; William of Newburgh, p. 223.

fitness for the office. His election had been confirmed by the
Pope, and certainly his father, who had secured his election in the
first place, would not have objected to his consecration. Geoffrey, who was with his father in Normandy, therefore must have
meant what he said when he wrote, shortly before Easter 1181:

> To the venerable father and Lord Richard, by the grace of God
> Archbishop of Canterbury and Legate of the Apostolic See, Geoffrey,
> the son of the Lord King and Chancellor: greetings and due and
> devoted reverence.
>
> It has pleased your apostolic majesty and holiness to charge me to
> receive priestly orders and the dignity of the episcopal office at a
> stated time. I, however, considering that a great many bishops
> more mature and advanced in wisdom and age can scarcely be equal
> to such duties or fulfil perfectly the office of their bishoprics without
> peril to their souls, am afraid to take upon myself, being younger, a
> burden that has proved unbearable for those older than I, and this
> I do, not indeed from any light-mindedness, but out of reverence
> for the Sacrament.
>
> Having discussed this matter with the Lord King my father, and
> with my lords and brothers, the King and the Counts of Poitou and
> Brittany, the Bishops Henry of Bayeux, Froger of Séez, Reginald
> of Bath, and other bishops who were present, I have disposed other-
> wise of my life and station, wishing at this time to be a soldier in my
> father's service and to abstain from episcopal duties.
>
> I therefore, of my own accord, freely and wholly resign into your
> hands, holy Father, all the rights of my election and the Bishopric
> of Lincoln, and beg you, as my metropolitan, especially delegated for
> this by the Apostolic See, to release me both from the election and
> from the bishopric.
>
> May you fare well.[1]

Henry was preparing to return to England in April when he
received an urgent appeal for help from King Philip. The Count
of Flanders had broken the peace and invaded France in an effort
to regain his influence over the young King. Henry went at
once to meet Count Philip at Gisors. By bringing all his influence to bear on the Count, he at last induced him to give up
his designs. Henry then informed King Philip of his intention
of going to England and assured the French King that if he needed
any help in his absence, the young Henry would be his protector.[2]
Henry sailed from Cherbourg and landed at Portsmouth on

[1] *Gesta*, Vol. I, pp. 271-2.   [2] Ibid., Vol. I, p. 277.

July 26, 1181. Shortly afterwards he published the Assize of
Arms, defining the obligation of each free layman to provide
himself with arms suitable to his station in life, in order to be
ready to serve in the King's army. The arms appropriate to each
rank were specified, ranging from the hauberk or full coat of
chain mail, the helmet, the shield, and the lance of the knight to
the wambais or padded tunic of leather or canvas, probably rein-
forced with steel rings, the steel cap, and the lance of the simple
free man. These arms could not be sold or taken out of the
country but were to be passed on from father to son. The
penalty for failure to obey the assize was declared to be the loss,
not of lands or of chattels, but of bodily members. The stubborn
resistance the men of Yorkshire had offered to the Scots and the
defeat of the Flemings by the stout-hearted East Anglians had
taught Henry the value of the fyrd, or national levy of all free
men, as contrasted with the treachery and unreliability of the
feudal host of barons and knights, and he wanted to make sure
that the free men were well equipped.

Pope Alexander III died on September 20, 1181, after a ponti-
ficate of twenty-two years. On October 1, Ubaldo Allucingoli,
a Cistercian monk whom Adrian IV, the English Pope, had made
Cardinal Bishop of Ostia, was elected as his successor and took
the name of Lucius III.

Roger of Pont l'Évêque, Archbishop of York, died on November 21, 1181, and was buried in the choir of his cathedral, with
Bishop Hugh of Durham officiating. Roger, 'the special enemy
of Blessed Thomas the Martyr and the Church of Canterbury',[1]
had been a most grasping man, 'more interested in shearing the
Lord's sheep than in feeding them'.[2] He had obtained a ruling
from Pope Alexander to the effect that if any clerk in his jurisdiction failed to distribute his money with his own hands and
waited till he was on his deathbed to make his will, that will
should be invalid and the Archbishop might seize all his property.
By these and other means he had amassed a fortune of '£11,000
in the old money, £300 in gold, a golden cup, 7 silver cups, 9
silver goblets, 3 mazers, 3 silver salt-cellars, 40 silver spoons, 8
silver dishes, 1 big silver platter, and some silver basins'.[3]

Shortly before his death Roger had made a will leaving his

---

[1] Gervase of Canterbury, Vol. I, p. 297.   [2] William of Newburgh, p. 227.
[3] Ralph of Diceto, Vol. II, p. 12.

great wealth to be divided amongst the poor, the churches of his diocese, and his particular friends and kinsmen. When the King learned of his death and of the will he had made, he promptly despatched some of his officials to York to seize the whole treasure, since Roger had not made the division with his own hands before he fell ill. The justiciars heard that Bishop Hugh had received three hundred marks from Roger's estate and ordered him to turn the money over to the King.

'I have distributed those three hundred marks amongst the blind, the mute, the lame, and other poor people, and in the repairing of churches and bridges. If anyone wants them, let him try to get them back; I certainly will not do so,' Hugh told them. The King was so enraged that he had the Bishop's house at Durham taken away from him.[1]

In France, meanwhile, Philip's uncles found themselves continually excluded from the young King's councils and unable to induce him to listen to them. Philip was a self-willed, arrogant, spiteful, and scheming lad, of so cold a nature that he never made a friend in the whole course of his life. In a sudden shift of policy, the house of Blois now formed a league with Count Philip of Flanders, raised an army in December, and invaded the region around Beauvais. Many of the greatest French nobles, thoroughly disgusted with their new King, joined the rebellion.

Philip, in his dire need, turned to his brother-in-law. The young Henry, who had been charged by his father to go to Philip's aid if the need should arise, raised an army in Normandy, and he and his brothers Richard and Geoffrey joined forces with Philip. One may surmise that it was Richard's skill and resolution that enabled them to drive the rebels out, forced Count Stephen of Sancerre to submit, and trapped Count Philip in his castle at Crépy-en-Valois, where he was soon starved into submission.[2]

[1] *Gesta*, Vol. I, pp. 283, 289.
[2] *Gesta*, Vol. I, pp. 283-4; Ralph of Diceto, Vol. II, pp. 8-10.

XVII

'KING OF THE COURTEOUS AND EMPEROR OF THE VALIANT'

1182 - 1183

KING Henry held his Christmas court of 1181 at Winchester. The Pipe Roll for this year carries a charge of 70s. 'for painting the King's chamber at Winchester',[1] probably in preparation for the feast. The frescoes may have included the picture that Gerald of Wales describes:

> There was a chamber at Winchester most beautifully decorated with many-coloured pictures of various forms. By the King's order, a blank space had been left, where he afterwards caused to be depicted an eagle with four eaglets perched on it, one on each wing and the third on its back, tearing at the parent with talons and beaks whilst the fourth, no smaller than the others, sat on its neck and waited to tear its parent's eyes out.

> When some of his friends asked him what the picture meant, he said: 'The four eaglets are my four sons, who will not cease persecuting me until my death. And the last-born, whom I now embrace with such love, will inflict on me the gravest injuries and perils of all.'[2]

Henry sailed from Portsmouth on March 3, 1182, and landed at Barfleur. His eldest son joined him, and together they went to Senlis early in April for a conference with the King of France and the Count of Flanders. Again Henry succeeded in patching up a temporary peace between them. Count Philip was in a conciliatory frame of mind because of his recent reverses. He promised to make amends for the damage he had done, and, as usual, he renewed his homage and oath of fealty to Henry for the lands he held of him.[3]

Richard, meanwhile, was in deep trouble in his Duchy. The nobles of Aquitaine hated him and his iron rule. They said that 'he treated all men badly, his own men worse, and himself worst

[1] Pipe Roll 28 Henry II, p. 146.
[2] Gerald of Wales: *De Principis Instructione*, pp. 295-6.
[3] Ralph of Diceto, Vol. II, pp. 10-11; *Gesta*, Vol. I, pp. 285-6.

of all.   He seized the wives and daughters and relations of his
free men by force and made them his concubines, and when he
had glutted his lust on them he turned them over to his soldiers
to serve as their whores.'[1]

Fresh grievances, if any were needed, had been supplied in the
preceding summer.   On June 28, 1181, Richard had ordered the
people of Limoges to tear down their city walls, which left them
defenceless to their enemies.   Five days later Count Vulgrin of
Angoulême had died, leaving an only daughter, Matilda.   Richard
promptly claimed both her and her lands, a claim that was
vigorously contested by Vulgrin's brothers, William and Aymar,
who succeeded him as joint Counts of Angoulême.   They
appealed for help to their half-brother, Viscount Aymar of
Limoges, who was smarting from Richard's treatment of him
and eager for revenge.[2]

The lively imagination of the troubadour, Bertrand of Born,
saw in these events the seeds of a great coalition of the nobles of
the Angoumois, the Limousin, and Périgord against their Duke.
He poured out a series of poems urging them to action and re-
proaching them for their lack of zeal.   'I am making a sirvente
against the cowardly barons, and you will never again hear me
speak of them, for I have broken more than a thousand spurs in
them without being able to make a single one of them run or
even trot.'[3]   Bertrand, after the habit of poets, no doubt over-
estimated the effects both of his verse and of his actions, for the
brothers of Angoulême and Limoges needed little spurring to induce them to unite against Richard.

By the spring of 1182 the nobles of Aquitaine were in full
revolt.   Richard laid siege to Périgueux and to Excideuil, twenty
miles to the northeast, and ravaged all the country between the
two towns.   After Henry had made peace between the two
Philips he went to Grandmont around Whitsunday, May 20, and
summoned the Counts of Angoulême and Périgord and the Viscount of Limoges in an effort to compose the quarrel.[4]   He sent
his son Geoffrey of Brittany as the bearer of these messages,[5] and
Geoffrey thus had an opportunity to confer with the rebel barons,

[1] *Gesta*, Vol. I, p. 292.
[2] Geoffrey of Vigeois, in *Rerum Gallicarum Scriptores*, Vol. XII, p. 448.
[3] *Un sirventes fatz*, in Raynouard, Vol. IV, p. 147.
[4] Geoffrey of Vigeois, in *R.G.S.*, Vol. XVIII, p. 212.
[5] *Gesta*, Vol. I, p. 295.

express his sympathy for their sufferings under Richard's harsh rule, and suggest to them that his brother Henry, already crowned King and destined to succeed his father as Richard's overlord, might prove to be a kinder and more sympathetic ruler than the iron-willed Richard.

Perhaps as a result of Geoffrey's intrigues, when the rebels met Henry at Grandmont they refused to accede to his demands. Angered by their stubbornness, he determined to help Richard subdue them. While his son continued the siege of Excideuil, Henry attacked and captured Pierre-Buffière, ten miles south-southeast of Limoges.

The young Henry, at his father's orders, came to join them. On his way south he stopped at Limoges on June 30, the feast of St. Martial, the first Bishop of Limoges, whose body was enshrined there. The young King was given a tumultuously enthusiastic welcome by the townspeople, which would indicate that Geoffrey's suggestions had begun to bear fruit and that the people were coming to believe that the young King was the man to deliver them from the oppression of their Duke. Henry gave a hanging, ornately embroidered with 'Henricus Rex', to St. Martial's shrine and joined in the festivities.

On the next day he went to Périgueux, where he found his father and brother. Count Elias of Périgord surrendered to their combined forces, and the Viscount of Limoges followed his example. Viscount Aymar gave two of his sons as hostages, and Count Elias surrendered his castle at Périgueux to Richard, who promptly had the walls demolished. The two brothers at Angoulême continued to hold out, but the other rebels promised not to help them.[1] The revolt was thus crushed for the time being.

While Henry was in Aquitaine he received the news that his daughter Matilda and her husband and children had arrived in Normandy. Henry the Lion, Duke of Saxony, after a long quarrel with the Emperor Frederick Barbarossa, originating in the Duke's refusal to help the Emperor in his difficulties in Italy, had been deprived of all his territories and sentenced to exile. He and his wife sought refuge with her father and brought with them their sons Henry and Otto and a daughter, Matilda. The King hastened to meet them and to see his grandchildren. After a few

[1] Geoffrey of Vigeois, loc. cit.

days, Duke Henry set out on a pilgrimage to Compostella, while Matilda stayed at Argentan with her father and children.[1]

When the King left Aquitaine to meet his daughter, it is not recorded whether any of his sons went with him. Richard, at any rate, spent the autumn in his never-ending task of bringing his barons to submission.[2] The young Henry, after his heart-warming reception at Limoges, began to entertain the idea of allying himself with the nobles of Aquitaine and helping them against his brother, perhaps with the idea of supplanting him there. By the end of the year 'he had secretly accepted pledges from the counts and barons of Poitou that they would faithfully serve him as their liege lord and that they would not depart from his service'.[3]

Puffed up by the flattery of the Southerners, who kept urging him to show himself a king in deed as well as in name, he went to his father and renewed his demand, which he had renounced almost ten years earlier, that the King 'give him Normandy or some other land where he and his wife might dwell and from the revenues of which he could pay his knights for their service', which would indicate that he was still maintaining a costly entourage to follow him about from one tournament to another. The King refused; although his son was now twenty-eight years old, he would give him no authority whatever. The young Henry, in a fit of petulance, fled to France, took the Cross, and announced that he was going to Jerusalem.[4]

In addition to his troubles with his father, the young Henry had lost his best friend. Some of his entourage, jealous of the favour and high esteem in which William Marshal stood, accused him of being Queen Margaret's lover. Henry was too wounded to charge William with the accusation, and William was too proud to condescend to deny it. Henry's friendship turned to hatred, and William left his service. When these same envious men brought their tale to the elder King, his only comment was to deplore the great expense that his son's retinue entailed and to express the wish that most of these young knights would leave his son's service.[5]

Henry sent messenger after messenger to his son to beg him to

[1] *Gesta*, Vol. I, p. 288; Ralph of Diceto, Vol. II, p. 13.
[2] Geoffrey of Vigeois, in *R.G.S.*, Vol. XVIII, p. 213.
[3] *Gesta*, Vol. I, p. 292.
[4] Ibid., Vol. I, p. 289.
[5] *Histoire de Guillaume le Maréchal*, lines 5095-481, 5653-68.

T

come back to him. Although the young man had asked for a territory that he might govern as his own, the cares of administration had no charm for him. What he wanted was money to support him and his following in the magnificence that he felt was befitting to him. Realising his son's weakness, the King offered to give him an allowance of £25 sterling a day. He also, and this was the clinching offer, undertook to pay the wages of a hundred knights of his household for a year. At this bait, Henry returned to his father and swore, as he had sworn before, 'that henceforth he would not depart from his will and counsel or ask for anything more from him'.[1]

Just as he had done at Bures in 1175, the young Henry now insisted on making a public renewal of his allegiance to his father, with the intention of forcing the King, by receiving his homage, to show that he was fully forgiven and restored to favour. On New Year's Day, 1183, 'of his own accord, with no one forcing him, touching the Holy Gospels, in the presence of a great multitude of clerks and laymen, he swore that he would from that day and henceforth all the days of his life bear fealty to King Henry as his father and lord and show him all due honour and service'. Then, 'because he wished, as he said, to retain no malice or rancour in his soul, by which his father might afterwards be offended', he revealed his plot with the nobles of Aquitaine against Richard.

He had been driven to this alliance, he said, because his brother had built a fortress at Clairvaux, near the frontier between Poitou and Anjou, but within Anjou, the patrimony due to the young Henry upon his father's death.[2] Bertrand of Born had already twitted the young Henry about this encroachment:

> Between Poitiers and l'Ile-Bouchard and Mirebeau and Loudon and Chinon, someone has dared to build a fair castle at Clairvaux, in the midst of a plain. I should not like for the young King to know about it or see it, for he would not find it to his liking, but I am afraid, so white is the stone, that he can easily see it from Mateflon.[3]

The young Henry, after thus betraying his friends and allies in Aquitaine, begged his father to force Richard to give up the castle. Richard was reluctant to do so, for with the eye of an experienced warrior he had picked a strategic spot to defend his city of Poitiers from the north, but at his father's urging he at last

---

[1] *Gesta*, Vol. I, pp. 290–1.   [2] Ibid., Vol. I, p. 294.
[3] *Pus Ventedorn e Comborn e Segur*, in Raynouard, Vol. IV, pp. 145–7.

agreed to surrender it to him, to be disposed of as the King willed.[1] When word of their betrayal reached the barons of Aquitaine, Bertrand of Born composed a bitter poem of reproach, calling the young Henry 'the King of cowards'.[2]

His son's confession opened the King's eyes to the possibility that such quarrels among his sons after his death might dismember the empire he had so painstakingly built up. He accordingly, at Angers, had Henry, Richard, and Geoffrey swear eternal fealty to him against all men. Next he had them swear that they would keep perpetual peace among themselves and abide by his disposition of his territories among them.[3]

Henry's intention was that his eldest son should succeed him not only as King of England, Duke of Normandy, and Count of Anjou and Maine, but also as overlord of the remainder of his empire, so that it might thus be kept intact after his death. He therefore required Geoffrey, as Duke of Brittany by virtue of his marriage to Constance in 1181, and Richard, as Duke of Aquitaine, to swear fealty and do homage to their eldest brother, of whom they were to hold their lands when their father died.[4] Geoffrey willingly agreed, because the King of France had long ago decreed that the Dukes of Brittany should hold their land of the Dukes of Normandy.

When his father then asked Richard to do homage and swear fealty to his brother for Aquitaine, the young Duke flatly refused to do so. He was born of the same father and mother and was in no way inferior to the young Henry. If his elder brother was entitled to inherit his father's lands, he, the second son, was equally entitled to his mother's.[5] He held Aquitaine, not as a favour from his father, but as a gift from his mother. He had been crowned Duke of Aquitaine in his mother's presence and with her consent, and he had done homage for it to the King of France, the lawful overlord of the Dukes of Aquitaine. His brother had no claim to his homage, and he would not give it.

The King had little love for Richard. Richard, for his part, deeply loved and honoured his mother. The fact that Henry had been keeping her a prisoner for ten years must have led

---

[1] *Gesta*, Vol. I, pp. 294-5.
[2] *D'un sirventes nom qual far longor ganda*, in Raynouard, Vol. IV, pp. 148-9.
[3] *Gesta*, Vol. I, p. 295.
[4] Ibid., Vol. I, pp. 291-2.
[5] Ralph of Diceto, Vol. II, pp. 18-19.

Richard almost to hate his father. The young Duke was later called 'Richard Oc e Non'—'Richard Yea and Nay'—because he always said exactly what he meant; his yea meant yea and his nay meant nay. He never troubled to dissimulate, and he scorned lies, whereas his father used dissimulation as his major weapon. At this stormy interview, the young Duke, standing straight and tall, his blue eyes flashing as he defended his right to his mother's lands, minced no words in telling his father what he thought of Henry's treatment of his Queen. Richard never gave way to spectacular fits of rage, as his father did, but he shook with a cold fury that was the more fearful for being restrained.

Richard turned on his heel and strode out, 'leaving nothing behind save threats and defiance'. He hastened back to Poitou, put his cities and castles in a state of defence,[1] and began taking his revenge on the traitors who had allied themselves with his brother. Henry, smarting from Richard's defiance and the plain speaking that accompanied it, turned to his eldest son and bade him 'curb Richard's pride'.[2]

Thus authorised to do the very thing he had been plotting with the nobles of Aquitaine, the young Henry sent his brother Geoffrey to Brittany to collect the army of mercenaries that Geoffrey was maintaining there for just this purpose, while he set about gathering his forces. In order that his father might not hold a hostage for his fidelity, he sent his wife to stay with her brother, King Philip.[3] He then went to Aquitaine and was joyfully received by the Counts of Angoulême, Viscount Aymar of Limoges, and a host of other nobles, who immediately forgave him his slip and formed a league with him against their hated Duke. Geoffrey, with the scourings of Brittany, arrived at Limoges shortly after Candlemas, was welcomed by Aymar, and set to work fortifying the castle. The young Henry joined them soon afterwards, and they started making Limoges as nearly impregnable as possible.

Richard was in the northern part of Poitou when he learned of these developments. By riding for two days and nights he arrived near Limoges and found Viscount Aymar besieging a church that some of Richard's supporters had turned into a fortress. At the Duke's sudden approach, Aymar turned and fled.

[1] *Gesta*, Vol. I, p. 292.   [2] Ralph of Diceto, Vol. II, p. 19.
[3] *Gesta*, Vol. I, pp. 292-3, 296.

If their horses had not been utterly worn out, Richard's party would have captured the Viscount. Even so, they seized many of his soldiers, the loathsome Brabantines. These 'sons of darkness' were so universally detested that it was considered a worthy punishment for them when Richard drove some of them into the Vienne to drown, had others put to death, and blinded eighty more of them.[1]

When the King learned that the young Henry's punitive expedition was turning into a full-scale revolt of the barons of Aquitaine, he went to Limoges to put a stop to it. 'Confident of his sons, confident of his own men', he came with only a small escort. When he arrived before the city he was greeted by a shower of arrows. The citizens and soldiers poured out of the town, wounded one of his knights, and sent an arrow through the King's cloak. Richard, with his small party, had joined his father, and they were obliged to take refuge in the castle of Aixe, a few miles west of Limoges.

The young Henry, dressed in his coat of mail, came to his father that evening and attempted to excuse the attack. He swore that unless he could persuade the barons of Aquitaine to submit to the King he would leave them and come to his father. Henry welcomed his son's mediation and promised that he would make peace with the barons if they would submit to him and recognise his authority. The young man returned to Limoges, ostensibly to persuade his allies to submit to the King. Viscount Aymar had all the citizens to gather in the Basilica of St. Peter and swear fealty to the young Henry. They then set to work fortifying the city against the King. They dug moats, built walls, and constructed towers with incredible speed, tearing down a number of churches to obtain timber and stones.[2]

When the King saw this burst of activity, he rode up to Limoges to talk to his sons Henry and Geoffrey. Again he was greeted by a rain of arrows, while his sons stood idly by and watched. His horse suddenly raised its head and thus received an arrow that would otherwise have pierced the King's chest. Again the young Henry came to his father and assured him of his fidelity. As a sign of his good faith he turned his armour and horses over to the King, ate at the same table with him, and stayed with him for

[1] Geoffrey of Vigeois, in *R.G.S.*, Vol. XVIII, p. 213.
[2] *Gesta*, Vol. I, p. 296; Geoffrey of Vigeois, in *R.G.S.*, Vol. XVIII, pp. 213-14.

several days. While his elder brother was thus keeping their father occupied, Geoffrey led his Brabantines on a plundering expedition and worked fearful havoc on the neighbouring territories that had remained faithful to Richard. The young Henry then returned to his allies and renewed his oaths to them.

At last the son came to his father and told him that as a result of his persuasions the burgesses of the town were ready to surrender to him. The King promised to receive them, and the young Henry led in a party of townspeople, who fell on their knees before him and begged for mercy. Henry granted them his peace, provided that they would give hostages to assure him that they would afford no help to the rebels in the castle. They returned to the town, and when the King sent some of his men to receive the hostages they fell on the messengers and almost killed them. Then the young Henry, to see how far he could carry the farce, sent a messenger to his father asking him to send some of his barons to him under a flag of truce. The King, still unable to believe in his son's treachery, did so, and while the young Henry and the envoys stood talking his allies attacked the envoy's servants and killed them.[1]

The King's eyes were opened at last, and he realised that his son was betraying him. He also realised for the first time the gravity of the situation. This was no mere local uprising, confined to the perpetually rebellious Limousin. Philip of France was sending mercenaries to his brother-in-law.[2] At the same time, Bertrand of Born was calling on the French and the Flemings to attack Normandy. 'This began in the Limousin, but before it is finished, between France and Normandy, towards Gisors and towards Neufmarché, I hope one may hear them cry "Arras!" and "Montjoie!" and "God help us!" '[3] (the battle cries of the Flemings, the French, and the Normans respectively).

Ten years earlier, Henry had ignored the beginnings of just such a revolt, and he had almost lost his crown as a consequence. Now he determined to quench it before it had an opportunity to spread. Both he and Richard had been handicapped by the lack of troops. He now summoned help from his domains to the north, and soon 'innumerable tents of noble men' surrounded the

---

[1] *Gesta*, Vol. I, pp. 297-8.
[2] Geoffrey of Vigeois, in *R.G.S.*, Vol. XVIII, p. 215.
[3] *Ieu chan*, in Raynouard, Vol. IV, pp. 157-60.

city of Limoges.[1] He also made sure that the leaders of the
earlier revolt were in no position to cause trouble in England while
his back was turned. The Earls of Norfolk and Chester were
dead. The Chief Justiciar on Henry's order put the Earl of
Leicester and Countess Petronilla in prison, confiscated their land,
and sold their chattels.[2]

Henry laid siege to Limoges, held by his sons Henry and
Geoffrey and by Viscount Aymar, on March 1, 1183.[3] Richard,
shortly afterwards, left his father encamped before the walls and
went to drive the marauding bands of mercenaries, turned loose
on the country by Geoffrey and by Philip of France, out of the
Saintonge. Although Bertrand of Born had been commissioned
by the young King to write his sirvente, *Ieu chan*,[4] he could not
help speaking admiringly in it of Richard's prowess:

> We shall know, when the game is played out, which of the sons
> will have the land. The young King would soon have conquered
> it if the Count [Richard] had not learned the game so well, but he so
> closes them in and presses them that he has conquered the Angou-
> mois by force and freed all the Saintonge as far as the borders of
> Brittany. Thus the Count can do his will, provided his sworn men
> do not sell him out, and free it all from chains; for we have never
> seen a wild boar more enraged, when one sticks it and chases it, than
> he, but he never swerves from his course.

The young Henry, 'who was not so much generous as prodi-
gal', was soon in dire straits for money with which to pay his
army of mercenaries. Their clamours for their pay were the
more peremptory because they were quite willing to desert him
at a moment's notice if the elder King should offer them better
wages. First the young Henry borrowed, as he called it, all the
money he could wring out of the townspeople. After that had
vanished into the bottomless pit of the mercenaries' pockets, he
turned to the Abbey of St. Martial, where the body of the Apostle
of the Limousin was preserved in a rich shrine. Henry turned
the monks 'and even the boys and the poor scholars' out of the
abbey and plundered the shrine, stripping it of all its gold and
silver and taking even the consecrated chalices and the crosses
from the altars.[5]

[1] Geoffrey of Vigeois, loc. cit.   [2] Pipe Roll 29 Henry II, p. 153.
[3] Geoffrey of Vigeois, loc. cit.   [4] Bertrand of Born, loc. cit.
[5] Geoffrey of Vigeois, in *R.G.S.*, Vol. XVIII, p. 216.

After this act of sacrilege, he contrived to pass through the besiegers' lines and went to Angoulême at Easter, April 17, leaving his brother and Aymar to defend the town while he joined the Counts of Angoulême and with them attacked the castles loyal to Richard. When he returned to Limoges the outraged citizens, appalled at the desecration of their holiest shrine and aware at last of the character of their ally, stoned him from their walls, shouting: 'We will not have this man to reign over us!'

The young King and his band went to Grandmont, the home of the Poor Men, universally venerated for their saintly lives. He took from the church what few treasures it had, including a golden pyx in the form of a dove that his father had given the monks. He next marched about fifty miles to the south, to Uzerche. There, on May 26, Duke Hugh of Burgundy and Count Raymond of Toulouse joined him. The accession of these two men to his cause showed the young King the possibility of capturing the whole of Aquitaine and perhaps more.

On the next day, Friday the 27th, the party marched further south, plundering and spreading terror as they passed, and reached Donzenac. The young King was seized by an attack of fever, but he nevertheless insisted that they continue their raid. On the following day they reached Martel. From there Henry went to Rocamadour, eight miles to the south, to Our Lady's shrine, one of the most famous in France. Seeking always for money with which to pay his lawless band, he committed his crowning act of sacrilege and robbed the shrine of everything of any value.

When he returned to Martel with his loot he became gravely ill with fever and dysentery. William Marshal, whom he had summoned from France, joined him there. Henry found lodgings in the house of one Stephen the Smith, and there, on Tuesday, June 7, Bishop Gerald of Cahors visited him and found him so ill that he knew he was going to die. With the approach of death came a return to reason and repentance for his sins. He made his confession to the Bishop and then prostrated himself naked in the dust to adore the Blessed Sacrament and receive Holy Communion.

Henry sent messengers to his father to inform him of his illness and to beg him to come to him. The King was ready to start immediately, but his advisers, fearing some trick on the part of the treacherous young man, dissuaded him. As a token of his forgiveness, however, he sent Count Rotrou of Perche and Bishop Bertrand of Agen to him with a precious ring he had inherited from his grandfather, King Henry I.[1]   When they arrived, the dying man pressed the ring to his lips and then dictated a letter to his father.

'Remember not the sins of my youth and my follies,' he began. He begged his father to treat his mother more kindly, to provide liberally for his wife, the young Margaret, to make peace with his allies and especially with Viscount Aymar and the people of Limoges, and to make restitution for the treasures he had stolen from the churches.   Lastly, he directed that his body be buried in Our Lady's Cathedral at Rouen.   He had the letter sealed both with his own seal and with the ring his father had given him.[2]

On Saturday, June 11, as his end drew near, the young King received Extreme Unction an hour after sunrise.   Then he confessed his sins and was given the Viaticum.   He had himself wrapped in his cloak with the Crusader's cross, which he had taken in a fit of petulance.   After resting in its folds for a few moments he gave it to the faithful William Marshal and begged him to carry it to Jerusalem and lay it on the Holy Sepulchre in his stead.[3]

The dying King ordered that a bed of ashes be made on the floor.   He had his attendants strip him of his rich garments, clothe him in a shirt of haircloth, and place him on the ashes. He lay there, with a great stone at his head and one at his feet, till late in the afternoon, when he died.[4]

As soon as it had become evident that the young King's illness would be fatal, his entourage faded away.   Duke Hugh of Burgundy and Count Raymond of Toulouse 'made haste to go about their own business'.   The mercenary soldiers, as soon as they had received the spoils their leader had taken from Rocamadour, vanished in search of other employment.   Only the knights and servants of his own household remained, to carry his body northwards.   When they reached Uzerche on the following day, a serene, radiant day of high mid-summer, they were so destitute and hungry that they begged food from the monks.   They

[1] Geoffrey of Vigeois, in *R.G.S.*, Vol. XVIII, p. 217.
[2] Ibid., in *R.G.S.*, Vol. XVIII, p. 220.
[3] Ibid., in *R.G.S.*, Vol. XVIII, p. 217.
[4] Roger of Hoveden, Vol. II, p. 279.

traded their master's most valuable horse for food, and one of the knights, 'not without shame', offered to exchange his dogs for something to eat.

Viscount Aymar and a few of his knights met the cortège at Uzerche. Early on Monday morning a funeral Mass was said for the young Henry, and his allies left. His few faithful knights, retracing the steps of his last wild foray, carried his body to Grandmont, where it was prepared for burial. His eyes, brains, and entrails were removed and buried there. The body was filled with salt and spices, dressed in the linen robe he had worn at his coronation, and sewn up in stout leather hides.

A monk of Grandmont was sent to tell the King of his son's death. He found Henry outside Limoges, taking shelter from the heat in a peasant's cottage, around the middle of the afternoon.

'What news have you?' asked the King.

'I am not a bearer of good news,' the monk replied.

Henry burst into wild cries of grief and shut himself up alone in the cottage with his sorrow. Shortly afterwards he sent a message to Richard, who was besieging Aixe, to bring up a great siege engine that he had ordered on the previous day, so that the assault on Limoges might be prosecuted with redoubled fury.

On the following day, Tuesday, June 13, Bishops Theobald of Nevers and Bertrand of Agen and Abbot Theobald of Cluny celebrated the young Henry's funeral at Grandmont. The King did not attend the rites, although he was only twenty miles away.[1]

As the young King's knights carried the body northwards on their shoulders into Anjou, the people lined the roads, weeping for a King of whom nothing good was recorded save his beauty, his charm, his courteous manners, and his gentle speech.

'King of the courteous and emperor of the valiant you would have been, my lord, had you but lived, for you had already gained the name of the Young King, and you were the chief and the father of the young,' lamented Bertrand of Born.[2] 'Chivalry was changed into loafing and idleness; generosity became an orphan; and all the world was darkened, when Fortune thus turned vile,' the biographer of William Marshal declared.[3] Even the matter-of-fact Robert of Torigni, who contented himself

---

[1] Geoffrey of Vigeois, in *R.G.S.*, Vol. XVIII, pp. 218-19; Ralph of Diceto, Vol. II, p. 20. [2] *Mon chan fenisc*, in Raynouard, Vol. IV, p. 49.
[3] *Histoire de Guillaume le Maréchal*, lines 6873-8.

with describing only the bare bones of the great events of his time, speaks of him as 'our dearest lord, the young King, a man to be mourned by everyone, for he was most beautiful in appearance, honest in his manners, munificent in his gifts, above all whom we have seen in our time. . . . He was such a knight as had no peer, but princes and counts and even kings feared him.'[1]

When the procession arrived at Le Mans, the Bishop and people would not allow them to take the body on to Rouen; they buried the young Henry beside his grandfather, Count Geoffrey the Fair.[2] Beside the young King they buried one of his followers, a lad who had refused through grief to eat or drink after his master's death and thus died in his sorrow.

The King meanwhile continued the siege of Limoges. On June 24 Viscount Aymar surrendered and agreed to give no further help to his brothers of Angoulême. Henry had the castle and the walls of the city demolished and the moat filled in. With the death of the young Henry and the surrender of Aymar, the revolt in Aquitaine collapsed. By the end of June peace had been so far restored that Henry left Richard to wipe out the last strongholds of resistance while he went back across the Loire.[3]

With the greater men out of the way, the chief rebel was now Bertrand of Born. King Alfonso of Castile joined Richard, and together they laid siege to Bertrand's castle of Hautefort. When their provisions began to run low, King Alfonso, an old friend of Betrand's, asked him to send them some meat and bread and wine. The Lord of Hautefort courteously complied with the King's request and added a private message to Alfonso that he would be grateful if the besiegers would aim their stone-throwers at some other part of his castle, for the wall they were then battering was greatly weakened and on the point of collapse.

King Alfonso treacherously passed this information on to Richard, who redoubled his attacks on the spot indicated. Bertrand then had no choice but to surrender his castle, which Richard straightway gave to Bertrand's brother, Constantine. When Bertrand appealed to Richard's generosity, the young Duke sent him to his father.

'I thought you boasted that you were so clever that you never

<hr>

[1] P. 305.
[2] *Gesta*, Vol. I, p. 303.
[3] Geoffrey of Vigeois, in *R.G.S.*, Vol. XVIII, pp. 218-19.

had to use more than half your wits,' said Henry, referring to one of Bertrand's poems. 'Where are your wits now?'

'My lord, I lost them on the day when the valiant young King, your son, died.'

Henry burst into tears and restored his castle to Bertrand.[1]

When the King reached Le Mans he found that the Archbishop and people of Rouen were on the verge of declaring war on the people of Le Mans. They swore that unless the people of Le Mans gave up the body of the young Henry they would destroy the city. Henry decreed that his son should be buried in the place he had designated in his will. The body was disinterred, carried to Rouen, and buried in the cathedral there.[2] Those who had sympathised with the young Henry in his revolt against his father immediately began circulating stories that the sick were being miraculously healed at his tomb. 'The number of fools,' concludes William of Newburgh wearily, 'is infinite.'[3]

Henry summoned Richard and Geoffrey to him at Angers for the formal conclusion of the rebellion in Aquitaine. Geoffrey, whom some of the chroniclers credit with having been the evil genius behind his brother's revolt, begged forgiveness for having helped his brother against his father and renewed his oath of fealty. Henry punished him by taking away from him all his castles in Brittany and forced him to beg forgiveness and make peace with Richard, whose land he had invaded.[4]

Now that her husband was dead, Philip of France demanded that the King surrender Margaret's dowry, Gisors and the Norman Vexin. More pressing issues than his widow's dower, however, were raised by the young Henry's death. The disposition of the whole great empire after the King's death was now open. At some time before Michaelmas Henry sent to England for his son John. When he arrived, Henry summoned Richard from Poitou. He then ordered Richard to surrender his Duchy of Aquitaine to his youngest brother. He said nothing whatever about making Richard his heir to the patrimony that would have gone to the young Henry had he lived.

Richard was staggered by such a demand. Instantly he suspected that his father was planning to disinherit him. Was John, already acknowledged as his father's favourite, to have not only

---

[1] Léon Clédat: *Du rôle historique de Bertrand de Born* (Paris, 1879), pp. 57-58.
[2] *Gesta*, Vol. I, pp. 303-4.   [3] P. 234.   [4] *Gesta*, Vol. I, p. 304.

England and Normandy and Anjou and Maine, but Aquitaine as well? What else could his father mean by this order? In any case, even if John were crowned King of England, Duke of Normandy, and Count of Anjou and Maine on the spot, it would have meant little to Richard as long as he had Aquitaine. Aquitaine was his; it was his mother's gift to him; it was his home or as near a home as he had ever had; he had devoted his life to making it his, to bringing its unruly barons to submission, and to making his authority acknowledged in every part of it. In Richard's eyes it was the fairest and richest province in all Christendom, with its broad, fertile valleys, its rich vineyards, its glowing fields, its cities gleaming in the Southern sun. What cared he for the little fog-bound northern island or the hard-faced Norman barons? Aquitaine was his.

Richard was growing wise. He could hide his feelings, when necessary, under a blank face, and with a blank face he replied: 'Give me two or three days to ask the advice of my friends, and then I will make you such an answer as will please you.'

When his father agreed, Richard left the court and, although it was already dusk, rode back to Poitou as fast as his horse could carry him. Once safely there, he sent a message to his father that he would never consent that anyone except himself should have Aquitaine.[1]

King Philip constantly renewed his demands for the surrender of his sister's dower. At last, on December 6, Henry met him at their usual conference place beneath a great elm, between Gisors and Trie. Henry opened the proceedings by doing homage to Philip for all the lands he held on the French side of the Channel: Normandy, Anjou, Maine, Brittany, and Aquitaine. Philip had not asked for his homage, which Henry had given to Louis but had not as yet paid to his son, and it may be that Henry, in addition to putting Philip in a good frame of mind, wanted to establish clearly the fact that Aquitaine belonged to him, in view of Richard's recalcitrant stand.

Philip then relinquished his claim to Margaret's dower in exchange for Henry's promise to pay her £2,700 Angevin every year as long as she lived. As for Gisors, he agreed that it was to be part of the dowry of his sister Alice, to be given with her to whichever of the King's sons Henry pleased. Geoffrey was al-

[1] Ibid., Vol. I, pp. 305, 308.

ready married to Constance of Brittany; John was betrothed to Hadwisa of Gloucester; and Richard had been betrothed to Alice for almost fourteen years. By introducing this further element of uncertainty, Henry may have wished to impress upon Richard that both his inheritance and his intended bride were in his father's possession. Henry was keeping Alice at Winchester, safely beyond the reach both of her brother and of her intended husband.[1]

Henry held his Christmas court at Le Mans. John was the only member of his family who was with him. Geoffrey was in Brittany, and Richard, from his Duchy, replied to his father's repeated orders to surrender Aquitaine, or at least a part of it, to John with the defiant declaration that he would never give any part of Aquitaine to anyone, as long as he lived.[2]

[1] *Gesta*, Vol. I, p. 306.   [2] Ibid., Vol. I, pp. 310-11.

XVIII

JOHN, LORD OF IRELAND
1184 - 1185

ONE of the many causes for contention between Henry's cousin, the dashing Count Philip of Flanders, and the King of France was the County of Vermandois, which Philip had acquired as his wife's dowry. Since he had had no children by her, he had promised the King to settle it, after his death, upon his niece, Isabel, whom the King had recently married. When the Count's wife died in 1182, however, the King demanded immediate possession of Vermandois.

Henry had on several occasions restrained his impetuous kinsman when he had attempted to make war on King Philip, and although Henry's efforts were largely directed toward protecting his liege lord, the King of France, he had nevertheless retained the respect and confidence of Count Philip. Henry had no love for the French King; no one could love that cold, selfish, and unscrupulous young man, and Henry came to his defence only from a sense of duty.

Early in 1184 Henry gave Count Philip some stirring advice. Why sit back supinely, he asked, and let both Vermandois and all of Flanders fall into King Philip's covetous grasp, thus bringing him, incidentally, to the shores of the English Channel, from which he was now barred by Normandy and Flanders? Why not marry again, Henry proposed, and provide an heir of his own to his rich lands?

Henry suggested Beatrice, the daughter of Alfonso, King of Portugal, as a suitable bride for his cousin. When the marriage was arranged, the King had his own ship, the Esnecca, repaired and fitted out at great expense and sent her and two other ships to Lisbon to carry the young woman in fitting style to La Rochelle.[1]

King Philip got word of the scheme to defraud him, as he thought, of the territories, and peremptorily forbade the Count

[1] Pipe Roll 30 Henry II, pp. 80, 86-87, 137.

of Flanders to marry Beatrice until he had turned the County of
Vermandois over to him. The Count refused, and both sides
prepared for war. Henry again intervened as peace-maker between his cousin and his young lord. He persuaded the two to
meet him at Choisy-au-Bac early in June 1184, but he was unable
to induce them to make a formal treaty of peace. He succeeded
only in persuading them to declare a truce to last till Christmas
1185.

Beatrice, meanwhile, had landed at La Rochelle and was met
by a magnificent escort provided by King Henry. She was conducted through his lands with the greatest honour and was met
at the Flemish border by Count Philip, who married her immediately, lest King Philip contrive to stop the marriage.[1]

Henry, his daughter Matilda, and her children crossed over to
England at the middle of June. After paying his customary visit
to St. Thomas's shrine, the King went to London. He gave
orders that Queen Eleanor, who had been under close custody for
eleven years, be released and permitted to join her daughter at
Winchester. Shortly thereafter, Matilda gave birth to a son,
William, called 'of Winchester', who was destined to be the
ancestor of the Dukes of Brunswick and hence of King George I.[2]

Rejoicing in her freedom, the Queen laid in a stock of clothes
and wine during the summer:

> For clothes for the Queen and wine for her and the Duchess of
> Saxony at Berkhamstead and for the cost of hauling the aforesaid
> wine and for gold of the weight of 14 pennies and for cloaks and
> covers of grey fur and a hood of fine linen, £33 11s.
> For clothes and hoods and cloaks and for the trimming for 2 capes
> of samite and for the clothes of the Queen and of Bellebelle, for the
> King's use, £55 17s., by the King's writ.[3]

One can only surmise that 'Bellebelle (Pretty-pretty), for the
King's use', was one of Henry's mistresses; if she were the Queen's
maid she would hardly be styled 'for the King's use'.

William, King of Scots, who was then forty-one years old,
asked the King to give him Matilda, the daughter of the Duke
and Duchess of Saxony, as his wife. Inasmuch as the girl's
parents were penniless exiles, William's only motive could have

[1] *Gesta*, Vol. I, pp. 310, 312; Ralph of Diceto, Vol. II, pp. 28-29.
[2] Gervase of Canterbury, Vol. II, p. 30; *Gesta*, Vol. I, pp. 313, 316.
[3] Pipe Roll 30 Henry II, pp. 134-5.

been a desire to ally himself even more closely with the King. William and Matilda were related within the forbidden degree, however, since she was his second cousin twice removed, and it was necessary to secure a dispensation from the Pope. Henry gave his consent to the match, provided the papal permission could be obtained.[1]

While Henry was at Worcester in July, evidence of further misdeeds on the part of Rannulf of Glanville came to light. A certain Gilbert of Plumpton, a young man of a good Yorkshire family, had married, without the King's leave, the heiress of Roger of Guilevast. Since she was the heiress of a Crown tenant, she was in the King's gift. To marry such an heiress without having purchased the King's leave was a common offence, punished at the most by an amercement varying according to the value of the heiress. Rannulf, however, had intended the young woman as a prize for his steward, Reiner, who was acting as his under-sheriff in Yorkshire.

Rannulf, who was Sheriff of Yorkshire as well as Chief Justiciar, had the young man thrown into chains, seized his lands, and sold his movable property. The Pipe Roll for this year shows that the chattels brought £19 19s. 9d., which would indicate that he was a man of some substance. The same Roll shows a charge of 14s. 'for taking Gilbert of Plumpton and his companions from York to Worcester',[2] the inference being that Rannulf was afraid to press his charges before men who knew Gilbert and the circumstances of his offence.

Once he had him at Worcester, Rannulf accused Gilbert of having broken into Roger's house, torn down six doors, and carried away a huntsman's horn and a halter, in addition to the heiress. That constituted thievery and robbery, and Rannulf demanded the death penalty. Young Gilbert denied having taken anything beyond the young woman, who was now his wife, and he offered to 'stand to the law', that is, to prove his innocence by fighting a duel with his accuser. The Chief Justiciar brought the great weight of his influence, second only to the King's, upon the judges, who were in any case his colleagues and probably his creatures. They condemned the young man to be hanged.

On Sunday, July 22, 1184, this rank injustice was reported to

_____
[1] *Gesta*, Vol. I, pp. 313-14.   [2] Pipe Roll 30 Henry II, pp. 29, 38.

U

Baldwin, 'a gentle and a holy man', a Cistercian monk who had become Bishop of Worcester after Roger, the King's cousin, had died in 1179. Baldwin mounted his horse, rode to the gallows, and found young Gilbert with his hands tied behind his back, a green hood turned down over his eyes, and an iron chain about his neck. The executioners were ready to draw him up and let him die of the slow strangulation that resulted from hanging before the drop was introduced.

The Bishop dismounted, ran to Gilbert's side, and shouted: 'I forbid you, on behalf of God and Blessed Mary Magdalene and under pain of anathema, to hang this man today, for it is Sunday and the feast of Blessed Mary Magdalene, and therefore you cannot defile this day.'

'Who are you,' asked the executioners, 'and what madness leads you to obstruct the King's justice?'

'No madness brings me here, but God's mercy; not to obstruct the King's justice, but to check your folly, lest by defiling this holy day you bring down upon yourselves and the King the wrath of the Eternal King.'

The Bishop at last prevailed upon the executioners to take Gilbert back to his prison, while Baldwin laid the story before the King. Henry ordered the young man to be reprieved till he could investigate the matter.[1]

This incident brought Baldwin to the King's attention, and because of the Bishop's courage and uprightness Henry began to entertain a great admiration for him and marked him for further advancement. Archbishop Richard of Canterbury had died on February 17. After the usual prolonged and bitter struggle between the bishops and the monks of Canterbury, the King succeeded, in the following December, in forcing them to elect Baldwin as Archbishop.

It is not recorded that the King was disturbed by Rannulf's evil doings or lost any confidence in him. The story would seem to have a happy ending, for although Roger of Hoveden says that Rannulf kept Gilbert in prison until the King's death, the Pipe Roll accounts for his lands only till the following Easter, when one may presume that they were restored to him.[2]

At a meeting of the Great Council at Woodstock in August,

---

[1] *Gesta*, Vol. I, pp. 314-16.
[2] Roger of Hoveden, Vol. II, p. 286; Pipe Roll 31 Henry II, p. 76.

Henry published the last of his legal measures, the Assize of Forests. The King required a veritable army of foresters to protect the royal forests, covering as they did almost a third of the country and embracing even lands that belonged to private individuals if those lands were wooded and sheltered 'the beasts of the chase', the deer and wild boar.

Offences against the forest law fell broadly into four classes: the killing of game within the purlieus of the forest, whether by the upper classes for sport or by the hungry peasants for food; the felling of timber, either for building materials or for firewood; the clearing of forest land to bring it under cultivation in areas where an increasing population had outstripped the supply of arable land; and the unlicensed pasturing of cattle, sheep, and swine within the forest, to the detriment of the food supply of the King's game.

Henceforth, declared the King, there would be no amercements for forest offences; the guilty ones would answer with their own persons and be subject to blinding and castration. Most of the other articles were repetitions of the existing laws. No-one might keep bows and arrows and dogs within a forest. Owners of private woods within the forest might cut timber for their own use, but only under the supervision of one of the King's foresters, who were to have charge of privately employed foresters. Twelve knights were to be appointed in each county in which the King's forest lay to guard 'vert and venison', or all green growth and game. A register was to be kept of all authorised buildings and clearings within the forest, for which a yearly rent was exacted.

The threat of mutilation applied only to villeins, if at all, apparently, for the King was too thrifty to give up the amercements that formed a sizable part of his revenue. Pleas of the forest were held all over the country during the next year, and amercements were levied as usual, with no record of any mutilations being performed.

Before he left Normandy, Henry, exasperated by Richard's repeated refusals to surrender any part of Aquitaine to John, had 'granted to his son John to lead an army into the land of Richard his brother to make war upon him, that thus at least he might try to get what he was asking for'.[1] John, who was seventeen at the

[1] *Gesta*, Vol. I, p. 311.

time, was far too young and inexperienced to attempt to match forces with such a seasoned warrior as Richard, and Henry could hardly have expected his petulant outburst to be taken seriously.

In the background, however, was Geoffrey of Brittany, who had organised the Poitevin barons against his brother in the preceding years and who was consumed with jealousy of Richard. Geoffrey's peninsula of Brittany was the poorest of his father's domains, and he envied Richard both his rich Duchy and his growing reputation as a warrior.

After Henry went to England, Geoffrey persuaded his feckless brother to take advantage of their father's permission, step into the young Henry's shoes, and attempt to take Aquitaine from Richard, an enterprise so harebrained that only a foolish lad and a man blinded by jealousy would attempt it. John had little money and no army, but Geoffrey was in possession of the revenues of Brittany, a favourite haunt of mercenary soldiers.

The precious pair between them raised an army and invaded Richard's territory, burning towns and pillaging in the true style of Brabantines. None of the barons of Aquitaine joined in this invasion or seized the opportunity to revolt. They knew Geoffrey for what he was, and they were beginning at last to respect the prowess of their young Duke. Richard replied with blazing fury. He drove the invaders out, chased them back into Brittany, and treated Geoffrey's land as his own had been treated.

Henry knew what Richard was like when he was aroused, and he also knew how little chance the younger sons had against their brother. He therefore ordered all three to come to him in England. His court at Westminster on St. Andrew's Day, November 30, 1184, was both a family reunion and a general peace-making. Queen Eleanor was there, to greet the most dearly loved of her sons. The King's three sons, his daughter Matilda, her husband, and their children were all present. Henry forced his sons to make peace among themselves.[1]

In December the King despatched Geoffrey to Normandy to take charge of the Duchy for him. This was an extraordinary move, for Geoffrey had shown no signs of administrative ability. It may have been intended to impress upon Richard's mind the fact that the succession was not yet settled and that if he persisted in clinging to Aquitaine against his father's orders he might well

[1] *Gesta*, Vol. I, pp. 319-20.

find himself, at Henry's death, Duke of Aquitaine and nothing more.   Immediately after Christmas the King sent Richard back to Poitou, thus admitting that he could not shake his son's determination to hold on to his Duchy and that he had given up the effort to induce him to cede it to John.[1]

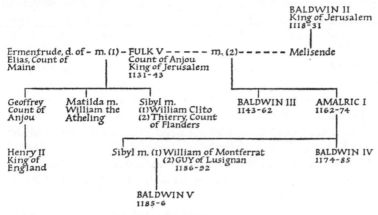

VIII KINGS OF JERUSALEM

Affairs in the Holy Land meanwhile were approaching a crisis. The King of Jerusalem, Baldwin IV, was a leper and knew that he had not much longer to live.   By the autumn of 1184 he was bedfast, with the flesh of his arms and legs beginning to rot away. The apparent heir to the crown of Jerusalem was Baldwin's nephew, a mere child, the son of his sister Sibyl and William of Montferrat.   The great Saracen leader, Saladin, was now approaching the height of his power.   With both Syria and Egypt under his control, he posed a threat to the Holy Land so deadly that King Baldwin recognised that neither an invalid nor a child could hope to meet it.   He turned then for help to his cousin Henry, the head of the House of Anjou, the grandson of King Fulk, and the most powerful King in Christendom.   He sent Heraclius, the Patriarch of Jerusalem, to beg Henry to come at once to accept the crown of Jerusalem and to defend the Holy Land.

When Henry learned of the envoy's arrival at Canterbury on January 29, 1185, he went to meet him at Reading.   The

[1] Ibid., Vol. I, p. 334.

Patriarch fell at his feet and offered him the banner of the Kingdom of Jerusalem and the keys of the city and of the Holy
Sepulchre.

'My Lord King,' he said, 'Our Lord Jesus Christ calls and the
cries of God's people urge you to the defence of the land of
Jerusalem. And here are the keys of the kingdom, which the
King and the princes of that land send you by me, for in you alone,
after God, do they have faith and hope for their salvation. Come,
therefore, my lord, and do not delay, and deliver us from the
hands of our enemies and from those who persecute us. For
Saladin, the leader of the enemies of Christ's Cross, and the whole
pagan people are hurling themselves shamelessly against the land
of Jerusalem to invade it, which God forbid!'

The King took the Patriarch's hand and raised him to his feet.
'May Our Lord Jesus Christ, the powerful King, be the defender
of His people and turn His anger away from His people, and we
will be His helper, inasmuch as we can, with the aid of Him to
Whom is honour and glory.'

Henry then said that so important a matter must be submitted
to his council, and he summoned the Great Council to meet at
Clerkenwell on March 18.[1]

The King spent the interval before the meeting of the council
in hunting at Clarendon with his son-in-law, the Duke of Saxony,
a man after his own heart. The Pipe Roll for this year shows an
outlay of 76s. 10d. 'for wheat and barley and honey to make beer
for the use of the Duke of Saxony'.[2]

Gerald of Wales, a pompous priest whom Henry had taken
into his service largely in order to have him under his eye rather
than allow him at large to stir up his fellow countrymen, chose
the inauspicious moment of Henry's preparations to start on the
chase to tell him what a great honour it was both for the King
and for the country that so eminent a man as the Patriarch should
come to him on such a mission.

Henry, ever the realist, replied: 'If the Patriarch or others come
to us, they are seeking their own advantage more than ours.'

Gerald was not willing to let the matter rest. 'You should
think it to your great advantage and honour, King, that you
alone should be chosen above all the other kings of the earth for
such service to Christ.'

[1] *Gesta*, Vol. I, pp. 335-6.   [2] Pipe Roll 31 Henry II, p. 206.

'Boldly indeed,' said Henry, 'can clerks urge us on to arms and perils, for they will receive no blows in the fight, nor will they bear any burden they can avoid.'[1]

When the Great Council assembled, Henry, in the presence of the Patriarch, put the question to them: 'Whether the King should go in his own person to succour Jerusalem or whether he should on no account cease to rule over the realm of the English, which he had formerly undertaken to govern in the sight of Mother Church?'

The members of the council, who had no doubt been given their cues beforehand, could answer such a question in only one way.   They reminded the King of his coronation oath.   'It therefore seemed better to all and much more healthful for the King's soul that he should govern his realm with due moderation and protect it from the onslaughts of barbarians and from foreigners than that he should look after the salvation of the Easterners in his own person.'[2]

Henry was a hard-headed and practical man with nothing romantic or idealistic about him.   It was all he could do to hold his scattered empire together; the thought of going off and leaving it to be torn asunder by his sons, by the ambitious barons of the North and the rebellious counts of the South, and by the Scots and Flemings and French who had once before tried to wrest it from him, while he chased a will-of-the-wisp at the other end of the world, seemed sheer madness to him.   Why should he, the King of England, the Duke of Normandy and Aquitaine, the Count of Anjou and Maine, the greatest ruler in the West, leave his vast domains in search of the Crown of Jerusalem, a petty principality racked by intrigues and plots and imminently threatened by a great and disciplined army led by a man whose genius as a fighter was common knowledge?

Henry had no taste for fighting.   What he had he had won by astuteness, by trickery, by knavery perhaps, but not by fighting. Let those who had nothing to lose, the young, the romantic, the landless knights, the followers of tournaments, embark on such adventures; as for him, he would hold fast to what he had. Lest the Patriarch should have made his long journey for nothing, however, Henry, as a devout Christian, offered to give

---

[1] Gerald of Wales: *De Principis Instructione*, p. 207.
[2] Ralph of Diceto, Vol. II, pp. 33-34.

him fifty thousand marks for the defence of the Holy Land.[1]

The Patriarch, with all his hopes dashed, warned him: 'Not in this way, King, will you save your soul or guard Christ's patrimony. We came to seek a prince, not pelf. Almost every part of the world sends us pelf, but none a prince. We want a man who lacks money, not money that lacks a man.'

He then asked Henry to give them one of his sons, even his lastborn, John, to be their prince, so that the blood of Fulk of Anjou might still rule in Jerusalem. John, carried away by the emotional pleading of the Patriarch, threw himself at his father's feet and begged to be sent to the Holy Land. Henry refused curtly; he had other designs for John.[2]

Richard, meanwhile, had returned to Poitou more convinced than ever that his father was going to try to take Aquitaine away from him. He armed all his castles and launched an attack on Geoffrey, to teach him to keep out of his Duchy. Henry thereupon prepared to return to Normandy to enforce peace between his warring sons.

On April 15, 1185, there was a great earthquake in England, a thing that had never happened before. Almost the whole of Lincoln Cathedral was demolished; only the west front, most of which was built by Remigius, Bishop from 1086 till 1092, survived. The diocese was again without a bishop, for Walter of Coutances, consecrated Bishop of Lincoln in 1183, had been elected Archbishop of Rouen to succeed Rotrou and had gone to Normandy in February 1185.[3]

On the day after the earthquake, Henry and the Patriarch went to Dover, to cross the Channel. Heraclius, now that he was at the end of his mission, made a final appeal to Henry to go to the Holy Land with him, and the King again refused. The Patriarch then reminded him of all the honours, the wide lands, the long reign, the glories, the success, and the victories that God had bestowed on him. And how, he asked, had Henry shown his gratitude? By breaking faith with his lord, King Louis, by making war on him, taking his lands away from him, and even stealing his wife. As a climax to his tirade, the Patriarch told Henry that he was as guilty of the murder of St. Thomas, since

---

[1] Gervase of Canterbury, Vol. I, p. 325.
[2] Gerald of Wales, op. cit., pp. 208-9.
[3] *Gesta*, Vol. I, pp. 334-5, 337.

he had sent his executioners to do the deed for him, as if he had slain him with his own hand.

That thrust went home. Henry turned on him, his eyes wild with rage. Heraclius bent his head and exposed his neck.

'Do to me what you did to Blessed Thomas,' the Patriarch said. 'I would as lief have my head cut off by you here in England as by the Saracens in Palestine, for you are worse than any Saracen!'

With an oath, the King replied: 'If all the men of my land were gathered in one body and spoke with one mouth, they would not dare to say such things to me!'

'Do you think then that they love you, when they look only to your wealth and not to your works? That crowd follows the booty, not the man; power, not the person, is venerated everywhere.'

Henry, his wrath somewhat cooled, tried to explain to the prelate that he could not leave, for if he did his sons would fall to fighting, even as they were then, and would take his lands away from him.

'No wonder,' replied the Patriarch; 'they came from the Devil, and to the Devil they will go.'[1]

One of them, at least, showed a disposition to go to the Devil as quickly as possible, for as such John's conduct in Ireland was to appear. Henry had knighted him at Windsor Castle on March 31 and ordered him to go to Ireland to curb his vicegerent, Hugh of Lacy, in whom his ever-suspicious mind had begun to detect pretentions to make himself King of Ireland. After Strongbow's death in 1176, Henry had sent William son of Aldelm to succeed him as viceroy.[2] William, however, was unable to keep order among the turbulent Irish, and he was replaced by Hugh of Lacy, to whom Henry had granted the whole of Meath. Hugh was fair, just, and stern in his dealings with both the Irish and the colonists. He got along so well with the Irish that he married the daughter of Rory O'Connor, King of Connaught. His popularity amongst the Irish, his stern curb upon the depredations of the English, and his failure to keep Henry adequately informed, as the King thought, of his doings, together with the complaints of some of the colonists, led Henry to think that Hugh was planning to set himself up as King of Ireland.[3]

[1] Gerald of Wales, op. cit., pp. 210-11.   [2] *Gesta*, Vol. I, pp. 125, 336.
[3] William of Newburgh, pp. 239-40.

John had been named Lord of Ireland in 1177, and it was natural that his father should turn to him, now that he was around nineteen years old, as the proper person to go to the island, check the designs of his vicegerent, restore peace, and compel the submission both of the petty Irish kings and of the colonists. The young man sailed from Milford Haven on April 24, 1185, with a fleet of sixty ships and an army of three hundred knights and many soldiers.[1] The most important member of John's entourage, at least in his own eyes, was Gerald of Wales, who had visited Ireland in 1183 and who had many kinsmen amongst the Welsh who had gone over in 1169.

John landed at Waterford on the 25th and was greeted by many of the Irish chieftains who were friendly to the English and who offered him the kiss of peace. The worthless young Normans whom John had chosen as his personal followers burst into derisive laughter at the sight of the Irish, attired, not after the latest Norman fashions, but in their native garb and wearing long beards. The silly young men pulled their beards and mocked them.

Thus on the very day of his landing John's mission was brought to naught, and every day that he stayed made the ruin more complete. 'The three pillars of Ireland', as Gerald of Wales called the Kings of Limerick, Connaught, and Cork, had been ready to submit to John in the hope that he could bring peace to the troubled land. When they learned of their compatriots' reception, they dropped their ancient enmities amongst themselves and swore to unite in resisting him.

John and his army went to Dublin and from there engineered their own downfall. Having alienated the Irish, John went on to offend the more responsible of the English, chief amongst whom was Hugh of Lacy. John took lands and castles away from the colonists and awarded them to his own favourites, who were boasters, swearers of great oaths, scornful of others, mercenary, and addicted to wine and women.[2] While their leaders were wasting their time in idleness and carousing, the common soldiers went without their pay, which John put into his own pocket.[3]

[1] Gerald of Wales: *Expugnatio Hibernica*, pp. 380-1; *Annals of the Four Masters*, ed. John O'Donovan (Dublin, 1851), Vol. III, p. 67.
[2] Gerald of Wales, op. cit., pp. 389-91, 394-5.
[3] Roger of Hoveden, Vol. II, p. 305.

They turned first to plunder, and when they had stripped the land they deserted to the Irish.[1]

When the Irish had made their preparations, they struck to such good effect that they almost wiped out the English forces. Donell O'Brien, King of Limerick, defeated John's army with great slaughter.[2] The new arrivals were forced back into a few castles and towns along the coast, while Hugh of Lacy and the older settlers, mortally offended by the foolish youth and his silly followers, made no attempt to help him.

Short of getting himself and his whole army killed, John could hardly have made a more resounding failure of his expedition. Henry appointed John of Courcy his vicegerent and ordered his son to return to England. John landed on December 17,[3] leaving behind him, in addition to the ruin of his reputation, the clerk Gerald of Wales, who stayed in Ireland till around Easter to take notes for a book he was planning to write, *The Topography of Ireland*.

While his youngest son was thus showing his utter irresponsibility, Henry, having gone to Normandy on April 16, resumed his efforts to bring his eldest son to obedience. Henry considered that he had made a great mistake when he had had the young Henry anointed and crowned King of England; he now went to the other extreme and deprived Richard, his heir apparent, of all his lands. He may have been putting into practice the favourite maxim of his mother, the Empress: 'If meat is often taken away from an untrained hawk and withdrawn or hidden, the hawk is made more eager and obedient and clings to its master.'[4]

At the end of April Henry ordered Queen Eleanor, under the escort of the Duke of Saxony, to come to him in Normandy. When Eleanor crossed the Channel for the first time since 1174, 'the King immediately ordered his son Richard to give up Poitou, with its appurtenances, without delay to Queen Eleanor, his mother, because it was her inheritance'. Henry had hit on the only possible way of inducing Richard to surrender Poitou, short of taking it from him by main force. Richard and his mother

[1] Gesta, Vol. I, p. 339.
[2] *Annals of the Four Masters*, loc. cit.; Gerald of Wales, op. cit., pp. 386-8.
[3] Ralph of Diceto, Vol. II, p. 39.
[4] Walter Map: *De Nugis Curialium*, p. 238.

had always had a deep affection for each other.   It was in her name that he held Poitou, and to her he surrendered it without a murmur.

Richard was both puzzled and deeply wounded by this arbitrary act that deprived him of his Duchy.   It could not have been as a punishment, for the King had apparently acquiesced in his refusal to give it to John when Henry had sent him back to Poitou at the beginning of the year.   It could not have been meant as a reflection on his government of Aquitaine, for he had shown that he alone was able to keep order in that turbulent region.   Was he to be thus rewarded, after he had fought side by side with his father before the walls of Limoges, while his brothers defied their father and sought his ruin?

'And then, like a tamed son, he remained with his father.'[1] Henry could smile at his success; he had withdrawn the meat, and the hawk had come to his wrist.

[1] *Gesta*, Vol. I, pp. 337-8.

XIX

RICHARD, DUKE OF AQUITAINE
1186 - 1187

ALTHOUGH Henry had repeatedly promised the King of France that he would pay an annuity to the widowed Queen Margaret and that Richard should marry Alice, he still had Alice in his keeping and her marriage seemed as far off as ever. Furthermore, it is probable that he had not yet made any payments to Margaret. Philip pressed Henry again about his promises. On March 10, 1186, the Kings of England and France, the Count of Flanders, and Queen Margaret met at Gisors. Henry renewed his former promises to pay his daughter-in-law £2,700 Angevin yearly and to see to it that Richard and Alice were married without further delay. Philip in turn agreed to relinquish Gisors to Henry and his heirs and to make no further claim to it.[1]

It was by now obvious that Richard was the only person who could keep order in Aquitaine, for as soon as he was out of the Duchy Count Raymond of Toulouse seized the opportunity to invade the Quercy, to the north of his County, and the men whom Henry had sent to govern Aquitaine were not able to cope with him. Without restoring his titles or lands to him, Henry gave Richard 'an infinite sum of money' and sent him to deal with Raymond. Richard, welcoming the prospect of activity after being idle in Normandy for a year, raised an army and hastened southward.

Having thus soothed Philip with promises and Richard with the sort of employment dearest to his heart, Henry sailed from Barfleur and landed at Southampton on April 27. He took Queen Eleanor with him in the same ship; the days were long past when he could trust her to rule Aquitaine in his absence. Their granddaughter Matilda sailed with them. Her father, the Duke of Saxony, through Henry's intercession, had succeeded in in-

[1] *Gesta*, Vol. I, pp. 343-4.

ducing the Emperor to lift his sentence of banishment. Of all his vast estates, however, only Brunswick was restored to him. He had returned to Germany in the previous autumn, leaving his wife and children behind.[1]

Seven bishoprics were now vacant in England. Shortly after he returned, Henry summoned the clergy to fill some of them. Except for the brief time that Walter of Coutances had held the see before his promotion to Rouen, Lincoln had had no bishop since the death of Robert of Chesney in 1166. With the major part of their cathedral in ruins and the diocese vacant for almost twenty years, the people of Lincoln may well have felt that their diocese, the largest in England, was doomed to extinction.

At a council held at Eynsham, near Oxford, on May 24, the canons of Lincoln presented the names of three of their number to the King. One of them was that of Herbert, Archdeacon of Canterbury, a bastard son of Richard of Ilchester, Bishop of Winchester; another was that of Richard, the King's Treasurer and the son of Bishop Nigel of Ely; the third was that of Godfrey of Luci, one of the King's justiciars.

To the consternation of the canons, Henry would have none of them. He said that 'they were rich enough already, and henceforth he would never give a bishopric to anyone for love, or because of kinship, or at the counsel or request of another, or for a price, but only to those whom the Lord had chosen for Himself'. In this case, he announced, the Lord had chosen for Himself Hugh, the Prior of the little Carthusian monastery that the King had founded at Witham, and he forced the canons to elect him.[2]

Hugh was filled with dismay at the tidings of his election. His nimble wit saved him for the time being. He sent word to the King that valid elections of bishops were conducted, not in royal palaces or in councils of bishops, but in the chapter-houses of cathedrals. Since his election was patently invalid, he refused to accept it. Henry, not to be thwarted, sent the canons back to Lincoln and ordered them to elect Hugh in the manner he had specified. To this second election Hugh replied that he was under a vow of obedience to his superior, the Prior of the Grande Chartreuse, and he would not leave Witham except at his order.

---

[1] *Gesta*, Vol. I, p. 345; Ralph of Diceto, Vol. II, pp. 38, 40.
[2] *Gesta*, Vol. I, pp. 345-6.

The King then despatched letters to the Grande Chartreuse, requesting Hugh's release.[1]

Messengers from Bela III, King of Hungary, came to Henry at about this time with a proposal of marriage from their master to Henry's granddaughter Matilda. She was already promised to William, King of Scots, if a dispensation could be obtained, and Henry furthermore had no desire to send the girl to those remote

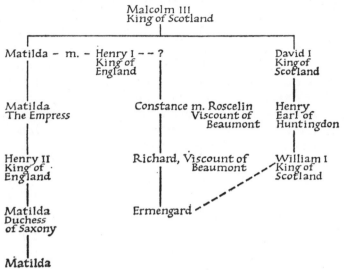

IX MARRIAGE OF THE KING OF SCOTLAND

parts to marry an obscure king. He saw in the proposals, however, a chance to stop one of King Philip's most persistent complaints. He suggested to the Hungarians that they go to Paris and see King Philip, who had a most beautiful sister, the widow of Henry's eldest son. Philip assented gladly to the match. Margaret left on August 24 for Hungary, a region so remote that Henry felt sure that he would hear no further claims for her dower or the annuity he had promised her.[2]

The Pope, meanwhile, had refused to grant a dispensation for the marriage of Matilda and King William. When the King of Scots came to visit him, Henry informed him of his great sorrow

[1] *Magna Vita S. Hugonis*, pp. 102-9.
[2] Gervase of Canterbury, Vol. I, pp. 336-7; *Gesta*, Vol. I, p. 346; Ralph of Diceto, Vol. II, p. 41.

that the marriage could not take place. He proposed instead that they become allied by means of another marriage, and he offered William the hand of Ermengard, the daughter of Viscount Richard of Beaumont, who was the son of Constance, a bastard daughter of King Henry I. William agreed to the marriage, and Henry sent messengers to Viscount Richard to tell him of the brilliant match he had made for his daughter.[1]

In August Henry learned that Hugh of Lacy had been murdered by the Irish on July 25. He rejoiced to hear of Hugh's death, for John, with smooth plausibility, had fanned his father's previous suspicions of Hugh and had succeeded in laying the blame for his own failure in Ireland on Hugh's shoulders, alleging that he 'had prevented the Irish kings from sending him either tribute or hostages'.[2] John had so convincingly excused his conduct in Ireland and Henry was so blind to the true character of his youngest son that he determined to send him back to Ireland to take over Hugh's great holdings in Meath.[3]

Before John could embark on further follies, however, Henry received news that caused him to recall his son. Geoffrey of Brittany, smarting from the drubbing that Richard had given him, went to King Philip, did homage to him for Brittany, and with Philip's encouragement began to lay plans for the conquest of Normandy. Philip made him Seneschal of France, an office that had been held by the young Henry, and began grooming him as the best possible weapon he could use against the King of England.

Geoffrey, like his brother Henry, was addicted to 'those detestable fairs called tournaments'. In the course of a tournament at Paris he and his horse were thrown to the ground by several knights who had joined together to attack him. When he refused to yield to them, 'he was so trodden by the hoofs of the horses and so severely shaken by the blows of the aforesaid knights that he shortly finished his life'. Geoffrey died on August 19, 1186. Philip had him buried before the high altar of Our Lady's Cathedral at Paris, and according to Gerald of Wales he was so overcome by grief that he had to be forcibly restrained from throwing himself into the grave.[4]

[1] *Gesta*, Vol. I, pp. 322, 347-8.
[2] *Annals of the Four Masters*, Vol. III, pp. 67-69, 71-75.
[3] *Gesta*, Vol. I, p. 350.
[4] *Gesta*, Vol. I, p. 350; Gerald of Wales: *De Principis Instructione*, p. 176.

Henry now had only two sons left, and he considered John too precious a treasure to risk sending him to Ireland. Henceforth he kept him at his side as much as possible.

Early in September the Viscount of Beaumont and his daughter arrived in England. Henry, to console King William for not being able to marry Matilda, determined to make his marriage to Ermengard as brilliant an affair as possible. He summoned his bishops and barons to meet at Woodstock, and there, on September 5, William and Ermengard were married by Archbishop Baldwin of Canterbury. Henry gave the bride as her dowry Edinburgh Castle, which he had been holding since William's rebellion. He moved out of his own palace and gave it up to the newly married couple for their wedding feast, for which he supplied all that was necessary.

The Prior of the Grande Chartreuse meanwhile had ordered Hugh to accept the Bishopric of Lincoln. As a bishop-elect he received a summons to a meeting of the Great Council at Marlborough. Some of the canons of Lincoln Cathedral went to Witham to escort him to the council, to his consecration, and then to his installation. The dignitaries, as befitted their station in life, were richly dressed and mounted on horses whose trappings gleamed with gold. To their intense mortification, their new Bishop, clad in his Carthusian habit of coarse wool, mounted a sorry nag with the plainest of saddles and had all his baggage, consisting of a shabby sheepskin cloak such as peasants wore in the fields, tied on behind his saddle.

As this odd procession rode along, the clerks begged Hugh at least to have his bundle put on one of the pack horses, laden with the rich robes of the escort, but he pretended not to hear them. At last, as they approached Marlborough, where the King and his bishops and barons were gathered in solemn state, the clerks contrived to cut the cords that bound the bundle to the saddle and thus relieved their Bishop of his burden, so that he might not shame them in the eyes of the mighty.[1]

At the conclusion of the council at Marlborough, the King and his bishops went to London, where, on September 21, Archbishop Baldwin consecrated Hugh Bishop of Lincoln. Seeing that he had literally nothing more than the clothes on his back, the King had him fitted out with clothes, vestments, and gold and silver

[1] *Magna Vita S. Hugonis*, pp. 109, 113-14.

vessels, at a cost of £23 6s. 8d.[1]   Hugh then went to take possession of the ruins of his cathedral.   He was enthroned on the 20th
by Herbert, Archdeacon of Canterbury, who had the right of
installing the bishops of the Southern Province. When Herbert demanded the customary gifts from the new Bishop, Hugh replied:
'As much as I paid for my election, so much and no more will I
pay for my cathedral.'[2]

The Pipe Roll for this year is our only authority for the introduction of the last of Henry's great contributions to legal procedure.   The previous assizes, such as those of Novel Disseisin
and of Mort d'Ancestor, were concerned with rather specialised
disputes concerning the possession of land.   The idea underlying
them, that of substituting the sworn testimony of reputable men
of the neighbourhood for the trial by battle between the accuser
and the accused, was so eminently practical and fair that Henry,
at some time during this year, extended the procedure to all disputes concerning land.   This was not as yet trial by jury as we
now know it, but it was a long step in that direction.   In the
Great Assize, as it is called for the first time in the Pipe Roll of
this year, a sworn jury of law-worthy men gave their testimony
as to the facts in dispute before the King's justiciar, who then
pronounced the verdict.   Those who asked for this special procedure had to pay for it, as did all those who availed themselves
of the superior facilities offered by the King's court, and thus their
names found their way into the Pipe Roll.[3]

Although Geoffrey's death had put an end to King Philip's
plans for using him to stir up trouble in Normandy and Brittany
and possibly to lead another revolt, it provided him with material
for a fresh complaint against Henry.   In addition to his claim for
the marriage of Richard and Alice, Philip, as Geoffrey's overlord,
now demanded the wardship of his infant daughter, Eleanor, and
the custody of Brittany until her marriage.   He also demanded
that Richard, who had driven Count Raymond of Toulouse out
of the Quercy, cease making war on Philip's vassal.   If he did not,
Philip threatened, he would invade Normandy in retaliation.

The situation was so grave that Henry sent an embassy headed
by three of the most important and experienced men in his realms,

[1] Pipe Roll 32 Henry II, p. 84.
[2] *Magna Vita*, pp. 114-15; *Gesta*, Vol. I, pp. 352-3.
[3] Pipe Roll 32 Henry II, pp. 18, 173, 192.

Rannulf of Glanville, his Chief Justiciar, William of Mandeville, Earl of Essex, and Walter of Coutances, Archbishop of Rouen, to try to pacify Philip. With great difficulty they induced the French King to agree to a truce till the following Hilary-tide, January 14, 1187.[1]

The King and his son John kept their Christmas at Guildford. On the following day Henry learned that two Papal Legates had landed in England. He had sent Hugh of Nonant, Bishop-elect of Coventry, to the new Pope, Urban III, who had succeeded Lucius III on December 1, 1185, to request permission to crown one of his sons King of Ireland. Urban not only granted the permission; he sent Cardinal Octavian, with a crown made of gold and peacock feathers, to perform the ceremony. The King received them with a solemn procession in Westminster Abbey on January 1, 1187. He accepted the peacock crown with all due gratitude, but affairs in France were assuming such a perilous aspect that he deferred John's coronation until a more propitious moment.[2]

It was clear to Henry and his advisers that only his presence in Normandy would induce Philip to keep the peace. He sent John ahead of him, while he collected a body of knights and soldiers to accompany him. He landed on February 17, and around March 25 he and Philip began making arrangements for a conference on April 5. In the meantime, on Easter Sunday, March 29, Constance of Brittany, Geoffrey's widow, gave birth to a son. The King ordered that this latest grandson was to be named after himself, but the Bretons, delirious with joy that this child had come to deliver them from the hated Normans, 'by solemn acclamation' had him christened Arthur, after their national hero. Later in the year Henry gave Constance in marriage to Rannulf of Blondeville, the young Earl of Chester.[3]

The birth of the child made no difference in Philip's contentions, save that when he met Henry near Nonancourt he included the custody of Arthur among his other demands. Henry would agree to none of them, or, rather, one suspects, Philip would no longer agree to be put off by promises that Henry obviously had

[1] *Gesta*, Vol. I, pp. 353-5; Ralph of Diceto, Vol. II, pp. 43-44.
[2] *Gesta*, Vol. I, p. 339; Vol. II, pp. 3-4.
[3] *Gesta*, Vol. II, pp. 4-5; Ralph of Diceto, Vol. II, p. 48; William of Newburgh, p. 235.

no intention of keeping, and both sides prepared for war. Henry had 520 foot sergeants, 52 mounted sergeants, and 3 'masters of the same sergeants' sent over from the Welsh marches.[1]

Henry divided his forces into four armies around May 17. One he assigned to Richard and another to John; the third to William of Mandeville, and the fourth to his bastard son and Chancellor, Geoffrey. Richard and John hastened to Châteauroux to anticipate an attack through Berri. As Richard had foreseen, Philip made his initial assault through that province and laid siege to Richard and John. They sent word to their father, who came to their relief with a large army. Philip then abandoned the siege and prepared for a pitched battle, a most rare occurrence in medieval warfare, which consisted almost wholly of sieges relieved by occasional skirmishes.[2]

While the two armies were thus facing each other, Count Philip of Flanders came to his young cousin Richard and reminded him that, except for England, any lands he might hope to have after his father's death would be held of Philip, against whom he was now preparing to do battle.

'My lord Count,' he said, 'it seems to me and to many others that you are acting extremely foolishly and not using good advice when you come armed and leading an army to make war against your lord, the King of France, from whom you have received many gifts and hope to receive many more. How or why should he feel any friendship for you in the future or why should he confer on you any of the benefits you will some day expect from him? He is not to be despised because of his youth. He is young in years, it is true, but he is old in wisdom, prudent and strenuous in his deeds, ever mindful of evil and never forgetful of benefits done to him. Believe those who have had experience. I was once at odds with him and spent a great deal of money, but I regret it now. What a wonderful and profitable thing it would be if you enjoyed the good will and favour of your lord!'

Richard, fully aware of all this, replied extravagantly: 'I would be willing to go barefooted to Jerusalem if I might have my lord's favour as I should.'

'You do not have to undertake such a painful journey,' said Count Philip. 'Here is the King of France near at hand. You need not walk to him, either barefooted or otherwise. Approach

[1] Pipe Roll 33 Henry II, pp. 40, 63, 131, 215.   [2] *Gesta*, Vol. II, pp. 5-7.

him, armed just as you are, sitting on your horse with its splendid
trappings, and you can easily win your lord's favour, God willing.'

Richard then passed through the lines, had a private conference
with King Philip, and returned to his knights. Before the results
of this meeting could be made known, Henry, 'suspecting not
peace but perfidy', asked some of the leading French noblemen
to come to him. His situation was perilous, and he knew it.
Having exhausted every device of promises made and never kept,
he had now manoeuvred himself into a position where war, and
a real war at that, rather than a mere border clash or a trifling
siege, seemed inevitable. He was not a skilled warrior, and his
chief aim had been to avoid war by every means at his command.
He now cast about for some way to extricate himself from the
situation and hit upon a device that had worked once before with
Philip's father.

When the Archbishop of Rheims, Count Theobald of Blois,
the Count of Flanders, Count Robert of Dreux, and a number of
others came in response to his invitation, Henry said: 'My lords
and friends and kinsmen, I acknowledge to you that I am a sinner
and that up till now I have led an evil life in many respects. But
now I want to mend my life and my errors, and, while I still have
time, I want to be reconciled with God. Now that I have the
money and the men, I will go against the pagans, if it pleases my
lord, the King of France. Do you therefore beg my lord on my
behalf to grant me a truce for two years. If he will not grant it,
beyond any doubt he will have to answer before God for my
soul's health. And you also will have to answer for it if you do
not bear this message to the Lord King.'

Henry then burst into tears at the thought of the extremity to
which he was reduced.

When his nobles reported this interview to Philip, he laughed
heartily and asked them: 'And do you believe him?' Henry had
taken the Cross and promised to go on Crusade so often that
Philip considered it a rare joke that he should fall back on that
hoary stratagem.

The nobles refused to commit themselves as to Henry's sincerity,
but they were anxious to avoid a battle from which little good
could come. 'He begged us to report this to you, and we advise
you to do as he asked,' they replied. Philip agreed.

When they returned to the English King, however, they found

that he had changed his mind. Henry was beginning to realise that Philip, unlike his father, Louis, would not be fobbed off indefinitely with empty promises. If he granted a truce on condition that Henry go on Crusade, Henry could be sure that Philip would do his best to make him keep that promise. Henry felt that he might just as well renounce his crown as go off to the Holy Land. He therefore told the envoys that he would not accept the truce for which he had just been begging. With great mortification they brought the news back to Philip. The French King was eager for a battle, which is a certain indication that he was sure of winning. Early the next morning he had his army drawn up in battle array.

Henry, in despair and terror at the prospect of the decisive battle that he had been avoiding for over thirty years, summoned Richard. 'What shall we do?' he asked his son. 'What advice do you give me in this extremity?'

'What advice can I give you, when yesterday you refused to accept the truce you had asked for and been granted? Now we cannot ask for a truce again without bringing great shame on ourselves.'

When he saw that his father was at his wits' end, Richard swallowed his own pride. 'Although it is a shameful thing to do, my lord father, if you want me to, I will go to our lord the King and see if I can persuade him to grant the truce that you asked for yesterday.'

Sorely though it went against his fiery pride, Richard crossed over to the French lines, offered his sword to Philip, knelt bareheaded before him, and humbly asked for a truce. He promised that if his father broke it in any way he himself would submit his own body to the judgment of Philip's court in Paris. After consulting his nobles, Philip again granted the truce, but grudgingly. Each army went back to its own country rejoicing. Philip took Richard to Paris with him, ostensibly to show the concord that was between them, but more probably to have him at hand as a hostage.[1]

While Richard was his guest in Paris, Philip 'so honoured him for a long time, that every day at the same table they ate from the same dish and at night the bed did not separate them. And the King of France loved him as his own soul, and they loved each

[1] Gervase of Canterbury, Vol. I, pp. 370-3.

other so much that because of the vehemence of the love that was between them the Lord King of England, seized with a great astonishment, wondered what this was.' Henry even postponed returning to England till he could discover what this sudden intimacy foreboded.[1]

Once he had the Duke of Aquitaine as his guest, Philip's cunning mind seized on the possibility of grooming him as the successor to the young Henry and to Geoffrey as the leader of a revolt that would break Henry's power and thus bring his continental empire under the sway of the King of France, a plan that Philip's father had devised more than twenty years before this. Philip therefore showed Richard a letter that Henry had written him while they were before Châteauroux, to propose terms of peace. The conditions Henry had put forth were that Alice, who had been betrothed to Richard for eighteen years, should marry John, to whom Henry would then give all his lands save England and Normandy.[2]

Richard had never shown the slightest interest in Alice and probably did not care in the least whom she married. The revelation that his father intended to strip him of the dearest portion of his inheritance, which Richard had long suspected, drove him to fiery rage. His father sent messenger after messenger to recall him. When he became convinced of his father's treachery Richard went to Chinon, seized the treasure there, and fled to his beloved Poitou to arm his castles.

Henry continued to send messengers to him, assuring him of his love and his good intentions and promising to grant all his just requests. It was always difficult for Richard to believe that the rest of the world was not as straightforward as he was. At last he became convinced that he had judged his father wrongly. When Richard submitted, he submitted whole-heartedly. He met his father at Angers, 'where the son became his obedient man to his father and in the sight of many swore fealty to him against all men, with his hand on the Holy Gospels. He also swore that he would not depart from his counsel.'[3]

During this autumn the news of the disasters in the Holy Land reached Western Europe. Before the Patriarch Heraclius had

---

[1] *Gesta*, Vol. II, p. 7.
[2] Gerald of Wales: *De Principis Instructione*, pp. 231-3.
[3] *Gesta*, Vol. II, p. 9.

returned from his fruitless mission, King Baldwin IV was delivered from his sufferings, in March 1185. He was succeeded by Baldwin V, the eight-year-old son of his sister, Sibyl, and William of Montferrat. When this sickly lad died in August 1186, Sibyl conferred the crown on her second husband, Guy of Lusignan.

On July 4, 1187, at Hattin, Saladin wiped out the Christian army and captured not only King Guy but also the holiest relic in all Christendom, the True Cross itself. Pope Urban III is said to have died of grief, on October 20, when he learned of this calamity. Two days later his chancellor, the Cardinal Albert, who had absolved King Henry at Avranches, was elected as his successor and took the name of Gregory VIII. He reigned less than two months. He died on December 17, and on the 19th Cardinal Paul Scolari, Bishop of Palestrina, succeeded him as Clement III.[1]

Richard received the news of the calamities in the Holy Land late one afternoon at the beginning of November. Early the next morning he took the Cross at the hands of Bartholomew, Archbishop of Tours.[2] This was no mere empty promise, such as his father had made many times before; from this day the whole course of Richard's life was changed. He had been content up till now to govern Aquitaine to the best of his ability and to attempt to puzzle out his father's intentions in regard to him; henceforth he would fight, not against petty rebellious barons, but against Saladin himself.

When Henry learned what his son had done he was filled with consternation and suspended all business for four days.[3] Richard's precipitate action threatened to bring to a crisis all those issues that Henry had been evading for many years. The succession to the throne, the disposition of Henry's empire at his death, the troublesome question of Alice, and the whole matter of Henry's relations with Philip would have to be settled in some manner or other before the King's elder son could or would embark on his hazardous venture.

Henry held his Christmas court at Caen and then went to Barfleur with the intention of crossing over to England, perhaps

---

[1] Gesta, Vol. II, pp. 14, 19-20.
[2] Gerald of Wales, op. cit., p. 239; William of Newburgh, p. 271.
[3] Gervase of Canterbury, Vol. I, p. 389.

with the hope of escaping these embarrassing questions for as long as possible. Before he could sail, however, he learned that Philip had collected an army, with the intention of invading and devastating Normandy unless Henry either surrendered Gisors to him or had Alice married to Richard immediately.[1]

The two Kings met for a conference at Gisors on January 22, 1188.[2] They had scarcely begun their parley when the Archbishop of Tyre arrived with the news that Jerusalem itself had fallen into the hands of the infidel on October 2, 1187. In the face of such a disaster, the two Kings could not in common decency continue their quarrel over matters that had paled into insignificance. Both Henry and Philip received the Cross from the Archbishop. They were followed by the Duke of Burgundy, the Counts of Flanders and Blois, the Archbishops of Rouen and Rheims, and almost all the other nobles present.[3] Henry was trapped at last and forced into a more definite commitment than any he had yet made. He had not the slightest desire to go to the Holy Land, but he could hardly have called himself a Christian if he had stood aloof while Philip and all the others took the Crusader's vows.

Henry and Philip agreed to set out at Easter 1189 and to lay a tax of a tenth of all personal property on their subjects to pay the expenses of the expedition.[4] It was all well enough for Henry and Philip to promise to start for the Holy Land a year from the next Easter, which to anyone who knew them meant some indefinite time in the future, if at all. Richard had taken his oath; he meant to keep it; and he intended to leave at the earliest possible moment, which would be the next summer.

Before he could set out, however, two things were necessary. First of all, he needed money. Secondly, as the elder son of a King who was almost fifty-five years old, rather an advanced age for those times, and as the son of a King who had, moreover, obstinately, repeatedly, and inexplicably refused to declare his intentions as to the succession, Richard had to have some assurance concerning his inheritance before he went to the other end of the world and left his father with a younger son for whom he showed a pronounced and even foolish preference.

---

[1] *Gesta*, Vol. II, pp. 28-29.   [2] Ralph of Diceto, Vol. II, p. 51.
[3] William of Newburgh, p. 272; Gervase of Canterbury, Vol. I, p. 406.
[4] Gerald of Wales, op. cit., p. 240.

Richard therefore asked his father either to lend him money for his journey on the pledge of his Duchy or to allow him to borrow the money from someone faithful both to his father and to him, giving his Duchy as security. Secondly, he asked that, 'because he was about to set out on such a long and perilous journey and lest his long absence become the occasion for malicious machinations to his prejudice', he be allowed to receive the fealty of his father's nobles, both English and French, in recognition of his hereditary rights, 'saving in all things the fealty first shown and due to his father'.

'Together, my dearest son,' Henry answered, 'together, not separately, we will set out on the road, and we will have, not money alone, but all things necessary for our journey in common, as is fitting. Nor need you lack for anything of which I have an abundance, for nothing save death itself, which spares no man, can separate us from each other.'

This was no doubt a beautiful speech, but it was also a plain refusal either to help Richard or to assure him of his future. 'When the Count could get no other answer, his eyes were opened to his father's envy and malice, and the son went away from the father, both in body and in heart.' Richard went back to Poitou and made what preparations he could for the journey on which he had set his heart, while his father, on January 29, sailed for England.[1]

[1] Gerald of Wales, op. cit., pp. 244-5; *Gesta*, Vol. II, p. 32.

XX

THE VANQUISHED KING
1188 - 1189

HENRY landed at Winchelsea on January 30, 1188 and immediately issued a summons for a meeting of the Great Council at Geddington, in Northamptonshire, on February 11. When his earls and barons had gathered, the King had the ordinances concerning the collection of the Saladin Tithe, to finance his expedition to the Holy Land, read to them. All men, both clerk and lay, were to give a tenth of their income and movables, excepting only the necessary equipment of a priest or a knight. Those who took the Cross were to receive extraordinary benefits, both spiritual and temporal. The Pope promised them a full pardon for all the sins for which they repented and which they confessed. The King not only released them from the obligation of paying the tax; all lords of fiefs who went on the Crusade were to be given the tithes collected from their men, which they could use for their own expenses.

After the Ordinance had been read, both Archbishop Baldwin and Bishop Gilbert of Rochester 'preached wondrously on that day, before the King and his princes, the word of God and the healing mystery of the Cross. Through their preaching many, both clerk and lay, took the Cross.'[1] It is evident, however, that there was little real enthusiasm for this new Crusade. William of Newburgh says candidly that although many did indeed take the Cross through true devotion, many others took it either at the King's command or in order to gain his favour and to forestall his command. According to Gerald of Wales, Henry made his friends and servants take the Cross by blandishments and promises and his enemies by threats and force.[2]

England had been hearing about Crusades and the Holy Land

---

[1] *Gesta*, Vol. II, p. 33.
[2] William of Newburgh, p. 275; Gerald of Wales: *De Principis Instructione*, p. 251.

for a hundred years now, and men could no longer be swept off
their feet at the thought of going there. They well knew, from
the tales of returned Crusaders, what had been going on in the
Holy Land; they knew how the Franks of Outremer had fought
and intrigued among themselves more bitterly than they had ever
done battle with the Saracen. Though bishops might preach
about rescuing the Holy Cross, the more cynical of their listeners
thought that their help was being sought to regain the Crown of
Jerusalem for a set of squabbling Franks who were nearer in their
hearts to the Muslim foe than to their Christian brothers.

The Saladin Tithe was considered a most unjust exaction.
William of Newburgh says: 'He never laid any heavy burden on
the realm of the English or his lands across the sea until that last
tithe for the sake of the expedition to Jerusalem.'[1]   Taxation until
this time had been a haphazard affair, based on the number of fiefs
a tenant held or upon the ability of the towns to meet the King's
demands, and it had been levied, at least in theory, only in order
to meet the expenses of a war. The notion of taxing everyone,
rich and poor, clerk and lay, alike, a certain proportion of his
income was a new idea, conceived apparently by the Pope. Once
it was introduced into England it was taken up enthusiastically by
succeeding kings, who found it an admirable means of increasing
their revenues.

After the promulgation of the Ordinance, Henry sent his
officials all over the country to collect the tithe from the lesser
folk, while he himself extracted it from his wealthier subjects.

He had all the rich men selected from every town in all England,
to wit, two hundred from London and a hundred from York and
from the other towns according to their number and wealth, and he
had them all to present themselves before him at stated times and
places. From them he took a tenth of their revenues and movables,
according to the estimate of faithful men who knew their revenues
and movables. If, however, he found any of them rebellious, he
had them straightway put in prison and kept in chains until they had
paid the last farthing. He did likewise with the Jews of his land,
from whom he acquired an inestimable sum of money for himself.[2]

In addition to the exaction of the Saladin Tithe, the people
complained bitterly of the oppression and injustice of the forest
law. The justice dispensed by the King's courts was sometimes of

[1] William of Newburgh, p. 282.   [2] *Gesta*, Vol. II, p. 33.

a dubious quality, but at least they operated in the open and according to the accepted principles of judicial procedure. The forest courts, on the other hand, were conducted, not according to the testimony of law-worthy men, but after the absolute authority of the Forest Justiciar, Geoffrey Fitz Peter, and his men. The forest laws were felt to be unjust in the first place, concerned only, as they were, with the preservation of the King's game regardless of the hardships inflicted on the men dwelling in or near the forests. When to this injustice was added the autocratic and irresponsible behaviour of the forest officials, men complained that the tyranny of the foresters was the chief bane of the realm. 'To them, violence is law, pillage is praiseworthy, justice is hateful, and innocence is guilt. From their evil ferocity no condition or rank of men save the King himself can escape unharmed.'[1]

The Pipe Rolls abound in the fines and amercements imposed by Geoffrey Fitz Peter and his delegates. In 1188, for instance, in Oxfordshire, a man 'renders account of £100 that he may go forth from the King's prison in which he was put for a forest offence and that he may be at right therein [i.e., stand his trial] when the King orders'.[2] To force a man to pay such a sum, not for an offence for which he was found guilty, but merely in order that he might be tried for the offence of which he was accused, was indeed a refinement of injustice.

One man, at least, had the courage to defy the Chief Forester. When Geoffrey Fitz Peter began persecuting the men under the jurisdiction of Bishop Hugh of Lincoln, that fearless man, without consulting the King, excommunicated Geoffrey. Although he had renounced most of the provisions of the Constitutions of Clarendon, Henry still clung to the one that forbade clerks to excommunicate any of his officials or tenants in chief without first notifying him. The King, when he learned what his favourite bishop had done, broke forth in 'vehement wrath'.

Shortly after this, when a prebend fell vacant at Lincoln, Henry sent a letter to Bishop Hugh, asking him to give it to one of Henry's clerks. Hugh refused. 'Ecclesiastical benefices,' he said, 'should be conferred, not on courtiers, but on clerks who will serve, not the palace or the Treasury or the Exchequer, but the altar, as Scripture teaches. The King has wherewith to reward those who serve his affairs; he has wherewith to compensate with

---

[1] *Magna Vita S. Hugonis*, p. 125.   [2] Pipe Roll 34 Henry II, p. 155.

temporal goods those who labour for him in temporal affairs. It would be a good thing for him if he would allow those who fight for the King of Kings to enjoy provision for their needs and not try to take their due rewards away from them.'

When this was reported to Henry, he summoned Bishop Hugh to his presence. The Bishop found the King and his courtiers seated in a circle on the ground in a pleasant spot in the woods. No-one rose as he approached, and no-one, in obedience to the King's orders, returned his courteous greeting. Hugh laid his hand on the shoulder of the courtier sitting next the King and took his place at Henry's side. The King ignored him and called for a needle and thread. While the members of the circle watched in silence, Henry set to work sewing up a rough bandage he had wrapped around a cut on his left hand. Hugh observed this operation gravely and then remarked: 'How like you are to your cousins of Falaise!'

Henry burst into peals of laughter and fell on his face on the ground in his merriment. When he had regained his composure he explained to the assembly that the Bishop was referring to William the Conqueror's mother, a woman of low degree from Falaise, a town noted for its leather-workers.

'Now, my good man,' asked the King, 'what did you think you were doing when you laid an anathema on our Chief Forester without consulting us, and when you so disregarded our modest request that you neither came to us to explain your refusal nor sent us a civil explanation by our messengers?'

Hugh defended his actions so ably that Henry in the end agreed with him on every point. Geoffrey Fitz Peter and his accomplices submitted to a public scourging and then were absolved by the Bishop. Geoffrey, to his credit, showed a great love for the saintly Hugh for the rest of his life and looked after his affairs as his special friend.[1]

Richard, meanwhile, was interrupted in his preparations for the Crusade by an insurrection on the part of those perpetual rebels, Aymar of Angoulême, Geoffrey of Rancogne, and Geoffrey of Lusignan, who started their rebellion by treacherously slaying one of Richard's dearest friends. Both Ralph of Diceto and Gerald of Wales say that King Henry himself secretly inspired the revolt and sent money to the Poitevin barons and,

[1] *Magna Vita S. Hugonis*, pp. 126-31.

adds Gerald of Wales, to Count Raymound of Toulouse as well, to induce them to make war on his son and thus prevent him from setting out on the Crusade.[1]

Richard drove them into Taillebourg and then captured the castle and more than sixty of the leading rebels. He would set them free only on condition that they take the Cross, by which means he could get the rebels out of the country during his intended absence and also assure himself of knights for his army.

Scarcely had this uprising been put down than Count Raymond of Toulouse, perhaps at Henry's suggestion, captured some Poitevin merchants who were passing through his territory. Some of them he cast into prison; some he had blinded and castrated; and others he had put to death. Richard immediately raised an army and invaded Toulouse to avenge this barbarous insult. He captured a number of Raymond's men and imprisoned them.

Raymond retaliated by seizing two knights of King Henry's household who were passing through Toulouse on a roundabout way back to England from a pilgrimage to Compostella. One of the fundamental tenets of Christian behaviour at this time was that pilgrims were not to be molested and were to be allowed to pass freely through any country. Richard was outraged that Count Raymond should have so little respect for common decency. He refused to exchange prisoners 'for prayer or price' and said that he would greatly offend God and His blessed Apostle James if he were to connive at such an exchange, for the respect due to pilgrims should be sufficient reason for setting them free.

King Philip, learning of the outbreak of hostilities between Richard and Raymond, came south in an effort to make peace between his vassals. He shared Richard's view of Raymond's conduct, for he ordered the Count of Toulouse 'to let those pilgrims go, not through love of the King of England or of Count Richard his son, but through reverence and love of the blessed Apostle James'.

Raymond stubbornly refused to let them go unless Richard freed his men. 'Then the King of France, seeing that he could make no peace between the aforesaid Counts, left them inflamed with wrath and mortal hatred and went back to France.' Richard

---

[1] Ralph of Diecto, Vol. II, pp. 54-55; Gerald of Wales: *De Principis Instructione*, p. 245.

afterwards asserted that Philip gave him leave to make war on
Raymond because 'he had refused to be within the truce and
peace that the King of France and [the King of England] had
made'.[1]   At any rate, fired with impatience to bring Count Raymond to subjection and thus be free to get on with his preparations for the Crusade, Richard seized the Quercy, invaded the
County of Toulouse in grim earnest, captured seventeen castles,
and threatened the city of Toulouse itself.

Raymond appealed to King Philip for help, and Philip in turn
sent messengers to Henry to remonstrate upon his son's conduct.
Henry replied 'that Richard his son did none of those things by
his counsel and will, and that he could not justify him'.   Although Philip would not help Raymond directly, he now saw his
chance, while Richard was occupied in the south, of striking at
the northeastern border of Poitou, where Richard's defences were
weakest.   He took Issoudun, captured Châteauroux on June 16,
1188, and soon was master of all Berri except Loches and a few
other castles.[2]

Henry immediately sent Archbishop Baldwin and Bishop Hugh
of Lincoln to Philip to try to restrain him, but they could make
no impression on him.   Henry knew that only his own presence
in Normandy, backed up by an imposing army, would have any
effect on Philip.   He despatched Rannulf of Glanville to raise an
army of Welsh mercenaries, and he sent John to Normandy ahead
of him.

While he was at Portsmouth, preparing to cross the Channel,
his kinswoman Margaret of Bohun, the sister of King William
and the widow successively of Conan of Brittany and of Humphrey of Bohun, came to the King and warned him of the rising
dissatisfaction of his people.

'My lord, I have never felt so much fear concerning your state
as I do now,' she told him.   'In the past, whenever adversity
came upon you, the blessings of your people always followed
you in your doings, but now, I grieve to say, the contrary is
true.'

When Henry asked her the reason for this, she told him that it
was the exaction of the Saladin Tithe.   Henry fell into a rage.
'These vile people have no cause to curse me.' he cried.   'In the

[1] *Gesta*, Vol. II, pp. 34-36, 40.
[2] *Gesta*, Vol. II, p. 39; Ralph of Diceto, Vol. II, p. 55.

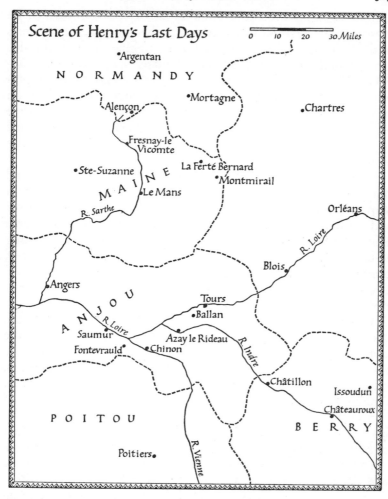

Scene of Henry's Last Days

0   10   20   30 Miles

•Argentan

N O R M A N D Y

•Mortagne

Alençon.   •Chartres

Fresnay-le Vicomte

La Ferté Bernard

• Ste-Suzanne   •Montmirail

M A I N E   •Le Mans

R. Sarthe   Orléans

R. Loire

Blois,

•Angers   A N J O U   Tours   R. Loire   •Ballan   Azay le Rideau   R. Indre

Saumur

Fontevrauld•   •Chinon

•Châtillon

Issoudun

Châteauroux

P O I T O U   B E R R Y

Poitiers•   R. Vienne

future, if I live and am able to return, they will indeed curse me, and not without cause.'[1]

It may have been at this same time that Henry drew aside from the throng Archbishop Baldwin and Bishop Hugh, who had reported to him their failure to restrain King Philip, and gave vent to the bitterness of his heart.

'Why should I worship Christ?' he asked the horified prelates. 'Why should I deign to honour Him Who takes away my earthly

[1] Gerald of Wales, op. cit., p. 253.

Y

honour and allows me thus ignominiously to be confounded by a
mere boy?' He broke into further blasphemies, refused all efforts
of the bishops to reason with him, and, digging his spurs into his
horse, rode back into the crowd as though beside himself.[1]

Leaving Eleanor either in confinement or under close supervision, Henry sailed from Portsmouth, landed at Barfleur on
July 10, and went to Alençon to assemble his army.[2] The Pipe
Roll accounts for the pay of 1695 foot soldiers and 107 mounted
men from Shropshire, Herefordshire, and Gloucestershire 'who
went to London to cross over in the King's service'.[3]

While his father's forces were living in tents in Normandy and
doing nothing, save for raiding across the French border in
search of plunder, Richard abandoned his designs on Toulouse
and hurried to meet the danger threatened by Philip in Berri.
Philip, however, was always most cautious in warfare. Fearing
to be caught between Henry's forces coming from the north and
Richard advancing from the south, he prudently entrusted
Châteauroux to one of his captains and retired to his own territories.[4]

When Richard arrived before Châteauroux, some of the
garrison went out on a foray. He barred their return to the
castle and was working great havoc amongst them when the
remainder of the garrison, seeing the plight of their comrades,
came forth in strength. Richard's party was routed; Richard
himself was thrown from his horse; and only the intervention of
'a robust butcher' saved him from being captured.[5] Since Philip
had in any case withdrawn from Berri, Richard joined his father
in Normandy rather than begin a prolonged siege of Châteauroux.

Henry and Philip were alike in that each dreaded the expense
and dangers of warfare and resorted to it only when all other
means of gaining their ends had failed. Neither wanted to bring
on a full-scale war; each side kept up a constant harassment of
raids into the other's territory and avoided a general engagement,
jockeying all the while for small points at a series of fruitless
conferences.

Henry sent Archbishop Walter of Rouen, Bishop John of

[1] Gerald of Wales, pp. 256-7.
[2] *Gesta*, Vol. II, p. 40.
[3] Pipe Roll 34 Henry II, pp. 95, 106-7, 210.
[4] Ralph of Diceto, Vol. II, p. 55; *Gesta*, Vol. II, p. 45.
[5] Gervase of Canterbury, Vol. I, p. 434.

Evreux, and William Marshal, who had returned from the Holy Land before the great series of disasters had begun, to Philip to demand reparation for the damages he had done, with the threat that 'he would henceforth bear no fealty to him as his mortal enemy, but he would harm him in all ways as his foe and inflict all the damage he could on him and his land'. Philip replied that he would not cease what he had begun till he had all of Berri and the Norman Vexin in his power. Richard, realising that this stalemate might continue indefinitely, went back to Poitou to protect his own frontiers, 'promising the King his father that he would serve him well and faithfully'.[1]

Meanwhile both Kings were having to bear the heavy expense of maintaining large armies of mercenaries in order to lend force to their demands. As his ultimate aim, Philip hoped to drive Henry out of France; Henry, on the other hand, was determined to hold on to what he had. With the approach of the vintage, Philip dismissed part of his army[2] and requested a conference with Henry. The two Kings met at Gisors, under the great elm beneath which the Kings of England and France had met for conferences since time immemorial. The parley began on August 16, 1188, and lasted three days,[3] but the Kings could come to no agreement. When they parted, Philip in his wrath had the elm cut down, so that no conference could ever be held there again.

Philip had undertaken this war, if it could be called a war, against the advice of many of his nobles. When they saw that it promised to drag on indefinitely with no benefit to either side, Count Philip of Flanders, Count Theobald of Blois, and many others of his nobles laid down their arms and refused to help him any longer in this strife against a King who was their fellow Crusader, in name at least. They declared that they 'would never bear arms against Christians until they had returned from the pilgrimage to Jerusalem'. Alarmed by their desertion, Philip asked Henry for yet another conference.

The Kings met again, this time at Châtillon-sur-Indre, on the border between Berri and Touraine, on October 7. The long strain of supporting their armies and the knowledge that all Christendom was disgusted by the continued hostilities between two Crusaders made them more inclined to agree. They there-

---

[1] *Gesta*, Vol. II, p. 46.   [2] Gervase of Canterbury, loc. cit.
[3] Ralph of Diceto, loc. cit.

fore settled upon the device of having Philip relinquish Berri in
return for Richard's surrendering what he had taken from Count
Raymond. At the last moment Philip spoiled the plan by insisting that Henry turn over to him the castle of Pacy, on the
Norman border between Evreux and Mantes, as a pledge of his
good faith, a demand that Henry indignantly rejected.

On his way back to his own lands, Philip withdrew his mercenary soldiers from Châteauroux, with the promise to pay all
the arrears due them when they reached Bourges. The wily
Philip, however, once they were in territory occupied by his own
men, had their horses, arms and all their money taken away from
them 'and cast them out unarmed and naked'. Henry, who by
now had spent a vast sum in maintaining his army of Welshmen
and other mercenaries, dismissed them, for he realised that Philip
did not dare attack him at that juncture.

Richard, fiery and impatient, had now seen a whole year pass
since he had taken the Cross, and still he was no nearer Jerusalem.
As long as his father and Philip were at enmity he could not hope
to set out on the Crusade; Philip's incursion into Berri was evidence of what would happen if he were to leave before a firm
peace had been secured. The ostensible cause of the hostilities
had been Richard's attack on Toulouse. Although he was certain that his conduct had been justified, he got in touch with
Philip on his own initiative and offered to stand trial in Philip's
court for what he had done to Count Raymond. When Henry
heard of this he was greatly displeased and refused to agree to it.[1]

Even though peace were to be restored somehow, Richard still
could not start for the Holy Land until he had secured some
assurance concerning his inheritance. Now that he had opened
negotiations with Philip, Richard explained to the King of France,
his overlord, the difficulties and doubts that were torturing him.
If he did succeed at last in inheriting his father's continental
domains, he could hold them only by Philip's permission, and in
good faith and simplicity he laid bare his heart to him.

> Count Richard was reconciled with the King of France because
> he had heard that his father, the King of England, wanted to defraud
> him of the succession to the realm, in that he was trying, as was com-
> mon report, to place the crown of the realm on his younger son
> John. Disturbed at this, which is not surprising, Richard tried to

[1] *Gesta*, Vol. II, pp. 47-50.

soften the heart of the King of France before the conference, so that
if his father failed him he might at least find some help in him.[1]

With the intention of bringing matters to a head and forcing
his father, in the presence of his overlord, to declare his intentions,
Richard arranged for a conference between them at Bonsmoulins,
near Mortagne, on November 18. Philip began with the proposal that both sides give back whatever they had captured since
they had taken the Cross in the preceding January. Henry was
ready to agree to this, since he had succeeded in taking nothing.
Richard, however, vehemently rejected the proposition. He
had offered to stand trial for his actions, but he was not willing to
relinquish the Quercy and all his other conquests, which he declared were worth a thousand marks a year, for Châteauroux and
Issoudun and a few other castles.[2]

Philip then offered to give up all he had taken and to leave
Richard in possession of his gains if Henry would give Alice to
Richard for his wife and would have his barons, both of England
and of his other lands, swear fealty to Richard as his heir. This
Henry flatly refused to do. He would not give Alice to Richard,
although they had been betrothed for almost twenty years, and
he would not have his barons swear fealty to Richard.[3]

The three participants in the conference were conducting their
discussion, as was the custom, surrounded by a dense ring of
courtiers who heard and treasured every word. In the hearing
of all of them, Richard asked his father to recognise him as his
heir. Henry refused.

'Now at last,' said Richard, 'I believe what had before seemed
unbelievable to me.' He turned to the King of France, ungirded
his sword, and kneeling stretched out his hands, joined palm to
palm, in the gesture of feudal homage.[4] Philip took Richard's
hands between his, and Richard did homage to him 'for Normandy and Poitou and Anjou and Maine and Berri and Toulouse
and all the other fiefs on that side of the sea, and he swore fealty
to him against all men, saving the fealty that he owed his father
the King'. In return for his homage, Philip promised to give
Richard Châteauroux, Issoudun, and all the castles and lands he
had occupied in Berri.

---

[1] Gervase of Canterbury, Vol. I, p. 435.
[2] Ralph of Diceto, Vol. II, pp. 57-58.   [3] *Gesta*, Vol. II, p. 50.
[4] Gervase of Canterbury, Vol. I, p. 436.

Henry was too thunderstruck to do more than agree to a truce till the following Hilary-tide,[1] for winter had set in, 'when cold falls from the air and Frenchmen hate to go to war'.[2]   Richard and Philip rode away together, leaving Henry to wonder 'whither this unlooked-for conspiracy would lead'.

It should have been obvious to anyone who had the slightest knowledge of Richard's character that no-one could treat him as Henry had been doing without at last provoking him into some sort of desperate action.   For the past five years his father had kept him in a torment of doubt, uncertainty, and suspense. Richard was now thirty-one years old, a man already widely experienced both in war and in government, and it was little short of madness to expect him to be willing to continue indefinitely in the dark as to his prospects.   Now that Henry's design of disinheriting Richard and giving the crown to John, which Richard had long suspected and which Henry had at last tacitly acknowledged, had come to light, a man far less experienced than Henry might be certain that Richard would resist such a plan with all his strength.

For the time being, at any rate, Henry was protected by the truce.   He sent his Chancellor and bastard son, Geoffrey, to secure the fortresses of Anjou while he made a hurried excursion into Aquitaine.[3]   Curiously enough, nothing is said about John's whereabouts.   After he landed ahead of his father in Normandy in July 1188, he is not mentioned again till the following June.

Henry held his Christmas court at Saumur in Anjou.   It must have been a cheerless feast, for now Henry learned that many of his earls and barons had left him and gone over to Richard.   The Bretons, who hated him more cordially than did any other of his subjects, also joined Richard.   When the truce expired, on January 14, 1189, Richard and Philip 'invaded the lands of the King of England and devastated them as much as they could',[4] but it was not a favourable season for extended military operations.

Henry fell ill during the winter and spent most of his time at Le Mans.[5]   He had developed an anal fistula, which by March was badly abscessed.[6]   Philip asked him to meet him for a con-

[1] Gesta, loc. cit.   [2] Histoire de Guillaume le Maréchal, lines 7874-5.
[3] Gervase of Canterbury, loc. cit.   [4] Gesta, Vol. II, pp. 60-61.
[5] Histoire de Guillaume le Maréchal, lines 8065-7.
[6] Gerald of Wales: De Principis Instructione, p. 259.

ference, but the King was so ill that he postponed the meeting, first till Candlemas and then till after Easter. Meanwhile he sent Archbishop Baldwin to Richard to try to induce him to return. Richard by now was so completely convinced of his father's intention to disinherit him and so wary of the wiles that had formerly deceived him and led him back to his treacherous father that he would have nothing to do with him and refused even to listen to the Archbishop.[1]

By Easter, April 18, Henry had sufficiently recovered from his illness to meet Richard and Philip several times between then and Whitsunday, May 28, for a series of fruitless conferences.[2] A new turn was given the negotiations by the arrival of the Papal Legate, Cardinal John of Anagni, whom Clement III had sent with full powers to bring to an end, in so far as the authority of the Church could, the strife between the two Kings, which had become the scandal of all Christendom and the chief hindrance to the projected Crusade. The Legate persuaded Henry and Philip to agree to submit their differences to the arbitration of the Cardinal and the Archbishops of Rheims, Bourges, Rouen, and Canterbury, with the threat that he would excommunicate them both if they did not make peace and set out for Jerusalem. To show that this was no empty talk, the Cardinal then and there pronounced the sentence of excommunication upon all disturbers of the peace, excepting only the persons of the two Kings.

At the end of May or early in June, Richard and Philip met Henry at La Ferté-Bernard, twenty-five miles northeast of Le Mans, in the presence of the Legate, the four Archbishops, and a host of bishops, earls, and barons from both sides. As his conditions for making peace, Philip demanded that Henry give Alice to Richard as his wife, that he give Richard an assurance that he would be his father's heir, and that John take the Cross and go to Jerusalem with the crusading army. This last condition was added to make sure that John would be under Richard's eye and thus unable to take the kingdom away from him in his absence. Richard seconded Philip's demands and said that he would not go to Jerusalem unless John went with him.[3]

Henry refused all these demands and countered with an offer

[1] Gervase of Canterbury, Vol. I, pp. 438-9.
[2] Gerald of Wales, op. cit., p. 260.
[3] *Gesta*, Vol. II, pp. 61, 66.

that he knew neither Philip nor Richard would accept: he proposed that John marry Alice, thus showing that he still clung to
his intention of making John his heir.[1]

When Richard and Philip indignantly rejected this, Cardinal
John turned on Philip and most unreasonably placed all the blame
on him, telling him that unless he made peace with Henry, presumably on Henry's terms, he would place all his lands under
interdict.   Philip stoutly replied that he did not fear the Legate's
sentence and would not obey it.   It did not concern the Roman
Church, he said, if the King of France, to avenge his injuries and
the insults to his crown, put down his unworthy and rebellious
vassals.   Finally, he added, the Cardinal 'stank of the King's
sterling'.[2]   That insult brought the conference to a close.

Henry returned to Le Mans, and neither the bishops nor his
barons nor the members of his household could make him see the
danger of his present position or induce him to go to some safer
stronghold.[3]   He promised the citizens of Le Mans that he would
never leave them, for his father was buried there, he himself had
been born there, and he loved it more than any other city.
Philip, meanwhile, was marching almost unopposed through
Maine and taking every castle of any importance that stood between him and Le Mans.[4]

Richard and Philip, at the head of their army, appeared before
Le Mans on Sunday, June 11,[5] and prepared to attack the city
early the next morning.   Henry, seeking as usual to avoid a
battle, had one of the suburbs fired in order to drive the French
army away.   The wind suddenly changed and, instead of carrying the fire into the French camp, set the city itself ablaze.[6]   The
French, finding the gates open, poured into the city.[7]

Henry, with seven hundred of his knights, took to flight.[8]
When they reached a hill a few miles north of the city, he drew up
his horse and looked back at the cloud of smoke hanging over Le
Mans.   'O God,' he cried, 'since You have so vilely taken away
from me today the city that I loved most on earth in order to heap
up confusion on me and increase my shame, the city where I was
born and bred, the city where my father is buried, the city where

[1] Roger of Hoveden, Vol. II, p. 363.   [2] *Gesta*, Vol. II, pp. 66-67.
[3] Ralph of Diceto, Vol. II, p. 63.   [4] *Gesta*, Vol. II, p. 67.
[5] Ralph of Diceto, loc. cit.   [6] Gerald of Wales, op. cit., p. 283.
[7] Ralph of Diceto, loc. cit.   [8] *Gesta*, loc. cit.

St. Julian is enshrined, I will pay You back as best I can: I will take
away from You what You love best in me!'[1]

Henry could not long indulge his wrath and despair, for a party
of the enemy set out in pursuit of him. As the King and his little
army pressed frantically on to the north, William Marshal covered
their retreat. Richard himself, armed only in a quilted doublet
and a steel cap, led the pursuit. When he caught up with the
rearguard, the Marshal turned, levelled his lance, and charged the
Duke.

'By God's legs, Marshal!' cried Richard, 'do not kill me!
That would be an evil thing to do, for I am unarmed.'

'No, let the Devil kill you,' the Marshal replied, 'for I will not.'
He ran his lance into Richard's horse, killing it instantly. Richard
was thrown to the ground, and the pursuit was abandoned.[2]

In the confusion of the flight from Le Mans, John, who is now
mentioned for the first time since his arrival in Normandy in the
preceding summer, quietly disappeared.[3] Henry was accompanied in his flight by his faithful friend, William of Mandeville,
Earl of Essex; his bastard son Geoffrey; William Marshal; and the
seven hundred knights who had escaped from Le Mans. The
weather was so hot and the pace so fast that many knights perished
by the wayside.

After a wild ride of twenty miles, they reached Fresnay-le-
Vicomte. The castle was so small that most of Henry's followers
had to lodge in the town. Geoffrey wanted to stand guard
against a surprise attack with the forces in the town, but his father
insisted that he stay with him. After they had eaten, the King
was so consumed with anger and anxiety that he would not un-
dress for the night but threw himself on the bed fully clothed.
Geoffrey covered him with his cloak when his father at last fell
into a troubled sleep.

They were only ten miles from Alençon, on the Norman
border. On the next morning, Tuesday, June 13, all his advisers
counselled the King to press on to Normandy, where he could
meet his army and whence he could send to England for help.
Henry, for some utterly incomprehensible reason, refused, and

---

[1] Gerald of Wales, loc. cit.
[2] *Histoire de Guillaume le Marcéhal*, lines 8837-47.
[3] *Gesta*, Vol. II, p. 72; William of Newburgh, p. 277; Gerald of Wales: *De Vita Galfridi*, pp. 368-9.

thus he sealed his fate. He would go to Anjou, he said, and from that decision no-one could budge him and no pleading could move him. Anjou was the homeland of the race from which he sprang, and now in his dire extremity, hunted by his son and by the King of France and guarded by only a few faithful friends, it was to Anjou that he would go. He had the Seneschal of Normandy and the Earl of Essex swear that if anything untoward should happen to him they would deliver up the castles of Normandy to no-one save his dearest son John.

He put Geoffrey in command of the remnant of his army and sent them all to Alençon.[1] There they found the Norman barons assembled, but they were so afraid of Philip's army that they dared not go to aid their Duke. Henry, meanwhile, started out on a wide swing to the west of Le Mans, for Philip held all of Maine east of the city, in an effort to reach Anjou. He spent the night of the 13th at Ste-Suzanne, twenty miles southwest of Fresnay, but he had little rest, for the feverish excitement and the hard riding had brought on a recurrence of his illness.[2]

The hunted King continued his way through the forests, and as he doggedly rode to the south his son Geoffrey, who had fulfilled his mission at Alençon, rejoined him with a company of a hundred picked knights. Philip's forces were now patrolling all the roads. Henry, Geoffrey, and their little band stole silently through the forests and reached Chinon,[3] south of the Loire, an amazing journey of a hundred and twenty miles as the crow flies, but probably close to two hundred by the trails they followed. When they arrived at Chinon, Henry sent word to William Marshal to come to him, bringing with him only the men who followed the Marshal's banner and leaving the others behind.[4] Henry was past any help from his armies now; all he sought was the support of a few loyal friends.

Philip meanwhile was carrying all before him. After taking Le Mans and making himself master of the surrounding country, he led his army south, towards Tours, and captured all the castles between the two cities. Philip and Richard arrived before Tours on Friday, June 30,[5] and sent a message to Henry to meet them

[1] Gerald of Wales, op. cit., p. 369.
[2] Histoire de Guillaume le Maréchal, lines 8899-910.
[3] Gerald of Wales, op. cit., p. 371.
[4] Histoire de Guillaume le Maréchal, lines 8915-20.
[5] Gesta, Vol. II, pp. 68-69.

at Azay-le-Rideau, midway between Tours and Chinon. Henry was seized with a violent fever on that day, and although he apparently went to Azay he sent word that he was too ill to meet them. Richard and Philip declared that this was merely one more ruse on Henry's part and refused to believe that he was ill. They disposed their forces for an assault on Tours on the following Monday, while Henry remained shut up at Azay.[1]

On Sunday, July 2, Henry's best friends at the French court, his cousins Count Philip of Flanders, Archbishop William of Rheims, and Count Theobald of Blois, came to him to try to induce him to make peace. They had no authority to negotiate on behalf of the King of France, who had assured them before they left that regardless of the results of the interview he was determined to take Tours on the following day, but they could attempt to point out to Henry the hopelessness of his position and the futility of holding out any longer. Henry would not listen to them.[2]

The most curious feature of these closing days of Henry's life, which such English chroniclers as Gervase of Canterbury and Roger of Hoveden considered so shameful that the one drew a veil over them 'through reverence for the royal majesty' and the other depicted a deathbed scene that does not accord with any other account,[3] is the fact that with all the resources of his vast empire and with the ample warning he had had, Henry apparently made no effort to summon help and that his subjects lifted not a finger to help him. They stood aside and watched as the King and Richard played out the last act of Henry's tragedy, unwilling to help the father and apparently equally unwilling to commit themselves in Richard's favour while the issue was still undecided.

It did not long remain undecided. On Monday, July 3, Philip launched his attack against Tours. The hot, dry summer had reduced the Loire to a mere trickle. The French troops easily forded it and set up their scaling ladders against the walls at their weakest points. The city fell by mid-morning, and Philip captured eighty knights and a hundred soldiers.[4] Philip thus showed, if further demonstration were needed, that he was master of the

[1] Gerald of Wales: *De Principis Instructione*, p. 286.
[2] *Gesta*, Vol. II, p. 69.
[3] Gervase of Canterbury, Vol. I, p. 449; Roger of Hoveden, Vol. II, p. 367.
[4] *Gesta*, Vol. II, p. 69.

situation and had Henry completely at his mercy. Again he summoned Henry to a conference without delay, this time between Azay and Tours, on the following day, July 4.

Geoffrey could not bear to witness his father's humiliation and begged to be excused from accompanying him.[1] Racked with pain and fever, Henry nevertheless went to Ballan, five miles southwest of Tours, and arrived there before Richard and Philip. When the party reached Ballan, Henry stopped at the house of the Knights Templars and complained to William Marshal of the agony the journey had caused him. 'Marshal, sweet gentle sir, I must tell you of my pain. A cruel pain seized first my toes and next my feet and then pierced my legs. Now I am shaken with pain all over, and it grips my heart. Now I have neither body nor heart nor limbs.' When the Marshal saw his face turn first red and then black, he induced the King to go to bed.

When Richard and Philip reached the conference place, Philip asked where the King of England was. Some of his followers replied that he was nearby but so sick that he could neither sit nor stand. Richard declared that his father was but feigning illness. Henry's friends then urged him to go to the meeting at whatever price. The King had his followers place him on his horse and attend him to the conference.[2]

As Henry rode up, the sight of his face, ashen-grey and twisted with pain, moved even Philip's cold heart to pity. In the presence of the man whose most generous and unselfish actions had been to rescue that same Philip, over and over again, from the consequences of his youthful folly and to prevent him from tearing the kingdom of France asunder by civil wars, Philip ordered a mantle to be folded and placed on the ground, and he invited Henry to sit on it to ease his pain. Henry replied that he had not come there to sit with Philip but to hear what he demanded of him and to ask why he took his land away from him.[3]

It was a still, hot, summer day, with not a cloud in the sky. As the two Kings conferred, a thunderclap rent the air, and then another. Henry was in such agony that his followers had to hold him on his horse as the terms that Philip dictated were read to him.[4] They were terms of such abject surrender and of a humiliation so

[1] Gerald of Wales: *De Vita Galfridi*, p. 370.
[2] *Histoire de Guillaume le Maréchal*, lines 8955-99.
[3] Ibid., lines 9013-28.   [4] Roger of Hoveden, Vol. II, p. 366.

complete that the anguish in Henry's heart as he heard them must have equalled the pain that racked every nerve in his body.

'Henry, King of England, places himself wholly at the counsel and will of Philip, King of France, in such wise that whatever the King of France may devise and ordain, that the King of England will do with all his might and without gainsaying,' the treaty began. Henry was forced to do homage to Philip for all his continental territories. He promised to give up Alice, who was to be put under the guardianship of one of five men whom Richard should name, to be married to Richard when he returned from Jerusalem. Henry further agreed that Richard was to receive the fealty of his father's subjects on both sides of the sea as lawful heir to all his father's lands.

To prevent Henry from revenging himself on any of his barons who had deserted him, it was provided that no baron or knight who had left Henry and joined Richard was to return to the King until a month before the two Kings and Richard should set out on the Crusade, for which purpose they were to meet at Vézelay on the following Mid-Lent. To reimburse Philip for his expenses in the war, Henry agreed to pay him twenty thousand marks.

Finally, to make sure that Henry kept the treaty, all his barons were to swear that if he did not, they would go over to Richard and Philip and with all their strength help them to force him to do so. As a further pledge for his good faith, Henry was to surrender either Le Mans, Tours, and two castles in Anjou or the three most important fortifications on the Norman border, Gisors, Pacy, and Nonancourt.[1]

As a last and crowning humiliation, Henry was required to give Richard the kiss of peace. As he drew back from embracing his son, the King whispered fiercely: 'God grant that I may not die till I have had a fitting revenge on you!'[2]

When the conference was concluded, Henry was past any riding. While he was being carried back to Chinon in a litter,[3] he sent one of his household, Roger Malchael, to Tours to secure from Philip the names of those who had deserted him and who were to be exempt from punishment. When Roger returned to Chinon with the list, Henry ordered him to read it aloud.

[1] *Gesta*, Vol. II, pp. 70-71.
[2] Gerald of Wales: *De Principis Instructione*, p. 296.
[3] Gerald of Wales: *De Vita Galfridi*, p. 370.

'Sir, may Jesus Christ help me!' exclaimed Roger. 'The first name written here is Count John, your son.'[1]

Henry sat up in his anguish and cried: 'Is it true that John, my heart, has left me—John, whom I loved more than all my sons—John, for whose sake I have brought on myself all these evils?' Falling back on his bed, he turned his face to the wall and murmured: 'Now all the rest may go as it will; I care no more for myself or for anything else in the world.'[2]

As his fever increased, Henry lapsed into delirium. Occasionally he broke into wild cries of pain and of grief. Geoffrey supported his father's head and shoulders on his breast, while one of Henry's knights held his swollen feet on his lap. Geoffrey fanned away the flies, thick in the summer heat, and tried to cool his father's face and ease his pain. Henry opened his eyes, looked up into his son's face, and recognised him.

'My dearest son!' he whispered. 'You have always shown me all the faithfulness and gratitude that a son could show his father. If God grants that I recover from this illness, I will reward you as the best of fathers, and I will place you among the greatest and most powerful men of my realm. But if I die and cannot reward you, may God reward you, for in all my fortunes you have shown yourself a true son to your father.'

'Your health and prosperity are all I want, Father,' Geoffrey replied. 'If God will grant that, I can ask for nothing more.' He burst into tears and stumbled blindly from the room, unable to listen any longer to his father's heartbreaking cries as he fell again into delirious ravings.

All day Wednesday the King lay in his death-agony, now seeming to sleep, now crying out confused words of grief and shame when his mind cleared momentarily and reverted to his humiliation and final betrayal. On Thursday, in a few lucid moments, he again recognised Geoffrey, bending over his bed, and in broken words told him of his desire to make him Bishop of Winchester or, better still, Archbishop of York. He sent a golden ring with the device of a panther on it to his son-in-law, King Alfonso of Castile, with his blessing, and he gave another ring, set with a sapphire of great price, to Geoffrey.[3]

---

[1] *Histoire de Guillaume le Maréchal*, lines 9047-78.
[2] Gerald of Wales: *De Principis Instructione*, p. 295.
[3] Gerald of Wales: *De Vita Galfridi*, pp. 370-1.

Although he had always travelled with a group of prelates in his train, in his last hours Henry had no bishop beside him to give him the sacraments of the dying.   Only a few of his most faithful knights remained; the others plundered him of all they could find and then fled.

In his last agony he cried over and over again: 'Shame, shame on a vanquished King!'   Thus crying, he died on Thursday, July 6, 1189.[1]   His servants stripped him of his jewels, his money, and even his clothes and left him lying on the earth, clad only in his shirt and drawers.   His knights found him thus, and one of them, William Trihan, hastily covered the body with his own light summer cloak, which scarcely reached the King's knees. Thus Henry Curt Mantle lay till William Marshal could take charge of the situation and have the body prepared for burial.[2]

In the disorder and confusion, it was with the greatest difficulty that his friends could dress Henry's body in something approaching royal state.   They put a ring on his finger, a makeshift sceptre in his hand, and about his head a band of tattered gold embroidery as a travesty of a crown.[3]   The procession started out for Fontevrault the next morning, with Geoffrey following his father's bier on foot.[4]   At the bridge across the Vienne the poor from all the neighbourhood were gathered in expectation of the alms that were customarily distributed at the funerals of notable men. William Marshal turned to Stephen of Marzai, Seneschal of Anjou.

'Seneschal, we must have some money.   Here is the King of England, whom death has brought to his end.   It would be right to pay honour to such a great man by giving all these poor people some of his money, for he has no longer need of anything.'

'Dear gentle sir,' replied Stephen, 'truly, I have none of his money.'

'Sir, if you have none of his, you have plenty of your own that you have piled up in his service, for through him you have long had great wealth and great honour.'

Stephen still denied having anything, and so the poor were sent empty away.

[1] Gerald of Wales: *De Principis Instructione*, pp. 296-7, 304.
[2] *Histoire de Guillaume le Maréchal*, lines 9138-64.
[3] Gerald of Wales, op. cit., p. 305.
[4] Gerald of Wales: *De Vita Galfridi*, p. 372.

The nuns of Fontevrault formed a procession to meet the King who had bestowed many benefits on them. The bier was placed before the high altar, and the nuns kept watch over it, chanting the Office of the Dead and 'praying God, if it pleased Him, to have mercy on King Henry'.[1]

Thus Henry, King of England, Duke of Normandy and Aquitaine, Count of Anjou and Maine, lay in borrowed robes and tawdry mockery of royal state, mourned only by his bastard son, a few loyal friends, and the veiled nuns, his empire seemingly shattered and his ambitions brought to nothing, pursued to his death by one son and betrayed at the last by the other.

Far from the sunny slopes of Anjou lay his island realm, where in centuries to come men would count his name among the greatest Kings of England. They would forget his faults, his passionate temper, his cruelties and injustices to his wife, his sons, and his subjects. They would remember, rather, that he had rescued England from feudal anarchy and that he had established a strong and capable government of almost unbelievable efficiency when compared with that of other realms of the time, manned by servants so well trained in law and finance and administration that it could function smoothly for ten full years with hardly a glance from his successor.

Most of all they would remember that he had made the royal power supreme in England through a series of legal innovations that laid the foundation for the development of English law. Faulty though it was, permeated by favouritism and corruption, regarded often as a means of raising money rather than of administering justice, the legal system that Henry established opened men's eyes to the concept of equal justice under law. Once their eyes had been opened to that ideal, Englishmen might perforce submit to tyranny and injustice, but never willingly and never for long. The sworn jury of twelve law-worthy men would in the end prove the match for any tyrant; once Henry had established it as the normal procedure in English courts, his greatest work was done.

William Marshal had notified Richard of his father's death. As the body lay in the church, Richard came and gazed impassively at his father's face. 'One could not tell from his expression whether he felt joy or sorrow, grief, anger, or satisfac-

[1] *Histoire de Guillaume le Maréchal*, lines 9173-211, 9229-44.

tion.'[1]   He shuddered with horror to see the stream of blood that
poured from Henry's nostrils as long as his son was in the church
and that announced to all the beholders that the corpse was
accusing its murderer.   Richard knelt before the altar for less time
than it would take to say a Pater Noster[2] and then motioned to
William Marshal to follow him outside.

'Marshal, fair sir, the other day you tried to kill me, and no
doubt you would have done so if I had not turned your lance
aside with my arm.   That would have been a bad day's work.'

William explained that he had had no intention of killing him.
'Otherwise it would have been as easy, if I had wanted to, to
strike your body as your horse's.   If I killed your horse, I do not
think it was wrong, nor am I yet sorry for it.'

Richard at once forgave him, as he forgave and took into his
highest favour all those who had remained faithful to his father.
After Henry was buried at Fontevrault on the following day,
with Archbishop Bartholomew of Tours officiating at the funeral,
Richard sent William Marshal to England 'to guard my realm
and all my other affairs'.

William's first concern, at Richard's order, was to have Queen
Eleanor released from her prison at Winchester.[3]

> The Lady Queen Eleanor was set free from her husband's prison,
> where she had been long detained, and, gathering about her a
> queenly court, she made a royal progress from city to city and from
> castle to castle, at her will.   And she ordered that all prisoners be set
> free from their prisons and places of detention, for in her own person
> she had had proof that prisons are irksome to men and that it is a
> most delightful refreshment to the soul to come forth therefrom.[4]

[1] Ibid., lines 9294-8.   [2] Gerald of Wales: *De Principis Instructione*, p. 305.
[3] *Histoire de Guillaume le Maréchal*, lines 9319-54, 9503-10; Ralph of Diceto,
Vol. II, p. 65.   [4] *Gesta*, Vol. II, p. 74.

z

BIBLIOGRAPHY

For a much more complete bibliography covering every aspect of the period, the reader is referred to *From Domesday Book to Magna Carta* (see below).

Most of the contemporary chronicles have been published in *Chronicles and Memorials of Great Britain and Ireland during the Middle Ages*, usually referred to as the Rolls Series.

Annales de Wintonia, in *Annales Monastici*, ed. H. R. Luard (5 vols., Rolls Series, 1864-9), Vol. II.

Annals of the Four Masters, ed. John O'Donovan (7 vols., Dublin, 1851).

Brooke, G. C.: *English Coins* (London, 1950).

Brown, R. Allen: *English Medieval Castles* (London, 1954).

— 'Royal Castle Building in England, 1154-1216', *English Historical Review*, Vol. LXX (1955).

Clédat, Léon: *Du role historique de Bertrand de Born* (Paris, 1879).

Continuatio Beccensis, ed. Richard Howlett, in *Chronicles of the Reigns of Stephen, Henry II, and Richard I* (4 vols., Rolls Series, 1884-90), Vol. IV.

Corbett, W. J.: 'The Development of the Duchy of Normandy and the Norman Conquest of England', *The Cambridge Medieval History* (8 vols., Cambridge, 1911-36), Vol. V.

Delisle, L. V., and Berger, Élie: *Recueil des actes de Henri II* (2 vols., Paris, 1916-20).

Geoffrey of Vigeois: *Chronicle*, in *Rerum Gallicarum Scriptores*, Vols. XII and XVIII (Paris, 1781).

Gerald of Wales: *Opera* (8 vols., Rolls Series, 1861-91):
I. *De Rebus a se gestis*, ed. J. S. Brewer.
IV. *De Vita Galfridi Archiepiscopi Eboracensis*, ed. J. S. Brewer.
V. *Expugnatio Hibernica*, ed. J. F. Dimock.
VI. *Descriptio Kambriae*, ed. J. F. Dimock.
VIII. *De Principis Instructione*, ed. G. F. Warner.

Gervase of Canterbury: *Chronicle*, ed. William Stubbs (2 vols., Rolls Series, 1879-80).

Gesta Regis Henrici Secundi, ed. William Stubbs (2 vols., Rolls Series, 1867).

Gesta Stephani, ed. K. R. Potter (Nelson's Medieval Classics, 1955). (This edition contains the recently discovered final section and is therefore to be preferred to the one in the Rolls Series.)

344

Henry of Huntingdon: *Historia Anglorum*, ed. Thomas Arnold (Rolls Series, 1879).
Histoire de Guillaume le Maréchal, ed. Paul Meyer (3 vols., Paris, 1891-1901).
Historia Gaufridi Ducis Normannorum et Comitis Andegavorum, ed. Louis Halphen and René Poupardin, in *Collection des textes pour l'étude de l'histoire*, Vol. XLVIII (Paris, 1913).
Historic and Municipal Documents of Ireland, ed. J. T. Gilbert (Rolls Series, 1870).
Jenkinson, Sir Hilary: 'William Cade, a Financier of the Twelfth Century', *English Historical Review*, XXVIII (April 1913).
Jocelin of Brakelond: *Chronicle*, ed. H. E. Butler (Nelson's Medieval Texts, 1949).
John of Salisbury: *Historia Pontificalis*, ed. Marjorie Chibnall (Nelson's Medieval Texts, 1956).
John of Worcester: *Chronicle*, ed. J. R. H. Weaver. *Anecdota Oxonensia*, Medieval and Modern Series, Part 13 (Oxford, 1908).
Jordan Fantosme: *Chronicle*, ed. Richard Howlett, in *Chronicles of the Reigns of Stephen*, etc. Vol. III.
Knowles, Dom David: *The Episcopal Colleagues of Thomas Becket* (Cambridge, 1951).
Liber Niger Scaccarii, ed. Thomas Hearne (London, 1774).
Lloyd, J. E.: *History of Wales* (2 vols., London, 1948).
Magna Vita Sancti Hugonis Episcopi Lincolniensis, ed. J. F. Dimock (Rolls Series, 1864).
Materials for the History of Thomas Becket, ed. J. C. Robertson (Vols. I-VI) and J. B. Sheppard (Vol. VII), (Rolls Series, 7 vols., 1875-85).
Matthew Paris: *Historia Anglorum*, ed. Frederic Madden (3 vols., Rolls Series, 1866-9).
Norgate, Kate: *England under the Angevin Kings* (2 vols., London, 1887).
— *Richard the Lion Heart* (London, 1924).
Peter of Blois: *Epistolae*, in Migne's *Patrologia Latina*, Vol. CCVII.
Peter the Venerable: *Epistolae*, in *MPL*, Vol. CLXXXIX.
The Peterborough Chronicle, ed. Cecily Clark (Oxford, 1958).
Pipe Rolls, 2 Henry II-1 Richard I. The Pipe Roll for the first year of Henry's reign is missing. The Rolls for 2-4 Henry II and 1 Richard I, ed. J. Hunter, were published by the Record Commission in 1833 and 1844. The remainder were published by the Pipe Roll Society.
Pollock, F., and Maitland, F. W.: *History of English Law* (2nd ed., Cambridge, 1911).
Poole, A. L.: *From Domesday Book to Magna Carta* (Oxford, 1951).

Poole, R. L.: 'Two Documents Concerning Archbishop Roger of York', *Speculum*, III (Jan. 1928).

Rodolfus Glaber: *Historia*, in *Rerum Gallicarum Scriptores*, Vol. X (Paris, 1760).

Ralph of Diceto: *Opera*, ed. William Stubbs (2 vols., Rolls Series, 1876).

Ramsay, J. H.: *History of the Revenues of the Kings of England, 1066-1399* (2 vols., Oxford, 1925).

Raynouard, F. J. M.: *Choix des poésies originales des troubadours* (6 vols., Paris, 1816-20).

Richard son of Nigel: *Dialogus de Scaccario*, ed. Charles Johnson (Nelson's Medieval Texts, 1950).

Robert of Torigni: *Chronicle*, ed. Richard Howlett, in *Chronicles of the Reigns of Stephen*, etc., Vol. IV.

Roger of Hoveden: *Chronicle*, ed. William Stubbs (4 vols., Rolls Series, 1868-71).

Rotrou, Archbishop of Rouen: *Epistolae*, in *MPL*, Vol. CCVII.

Round, J. H.: *Feudal England* (London, 1909).

Select Charters, ed. William Stubbs (9th ed., Oxford, 1913).

Simpson, A. W. B.: *An Introduction to the History of the Land Law* (Oxford, 1961).

Stenton, F. M.: *The First Century of English Feudalism 1066-1166* (Oxford, 1950).

Stephen of Rouen: *Draco Normannicus*, ed. Richard Howlett, in *Chronicles of the Reigns of Stephen*, etc., Vol. II.

Walter Map: *De Nugis Curialium*, ed. M. R. James (Oxford, 1914).

William of Malmesbury: *Historia Novella*, ed. K. R. Potter (Nelson's Medieval Texts, 1955).

William of Newburgh: *Historia Rerum Anglicarum*, ed. Richard Howlett, in *Chronicles of the Reigns of Stephen*, etc., Vol. I.

INDEX

Persons are listed under their Christian names. Cities frequently mentioned, such as London and Winchester, are omitted.

The following abbreviations are used: Abp., Archbishop; Bp., Bishop; Ct., Count; Ctss., Countess; d., daughter; E., Earl; illeg., illegitimate; K., King; Q., Queen; Vct., Viscount.

347

DATE DUE

JAN 28			
JA 21 '68			
DE 15 '91			
JAN 25 '96			
OCT 2 4 2001			
GAYLORD			PRINTED IN U.S.A.

WITHDRAWN